BLOOM'S PERIOD STUDIES

The Victorian Novel

Edited and with an introduction by
Harold Bloom
Sterling Professor of the Humanities
Yale University

CHELSEA HOUSE
PUBLISHERS
A Haights Cross Communications Company

Philadelphia

©2004 by Chelsea House Publishers, a subsidiary of
Haights Cross Communications.

A Haights Cross Communications ⌇ Company

Introduction © 2004 by Harold Bloom.

Printed and bound in the United States of America.
10 9 8 7 6 5 4 3 2 1

Library of Congress Cataloging-in-Publication Data
Applied For
   ISBN: 0-7910-7678-4

Chelsea House Publishers
1974 Sproul Road, Suite 400
Broomall, PA 19008-0914

http://www.chelseahouse.com

Contributing Editor: Amy Sickels

Cover designed by Terry Mallon

Cover photo "Christmas Morn" by W.C. Bauer. Library of
   Congress, LC-USZC4-2023

Layout by EJB Publishing Services

Contents

Editor's Note

My Introduction begins with a discussion of the relationship between Thackeray the narrator and Becky Sharp in *Vanity Fair*, and then passes to what Ruskin called "stage fire" in Dickens, particularly as manifested in two of his masterpieces, *David Copperfield* and *Bleak House*. Following is an analysis of Emily Brontë's *Wuthering Heights* and Charlotte Brontë's *Jane Eyre* as Byronic "Northern romances." George Eliot's *Middlemarch*, perhaps *Bleak House*'s true rival as the greatest novel of the age, is read here as a romance of the Protestant Will. My Introduction then concludes with exegeses of two of Thomas Hardy's strongest novels, *The Return of the Native* and *The Mayor of Casterbridge*.

Lionel Stevenson finds in Victorian fiction most of the aesthetic values that so many of us consider "Modern," after which Michael Wheeler attempts to locate the starting-points of the Victorian sensibility.

In a shrewd essay, Julia Prewitt Brown examines the complex relations between finances and marriage in early Victorian fiction, while Christopher S. Nassaar gives us a useful overview of social contexts in the Victorian novel.

Robin Gilmour deftly juxtaposes Wilkie Collins, Trollope, and George Eliot, while Frederick R. Karl presents the Brontës as visionaries of the outsider.

Dickens, Thackeray, and Trollope are seen by S. Diana Neill against the London background, after which the eclectic J. Hillis Miller contemplates temporal intensities in the greater Victorian storytellers.

The heroines of Charlotte Brontë and of George Eliot are confronted by the distinguished Feminist critic Elaine Showalter, after which Jeff Nunokawa sensitively perceives some of the vagaries of Victorian sexual passion.

John R. Reed considers survivals of the Romantic Will in George Meredith, Samuel Butler, Thomas Hardy, and the very minor Theodore Watts-Dunton, while the poet T.S. Eliot compares melodrama with drama in Wilkie Collins and in Dickens.

Founders of Feminist Criticism, Sandra M. Gilbert and Susan Gubar chart the development of Jane Eyre's greatness, after which George Levine strongly concludes this volume by contrasting Charles Darwin and Charles Dickens.

HAROLD BLOOM

Introduction

G.K. Chesterton, saluting Thackeray as the master of "allusive irrelevancy," charmingly admitted that "Thackeray worked entirely by diffuseness." No celebrator of form in the novel has ever cared for Thackeray, who, like his precursor Fielding, always took his own time in his writing. Thackeray particularly follows Fielding, who was the sanest of novelists, in judging his own characters as a magistrate might judge them, a magistrate who was also a parodist and a vigilant exposer of social pretensions. Charlotte Brontë, Thackeray's fierce admirer, in her preface to the second edition of *Jane Eyre* said that he "resembles Fielding as an eagle does a vulture." This unfortunate remark sounds odd now, when no critic would place Thackeray anywhere near Fielding in aesthetic eminence. Nor would any critic wish to regard Thackeray as Dickens's nearest contemporary rival, a once fashionable comparison. Thackeray, we all agree, is genial but flawed, and until recently he did not have much following among either novelists or critics. Trollope and Ruskin sometimes seem, respectively, the last vital novelist and great critic to regard Thackeray with the utmost seriousness. Splendid as he is, Thackeray is now much dimmed.

Though *Henry Esmond* is a rhetorical triumph in the genre of the historical novel, *Vanity Fair*, itself partly historical, is clearly Thackeray's most memorable achievement. Rereading it, one encounters again two superb characters, Becky Sharp and William Makepeace Thackeray. One regrets that Becky, because of the confusion of realms that would be involved, could not exercise her charms upon the complaisant Thackeray, who amiably described his heroine's later career as resembling the slitherings of a mermaid. Anyway, Thackeray probably shared the regret, and what I like best in *Vanity Fair* is how much Thackeray likes Becky. Any reader who does not like Becky is almost certainly not very likeable herself or himself.

1

Such an observation may not seem like literary criticism to a formalist or some other kind of plumber, but I would insist that Becky's vitalism is the critical center in any strong reading of *Vanity Fair*.

Becky, of course, is famously a bad woman, selfish and endlessly designing, rarely bothered by a concern for truth, morals, or the good of the community. But Thackeray, without extenuating his principal personage, situates her in a fictive cosmos where nearly all the significant characters are egomaniacs, and none of them is as interesting and attractive as the energetic Becky. Her will to live has a desperate gusto, which is answered by the gusto of the doubtlessly fictive Thackeray who is the narrator, and who shares many of the weaknesses that he zestfully portrays in his women and men. Perhaps we do not so much like Becky because Thackeray likes her, as we like Becky because we like that supreme fiction, Thackeray the narrator. Sometimes I wish that he would stop teasing me, and always I wish that his moralizings were in a class with those of the sublime George Eliot (she would not have agreed, as she joined Trollope and Charlotte Brontë in admiring Thackeray exorbitantly). But never, in *Vanity Fair*, do I wish Thackeray the storyteller to clear out of the novel. If you are going to tour Vanity Fair, then your best guide is its showman, who parodies it yet always acknowledges that he himself is one of its prime representatives.

Does Thackeray overstate the conventional case against Becky in the knowing and deliberate way in which Fielding overstated the case against Tom Jones? This was the contention of A. E. Dyson in his study of irony, *The Crazy Fabric* (1965). Dyson followed the late Gordon Ray, most genial and Thackerayan of Thackerayans, in emphasizing how devious a work *Vanity Fair* is, as befits a narrator who chose to go on living in Vanity Fair, however uneasily. Unlike Fielding, Thackeray sometimes yields to mere bitterness, but he knew, as Fielding did, that the bitter are never great, and Becky refuses to become bitter. An excessively moral reader might observe that Becky's obsessive lying is the cost of her transcending of bitterness, but the cost will not seem too high to the imaginative reader, who deserves Becky and who is not as happy with her foil, the good but drab Amelia. Becky is hardly as witty as Sir John Falstaff, but then whatever other fictive personage is? As Falstaff seems, in one aspect, to be the child of the Wife of Bath, so Becky comes closer to being Falstaff's daughter than any other female character in British fiction. Aside from lacking all of the Seven Deadly Virtues, Becky evidently carries living on her wits to extremes in whoredom and murder, but without losing our sympathy and our continued pleasure in her company.

I part from Dyson when he suggests that Becky is Vanity Fair's Volpone, fit scourge for its pretensions and its heartlessness, of which she shares only the latter. Becky, like her not-so-secret sharer, Thackeray the narrator, I judge to be too good for Vanity Fair, though neither of them has the undivided inclination to escape so vile a scene, as we might wish them to do. Becky's most famous reflection is "I think I could be a good woman if I had five thousand a year." This would go admirably as the refrain of one of those ballads that Brecht kept lifting from Kipling, and helps us to see that Becky Sharp fits better into Brecht's world than into Ben Jonson's. What is most winning about her is that she is never morose. Her high-spirited courage does us good, and calls into question the aesthetics of our morality. Thackeray never allows us to believe that we live anywhere except in Vanity Fair, and we can begin to see that the disreputable Brecht and the reputable Thackeray die one another's lives, live one another's deaths, to borrow a formulation that W. B. Yeats was too fond of repeating.

Thackeray, a genial humorist, persuades the reader that *Vanity Fair* is a comic novel, when truly it is as dark as Brecht's *Threepenny Opera*, or his *Rise and Fall of the City of Mahagonny*. The abyss beckons in nearly every chapter of *Vanity Fair*, and a fair number of the characters vanish into it before the book is completed. Becky survives, being indomitable, but both she and Thackeray the narrator seem rather battered as the novel wanes into its eloquent and terribly sad farewell:

> Ah! *Vanitas Vanitatum!* Which of us is happy in this world? Which of us has his desire? or, having it, is satisfied?—Come children, let us shut up the box and the puppets, for our play is played out.

II

Courage would be the critical virtue most required if anyone were to attempt an essay that might be called "The Limitations of Shakespeare." Tolstoy, in his most outrageous critical performance, more or less tried just that, with dismal results, and even Ben Jonson might not have done much better, had he sought to extend his ambivalent obiter dicta on his great friend and rival. Nearly as much courage, or foolhardiness, is involved in discoursing on the limitations of Dickens, but the young Henry James had a critical gusto that could carry him through every literary challenge. Reviewing *Our Mutual Friend* in 1865, James exuberantly proclaimed that "*Bleak House* was forced; *Little Dorrit* was labored; the present work is dug out as with a spade and pickaxe." At about this time, reviewing *Drum-Taps*, James memorably dismissed Whitman as an essentially prosaic mind seeking to lift itself, by muscular exertion, into poetry. To reject some of the major works of the strongest English novelist and the greatest American poet, at about the same moment, is to set standards for critical audacity that no one since has been able to match even as no novelist since has equalled Dickens, nor any poet, Walt Whitman.

James was at his rare worst in summing up Dickens's supposedly principal inadequacy:

> Such scenes as this are useful in fixing the limits of Mr. Dickens's insight. Insight is, perhaps, too strong a word; for we are convinced that it is one of the chief conditions of his genius not to see beneath the surface of things. If we might hazard a definition of his literary character, we should, accordingly, call him the greatest of superficial novelists. We are aware that this definition confines him to an inferior rank in the department of letters which he adorns; but we accept this consequence of our proposition. It were, in our opinion, an offence against humanity to place Mr. Dickens among the greatest novelists. For, to repeat what we have already intimated, he has created nothing but figure. He has added nothing to our understanding of human character. He is a master of but two alternatives: he reconciles us to what is commonplace, and he reconciles us to what is odd. The value of the former service is questionable; and the manner in which Mr. Dickens performs it sometimes conveys a certain impression of charlatanism. The value of the latter service is incontestable, and here Mr. Dickens is an honest, an admirable artist.

This can be taken literally, and then transvalued: to see truly the surface of things, to reconcile us at once to the commonplace and the odd—these are not minor gifts. In 1860, John Ruskin, the great seer of the surface of things, the charismatic illuminator of the commonplace and the odd together, had reached a rather different conclusion from that of the young Henry James, five years before James's brash rejection:

> The essential value and truth of Dickens's writings have been unwisely lost sight of by many thoughtful persons merely because he presents his truth with some colour of caricature. Unwisely, because Dickens's caricature, though often gross, is never mistaken. Allowing for his manner of telling them, the things he

tells us are always true. I wish that he could think it right to limit his brilliant exaggeration to works written only for public amusement; and when he takes up a subject of high national importance, such as that which he handled in *Hard Times*, that he would use severer and more accurate analysis. The usefulness of that work (to my mind, in several respects, the greatest he has written) is with many persons seriously diminished because Mr. Bounderby is a dramatic monster, instead of a characteristic example of a worldly master; and Stephen Blackpool a dramatic perfection, instead of a characteristic example of an honest workman. But let us not lose the use of Dickens's wit and insight, because he chooses to speak in a circle of stage fire. He is entirely right in his main drift and purpose in every book he has written; and all of them, but especially *Hard Times*, should be studied with close and earnest care by persons interested in social questions. They will find much that is partial, and, because partial, apparently unjust; but if they examine all the evidence on the other side, which Dickens seems to overlook, it will appear, after all their trouble, that his view was the finally right one, grossly and sharply told.

To say of Dickens that he chose "to speak in a circle of stage fire" is exactly right, since Dickens is the greatest actor among novelists, the finest master of dramatic projection. A superb stage performer, he never stops performing in his novels, which is not the least of his many Shakespearean characteristics. Martin Price usefully defines some of these as "his effortless invention, his brilliant play of language, the scope and density of his imagined world." I like also Price's general comparison of Dickens to the strongest satirist in the language, Swift, a comparison that Price shrewdly turns into a confrontation:

> But the confrontation helps us to define differences as well: Dickens is more explicit, more overtly compassionate, insisting always upon the perversions of feeling as well as of thought. His outrage is of the same consistency as his generous celebration, the satirical wit of the same copious extravagance as the comic elaborations. Dickens's world is alive with things that snatch, lurch, teeter, thrust, leer; it is the animate world of Netherlandish genre painting or of Hogarth's prints, where all space is a field of force, where objects vie or intrigue with each other, where every

human event spills over into the things that surround it. This may become the typically crowded scene of satire, where persons are reduced to things and things to matter in motion; or it may pulsate with fierce energy and noisy feeling. It is different from Swift; it is the distinctive Dickensian plenitude, which we find again in his verbal play, in his great array of vivid characters, in his massed scenes of feasts or public declamations. It creates rituals as compelling as the resuscitation of Rogue Riderhood, where strangers participate solemnly in the recovery of a spark of life, oblivious for the moment of the unlovely human form it will soon inhabit.

That animate, Horgarthian world, "where all space is a field of force," indeed is a plenitude and it strikes me that Price's vivid description suggests Rabelais rather than Swift as a true analogue. Dickens, like Shakespeare in one of many aspects and like Rabelais, is as much carnival as stage fire, a kind of endless festival. The reader of Dickens stands in the midst of a festival, which is too varied, too multiform, to be taken in even by innumerable readings. Something always escapes our ken; Ben Jonson's sense of being "rammed with life" is exemplified more even by Dickens than by Rabelais, in that near-Shakespearean plenitude that is Dickens's peculiar glory.

Is it possible to define that plenitude narrowly enough so as to conceptualize it for critical use, though by "conceptualize" one meant only a critical metaphor? Shakespearean representation is no touchstone for Dickens or for anyone else, since above all modes of representation it turns upon an inward changing brought about by characters listening to themselves speak. Dickens cannot do that. His villains are gorgeous, but there are no Iagos or Edmunds among them. The severer, more relevant test, which Dickens must fail, though hardly to his detriment, is Falstaff, who generates not only his own meaning, but meaning in so many others besides, both on and off the page. Probably the severest test is Shylock, most Dickensian of Shakespeare's characters, since we cannot say of Dickens's Shylock, Fagin, that there is much Shakespearean about him at all. Fagin is a wonderful grotesque, but the winds of will are not stirred in him, while they burn on hellishly forever in Shylock.

Carlyle's injunction, to work in the will, seems to have little enough place in the cosmos of the Dickens characters. I do not say this to indicate a limitation, or even a limit, nor do I believe that the will to live or the will to power is ever relaxed in or by Dickens. But nothing is got for nothing, except perhaps in or by Shakespeare, and Dickens purchases his kind of plenitude at the expense of one aspect of the will. T. S. Eliot remarked that "Dickens's characters are real because there is no one like them." I would modify that to "They are real because they are not like one another, though sometimes they are a touch more like some of us than like each other." Perhaps the will, in whatever aspect, can differ only in degree rather than in kind among us. The aesthetic secret of Dickens appears to be that his villains, heroes, heroines, victims, eccentrics, ornamental beings, do differ from one another *in the kinds of will that they possess.* Since that is hardly possible for us, as humans, it does bring about an absence in reality in and for Dickens. That is a high price to pay, but it is a good deal less than everything and Dickens got more than he paid for. We also receive a great deal more than we ever are asked to surrender when we read Dickens. That may indeed be his most Shakespearean quality, and may provide the critical trope I quest for in him. James and Proust hurt you more than Dickens does, and the hurt is the meaning, or much of it. What hurts in Dickens never has much to do with meaning, because there cannot be a poetics of pain where the will has ceased to be common or sadly uniform. Dickens really does offer a poetics of pleasure, which is surely worth our secondary uneasiness at his refusal to offer us any accurately mimetic representations of the human will. He writes always the book of the drives, which is why supposedly Freudian readings of him always fail so tediously. The conceptual metaphor he suggests in his representations of character and personality is neither Shakespearean mirror nor Romantic lamp, neither Rabelaisian carnival nor Fieldingesque open country. "Stage fire" seems to me perfect, for "stage" removes something of the reality of the will, yet only as modifier. The substantive remains "fire." Dickens is the poet of the fire of the drives, the true celebrant of Freud's myth of frontier concepts, of that domain lying on the border between psyche and body, falling into matter, yet partaking of the reality of both.

III

If the strong writer be defined as one who confronts his own contingency, his own dependent relation on a precursor, then we can discover only a few writers after Homer and the Yahwist who are strong without that sense of contingency. These are the Great Originals, and they are not many; Shakespeare and Freud are among them and so is Dickens. Dickens, like Shakespeare and Freud, had no true precursors, or perhaps it might be more accurate to say he swallowed up Tobias Smollett rather as Shakespeare devoured Christopher Marlowe. Originality, or an authentic freedom from contingency, is Dickens's salient characteristic as an author. Since Dickens's influence has been so immense, even upon writers so unlikely as Dostoevsky and Kafka, we find it a little difficult now to see at first how overwhelmingly original he is.

Dickens now constitutes a facticity or contingency that no subsequent novelist can transcend or evade without the risk of self-maiming. Consider the difference between two masters of modern fiction, Henry James and James Joyce. Is not Dickens the difference? *Ulysses* comes to terms with Dickens, and earns the exuberance it manifests. Poldy is larger, I think, than any single figure in Dickens, but he has recognizably Dickensian qualities. Lambert Strether in *The Ambassadors* has none, and is the poorer for it. Part of the excitement of *The Princess Casamassima* for us must be that, for once, James achieves a Dickensian sense of the outward life, a sense that is lacking even in *The Portrait of a Lady*, and that we miss acutely (at least I do) amidst even the most inward splendors of *The Wings of the Dove* and *The Golden Bowl*.

The Personal History of David Copperfield, indeed the most personal and autobiographical of all Dickens's novels, has been so influential upon all subsequent portraits of the artist as a young man that we have to make a conscious effort to recover our appreciation of the book's fierce originality. It is the first therapeutic novel, in part written to heal the author's self, or at least to solace permanent anxieties incurred in childhood and youth. Freud's esteem for *David Copperfield* seems inevitable, even if it has led to a number of unfortunate readings within that unlikely compound oddly called "Freudian literary criticism."

Dickens's biographer Edgar Johnson has traced the evolution of *David Copperfield* from an abandoned fragment of autobiography, with its powerful but perhaps self-deceived declaration: "I do not write resentfully or angrily: for I know how all these things have worked together to make me what I am." Instead of representing his own parents as being David Copperfield's, Dickens displaced them into the Micawbers, a change that purchased astonishing pathos and charm at the expense of avoiding a personal pain that might have produced greater meaningfulness. But *David Copperfield* was, as Dickens said, his "favourite child," fulfilling his deep need to become his own father. Of no other book would he have said: "I seem to be sending some part of myself into the Shadowy World."

Kierkegaard advised us that "he who is willing to do the work gives birth to his own father," while Nietzsche even more ironically observed that "if one hasn't had a good father, then it is necessary to invent one." *David Copperfield* is more in the spirit of Kierkegaard's adage, as Dickens more or less makes himself David's father. David, an illustrious novelist, allows himself to narrate his story in the first person. A juxtaposition of the start and conclusion of the narrative may be instructive:

> Whether I shall turn out to be the hero of my own life, or whether that station will be held by anybody else, these pages must show. To begin my life with the beginning of my life, I record that I was born (as I have been informed and believe) on a Friday, at twelve o'clock at night. It was remarked that the clock began to strike, and I began to cry, simultaneously.
>
> In consideration of the day and hour of my birth, it was declared by the nurse, and by some sage women in the neighbourhood who had taken a lively interest in me several months before there was any possibility of our becoming personally acquainted, first, that I was destined to be unlucky in life; and secondly, that I was privileged to see ghosts and spirits; both these gifts inevitably attaching, as they believed, to all unlucky infants of either gender, born towards the small hours on a Friday night.
>
> I need say nothing here, on the first head, because nothing can show better than my history whether that prediction was verified or falsified by the result. On the second branch of the question, I will only remark, that unless I ran through that part of my inheritance while I was still a baby, I have not come into it yet. But I do not at all complain of having been kept out of this property; and if anybody else should be in the present enjoyment of it, he is heartily welcome to keep it.

> And now, as I close my task, subduing my desire to linger yet, these faces fade away. But one face, shining on me like a Heavenly light by which I see all other objects, is above them and beyond them all. And that remains.
>
> I turn my head, and see it, in its beautiful serenity, beside me. My lamp burns low, and I have written far into the night; but the dear presence, without which I were nothing, bears me company.
>
> O Agnes, O my soul, so may thy face be by me when I close my life indeed; so may I, when realities are melting from me, like the shadows which I now dismiss, still find thee near me, pointing upward!

No adroit reader could prefer the last four paragraphs of *David Copperfield* to the first three. The high humor of the beginning is fortunately more typical of the book than the sugary conclusion. Yet the juxtaposition does convey the single rhetorical flaw in Dickens that matters, by which I do not mean the wild pathos that marks the death of Steerforth, or the even more celebrated career of the endlessly unfortunate Little Em'ly. If Dickens's image of voice or mode of representation is "stage fire," then his metaphors always will demand the possibility of being staged. Micawber, Uriah Heep, Steerforth in his life (not at the end) are all of them triumphs of stage fire, as are Peggotty, Murdstone, Betsey Trotwood, and even Dora Spenlow. But Agnes is a disaster, and that dreadful "pointing upward!" is not to be borne. You cannot stage Agnes, which would not matter except that she does represent the idealizing and self-mystifying side of David and so she raises the question, Can you, as a reader, stage David? How much stage fire got into him? Or, to be hopelessly reductive, has he a will, as Uriah Heep and Steerforth in their very different ways are wills incarnate?

If there is an aesthetic puzzle in the novel, it is why David has and conveys so overwhelming a sense of disordered suffering and early sorrow in his Murdstone phase, as it were, and before. Certainly the intensity of the pathos involved is out of all proportion to the fictive experience that comes through to the reader. Dickens both invested himself in and withdrew from David, so that something is always missing in the self-representation. Yet the will—to live, to interpret, to repeat, to write—survives and burgeons perpetually. Dickens's preternatural energy gets into David, and is at some considerable variance with the diffidence of David's apparent refusal to explore his own inwardness. What does mark Dickens's representation of David with stage fire is neither the excess of the early sufferings nor the tiresome idealization of the love for Agnes. It is rather the vocation of novelist, the drive to tell a story, particularly one's own story, that apparels David with the fire of what Freud called the drives.

Dickens's greatness in *David Copperfield* has little to do with the much more extraordinary strength that was to manifest itself in *Bleak House*, which can compete with *Clarissa*, *Emma*, *Middlemarch*, *The Portrait of a Lady*, *Women in Love*, and *Ulysses* for the eminence of being the inescapable novel in the language. *David Copperfield* is of another order, but it is the origin of that order, the novelist's account of how she or he burned through experience in order to achieve the Second Birth, into the will to narrate, the storyteller's destiny.

IV

Bleak House may not be "the finest literary work the nineteenth century produced in England," as Geoffrey Tillotson called it in 1946. A century that gave us *The Prelude* and Wordsworth's major crisis lyrics, Blake's *Milton* and *Jerusalem*, Byron's *Don Juan*, the principal poems of Shelley, Keats, Tennyson, and Browning, and novels such as *Pride and Prejudice*, *Emma*, *Middlemarch*, and Dickens's own *Hard Times* and *Our Mutual Friend*, is an era of such literary plenitude that a single choice is necessarily highly problematic. Yet there is now something close to critical agreement that *Bleak House* is Dickens's most complex and memorable single achievement. W. J. Harvey usefully sketches just how formidably the novel is patterned:

> *Bleak House* is for Dickens a unique and elaborate experiment in narration and plot composition. It is divided into two intermingled and roughly concurrent stories; Esther Summerson's first-person narrative and an omniscient narrative told consistently in the historic present. The latter takes up thirty-four chapters; Esther has one less. Her story, however, occupies a good deal more than half the novel. The reader who checks the distribution of these two narratives against the original part issues will hardly discern any significant pattern or correlation. Most parts contain a mixture of the two stories; one part is narrated entirely by Esther and five parts entirely by the omniscient author. Such a check does, however, support the view that Dickens did not, as is sometimes supposed, use serial publication in the interest of crude suspense. A sensational novelist, for example, might well have ended a part issue with chapter 31; Dickens subdues the drama by adding another chapter to the number. The obvious exception to this only proves the rule; in the final double number the suspense of Bucket's search for Lady Dedlock is heightened by cutting back to the omniscient narrative and the stricken Sir Leicester. In general, however, Dickens's control of the double narrative is far richer and subtler than this.

I would add to Harvey the critical observation that Dickens's own narrative will in "his" thirty-four chapters is a will again different in kind than the will to tell her story of the admirable Esther Summerson. Dickens's (or the omniscient, historical present narrator's) metaphor of representation is one of stage fire: wild, free, unconditioned, incessant with the force of Freud's domain of those grandly indefinite frontier concepts, the drives. Esther's mode of representation is certainly not flat or insipid; for all of her monumental repressions, Esther finally seems to me the most mysteriously complex and profound personage in *Bleak House*. Her narrative is not so much plain style as it is indeed repressed in the precise Freudian sense of "repression," whose governing metaphor, in Esther's prose as in Freud's, is flight from, rather than a pushing down or pushing under. Esther frequently forgets, purposefully though "unconsciously," what she cannot bear to remember, and much of her narrative is her strong defense against the force of the past. Esther may not *appear* to change as she goes from little-girl to adult; but that is because the rhythm of her psyche, unlike Dickens's own, is one of unfolding rather than development. She is Dickens's Muse, what Whitman would have called his "Fancy," as in the great death-lyric "Goodbye, My Fancy!" or what Stevens would have called Dickens's "Interior Paramour."

Contrast a passage of Esther's story with one of Dickens's own narrative, from the end of chapter 56, "Pursuit," and towards the close of the next chapter, "Esther's Narrative":

> Mr. Jarndyce, the only person up in the house, is just going to bed; rises from his book, on hearing the rapid ringing at the bell; and comes down to the door in his dressing-gown.
>
> "Don't be alarmed sir." In a moment his visitor is confidential with him in the hall, has shut the door, and stands with his hand upon the lock. "I've had the pleasure of seeing you before. Inspector Bucket. Look at that handkerchief, sir, Miss Esther Summerson's. Found it myself put away in a drawer of Lady Dedlock's, quarter of an hour ago. Not a moment to lose. Matter of life or death. You know Lady Dedlock?"
>
> "Yes."
>
> "There has been a discovery there, to-day. Family affairs have come out. Sir Leicester Dedlock, Baronet, has had a fit—apoplexy or paralysis—and couldn't be brought to, and precious time has been lost. Lady Dedlock disappeared this afternoon, and left a letter for him that looks bad. Run your eye over it. Here it is!"
>
> Mr. Jarndyce having read it, asks him what he thinks?
>
> "I don't know. It looks like suicide. Anyways, there's more and more danger, every minute, of its drawing to that. I'd give a hundred pound an hour to have got the start of the present time.

Now, Mr. Jarndyce, I am employed by Sir Leicester Dedlock, Baronet, to follow her and find her—to save her, and take her his forgiveness. I have money and full power, but I want something else. I want Miss Summerson."

Mr. Jarndyce, in a troubled voice, repeats "Miss Summerson?"

"Now, Mr. Jarndyce"; Mr. Bucket has read his face with the greatest attention all along: "I speak to you as a gentleman of a humane heart, and under such pressing circumstances as don't often happen. If ever delay was dangerous, it's dangerous now; and if ever you couldn't afterwards forgive yourself for causing it, this is the time. Eight or ten hours, worth, as I tell you, a hundred pound a-piece at least, have been lost since Lady Dedlock disappeared. I am charged to find her. I am Inspector Bucket. Besides all the rest that's heavy on her, she has upon her, as she believes, suspicion of murder. If I follow her alone, she, being in ignorance of what Sir Leicester Dedlock, Baronet, has communicated to me, may be driven to desperation. But if I follow her in company with a young lady, answering to the description of a young lady that she has a tenderness for—I ask no question, and I say no more than that—she will give me credit for being friendly. Let me come up with her, and be able to have the hold upon her of putting that young lady for'ard, and I'll save her and prevail with her if she is alive. Let me come up with her alone—a harder matter—and I'll do my best; but I don't answer for what the best may be. Time flies; it's getting on for one o'clock. When one strikes, there's another hour gone; and it's worth a thousand pound now, instead of a hundred."

This is all true, and the pressing nature of the case cannot be questioned. Mr. Jarndyce begs him to remain there, while he speaks to Miss Summerson. Mr. Bucket says he will; but acting on his usual principle, does no such thing—following upstairs instead, and keeping his man in sight. So he remains, dodging and lurking about in the gloom of the staircase while they confer. In a very little time, Mr. Jarndyce comes down, and tells him that Miss Summerson will join him directly, and place herself under his protection, to accompany him where he pleases. Mr. Bucket, satisfied, expresses high approval; and awaits her coming, at the door.

There, he mounts a high tower in his mind, and looks out far and wide. Many solitary figures he perceives, creeping through the streets; many solitary figures out on heaths, and roads, and lying under haystacks. But the figure that he seeks is not among them. Other solitaries he perceives, in nooks of bridges, looking over; and in shadowed places down by the river's level; and a dark, dark, shapeless object drifting with the tide, more solitary than all, clings with a drowning hold on his attention.

Where is she? Living or dead, where is she? If, as he folds the handkerchief and carefully puts it up, it were able, with an enchanted power, to bring before him the place where she found it, and the night landscape near the cottage where it covered the little child, would he descry her there? On the waste, where the brick-kilns are burning with a pale blue flare; where the straw-roofs of the wretched huts in which the bricks are made, are being scattered by the wind; where the clay and water are hard frozen, and the mill in which the gaunt blind horse goes round all day, looks like an instrument of human torture; traversing this deserted blighted spot, there is a lonely figure with the sad world to itself, pelted by the snow and driven by the wind, and cast out, it would seem, from all companionship. It is the figure of a woman, too; but it is miserably dressed, and no such clothes ever came through the hall, and out at the great door, of the Dedlock mansion.

The transparent windows with the fire and light, looking so bright and warm from the cold darkness out of doors, were soon gone, and again we were crushing and churning the loose snow. We went on with toil enough; but the dismal roads were not much worse than they had been, and the stage was only nine miles. My companion smoking on the box—I had thought at the last inn of begging him to do so, when I saw him standing at a great fire in a comfortable cloud of tobacco—was as vigilant as ever; and as quickly down and up again, when we came to any human abode or any human creature. He had lighted his little dark lantern, which seemed to be a favourite with him, for we had lamps to the carriage; and every now and then he turned it upon me, to see that I was doing well. There was a folding-window to the carriage-head, but I never closed it, for it seemed like shutting out hope.

We came to the end of the stage, and still the lost trace was not recovered. I looked at him anxiously when we stopped to change; but I knew by his yet graver face, as he stood watching the ostlers, that he had heard nothing. Almost in an instant afterwards, as I leaned back in my seat, he looked in, with his lighted lantern in his hand, an excited and quite different man.

"What is it?" said I, starting. "Is she here?"

"No, no. Don't deceive yourself, my dear. Nobody's here. But I've got it!"

The crystallised snow was in his eyelashes, in his hair, lying in ridges on his dress. He had to shake it from his face, and get his breath before he spoke to me.

"Now, Miss Summerson," said he, beating his finger on the apron, "don't you be disappointed at what I'm a going to do. You know me. I'm Inspector Bucket, and you can trust me. We've come a long way; never mind. Four horses out there for the next stage up! Quick!"

There was a commotion in the yard, and a man came running out of the stables to know "if he meant up or down?"

"Up, I tell you! Up! Ain't it English? Up!"

"Up?" said I, astonished. "To London! Are we going back?"

"Miss Summerson," he answered, "back. Straight back as a die. You know me. Don't be afraid. I'll follow the other, by G—."

"The other?" I repeated. "Who?"

"You called her Jenny, didn't you? I'll follow her. Bring those two pair out here, for a crown a man. Wake up, some of you!"

"You will not desert this lady we are in search of; you will not abandon her on such a night, and in such a state of mind as I know her to be in!" said I, in an agony, and grasping his hand.

"You are right, my dear, I won't. But I'll follow the other. Look alive here with them horses. Send a man for'ard in the saddle to the next stage, and let him send another for'ard again, and order four on, up, right through. My darling, don't you be afraid!"

These orders, and the way in which he ran about the yard, urging them, caused a general excitement that was scarcely less bewildering to me than the sudden change. But in the height of the confusion, a mounted man galloped away to order the relays, and our horses were put to with great speed.

"My dear," said Mr. Bucket, jumping up to his seat, and looking in again—"you'll excuse me if I'm too familiar—don't you fret and worry yourself no more than you can help. I say nothing else at present; but you know me, my dear; now, don't you?"

I endeavoured to say that I knew he was far more capable than

I of deciding what we ought to do; but was he sure that this was right? Could I not go forward by myself in search of—I grasped his hand again in my distress, and whispered it to him—of my own mother.

"My dear," he answered, "I know, I know, and would I put you wrong, do you think? Inspector Bucket. Now you know me, don't you?"

What could I say but yes!

"Then you keep up as good a heart as you can, and you rely upon me for standing by you, no less than by Sir Leicester Dedlock, Baronet. Now, are you right there?"

"All right, sir!"

"Off she goes, then. And get on, my lads!"

We were again upon the melancholy road by which we had come; tearing up the miry sleet and thawing snow, as if they were torn up by a waterwheel.

Both passages are extraordinary, by any standards, and certainly "Pursuit" has far more stage fire than "Esther's Narrative," but this time her repressive shield, in part, is broken through, and a fire leaps forth out of her. If we start with "Pursuit" however, we are likelier to see what it is that returns from the repressed in Esther, returns under the sign of negation (as Freud prophesied), so that what comes back is primarily cognitive, while the affective aspect of the repression persists. We can remember the opening of *David Copperfield*, where Dickens, in his persona as David, disavows the gift of second sight attributed to him by the wise women and gossips. Inspector Bucket, at the conclusion of the "Pursuit" chapter, is granted a great vision, a preternatural second sight of Esther's lost mother, Lady Dedlock. What Bucket *sees* is stage fire at its most intense, the novelist's will to tell become an absolute vision of the will. Mounting a high tower in his mind, Bucket (who thus becomes Dickens's authorial will) looks out, far and wide, and sees the truth: "a dark, dark, shapeless object drifting with the tide, more solitary than all," which "clings with a drowning hold on his attention." That "drowning hold" leads to the further vision: "where the clay and water are hard frozen, and the mill in which the gaunt blind horse goes round all day." I suspect that Dickens here has a debt to Browning's great romance "Childe Roland to the Dark Tower Came," where another apparent instrument of human torture in a deserted, blighted spot is seen by a companionless figure as being in association with a starving blind horse, cast out from the Devil's stud, who provokes in Browning's narrator the terrible outcry that he never saw a beast he hated so, because: "He must be wicked to deserve such pain."

The ensuing chapter of "Esther's Narrative" brilliantly evokes the cognitive return of Esther's acknowledgment of her mother, under the sign of a negation of past affect. Here the narrative vision proceeds, not in the Sublime mode of Bucket's extraordinary second sight, but in the grave, meditative lyricism that takes us first to a tentative return from unconscious flight through an image of pursuit of the fleeing, doomed mother: "The transparent windows with the fire and light, looking so bright and warm from the cold darkness out of doors, were soon gone, and again we were crushing and churning the loose snow." That "crushing and churning" images the breaking of the repressive shield, and Dickens shrewdly ends the chapter with Esther's counterpart to Bucket's concluding vision of a Browningesque demonic water mill, torturing consciousness into a return from flight. Esther whispers to Bucket that she desires to go forward by herself in search of her own mother, and the dark pursuit goes on in the sinister metaphor of the sleet and thawing snow, shield of repression, being torn up by a waterwheel that recirculates the meaning of memory's return, even as it buries part of the pains of abandonment by the mother once more: "We were again upon the melancholy road by which we had come; tearing up the miry sleet and thawing snow, as if they were torn up by a waterwheel."

It is a terrifying triumph of Dickens's art that, when "Esther's Narrative" resumes, in chapter 59, we know inevitably that we are headed straight for an apocalyptic image of what Shakespeare, in *Lear*, calls "the promised end" or "image of that horror," here not the corpse of the daughter, but of the mother. Esther goes, as she must, to be the first to touch and to see, and with no affect whatsoever unveils the truth:

> I passed on to the gate, and stooped down. I lifted the heavy head,
> put the long dank hair aside, and turned the face. And it was my
> mother, cold and dead.

V

The three Brontë sisters—Charlotte, Emily Jane, and Anne—are unique literary artists whose works resemble one another's far more than they do the works of writers before or since. Charlotte's compelling novel *Jane Eyre* and her three lesser yet strong narratives—*The Professor, Shirley, Villette*—form the most extensive achievement of the sisters, but critics and common readers alike set even higher the one novel of Emily Jane's, *Wuthering*

Heights, and a handful of her lyrical poems. Anne's two novels—*Agnes Grey* and *The Tenant of Wildfell Hall*—remain highly readable, although dwarfed by *Jane Eyre* and the authentically sublime *Wuthering Heights*.

Between them, the Brontës can be said to have invented a relatively new genre, a kind of Northern romance, deeply influenced both by Byron's poetry and by his myth and personality, but going back also, more remotely yet as definitely, to the Gothic novel and to the Elizabethan drama. In a definite, if difficult to establish, sense, the heirs of the Brontës include Thomas Hardy and D. H. Lawrence. There is a harsh vitalism in the Brontës that finds its match in the Lawrence of *The Rainbow* and *Women in Love*, though the comparison is rendered problematic by Lawrence's moral zeal, enchantingly absent from the Brontës' literary cosmos.

The aesthetic puzzle of the Brontës has less to do with the mature transformations of their vision of Byron into Rochester and Heathcliff, than with their earlier fantasy-life and its literature, and the relation of that life and literature to its hero and precursor, George Gordon, Lord Byron. At his rare worst and silliest, Byron has nothing like this scene from Charlotte Brontë's "Caroline Vernon," where Caroline confronts the Byronic Duke of Zamorna:

> The Duke spoke again in a single blunt and almost coarse sentence, compressing what remained to be said, "If I were a bearded Turk, Caroline, I would take you to my harem." His deep voice as he uttered this, his high featured face, and dark, large eye burning bright with a spark from the depths of Gehenna, struck Caroline Vernon with a thrill of nameless dread. Here he was, the man Montmorency had described to her. All at once she knew him. Her guardian was gone, something terrible sat in his place.

Byron died his more-or-less heroic death at Missolonghi in Greece on April 19, 1824, aged thirty-six years and three months, after having set an impossible paradigm for authors that has become what the late Nelson Algren called "Hemingway all the way," in a mode still being exploited by Norman Mailer, Gore Vidal, and some of their younger peers. Charlotte was eight, Emily Jane six, and Anne four when the Noble Lord died and when his cult gorgeously flowered, dominating their girlhood and their young womanhood. Byron's passive-aggressive sexuality—at once sadomasochistic, homoerotic, incestuous, and ambivalently narcissistic—clearly sets the pattern for the ambiguously erotic universes of *Jane Eyre* and *Wuthering Heights*. What Schopenhauer named (and deplored) as the Will to Live, and Freud subsequently posited as the domain of the drives, is the cosmos of the Brontës, as it would come to be of Hardy and Lawrence. Byron rather than Schopenhauer is the source of the Brontës' vision of the Will to Live, but the Brontës add to Byron what his inverted Calvinism only partly accepted, the Protestant will proper, a heroic zest to assert one's own election, one's place in the hierarchy of souls.

Jane Eyre and Catherine Earnshaw do not fit into the grand array of heroines of the Protestant will that commences with Richardson's Clarissa Harlowe and goes through Austen's Emma Woodhouse and Fanny Price to triumph in George Eliot's Dorothea Brooke and Henry James's Isabel Archer. They are simply too wild and Byronic, too High Romantic, to keep such company. But we can see them with Hardy's Tess, and even more, his Eustacia Vye, and with Lawrence's Gudrun and Ursula. Their version of the Protestant will stems from the Romantic reading of Milton, but largely in its Byronic dramatization, rather than its more dialectical and subtle analyses in Blake and Shelley, and its more normative condemnation in Coleridge and in the Wordsworth of *The Borderers*.

VI

The Byronism of Rochester in *Jane Eyre* is enhanced because the narrative is related in the first person by Jane Eyre herself, who is very much an overt surrogate for Charlotte Brontë. As Rochester remarks, Jane is indomitable; as Jane says, she is altogether "a free human being with an independent will." That will is fiercest in its passion for Rochester, undoubtedly because the passion for her crucial precursor is doubly ambivalent; Byron is both the literary father to a strong daughter, and the idealized object of her erotic drive. To Jane, Rochester's first appearance is associated not only with the animal intensities of his horse and dog, but with the first of his maimings. When Jane reclaims him at the novel's conclusion, he is left partly blinded and partly crippled. I do not think that we are to apply the Freudian reduction that Rochester has been somehow castrated, even symbolically, nor need we think of him as a sacrificed Samson figure, despite the author's allusions to Milton's *Samson Agonistes*. But certainly he has been rendered dependent upon Jane, and he has been tamed into domestic virtue and pious sentiment, in what I am afraid must be regarded as Charlotte Brontë's vengeance upon Byron. Even as Jane Eyre cannot countenance a sense of being in any way inferior to anyone whatsoever, Charlotte Brontë could not allow Byron to be forever beyond her. She could acknowledge, with fine generosity, that "I regard Mr. Thackeray as the first of modern masters, and as the legitimate high priest of Truth; I study him accordingly with reverence." But *Vanity Fair* is hardly the seedbed of *Jane Eyre*, and the amiable and urbane Thackeray was not exactly a prototype for Rochester.

Charlotte Brontë, having properly disciplined Rochester, forgave him his Byronic past, as in some comments upon him in one of her letters (to W. S. Williams, August 14, 1848):

> Mr. Rochester has a thoughtful nature and a very feeling heart; he is neither selfish nor self-indulgent; he is ill-educated, misguided; errs, when he does err, through rashness and inexperience: he lives for a time as too many other men live, but being radically better than most men, he does not like that degraded life, and is never happy in it. He is taught the severe lessons of experience and has sense to learn wisdom from them. Years improve him; the effervescence of youth foamed away, what is really good in him still remains. His nature is like wine of a good vintage, time cannot sour, but only mellows him. Such at least was the character I meant to portray.

Poor Rochester! If that constituted an accurate critical summary, then who would want to read the novel? It will hardly endear me to feminist critics if I observe that much of the literary power of *Jane Eyre* results from its authentic sadism in representing the very masculine Rochester as a victim of Charlotte Brontë's will-to-power over the beautiful Lord Byron. I partly dissent, with respect, from the judgment in this regard of our best feminist critics, Sandra M. Gilbert and Susan Gubar:

> It seems not to have been primarily the coarseness and sexuality of *Jane Eyre* which shocked Victorian reviewers ... but ... its "anti-Christian" refusal to accept the forms, customs, and standards of society—in short, its rebellious feminism. They were disturbed not so much by the proud Byronic sexual energy of Rochester as by the Byronic pride and passion of Jane herself.

Byronic passion, being an ambiguous entity, is legitimately present in Jane herself as a psychosexual aggressivity turned both against the self and against others. Charlotte Brontë, in a mode between those of Schopenhauer and Freud, knows implicitly that Jane Eyre's drive to acknowledge no superior to herself is precisely on the frontier between the psychical and the physical. Rochester is the outward realm that must be internalized, and Jane's introjection of him does not leave him wholly intact. Gilbert and Gubar shrewdly observe that Rochester's extensive sexual experience is almost the final respect in which Jane is not his equal, but they doubtless would agree that Jane's sexual imagination overmatches his, at least implicitly. After all, she has every advantage, because she tells the story, and very aggressively indeed. Few novels match this one in the author's will-to-power over her reader. "Reader!" Jane keeps crying out, and then she exuberantly cudgels that reader into the way things are, as far as she is concerned. Is that battered reader a man or a woman?

I tend to agree with Sylvère Monod's judgment that "Charlotte Brontë is thus led to bully her reader because she distrusts him ... he is a vapid, conventional creature, clearly deserving no more than he is given." Certainly he is less deserving than the charmingly wicked and Byronic Rochester, who is given a lot more punishment than he deserves. I verge upon saying that Charlotte Brontë exploits the masochism of her male readers, and I may as well say it, because much of *Jane Eyre*'s rather nasty power as a novel depends upon its author's attitude towards men, which is nobly sadistic as befits a disciple of Byron.

"But what about female readers?" someone might object, and they might add: "What about Rochester's own rather nasty power? Surely he could not have gotten away with his behavior had he not been a man and well-financed to boot?" But is Rochester a man? Does he not share in the full ambiguity of Byron's multivalent sexual identities? And is Jane Eyre a woman? Is Byron's Don Juan a man? The nuances of gender, *within literary representation*, are more bewildering even than they are in the bedroom. If Freud was right when he reminded us that there are never two in a bed, but a motley crowd of forebears as well, how much truer this becomes in literary romance than in family romance.

Jane Eyre, like *Wuthering Heights*, is after all a romance, however Northern, and not a novel, properly speaking. Its standards of representation have more to do with Jacobean melodrama and Gothic fiction than with George Eliot and Thackeray, and more even with Byron's *Lara* and *Manfred* than with any other works. Rochester is no Heathcliff; he lives in a social reality in which Heathcliff would be an intruder even if Heathcliff cared for social realities except as fields in which to take revenge. Yet there is a daemon in Rochester. Heathcliff is almost nothing but daemonic, and Rochester has enough of the daemonic to call into question any current feminist reading of *Jane Eyre*. Consider the pragmatic close of the book, which is Jane's extraordinary account of her wedded bliss:

> I have now been married ten years. I know what it is to live entirely for and with what I love best on earth. I hold myself supremely blest—blest beyond what language can express; because I am my husband's life as fully as he is mine. No woman was ever nearer to her mate than I am; ever more absolutely bone of his bone and flesh of his flesh.
>
> I know no weariness of my Edward's society: he knows none of mine, any more than we each do of the pulsation of the heart that beats in our separate bosoms; consequently, we are ever together. To be together is for us to be at once as free as in solitude, as gay as in company. We talk, I believe, all day long: to talk to each other is but a more animated and an audible thinking. All my confidence is bestowed on him, all his confidence is devoted to me; we are precisely suited in character—perfect concord is the result.
>
> Mr. Rochester continued blind the first two years of our union: perhaps it was that circumstance that drew us so very near—that knit us so very close! for I was then his vision, as I am still his right hand. Literally, I was (what he often called me) the apple of his eye. He saw nature—he saw books through me; and never did I weary of gazing for his behalf, and of putting into words the effect of field, tree, town, river, cloud, sunbeam—of the landscape before us; of the weather round us—and impressing by sound on his ear what light could no longer stamp on his eye. Never did I weary of reading to him: never did I weary of conducting him where he wished to go: of doing for him what he wished to be done. And there was a pleasure in my services, most full, most exquisite, even though sad—because he claimed these services without painful shame or damping humiliation. He loved me so truly that he knew no reluctance in profiting by my attendance: he felt I loved him so fondly that to yield that attendance was to indulge my sweetest wishes.

What are we to make of Charlotte Brontë's strenuous literalization of Genesis 2:23, her astonishing "ever more absolutely bone of his bone and flesh of his flesh"? Is *that* feminism? And what precisely is that "pleasure in my services, most full, most exquisite, even though sad"? In her "Farewell to

Angria" (the world of her early fantasies), Charlotte Brontë asserted that "the mind would cease from excitement and turn now to a cooler region." Perhaps that cooler region was found in *Shirley* or in *Villette*, but fortunately it was not discovered in *Jane Eyre*. In the romance of Jane and Rochester, or of Charlotte Brontë and George Gordon, Lord Byron, we are still in Angria, "that burning clime where we have sojourned too long—its skies flame—the glow of sunset is always upon it—."

VII

Wuthering Heights is as unique and idiosyncratic a narrative as *Moby-Dick*, and like Melville's masterwork breaks all the confines of genre. Its sources, like the writings of the other Brontës, are in the fantasy literature of a very young woman, in the poems that made up Emily Brontë's Gondal saga or cycle. Many of those poems, while deeply felt, simply string together Byronic commonplaces. A few of them are extraordinarily strong and match *Wuthering Heights* in sublimity, as in the famous lyric dated January 2, 1846:

> No coward soul is mine
> No trembler in the world's storm-troubled sphere
> I see Heaven's glories shine
> And Faith shines equal arming me from Fear
>
> O God within my breast
> Almighty ever-present Deity
> Life, that in me hast rest
> As I Undying Life, have power in Thee
>
> Vain are the thousand creeds
> That move men's hearts, unutterably vain,
> Worthless as withered weeds
> Or idlest froth amid the boundless main
>
> To waken doubt in one
> Holding so fast by thy infinity
> So surely anchored on
> The steadfast rock of Immortality
>
> With wide-embracing love
> Thy spirit animates eternal years

Pervades and broods above,
Changes, sustains, dissolves, creates and rears

Though Earth and moon were gone
And suns and universes ceased to be
And thou wert left alone
Every Existence would exist in thee

There is not room for Death
Nor atom that his might could render void
Since thou art Being and Breath
And what thou art may never be destroyed.

We could hardly envision Catherine Earnshaw, let alone Heathcliff,
chanting these stanzas. The voice is that of Emily Jane Brontë addressing the
God within her own breast, a God who certainly has nothing in common with
the one worshipped by the Reverend Patrick Brontë. I do not hear in this
poem, despite all its Protestant resonances, any nuance of Byron's inverted
Miltonisms. *Wuthering Heights* seems to me a triumphant revision of Byron's
Manfred, with the revisionary swerve taking Emily Brontë into what I would
call an original gnosis, a kind of poetic faith, like Blake's or Emerson's, that
resembles some aspects (but not others) of ancient Gnosticism without in any
way actually deriving from Gnostic texts. "No coward soul is mine" also
emerges from an original gnosis, from the poet's knowing that her *pneuma* or
breath-soul, as compared to her less ontological psyche, is no part of the
created world, since that world fell even as it was created. Indeed the creation,
whether heights or valley, appears in *Wuthering Heights* as what the ancient
Gnostics called the *kenoma*, a cosmological emptiness into which *we have been
thrown*, a trope that Catherine Earnshaw originates for herself. A more overt
Victorian Gnostic, Dante Gabriel Rossetti, made the best (if anti-feminist)
observation on the setting of *Wuthering Heights*, a book whose "power and
sound style" he greatly admired:

It is a fiend of a book, an incredible monster, combining all the
stronger female tendencies from Mrs. Browning to Mrs.
Brownrigg. The action is laid in Hell,—only it seems places and
people have English names there.

Mrs. Brownrigg was a notorious eighteenth-century sadistic and
murderous midwife, and Rossetti rather nastily imputed to *Wuthering Heights*

a considerable female sadism. The book's violence is astonishing but appropriate, and appealed darkly both to Rossetti and to his close friend, the even more sadomasochistic Swinburne. Certainly the psychodynamics of the relationship between Heathcliff and Catherine go well beyond the domain of the pleasure principle. Gilbert and Gubar may stress too much that Heathcliff is Catherine's whip, the answer to her most profound fantasies, but the suggestion was Emily Brontë's before it became so fully developed by her best feminist critics.

Walter Pater remarked that the precise use of the term *romantic* did not apply to Sir Walter Scott, but rather:

> Much later, in a Yorkshire village, the spirit of romanticism bore a more really characteristic fruit in the work of a young girl, Emily Brontë, the romance of *Wuthering Heights*; the figures of Hareton Earnshaw, of Catherine Linton, and of Heathcliff— tearing open Catherine's grave, removing one side of her coffin, that he may really lie beside her in death—figures so passionate, yet woven on a background of delicately beautiful, moorland scenery, being typical examples of that spirit.

I have always wondered why Pater found the Romantic spirit more in Hareton and the younger Catherine than in Catherine Earnshaw, but I think now that Pater's implicit judgment was characteristically shrewd. The elder Catherine is the problematical figure in the book; she alone belongs to both orders of representation, that of social reality and that of otherness, of the Romantic Sublime. After she and the Lintons, Edgar and Isabella, are dead, then we are wholly in Heathcliff's world for the last half-year of his life, and it is in that world that Hareton and the younger Catherine are portrayed for us. They are—as Heathcliff obscurely senses—the true heirs to whatever societally possible relationship Heathcliff and the first Catherine could have had.

Emily Brontë died less than half a year after her thirtieth birthday, having finished *Wuthering Heights* when she was twenty-eight. Even Charlotte, the family survivor, died before she turned thirty-nine, and the world of *Wuthering Heights* reflects the Brontë reality: the first Catherine dies at eighteen, Hindley at twenty-seven, Heathcliff's son Linton at seventeen, Isabella at thirty-one, Edgar at thirty-nine, and Heathcliff at thirty-seven or thirty-eight. It is a world where you marry early, because you will not live long. Hindley is twenty when he marries Frances, while Catherine Earnshaw is seventeen when she marries the twenty-one-year-old Edgar Linton.

Heathcliff is nineteen when he makes his hellish marriage to poor Isabella, who is eighteen at the time. The only happy lovers, Hareton and the second Catherine, are twenty-four and eighteen, respectively, when they marry. Both patterns—early marriage and early death—are thoroughly High Romantic, and emerge from the legacy of Shelley, dead at twenty-nine, and of Byron, martyred to the cause of Greek independence at thirty-six.

The passions of Gondal are scarcely moderated in *Wuthering Heights*, nor could they be; Emily Brontë's religion is essentially erotic, and her vision of triumphant sexuality is so mingled with death that we can imagine no consummation for the love of Heathcliff and Catherine Earnshaw except death. I find it difficult therefore to accept Gilbert and Gubar's reading in which *Wuthering Heights* becomes a Romantic feminist critique of *Paradise Lost*, akin to Mary Shelley's *Frankenstein*. Emily Brontë is no more interested in refuting Milton than in sustaining him. What Gilbert and Gubar uncover in *Wuthering Heights* that is antithetical to *Paradise Lost* comes directly from Byron's *Manfred*, which certainly is a Romantic critique of *Paradise Lost*. *Wuthering Heights* is *Manfred* converted to prose romance, and Heathcliff is more like Manfred, Lara, and Byron himself than is Charlotte Brontë's Rochester.

Byronic incest—the crime of Manfred and Astarte—is no crime for Emily Brontë, since Heathcliff and Catherine Earnshaw are more truly brother and sister than are Hindley and Catherine. Whatever inverted morality—a curious blend of Catholicism and Calvinism—Byron enjoyed, Emily Brontë herself repudiates, so that *Wuthering Heights* becomes a critique of *Manfred*, though hardly from a conventional feminist perspective. The furious energy that is loosed in *Wuthering Heights* is precisely Gnostic; its aim is to get back to the original Abyss, before the creation-fall. Like Blake, Emily Brontë identifies her imagination with the Abyss, and her *pneuma* or breath-soul with the Alien God, who is antithetical to the God of the creeds. The heroic rhetoric of Catherine Earnshaw is beyond every ideology, every merely social formulation, beyond even the dream of justice or of a better life, because it is beyond this cosmos, "this shattered prison":

> "Oh, you see, Nelly! he would not relent a moment, to keep me out of the grave! *That* is how I'm loved! Well, never mind! That is not my Heathcliff. I shall love mine yet; and take him with me—he's in my soul. And," added she, musingly, "the thing that irks me most is this shattered prison, after all. I'm tired, tired of being enclosed here. I'm wearying to escape into that glorious world, and to be always there; not seeing it dimly through tears, and yearning for it through the walls of an aching heart; but really

with it, and in it. Nelly, you think you are better and more
fortunate than I; in full health and strength. You are sorry for
me—very soon that will be altered. I shall be sorry for *you*. I shall
be incomparably beyond and above you all. I *wonder* he won't be
near me!" She went on to herself. "I thought he wished it.
Heathcliff, dear! you should not be sullen now. Do come to me,
Heathcliff."

Whatever we are to call the mutual passion of Catherine and
Heathcliff, it has no societal aspect and neither seeks nor needs societal
sanction. Romantic love has no fiercer representation in all of literature. But
"love" seems an inadequate term for the connection between Catherine and
Heathcliff. There are no elements of transference in that relation, nor can we
call the attachment involved either narcissistic or anaclitic. If Freud is not
applicable, then neither is Plato. These extraordinary vitalists, Catherine and
Heathcliff, do not desire in one another that which each does not possess, do
not lean themselves against one another, and do not even find and thus
augment their own selves. They *are* one another, which is neither sane nor
possible, and which does not support any doctrine of liberation whatsoever.
Only that most extreme of visions, Gnosticism, could accommodate them,
for, like the Gnostic adepts, Catherine and Heathcliff can only enter the
pleroma or fullness together, as presumably they have done after Heathcliff's
self-induced death by starvation.

Blake may have promised us the Bible of Hell; Emily Brontë seems to
have disdained Heaven and Hell alike. Her finest poem (for which we have
no manuscript, but it is inconceivable that it could have been written by
Charlotte) rejects every feeling save her own inborn "first feelings" and every
world except a vision of earth consonant with those inaugural emotions:

> Often rebuked, yet always back returning
>   To those first feelings that were born with me,
> And leaving busy chase of wealth and learning
>   For idle dreams of things which cannot be:
>
> To-day, I will seek not the shadowy region;
>   Its unsustaining vastness waxes drear;
> And visions rising, legion after legion,
>   Bring the unreal world too strangely near.
>
> I'll walk, but not in old heroic traces,
>   And not in paths of high morality,

And not among the half-distinguished faces,
   The clouded forms of long-past history.

I'll walk where my own nature would be leading:
   It vexes me to choose another guide:
Where the gray flocks in ferry glens are feeding;
   Where the wild wind blows on the mountain side.

What have those lonely mountains worth revealing?
   More glory and more grief than I can tell:
The earth that wakes *one* human heart to feeling
   Can centre both the worlds of Heaven and Hell.

Whatever that centering is, it is purely individual, and as beyond gender as it is beyond creed or "high morality." It is the voice of Catherine Earnshaw, celebrating her awakening from the dream of heaven:

> "I was only going to say that heaven did not seem to be my home; and I broke my heart with weeping to come back to earth; and the angels were so angry that they flung me out, into the middle of the heath on the top of Wuthering Heights; where I woke sobbing for joy."

VIII

Even taken in its derivative meaning of outline, what is form but the limit of that difference by which we discriminate one object from another?—a limit determined partly by the intrinsic relations or composition of the object, & partly by the extrinsic action of other bodies upon it. This is true whether the object is a rock or a man.
                    —GEORGE ELIOT, "Notes on Forms in Art"

It was Freud, in our time, who taught us again what the pre-Socratics taught: *ethos* is the *daimon*, character is fate. A generation before Freud, George Eliot taught the same unhappy truth to her contemporaries. If character is fate, then in a harsh sense there can be no accidents. Character presumably is less volatile than personality, and we tend to disdain anyone who would say personality is fate. Personalities suffer accidents; characters endure fate. If we seek major personalities among the great novelists, we find many competitors: Balzac, Tolstoy, Dickens, Henry James, even the enigmatic Conrad. By general agreement, the grand instance of a moral character would be George Eliot. She has a nearly unique spiritual authority, best characterized by the English critic Walter Allen about twenty years ago:

> George Eliot is the first novelist in the world in some things, and they are the things that come within the scope of her moral interpretation of life. Circumscribed though it was, it was certainly not narrow; nor did she ever forget the difficulty attendant upon the moral life and the complexity that goes to its making.

Her peculiar gift, almost unique despite her place in a tradition of displaced Protestantism that includes Samuel Richardson's *Clarissa* and Wordsworth's poetry, is to dramatize her interpretations in such a way as to abolish the demarcations between aesthetic pleasure and moral renunciation. Richardson's heroine Clarissa Harlowe and Wordsworth in his best poems share in a compensatory formula: experiential loss can be transformed into imaginative gain. Eliot's imagination, despite its Wordsworthian antecedents and despite the ways in which Clarissa Harlowe is the authentic precursor of Dorothea Brooke in *Middlemarch*, is too severe to accept the formula of compensation. The beauty of renunciation in Eliot's fiction does not result from a transformation of loss, but rather from a strength that is in no way dependent upon exchange or gain. Eliot presents us with the puzzle of what might be called the Moral Sublime. To her contemporaries, this was no puzzle. F. W. H. Myers, remembered now as a "psychic researcher" (a marvelous metaphor that we oddly use as a title for those who quest after spooks) and as the father of L. H. Myers, author of the novel *The Near and the Far*, wrote a famous description of Eliot's 1873 visit to Cambridge:

> I remember how at Cambridge I walked with her once in the Fellows' Garden of Trinity, on an evening of rainy May; and she, stirred somewhat beyond her wont, and taking as her text the three words which had been used so often as the inspiring trumpet-call of men—the words God, Immortality, Duty— pronounced with terrible earnestness how inconceivable was the first, how unbelievable was the second, and yet how peremptory and absolute the third. Never, perhaps, have sterner accents confirmed the sovereignty of impersonal and unrecompensing Law. I listened, and night fell; her grave, majestic countenance

turned towards me like a sybil's in the gloom; it was as though she
withdrew from my grasp, one by one, the two scrolls of promise
and left me the third scroll only, awful with inevitable fates. And
when we stood at length and parted, amid that columnar circuit
of forest trees, beneath the last twilight of starless skies, I seemed
to be gazing, like Titus at Jerusalem, on vacant seats and empty
halls—on a sanctuary with no Presence to hallow it, and heaven
left empty of God.

However this may sound now, Myers intended no ironies. As the sybil
of "unrecompensing Law," Eliot joined the austere company of nineteenth-
century prose prophets: Carlyle, Ruskin, Newman, and Arnold in England;
Emerson in America; Schopenhauer, Nietzsche, Kierkegaard, and finally
Freud on the Continent. But this ninefold, though storytellers of a sort,
wrote no novels. Eliot's deepest affinities were scarcely with Dickens,
Thackeray, and Trollope, and yet her formal achievement requires us to read
her as we read them. This causes difficulties, since Eliot was not a great
stylist, and was far more immersed in philosophical than in narrative
tradition. Yet her frequent clumsiness in authorial asides and her hesitations
in storytelling matter not at all. We do not even regret her absolute lack of
any sense of the comic, which never dares take revenge upon her anyway.
Wordsworth at his strongest, as in "Resolution and Independence," still can
be unintentionally funny (which inspired the splendid parodies of the poem's
leech-gatherer and its solipsistic bard in Lewis Carroll's "White Knight's
Ballad" and Edward Lear's "Incidents in the Life of My Uncle Arly"). But I
have seen no effective parodies of George Eliot, and doubt their possibility.
It is usually unwise to be witty concerning our desperate need, not only to
decide upon right action, but also to will such action, against pleasure and
against what we take to be self-interest. Like Freud, Eliot ultimately is an
inescapable moralist, precisely delineating our discomfort with culture, and
remorselessly weighing the economics of the psyche's civil wars.

IX

George Eliot is not one of the great letter writers. Her letters matter because
they are hers, and in some sense do tell part of her own story, but they do not
yield to a continuous reading. On a scale of nineteenth-century letter-writing
by important literary figures, in which Keats would rank first, and Walter
Pater last (the Paterian prose style is never present in his letters), Eliot would
find a place about dead center. She is always herself in her letters, too much

herself perhaps, but that self is rugged, honest, and formidably inspiring. Our contemporary feminist critics seem to me a touch uncomfortable with Eliot. Here she is on extending the franchise to women, in a letter to John Morley (May 14, 1867):

> Thanks for your kind practical remembrance. Your attitude in relation to Female Enfranchisement seems to be very nearly mine. If I were called on to act in the matter, I would certainly not oppose any plan which held out a reasonable promise of tending to establish as far as possible an equivalence of advantages for the two sexes, as to education and the possibilities of free development. I fear you may have misunderstood something I said the other evening about nature. I never meant to urge the "intention of Nature" argument, which is to me a pitiable fallacy. I mean that as a fact of mere zoological evolution, woman seems to me to have the worst share in existence. But for that very reason I would the more contend that in the moral evolution we have "an art which does mend nature"—an art which "itself is nature." It is the function of love in the largest sense, to mitigate the harshness of all fatalities. And in the thorough recognition of that worse share, I think there is a basis for a sublimer resignation in woman and a more regenerating tenderness in man.
>
> However, I repeat that I do not trust very confidently to my own impressions on this subject. The peculiarities of my own lot may have caused me to have idiosyncrasies rather than an average judgment. The one conviction on the matter which I hold with some tenacity is, that through all transitions the goal towards which we are proceeding is a more clearly discerned distinctness of function (allowing always for exceptional cases of individual organization) with as near an approach to equivalence of good for woman and for man as can be secured by the effort of growing moral force to lighten the pressure of hard non-moral outward conditions. It is rather superfluous, perhaps injudicious, to plunge into such deeps as these in a hasty note, but it is difficult to resist the desire to botch imperfect talk with a little imperfect writing.

This is a strong insistence upon form in life as in art, upon the limit of that difference by which we discriminate one object from another. I have heard feminist critics decry it as defeatism, though Eliot speaks of "mere zoological evolution" as bringing about every woman's "worse share in existence." "A sublimer resignation in woman" is not exactly a popular goal these days, but Eliot never speaks of the Sublime without profundity and an awareness of human loss. When she praises Ruskin as a teacher "with the inspiration of a Hebrew prophet," she also judges him to be "strongly akin to the sublimest part of Wordsworth," a judgment clearly based upon the Wordsworthian source of Ruskin's tropes for the sense of loss that dominates the Sublime experience. The harshness of being a woman, however mitigated by societal reform, will remain, Eliot tells us, since we cannot mend nature and its unfairness. Her allusion to the Shakespearean "art which does mend nature," and which "itself is nature" (*Winter's Tale*, 4.4.88–96) subtly emends Shakespeare in the deliberately wistful hope for a moral evolution of love between the sexes. What dominates this letter to Morley is a harsh plangency, yet it is anything but defeatism. Perhaps Eliot should have spoken of a "resigned sublimity" rather than a "sublime resignation," but her art, and life, give the lie to any contemporary feminist demeaning of the author of *Middlemarch*, who shares with Jane Austen and Emily Dickinson the eminence of being the strongest woman writer in the English language.

X

Henry James asserted that "*Middlemarch* is at once one of the strongest and one of the weakest of English novels." The second half of that judgment was evidently defensive. By common consent, *Middlemarch* is equal, at least, to any other novel in the language. Dorothea Brooke is a crucial figure in that great sequence of the fictive heroines of the Protestant Will that includes Clarissa Harlowe, Elizabeth Bennet, Emma Woodhouse, Esther Summerson, Hester Prynne, Isabel Archer, Ursula Brangwen, and Clarissa Dalloway, among others. James complained that "Dorothea was altogether too superb a heroine to be wasted; yet she plays a narrower part than the imagination of the reader demands." Yet this is surely true of Isabel Archer also, since, like Dorothea Brooke, "she is of more consequence than the action of which she is the nominal centre." It could be argued that only Hester Prynne is provided with an action worthy of her, but then the superb Hester is called upon mostly to suffer. Dimmesdale, under any circumstances, seems as inadequate for Hester as Will Ladislaw seems too inconsequential for Dorothea, or as even Ralph Touchett seems weak in relation to Isabel. Except for Clarissa Harlowe confronting her equally strong agonist in Lovelace, the heroines of the Protestant Will are always involved with men less memorable than themselves. Lawrence attempted to defy this tradition, but failed, as we must acknowledge when we set the tendentious Birkin beside the vital Ursula.

"Of course she gets up spurious miracles," the young Yeats remarked in defense of Madame Blavatsky, "but what *is* a woman of genius to do in the Nineteenth Century?" What is Saint Theresa to do in the nineteenth century, and in England, of all countries? What is Isabel Archer, heiress of all the ages, to do in the nineteenth century? In America, is she to marry Caspar Goodwood, a prospect that neither she nor James can endure? In Europe, she marries the subtly dreadful Osmond, mock-Emersonian and pseudo-Paterian. Even Casaubon might have been better, George Eliot could have been sly enough to tell Henry James. The heroes of the Protestant Will may have existed in mere fact—witness Oliver Cromwell and John Milton—but they have not been persuasively represented in prose fiction.

Rereading *Middlemarch* makes me unhappy only when I have to contemplate Will Ladislaw, an idealized portrait of George Henry Lewes, George Eliot's not unworthy lover. Otherwise, the novel compels aesthetic awe in me, if only because it alone, among novels, raises moral reflection to the level of high art. There is Nietzsche of course, but then *Zarathustra* is not a novel, and *Zarathustra* is an aesthetic disaster anyway. The great moralists, from Montaigne through Emerson to Freud, do not write prose fiction, and yet George Eliot is of their company. If we can speak aesthetically of the Moral Sublime, then she must help inform our speaking. All versions of the Sublime seem to involve a surrender of easier pleasures in favor of more difficult pleasures, but the Moral Sublime, in Freud or George Eliot, necessarily centers upon a coming to terms with the reality principle.

How is it that Eliot can imbue her moralizings with an aesthetic authority, when such contemporary practitioners as Doris Lessing, Walker Percy, and even Iris Murdoch cannot? I think that there are two answers here, and they may be quite unrelated to one another. One is that Eliot is unmatched among all other novelists in cognitive strength; she has the same eminence in prose fiction as Emily Dickinson has in lyric poetry or Shakespeare in the drama. We ordinarily do not estimate imaginative writers in terms of intellect, but that may be one of the eternal weaknesses of Western literary criticism. And yet the puzzle is great. Walt Whitman, in my judgment, surpasses even Dickinson among American poets, yet compared to her he cannot think at all. Dickinson and George Eliot, like Blake, rethink everything in earth and in heaven for themselves, as Shakespeare, above all writers, would appear to have done for himself. Such cognitive originality clearly does become an aesthetic value, in combination with other modes of mastery, yet it scarcely exists in poets as superb as Whitman and Tennyson.

Unallied to her cognitive strength (so far as I can tell) is Eliot's other massive aesthetic advantage as a moralist: a lack of any of the crippling intensities of the wrong kind of self-consciousness concerning morals and moralization. We do not encounter hesitation or affectation in Eliot's broodings upon moral dilemmas. She contrives to be at once intricate and direct in such matters, as in the famous conclusion to Middlemarch:

> Certainly those determining acts of her life were not ideally beautiful. They were the mixed result of young and noble impulse struggling amidst the conditions of an imperfect social state, in which great feelings will often take the aspect of error, and great faith the aspect of illusion. For there is no creature whose inward being is so strong that it is not greatly determined by what lies outside it. A new Theresa will hardly have the opportunity of reforming a conventual life, any more than a new Antigone will spend her heroic piety in daring all for the sake of a brother's burial: the medium in which their ardent deeds took shape is for ever gone. But we insignificant people with our daily words and acts are preparing the lives of many Dorotheas, some of which may present a far sadder sacrifice than that of the Dorothea whose story we know.
>
> Her finely-touched spirit had still its fine issues, though they were not widely visible. Her full nature, like that river of which Cyrus broke the strength, spent itself in channels which had no great name on the earth. But the effect of her being on those around her was incalculably diffusive: for the growing good of the world is partly dependent on unhistoric acts; and that things are not so ill with you and me as they might have been, is half owing to the number who lived faithfully a hidden life, and rest in unvisited tombs.

Eliot is defending both of Dorothea's marriages, but I rapidly forget Dorothea, at least for a while, when I read and ponder that massive third sentence, at once a truism and a profound moment of wisdom writing: "For there is no creature whose inward being is so strong that it is not greatly determined by what lies outside it." Our overdetermination—by society, by generational position, by the familial past—could not be better expressed, nor could we be better reminded that we ourselves will overdetermine those who come after us, even heroines as intense as Saint Theresa, Antigone, and Dorothea Brooke.

Eliot's proleptic answer to Henry James's protest at the waste of the superb Dorothea is centered in one apothegm: "the growing good of the world is partly dependent on unhistoric acts." James might have agreed, but then would have murmured that the growing good of the world and of the art of fiction are somewhat different matters. It is George Eliot's peculiar strength that she comes closer than any other novelist to persuading us that the good of the world and of the novel are ultimately reconcilable.

XI

For Arthur Schopenhauer, the Will to Live was the true thing-in-itself, not an interpretation but a rapacious, active, universal, and ultimately indifferent drive or desire. Schopenhauer's great work *The World as Will and Representation* had the same relation to and influence upon many of the principal nineteenth- and early twentieth-century novelists that Freud's writings have in regard to many of this century's later, crucial masters of prose fiction. Zola, Maupassant, Turgenev, and Tolstoy join Thomas Hardy as Schopenhauer's nineteenth-century heirs, in a tradition that goes on through Proust, Conrad, and Thomas Mann to culminate in aspects of Borges and of Beckett, the most eminent living writer of narrative. Since Schopenhauer (despite Freud's denials) was one of Freud's prime precursors, one could argue that aspects of Freud's influence upon writers simply carry on from Schopenhauer's previous effect. Manifestly, the relation of Schopenhauer to Hardy is different in both kind and degree from the larger sense in which Schopenhauer was Freud's forerunner or Wittgenstein's. A poet novelist like Hardy turns to a rhetorical speculator like Schopenhauer only because he finds something in his own temperament and sensibility confirmed and strengthened, and not at all as Lucretius turned to Epicurus, or as Whitman was inspired by Emerson.

The true precursor for Hardy was Shelley, whose visionary skepticism permeates the novels as well as the poems and *The Dynasts*. There is some technical debt to George Eliot in the early novels, but Hardy in his depths was little more moved by her than by Wilkie Collins, from whom he also learned element of craft. Shelley's tragic sense of eros is pervasive throughout Hardy, and ultimately determines Hardy's understanding of his strongest heroines: Bathsheba Everdene, Eustacia Vye, Marty South, Tess Durbeyfield, Sue Bridehead. Between desire and fulfillment in Shelley falls the shadow of the selfhood, a shadow that makes love and what might be called the means of love quite irreconcilable. What M. D. Zabel named as "the aesthetic of incongruity" in Hardy and ascribed to temperamental causes is in a profound way the result of attempting to transmute the procedures of *The Revolt of Islam* and *Epipsychidion* into the supposedly naturalistic novel.

J. Hillis Miller, when he worked more in the mode of a critic of consciousness like Georges Poulet than in the deconstruction of Paul de Man and Jacques Derrida, saw the fate of love in Hardy as being darkened always by a shadow cast by the lover's consciousness itself. Hugh Kenner, with a distaste for Hardy akin to (and perhaps derived from) T. S. Eliot's in *After Strange Gods*, suggested that Miller had created a kind of Proustian Hardy, who turns out to be a case rather than an artist. Hardy was certainly not an artist comparable to Henry James (who dismissed him as a mere imitator of George Eliot) or James Joyce, but the High Modernist shibboleths for testing the novel have now waned considerably, except for a few surviving high priests of Modernism like Kenner. A better guide to Hardy's permanent strength as a novelist was his heir D. H. Lawrence, whose *The Rainbow* and *Women in Love* marvelously brought Hardy's legacy to an apotheosis. Lawrence, praising Hardy with a rebel son's ambivalence, associated him with Tolstoy as a tragic writer:

> And this is the quality Hardy shares with the great writers, Shakespeare or Sophocles or Tolstoi, this setting behind the small action of his protagonists the terrific action of unfathomed nature; setting a smaller system of morality, the one grasped and formulated by the human consciousness within the vast, uncomprehended and incomprehensible morality of nature or of life itself, surpassing human consciousness. The difference is, that whereas in Shakespeare or Sophocles the greater, uncomprehended morality, or fate, is actively transgressed and gives active punishment, in Hardy and Tolstoi the lesser, human morality, the mechanical system is actively transgressed, and holds, and punishes the protagonist, whilst the greater morality is only passively, negatively transgressed, it is represented merely as being present in background, in scenery, not taking any active part, having no direct connexion with the protagonist. Oedipus, Hamlet, Macbeth set themselves up against, or find themselves set up against, the unfathomed moral forces of nature, and out of this unfathomed force comes their death. Whereas Anna Karenina, Eustacia, Tess, Sue, and Jude find themselves up against the established system of human government and

morality, they cannot detach themselves, and are brought down. Their real tragedy is that they are unfaithful to the greater unwritten morality, which would have bidden Anna Karenina be patient and wait until she, by virtue of greater right, could take what she needed from society; would have bidden Vronsky detach himself from the system, become an individual, creating a new colony of morality with Anna; would have bidden Eustacia fight Clym for his own soul, and Tess take and claim her Angel, since she had the greater light; would have bidden Jude and Sue endure for very honour's sake, since one must bide by the best that one has known, and not succumb to the lesser good.

(*Study of Thomas Hardy*)

This seems to me powerful and just, because it catches what is most surprising and enduring in Hardy's novels—the sublime stature and aesthetic dignity of his crucial protagonists—while exposing also his great limitation, his denial of freedom to his best personages. Lawrence's prescription for what would have saved Eustacia and Clym, Tess and Angel, Sue and Jude, is perhaps not as persuasive. He speaks of them as though they were Gudrun and Gerald, and thus have failed to be Ursula and Birkin. It is Hardy's genius that they are what they had to be: as imperfect as their creator and his vision, as impure as his language and his plotting, and finally painful and memorable to us:

Note that, in this bitterness, delight,
Since the imperfect is so hot in us,
Lies in flawed words and stubborn sounds.

XII

I first read *The Return of the Native* when I was about fifteen, and had reread it in whole or in part several times through the years before rereading it now. What I had remembered most vividly then I am likely to remember again: Eustacia, Venn the red man, the Heath. I had almost forgotten Clym, and his mother, and Thomasin, and Wildeve, and probably will forget them again. Clym, in particular, is a weak failure in characterization, and nearly sinks the novel; indeed ought to capsize any novel whatsoever. Yet *The Return of the Native* survives him, even though its chief glory, the sexually enchanting Eustacia Vye, does not. Her suicide is so much the waste of a marvelous woman (or representation of a woman, if you insist upon being a formalist) that the reader finds Clym even more intolerable than he is, and is likely not to forgive Hardy, except that Hardy clearly suffers the loss quite as much as any reader does.

Eustacia underwent a singular transformation during the novel's composition, from a daemonic sort of female Byron, or Byronic witch-like creature, to the grandly beautiful, discontented, and human—all too human but hardly blameworthy—heroine, who may be the most desirable woman in all of nineteenth-century British fiction. "A powerful personality uncurbed by any institutional attachment or by submission to any objective beliefs; unhampered by any ideas"—it would be a good description of Eustacia, but is actually Hardy himself through the eyes of T. S. Eliot in *After Strange Gods*, where Hardy is chastised for not believing in Original Sin and deplored also because "at times his style touches sublimity without ever having passed through the stage of being good."

Here is Eustacia in the early "Queen of Night" chapter:

She was in person full-limbed and somewhat heavy; without ruddiness, as without pallor; and soft to the touch as a cloud. To see her hair was to fancy that a whole winter did not contain darkness enough to form its shadow: it closed over her forehead like nightfall extinguishing the western glow.

Her nerves extended into those tresses, and her temper could always be softened by stroking them down. When her hair was brushed she would instantly sink into stillness and look like the Sphinx. If, in passing under one of the Egdon banks, any of its thick skeins were caught, as they sometimes were, by a prickly tuft of the large *Ulex Europaeus*—which will act as a sort of hair-brush—she would go back a few steps, and pass against it a second time.

She had Pagan eyes, full of nocturnal mysteries, and their light, as it came and went, and came again, was partially hampered by their oppressive lids and lashes; and of these the under lid was much fuller than it usually is with English women. This enabled her to indulge in reverie without seeming to do so: she might have been believed capable of sleeping without closing them up. Assuming that the souls of men and women were visible essences, you could fancy the colour of Eustacia's soul to be flame-like. The sparks from it that rose into her dark pupils gave the same impression.

Hardy's Eustacia may owe something to Walter Pater's *The Renaissance*, published five years before *The Return of the Native*, since in some ways she makes a third with Pater's evocations of the Botticelli Venus and Leonardo's Mona Lisa, visions of antithetical female sexuality. Eustacia's flame-like quality precisely recalls Pater's ecstacy of passion in the "Conclusion" to *The Renaissance*, and the epigraph to *The Return of the Native* could well have been:

> This at least of flame-like our life has, that it is but the concurrence, renewed from moment to moment, of forces parting sooner or later on their ways.

This at least of flame-like Eustacia's life has, that the concurrence of forces parts sooner rather than later. But then this most beautiful of Hardy's women is also the most doom-eager, the color of her soul being flame-like. The Heath brings her only Wildeve and Clym, but Paris doubtless would have brought her scarce better, since as Queen of Night she attracts the constancy and the kindness of sorrow.

If Clym and Wildeve are bad actors, and they are, what about Egdon Heath? On this, critics are perpetually divided, some finding the landscape sublime, while others protest that its representation is bathetic. I myself am divided, since clearly it is both, and sometimes simultaneously so! Though Eustacia hates it fiercely, it is nearly as Shelleyan as she is, and rather less natural than presumably it ought to be. That it is more overwritten than overgrown is palpable:

> To recline on a stump of thorn in the central valley of Egdon, between afternoon and night, as now, where the eye could reach nothing of the world outside the summits and shoulders of heath-land which filled the whole circumference of its glance, and to know that everything around and underneath had been from prehistoric times as unaltered as the stars overhead, gave ballast to the mind adrift on change, and harassed by the irrepressible New. The great inviolate place had an ancient permanence which the sea cannot claim. Who can say of a particular sea that it is old? Distilled by the sun, kneaded by the moon, it is renewed in a year, in a day, or in an hour. The sea changed, the fields changed, the rivers, the villages, and the people changed, yet Egdon remained. Those surfaces were neither so steep as to be destructible by weather, nor so flat as to be the victims of floods and deposits.

With the exception of an aged highway, and a still more aged barrow presently to be referred to—themselves almost crystallized to natural products by long continuance—even the trifling irregularities were not caused by pickaxe, plough, or spade, but remained as long as the very finger-touches of the last geological change.

Even Melville cannot always handle this heightened mode; Hardy rarely can, although he attempts it often. And yet we do remember Egdon Heath, years after reading the novel, possibly because something about it wounds us even as it wounds Eustacia. We remember also Diggory Venn, not as the prosperous burgher he becomes, but as we first encounter him, permeated by the red ochre of his picturesque trade:

The decayed officer, by degrees, came up alongside his fellow-wayfarer, and wished him good evening. The reddleman turned his head and replied in sad and occupied tones. He was young, and his face, if not exactly handsome, approached so near to handsome that nobody would have contradicted an assertion that it really was so in its natural colour. His eye, which glared so strangely through his stain, was in itself attractive—keen as that of a bird of prey, and blue as autumn mist. He had neither whisker nor moustache, which allowed the soft curves of the lower part of his face to be apparent. His lips were thin, and though, as it seemed, compressed by thought, there was a pleasant twitch at their corners now and then. He was clothed throughout in a tight-fitting suit of corduroy, excellent in quality, not much worn, and well-chosen for its purpose; but deprived of its original colour by his trade. It showed to advantage the good shape of his figure. A certain well-to-do air about the man suggested that he was not poor for his degree. The natural query of an observer would have been, Why should such a promising being as this have hidden his prepossessing exterior by adopting that singular occupation?

Hardy had intended Venn to disappear mysteriously forever from Egdon Heath, instead of marrying Thomasin, but yielded to the anxiety of giving the contemporary reader something cheerful and normative at the end of his austere and dark novel. He ought to have kept to his intent, but perhaps it does not matter. The Heath endures, the red man either vanishes or is transmogrified into a husband and a burgher. Though we see Clym rather uselessly preaching to all comers as the book closes, our spirits are elsewhere, with the wild image of longing that no longer haunts the Heath, Hardy's lost Queen of Night.

XIII

Of Hardy's major novels, *The Mayor of Casterbridge* is the least flawed and clearly the closest to tragic convention in Western literary tradition. If one hesitates to prefer it to *The Return of the Native*, *Tess*, or *Jude*, that may be because it is the least original and eccentric work of the four. Henchard is certainly the best articulated and most consistent of Hardy's male personages, but Lucetta is no Eustacia, and the amiable Elizabeth-Jane does not compel much of the reader's interest. The book's glory, Henchard, is so massive a self-punisher that he can be said to leap over the psychic cosmos of Schopenhauer directly into that of Freud's great essay on the economics of masochism, with its grim new category of "moral masochism." In a surprising way, Hardy reverses, through Henchard, one of the principal topoi of Western tragedy, as set forth acutely by Northrop Frye:

> A strong element of demonic ritual in public punishments and similar mob amusements is exploited by tragic and ironic myth. Breaking on the wheel becomes Lear's wheel of fire; bear-baiting is an image for Gloucester and Macbeth, and for the crucified Prometheus the humiliation of exposure, the horror of being watched, is a greater misery than the pain. *Derkou theama* (behold the spectacle; get your staring over with) is his bitterest cry. The inability of Milton's blind Samson to stare back is his greatest torment, and one which forces him to scream at Delilah, in one of the most terrible passages of all tragic drama, that he will tear her to pieces if she touches him.

For Henchard "the humiliation of exposure" becomes a terrible passion, until at last he makes an exhibition of himself during a royal visit. Perhaps he can revert to what Frye calls "the horror of being watched" only when he knows that the gesture involved will be his last. Hence his Will, which may be the most powerful prose passage that Hardy ever wrote:

They stood in silence while he ran into the cottage; returning in a moment with a crumpled scrap of paper. On it there was pencilled as follows:—

"MICHAEL HENCHARD'S WILL
"That Elizabeth-Jane Farfrae be not told of my death, or made to grieve on account of me.
"& that I be not bury'd in consecrated ground.
"& that no sexton be asked to toll the bell.
"& that nobody is wished to see my dead body.
"& that no murners walk behind me at my funeral.
"& that no flours be planted on my grave.
"& that no man remember me.
"To this I put my name.
"MICHAEL HENCHARD."

That dark testament is the essence of Henchard. It is notorious that "tragedy" becomes a very problematical form in the European Enlightenment and afterwards. Romanticism, which has been our continuous Modernism from the mid-1740s to the present moment, did not return the tragic hero to us, though from Richardson's Clarissa Harlowe until now we have received many resurgences of the tragic heroine. Hardy and Ibsen can be judged to have come closest to reviving the tragic hero, in contradistinction to the hero-villain who, throughout Romantic tradition, limns his night-piece and judges it to have been his best. Henchard, despite his blind strength and his terrible errors, is no villain, and as readers we suffer with him, unrelievedly, because our sympathy for him is unimpeded.

Unfortunately, the suffering becomes altogether *too* unrelieved, as it does again with Jude Fawley. Rereading *The Mayor of Casterbridge* is less painful than rereading *Jude the Obscure*, since at least we do not have to contemplate little Father Time hanging the other urchins and himself, but it is still very painful indeed. Whether or not tragedy should possess some catharsis, we resent the imposition of too much pathos upon us, and we need some gesture of purification if only to keep us away from our own defensive ironies. Henchard, alas, *accomplishes nothing*, for himself or for others. Ahab, a great hero-villain, goes down fighting his implacable fate, the whiteness of the whale, but Henchard is a self-destroyer to no purpose. And yet we are vastly moved by him and know that we should be. Why?

The novel's full title is *The Life and Death of the Mayor of Casterbridge: A Story of a Man of Character*. As Robert Louis Stevenson said in a note to

Hardy, "Henchard is a great fellow," which implies that he is a great personality rather than a man of character. This is, in fact, how Hardy represents Henchard, and the critic R. H. Hutton was right to be puzzled by Hardy's title, in a review published in *The Spectator* on June 5, 1886:

> Mr. Hardy has not given us any more powerful study than that of Michael Henchard. Why he should especially term his hero in his title-page a "man of character," we do not clearly understand. Properly speaking, character is the stamp graven on a man, and character therefore, like anything which can be graven, and which, when graven, remains, is a word much more applicable to that which has fixity and permanence, than to that which is fitful and changeful, and which impresses a totally different image of itself on the wax of plastic circumstance at one time, from that which it impresses on a similarly plastic surface at another time. To keep strictly to the associations from which the word "character" is derived, a man of character ought to suggest a man of steady and unvarying character, a man who conveys very much the same conception of his own qualities under one set of circumstances, which he conveys under another. This is true of many men, and they might be called men of character *par excellence*. But the essence of Michael Henchard is that he is a man of large nature and depth of passion, who is yet subject to the most fitful influences, who can do in one mood acts of which he will never cease to repent in almost all his other moods, whose temper of heart changes many times even during the execution of the same purpose, though the same ardour, the same pride, the same wrathful magnanimity, the same inability to carry out in cool blood the angry resolve of the mood of revenge or scorn, the same hasty unreasonableness, and the same disposition to swing back to an equally hasty reasonableness, distinguish him throughout. In one very good sense, the great deficiency of Michael Henchard might be said to be in "character." It might well be said that with a little *more* character, with a little more fixity of mind, with a little more power of recovering *himself* when he was losing his balance, his would have been a nature of gigantic mould; whereas, as Mr. Hardy's novel is meant to show, it was a nature which ran mostly to waste. But, of course, in the larger and wider sense of the word "character," that sense which has less reference to the permanent definition of the stamp, and

more reference to the confidence with which the varying moods
may be anticipated, it is not inadmissible to call Michael
Henchard a "man of character." Still, the words on the title-page
rather mislead. One looks for the picture of a man of much more
constancy of purpose, and much less tragic mobility of mood,
than Michael Henchard. None the less, the picture is a very vivid
one, and almost magnificent in its fullness of expression. The
largeness of his nature, the unreasonable generosity and
suddenness of his friendships, the depth of his self-humiliation
for what was evil in him, the eagerness of his craving for
sympathy, the vehemence of his impulses both for good and evil,
the curious dash of stoicism in a nature so eager for sympathy,
and of fortitude in one so moody and restless,—all these are
lineaments which, mingled together as Mr. Hardy has mingled
them, produce a curiously strong impression of reality, as well as
of homely grandeur.

One can summarize Hutton's point by saying that Henchard is stronger
in pathos than in ethos, and yet ethos is the daimon, character is fate, and
Hardy specifically sets out to show that Henchard's character is his fate. The
strength of Hardy's irony is that it is also life's irony, and will become
Sigmund Freud's irony: Henchard's destiny demonstrates that there are no
accidents, meaning that nothing happens to one that is not already oneself.
Henchard stares out at the night as though he were staring at an adversary,
but there is nothing out there. There is only the self turned against the self,
only the drive, beyond the pleasure principle, to death.

The pre-Socratic aphorism that character is fate seems to have been
picked up by Hardy from George Eliot's *The Mill on the Floss*, where it is
attributed to Novalis. But Hardy need not have gleaned it from anywhere in
particular. Everyone in Hardy's novels is overdetermined by his or her past,
because for Hardy, as for Freud, everything that is dreadful has already
happened and there never can be anything absolutely new. Such a
speculation belies the very word "novel," and certainly was no aid to Hardy's
inventiveness. Nothing that happens to Henchard surprises us. His fate is
redeemed from dreariness only by its aesthetic dignity, which returns us to
the problematical question of Hardy's relation to tragedy as a literary form.

Henchard is burdened neither with wisdom nor with knowledge; he is
a man of will and of action, with little capacity for reflection, but with a spirit
perpetually open and generous towards others. J. Hillis Miller sees him as
being governed erotically by mediated desire, but since Miller sees this as the

iron law in Hardy's erotic universe, it loses any particular force as an observation upon Henchard. I would prefer to say that Henchard, more even than most men and like all women in Hardy, is hungry for love, desperate for some company in the void of existence. D. H. Lawrence read the tragedy of Hardy's figures not as the consequence of mediated desire, but as the fate of any desire that will not be bounded by convention and community.

> This is the tragedy of Hardy, always the same: the tragedy of those who, more or less pioneers, have died in the wilderness, whither they had escaped for free action, after having left the walled security, and the comparative imprisonment, of the established convention. This is the theme of novel after novel: remain quite within the convention, and you are good, safe, and happy in the long run, though you never have the vivid pang of sympathy on your side: or, on the other hand, be passionate, individual, wilful, you will find the security of the convention a walled prison, you will escape, and you will die, either of your own lack of strength to bear the isolation and the exposure, or by direct revenge from the community, or from both. This is the tragedy, and only this: it is nothing more metaphysical than the division of a man against himself in such a way: first, that he is a member of the community, and must, upon his honour, in no way move to disintegrate the community, either in its moral or its practical form, second, that the convention of the community is a prison to his natural, individual desire, a desire that compels him, whether he feel justified or not, to break the bounds of the community, lands him outside the pale, there to stand alone, and say: "I was right, my desire was real and inevitable, if I was to be myself I must fulfil it, convention or no convention," or else, there to stand alone, doubting, and saying: "Was I right, was I wrong? If I was wrong, oh, let me die!"—in which case he courts death.
>
> The growth and the development of this tragedy, the deeper and deeper realisation of this division and this problem, the coming towards some conclusion, is the one theme of the Wessex novels.
>
> (*Study of Thomas Hardy*)

This is general enough to be just, but not quite specific enough for the self-destructive Henchard. Also not sufficiently specific is the sympathetic judgment of Irving Howe, who speaks of "Henchard's personal struggle—the struggle of a splendid animal trying to escape a trap and thereby entangling itself all the more." I find more precise the dark musings of Sigmund Freud, Hardy's contemporary, who might be thinking of Michael Henchard when he meditates upon "The Economic Problem in Masochism":

> The third form of masochism, the moral type, is chiefly remarkable for having loosened its connection with what we recognize to be sexuality. To all other masochistic sufferings there still clings the condition that it should be administered by the loved person; it is endured at his command; in the moral type of masochism this limitation has been dropped. It is the suffering itself that matters; whether the sentence is cast by a loved or by an indifferent person is of no importance; it may even be caused by impersonal forces or circumstances, but the true masochist always holds out his cheek wherever he sees a chance of receiving a blow.

The origins of "moral masochism" are in an unconscious sense of guilt, a need for punishment that transcends actual culpability. Even Henchard's original and grotesque "crime," his drunken exploit in wife-selling, does not so much engender in him remorse at the consciousness of wrongdoing, but rather helps engulf him in the "guilt" of the moral masochist. That means Henchard knows his guilt not as affect or emotion but as a negation, as the nullification of his desires and his ambitions. In a more than Freudian sense, Henchard's primal ambivalence is directed against himself, against the authority principle in his own self.

If *The Mayor of Casterbridge* is a less original book than *Tess* or *Jude*, it is also a more persuasive and universal vision than Hardy achieved elsewhere. Miguel de Unamuno, defining the tragic sense of life, remarked that "the chiefest sanctity of a temple is that it is a place to which men go to weep in common. A *miserere* sung in common by a multitude tormented by destiny has as much value as a philosophy." That is not tragedy as Aristotle defined it, but it is tragedy as Thomas Hardy wrote it.

LIONEL STEVENSON

The Modern Values
of Victorian Fiction[1]

During the past twenty years, critical and scholarly opinion has undergone a radical transformation in its attitude toward the works of the mid-nineteenth-century novelists. Prior to the last war, the whole literature of the Victorian period languished in the depths of critical disfavor, and the novels were considered if possible even more contemptible than any of the other literary genres. When I was a graduate student I would scarcely have ventured to confess that I had read the works of Dickens, Thackeray, and the Brontës, let alone that I enjoyed them.

The principal reason for this neglect, of course, was the normal cycle of literary taste which inevitably revolts against the immediately preceding era, and only the more violently when that preceding era has been especially eminent and revered. As long as the Victorian age was reviled for smugness, sentimentality, and vulgar taste, the fiction that reproduced it so faithfully was bound to incur those strictures to the extremest degree.

A particular reason for the antipathy toward the novel was the rigid code of critical dogmas that began to come into effect after 1880. Henry James confidently proclaimed that the art of the novel depended essentially upon exact realism, with the corollary that the author's personal views and feelings ought to remain invisible. George Moore reinforced James's influence by propagating the French naturalistic school's doctrine that fiction must depict human behavior—mainly its violent and bestial manifestations—with the ruthless impartiality of an anatomist's dissection.

From *CLA Journal* IV, no.1 (1960). © 1960 by Lionel Stevenson.

Not only by practical example in their own novels but also by persuasion in their prefaces and critical essays, James and Moore established the primacy of realism so effectively that the English fiction of the preceding generation appeared hopelessly naïve and archaic. The authoritative treatises that were published in the 1920's, notably *The Craft of the Novel*, by Percy Lubbock, and *Aspects of the Novel*, by E. M. Forster, were written by devout Jamesians who could not conceive that his axioms could ever be challenged.

Being blissfully unaware of these austere axioms, the Victorian novelists had given emotional coloring to everything they wrote about; they had expressed their own attitudes and sympathies without constraint; they had written in individual styles that sometimes burst into the extravagance of oratory or the luxuriance of poetry; their complicated plots had often included melodramatic suspense or farcical absurdity; many of them were committed to overt social purpose, and yet paradoxically their earnest crusades were so mingled with genial laughter that literal-minded students could accuse them of irresponsibility.

The critics and scholars in the early twentieth century could not be oblivious to the fact that a great many people still enjoyed reading the fiction of the earlier era; but this became merely another count in the indictment. Anything that existed primarily to give pleasure to a wide indiscriminate audience was automatically debarred from the sacred canon of good literature.

A general revival of appreciation for Victorian literature was certain to occur as soon as the era faded far enough into the past to make possible a normal perspective. The artistic and intellectual stature of the Victorian authors, and their astonishing variety of achievement, began to be tentatively and grudgingly acknowledged by pontiffs of modern criticism such as T. S. Eliot and Edmund Wilson. As the tensions of this present age of anxiety increased, readers turned nostalgically to the literary landscape of an epoch that seemed to enjoy security and confidence. As soon as intelligent people started to read Victorian literature without preconceived notions, they discovered with amazement that the major authors, far from being the complacent optimists depicted in the accepted stereotype, were vitally concerned with the basic issues of social change and were distressed by most of the current trends of their century. A new explanation for the temporary eclipse of the great Victorians became apparent: the reading public of the early twentieth century had ignored them in an instinctive evasion of the disquieting warnings that the average person was unwilling to accept or even to perceive. The Victorians had been all too prescient in their anxiety about such a materialistic and competitive society as the modern world proceeded to adopt.

The Victorian novel naturally shared in the restored prestige of its period. The mid-nineteenth century was the first epoch when prose fiction had reached full parity with the other types of literature in critical esteem, and had surpassed them in popular appeal. Hence the combined opportunities of fame, profit, and influence attracted a wide assortment of ambitious and able authors, who might otherwise have expressed themselves in the older literary media. The energy and richness of Victorian fiction more than compensates for occasional deficiencies in technical skill. In fact, one of the most compelling reasons for studying Victorian fiction is that it offers a unique opportunity for observing a new literary genre in the very process of maturing. Each author was supplying his individual component, all were experimenting freely and borrowing from one another, while no rigid system of critical theory had yet come into existence to dictate practice and to prohibit innovation. By analysis of Victorian fiction we can learn a great deal about the processes of literary evolution.

To account for the abrupt accession of interest in the Victorian novelists, cynics may suggest that the pressure upon professors to find new material for publishable books and articles, and upon graduate students to select topics for dissertations, obliged them to venture beyond the approved areas of scholarly research, and that Victorian fiction by its very bulk proved to be a virtually inexhaustible territory for exploration. It is true that adequate interpretation and explication had been impossible without certain indispensable tools of a sort that can never be satisfactorily provided until a couple of generations have elapsed. The most noteworthy of these tools are Gordon Ray's massive edition of Thackeray's letters, Gordon Haight's of George Eliot's, Bradford Booth's of Trollope's, Edgar Johnson's exhaustive biography of Dickens and Ray's of Thackeray, all of which have appeared within the past fifteen years. Indeed, the solid three-volume Nonesuch collection of Dickens's letters, which was hailed as a scholarly landmark when it was published in 1938, is already so obsolete and undependable that a vast new edition, three or four times as extensive, is now in preparation.

Once provided with the essential sources of factual information, the analysers were able to work more confidently upon the novels. When Bradford Booth in 1945 cautiously started a journal to facilitate communication among the scattered scholars who shared his interest in Anthony Trollope, he was amazed by an inundation of articles on other Victorian novelists also; he changed the name of his periodical to *Nineteenth-Century Fiction*, and it is now firmly established among the important academic quarterlies.

The resurgence of Victorian fiction, however, cannot be attributed primarily to the quest for a new area of research, or to the provision of documents and biographical data and the establishment of new media of publication, or even to the general rehabilitation of all Victorian writers. A more definite reason can be found in the influence exerted upon critical theory by the psychological study of the unconscious.

The dominance of realism in the novels of the late nineteenth century was postulated upon the rationalistic assumptions of the physical scientists. Henry James concerned himself exclusively with the conscious processes in the minds of his characters; and in his determination to avoid overt discusssion of them he was obliged to show the characters engaged in interminable analytical discussion of their own and one another's motives and attitudes. Even the naturalists, who claimed to be displaying the primitive instincts of their characters rather than the intelligent decisions, nevertheless accepted the scientific method of tracing a logical train of cause and effect in human conduct. The novelists of the early twentieth century, such as Wells and Galsworthy, who enlarged their focus to include the study of social groups and movements, were just as fully committed to scientific principles.

All this cool reasonableness was invalidated when the theories of Freud and Adler and Jung gained currency. The psycho-analysts concentrated upon the irrational element in behavior; and since prose fiction is the literary form best suited to detailed recording of what goes on within individuals, the novelists promptly undertook to find ways of revealing the inner processes that are not susceptible to coherent exposition.

To communicate the impression of dreams and reveries and all the divagations of each individual's reactions to experience, it became apparent that the novelist must use distortions, metaphors, rhythm, incongruity, and any other possible stimuli to emotional and imaginative response that they could devise. Moreover, the psychoanalysts soon joined hands with the cultural anthropologists to emphasize the primitive and traditional elements in our mental equipment. Myths, folklore, and fairy tales gained new significance. The theories of Miss Maude Bodkin and Miss Jessie Weston about archetypes and symbolic ritual exerted immense influence upon critics and creative writers alike. In the second decade of the twentieth century the most enterprising writers of fiction were seeking for methods of combining these age-old intuitions and legends with the sophisticated externals of modern civilization.

The experimental fiction of half a century ago seemed to be radically new because it broke away from the tedious uniformity of external realism.

Ironically, however, scholars are now realizing that Lawrence and Joyce were at the same time paving the way for a restored appreciation of the Victorian novelists. Foreshadowings of the "stream of consciousness" have been recognized in early novels of Dickens, particularly in his studies of fear and guilt in such criminals as Bill Sikes and Jonas Chuzzlewit. Another recent critic has pointed out an affinity between Molly Bloom's drowsy reverie at the end of *Ulysses* and Flora Finching's scatterbrained conversation in *Little Dorrit.*

Once the shibboleths of external realism were abandoned, Dickens could no longer be dismissed as a mere caricaturist because he exaggerated and distorted the appearance and behavior of his characters, or as a mere sensationalist because he portrayed emotional agonies. Emily Brontë ceased to be regarded as a neurotic girl who spun an implausible horror-story out of her reading of Byron. George Meredith was relieved of the stigma of wilful obscurity and gratuitously oblique implications.

One result of the changed critical attitude has been a weakening of the artificial barrier between prose fiction and poetry. Simile and metaphor, rhythm and echo, fantasy and symbol are now accepted as serving valid functions in a novel as well as in a poem. And this in turn has led to a more exact study of the art of fiction. The old assumption used to be that the Victorian novelists were "natural story-tellers" who simply rambled on through interminable sequence of confused episodes. Now students are discovering structural design, verbal patterns, recurrent images, symbolic correspondences, and all manner of other technical subtleties that were previously invisible mainly because a novel is so much larger and more complex than a poem that its minute aesthetic details are less conspicuous.

In the long run, the chief value of the revulsion in critical and scholarly opinion is that intelligent people can now undertake the reading of Victorian fiction without a guilty conscience. Exempted from the tyranny of categorical condemnation, we can approach each novel with an open mind, ready to appreciate its particular merits and leniently to observe its incidental defects. One must remember, of course, that the relationship between author and reader was vastly different a hundred years ago. It would be unwise to pick up *Vanity Fair* or *Bleak House* or *Framley Parsonage* or *Middlemarch* like a paper-back murder-mystery at an airport newsstand, to while away the three hours of a jet flight. Most of the Victorian novels came out serially in weekly or monthly installments, often running for as long as two years; and ordinarily they were read aloud in the family circle, a few pages every evening, to prolong the enjoyment to the utmost. One of the most pleasurable features of Victorian fiction is the refuge that it provides from the precipitate tempo of the modern age. The ideal procedure in reading a novel by Thackeray or Dickens, Kingsley or Mrs. Gaskell, Borrow or Bulwer-Lytton is to forget about technical analysis and stylistic devices, to spread the reading over several weeks as an intermittent relief from more strenuous tasks, and to enter with imaginative sympathy the author's fully realized world, which is just as vivid as the actual world around us, just as unreasonable in its mixture of triviality and crisis, of absurdity and profundity, just as frustrating in its unreconciled tensions, and which nevertheless in some elusive way is an individual work of art, surviving apart from temporal vicissitudes. After one has finished reading such a novel for the sheer pleasure of the vicarious experience that it provides, one can then look back over its voluminous bulk and recognize the artistic dexterity and the creative insight with which it was constructed.

NOTE

1. An address, delivered at the Banquet Session of The College Language Association's Annual Meeting, North Carolina College, Durham, North Carolina, Friday evening, April 8, 1960.

MICHAEL WHEELER

Mid-Century Fiction: A Victorian identity: Social-Problem, Religious and Historical Novels

We now come to a remarkably productive phase in the history of the nineteenth-century English novel and the first in which both the fiction and the 'shared culture' of novelists and readers can be characterized as specifically Victorian. For in many spheres of life and culture, from politics and religion to painting and fashion, the areas of controversy and development of later decades were marked out at mid-century, when writers, artists and preachers addressed themselves to the issues confronting a newly expanded industrialized and urbanized society. For example, the Condition of England Question came to a head in the debates generated by the repeal of the Corn Laws in 1846 and by the Chartist uprisings of 1848. The most influential social-problem novels of the century were written between 1845 and 1855, by which time much of the very worst poverty experienced in the Hungry Forties had been at least partially relieved in a period of relative prosperity, itself the source of a complacency which provided Dickens and other reformist novelists with new subjects. An awareness, however, of living in a divided society and a consequent fear of revolution were to remain the legacies of this mid-century period. The Oxford Movement of the 1830s and 1840s and J. H. Newman's conversion to Roman Catholicism in 1845 left the Church of England deeply divided on High, Low and Broad Church party lines in the 1850s. While anti-Papist feeling ran high among churchmen and nonconformists following the restoration of the Catholic hierarchy in

From *English Fiction of the Victorian Period 1830–1890*. © 1994 by the Longman Group UK Limited.

England and the appointment of Nicholas Wiseman as Archbishop of Westminster in 1850, the more liberal Protestant thinkers were already registering the first tremors of the challenge to orthodoxy represented by science and German biblical criticism. Meanwhile regular religious observance and the maintenance of strict moral standards remained the norm in families of the dominant middle class. Against this complex background, religious fiction became a popular sub-genre in its own right.

Social, religious and other controversies, such as the arguments generated by the foundation of the Pre-Raphaelite Brotherhood of artists in opposition to the Academy in 1848, were closely followed by a greatly enlarged reading public, with access to a wide range of newspapers and periodicals which were now cheap and easily available. Thus the 1850s, variously described by twentieth-century writers as the Victorian Noon-Time, Victorian Noon and Victoria's Heyday,[1] saw the beginnings of mass participation, both directly, by means of rail travel to the Great Exhibition of 1851, the Academy exhibitions or the launchings of Brunel's great steamships, and indirectly, by reading about the exploits of Palmerston in diplomacy and Livingstone in exploration or the disastrous Crimean War and Indian Mutiny. Similarly, in the arts, prints of the most popular paintings of modern life sold in large quantities, as did the works of the new Poet Laureate, Tennyson.

The novel, however, was the most popular literary genre at mid-century. At one end of the social spectrum there were the journals which serialized popular romances, the staple diet of a large working-class readership. These publications threw up writers such as John Frederick Smith, the most popular novelist of the Victorian era. Having previously written some plays and two novels—*The Jesuit* (1832) and *The Prelate* (1840)—while leading a Bohemian life, Smith's break came when he returned from a Continental tour in 1849 to write for *The London Journal*. He raised the *Journal's* circulation to 100,000 copies that year, first with his short story 'Marianne, a Tale of the Temple' and then with instalments of his most ambitious novel, *Stanfield Hall*. Subsequently published as a three-decker, the novel traces the fortunes of the Stanfield family from the Middle Ages to the Restoration and combines historical romance (influenced by Scott) with anachronistic treatment of Victorian inventions. *Minnigrey* (1851–52), illustrated by John Gilbert, is said to have increased sales of *The London Journal* to half a million copies, for which newsagents had to send special wagons to the station. Smith's habit was to write in the printing office itself. He would closet himself with a bottle of port and a cigar or pipe, read the end of the previous instalment, and then write the next, drawing his fee when he handed over the text. He raised the tension from episode to episode until the mill girls of the North and the Midlands had to buy their own copies rather than wait to borrow one. The fact that neither the formulaic quality of his fiction (virtue, for example, is always rewarded) nor the sensationalist action of the weekly instalments is suited to novel publication did not prevent him from earning the salary of a Parliamentary Under-Secretary of State.

Meanwhile, even the expensive three-decker became much more widely available through Mudie's and other lending libraries. Most of Thackeray's major novels appeared in the cheap monthly number form with which Dickens had already achieved a series of huge popular successes. Dickens himself published fiction in serial form, including his own Christmas stories and *Hard Times*, Elizabeth Gaskell's *Cranford* and *North and South* and stories by Wilkie Collins, in his weekly family periodical, *Household Words*, founded in 1850. Although conditions were ideal for the novel to flourish at mid-century, the fact that so many major and minor novelists came to maturity or began their careers at this time is partly a happy historical accident. In those *anni mirabiles* of English fiction, 1847–48, Thackeray's *Vanity Fair* came out in monthly numbers alongside Dickens's *Dombey and Son*, Disraeli completed his trilogy of novels with *Tancred*, and an impressive list of writers published their first novels: Emily Brontë, *Wuthering Heights*; Charlotte Brontë, *Jane Eyre*; Anne Brontë, *Agnes Grey*; Elizabeth Gaskell, *Mary Barton*; Anthony Trollope, *The Macdermots of Ballycloran*; Charles Kingsley, *Yeast*; J. H. Newman, *Loss and Gain*. The rich variety of form and subject-matter represented here is characteristic of the mid-century literary scene.

For all their differences, the major mid-century novelists also share certain common concerns. The life of the individual in the family, in courtship and in marriage is related to larger historical, social, political or spiritual themes. The figure of the vulnerable, innocent child, a legacy of the Romantic movement and a key Victorian symbol, haunts many of the major novels of the period: Dickens's Florence Dombey and David Copperfield, Thackeray's Henry Esmond, Charlotte Brontë's Jane Eyre and Emily Brontë's Heathcliff are all memorable as children. Four of them are orphans and Florence has lost her mother. Their yearning for emotional and spiritual fulfilment in a hostile world, and the effect it has on themselves and those they encounter in their adult lives, suggests interesting parallels with mid-century poetry, especially Matthew Arnold's volumes of 1852 and 1853. As in the poetry of Arnold and Tennyson, the inner life is reflected in external objects and locations, and change and development in the individual is often related to external social change.

The reformist drive in much of the fiction of mid-century, evident in the social-problem novel and the broader vision of Dickens's major social novels, is often complemented by an attempt to place the changes of the present in the context of the historical past. Disraeli's political novels, for example, are informed by his reading of English history, and students of Victorian fiction should also examine the writings of contemporary historians such as Macaulay—extended prose narratives which often rivalled the novel in popularity. At a time of rapid change, both the historian and the novelist explored the central theme of progress. None of the major novelists, however, approached Macaulay in his optimistic reading of recent English history. Charlotte Brontë's reference to the 'warped system of things' in the preface to the second edition of *Jane Eyre* (1847) is characteristic of a period in which many novelists attacked received views on the position of women, or example, and, with Carlyle, saw cash as the sole nexus in a highly acquisitive society.

The work of Thackeray, the Brontës, Elizabeth Gaskell and Dickens will be discussed later in this chapter. (Trollope's novels are discussed in Ch. 3, which covers the most fertile period of his long career.) Before examining these individual novelists, however, I want to consider three of the most important sub-genres of the mid-century period, to which most of the major novelists also contributed: the social-problem novel, the religious novel and the historical novel.

Jean-Paul Sartre wrote: 'It seems that bananas have a better taste when they have just been picked. Works of the mind should likewise be eaten on the spot.'[2] Although this statement is of doubtful validity it is certainly pertinent to reformist literature, written with an educative purpose for a specific readership at a specific time. The Victorian social-problem novel represented an 'appeal' not only in the broad Sartrean sense of a writer's creation finding its 'fulfilment' in the reading,[3] but also in the more specific sense of demanding a response of some kind, such as a change of attitude or behaviour. In 1845, which I am taking as the first year of the mid-century period in the development of Victorian fiction, the journalist and playwright Douglas Jerrold wrote a prospectus to his new shilling magazine in which he reflected the spirit of the age in his own aims as editor: 'It will be our chief object to make every essay ... breathe WITH A PURPOSE. Experience assures us that, especially at the present day, it is by a defined purpose alone ... that the sympathies of the world are to be engaged, and its support ensured.'[4] The immediate purpose of the mid-century social-problem novelist was still that of educating the middle and upper classes. In the same year as Jerrold's prospectus, Disraeli wrote of the rich and the poor being 'as ignorant of each other's habits, thoughts, and feelings, as if they were dwellers in different zones, or inhabitants of different planets' (*Sybil*, 1845; II. 5). In *Mary Barton* (1848) and *North and South* (1854–55), Elizabeth Gaskell describes a kind of class apartheid in early Victorian Manchester, where members of the middle class can walk the streets of the town without ever entering the slum districts, thus remaining ignorant of poverty in their own 'zone'. It is no coincidence that Dickens makes education itself one of his central themes in *Hard Times* (1854), set in industrial Coketown. In country areas too, the innocent aristocrat and the knowing farm labourer can look at the same village or house and see different things, as Tregarva the gamekeeper suggests in Kingsley's *Yeast* (1848) when he unwittingly echoes Carlyle in saying that 'a man's eyes can only see what they've learnt to see' (3).

Any critical assessment of a Victorian social-problem novel must necessarily include some kind of judgement on its ideology and the way in which this shapes its diagnosis of social ills and ideas on possible cures. A strong authorial presence in the narrative is, of course, characteristic of Victorian fiction, but here it is of special significance, where novelists write as teachers, guides and even prophets. Most obviously and commonly, an author-narrator will introduce a passage of commentary on some fictional episode, often writing in the style of the religious tract, the statistical 'blue book', or the parliamentary report. But dialogue can also be weighted in such a way that the author's viewpoint emerges very clearly, as for example in Stephen Blackpool's interview with Mr Bounderby in Dickens's *Hard Times*, when they discuss divorce (I. 11)

This is not to say, however, that the social-problem novelists all wrote from positions which were fully worked out and strongly held. Indeed, the tensions within their novels betray the difficulties they faced as they analyzed the Condition of England Question. Perhaps the most extreme case is *Alton Locke* (1850), in which the 'Parson Lot' side of Kingsley–radical, Christian Socialist, reformist–struggles with the establishment clergyman who admired the more heroic variety of English aristocrat. In the revisions he made to the Cambridge chapters (12–13) in the edition of 1862, removing the original passages which had criticized the university and its undergraduates, Kingsley showed how he had come to resolve at least one problem of this kind. Two years previously, in 1860, he had been elected Regius Professor of Modern History at Cambridge, and now wished to acknowledge what he called the 'purification' which had gone on in the university since he had been an undergraduate!

Perhaps the most interesting example of this kind of tension or conflict is Elizabeth Gaskell's *Mary Barton*, for here the writer's difficulties are related to the problems of form and plotting in social-problem fiction. The opening chapters of the novel are one of the best portrayals of working-class life in nineteenth-century fiction, representing the grey masses of an alien class as a group of unique individuals, as different from each other as members of higher social groups are. Whereas Elizabeth Gaskell's detailed, often harrowing realism engages the sympathy of the reader in the lot of the poor, particularly of the Chartist and union man, John Barton, his daughter Mary and their friends the Wilsons, her portrayal of the wealthy mill-owning Carson family is unflatteringly stereotyped. (*North and South* was written partly in order to correct this imbalance.) Having, however, sympathetically illustrated the plight of the oppressed Manchester weavers and explained their arguments for militant action, she draws back from the brink of finally condoning either their attitudes or their actions, preferring to preach mutual understanding and education between the classes as a social palliative. Similarly, the happy ending of the two-volume novel has been much criticized as a fudging of the issues raised in the first volume, for Mary Barton simply sails away to a new life in Canada, married to her worthy working-class lover Jem Wilson, leaving the stark realities of the Manchester slums behind her.

Elizabeth Gaskell's pious wish that worker and master might love one another in the spirit of the Gospels is as inadequate a solution to the problems she exposes as Disraeli's appeals to the English aristocracy or Kingsley's suggested programme of sanitary reform. The limitations of her social analysis, as revealed in her plotting, also highlight other limitations of the social-problem novels of the period, for these mid-century novelists characteristically illustrate the general and unexceptional (in *Mary Barton*, the masters' exploitation of the workers and the workers' embittered response) through the particular and exceptional (John Barton's murder of his employer's son, Harry Carson, on behalf of the union).

Elizabeth Gaskell is typical in her use of a love plot to organize the particular and exceptional and in her abnegation of the role of social analyst in the process of working out that plot in the second volume. In shooting Harry Carson as an enemy of the weavers, John Barton also unknowingly kills his daughter's would-be seducer. The wadding he uses in the gun borrowed from Jem Wilson is a piece of an old valentine from Jem to Mary, on the blank part of which Mary had once copied Samuel Bamford's poem entitled 'God help the poor' (9, 21–22). The police arrest Jem as the owner of the gun, knowing that he has recently had an angry exchange with Carson, his rival lover. They pursue the line of reasoning which, for the reader, is symbolically represented by the valentine greeting on the card. The motive of the actual murderer is symbolically represented by the Bamford poem: Barton avenges the poor. This contrived and over-elaborate plotting epitomizes the social-problem novelists' attempts to accommodate the threatening forces of class conflict within a romance scheme, to which the ethics of the New Testament can then be applied. In her later, more mature novel, *North and South*, Elizabeth Gaskell still makes the central love plot her main focus, Margaret Hale's eventual marriage to the Milton-Northern manufacturer John Thornton being the culmination of their mutual education. As in *Mary Barton*, the conflation of the love plot and what might be called the social-problem plot is the source both of the narrative strength and the social-analytical weakness of *North and South*. For all its obvious shortcomings, however, *Mary Barton* is perhaps the most compelling of the mid-century social-problem novels, a moving if at times highly melodramatic parable for the times, portraying early Victorian Manchester as the town of Dives and Lazarus, in which Lazarus becomes an avenger.

Disraeli's *Sybil; or, The Two Nations* is in places just as melodramatic as *Mary Barton*. Yet in many ways his reformist novels differ from those of Elizabeth Gaskell, Charles Kingsley and the women novelists of the 1830s and 1840s mentioned in Chapter 1 (see pp. 20–1 above). He worked on a much larger canvas, for example, virtually creating the political novel in *Coningsby; or, The New Generation* (1844), whose theme is 'the derivation and character of the political parties' (General Preface to Novels and Tales', 1870–71), and completing his ambitious Tory trilogy with *Sybil*, on 'the condition of the people', and *Tancred; or, The New Crusade* (1847), on 'the duties of the Church'. Disraeli's ideas on the history and destiny of the English nation, ideas with which he launched his bid for the leadership of his party, are worked out in the novels through symbolic confrontations, such as the clash between Coningsby's grandfather, Lord Monmouth (the aristocrat of the old order) and his enemy Millbank (the model self-made industrialist who takes care to consume his own smoke), and the marriage of the noble hero Egremont to Sybil, an 'angel from heaven' (II. 14), the daughter of a Chartist overseer who turns out to be of aristocratic descent. This use of plots concerned with private lives, and particularly love lives, as vehicles for some kind of social message typifies the social-problem novelists' technique of domesticating large social issues in personal terms. In Disraeli's case, however, the grand scale of some of his ideas can work against this effect. Characters are often portrayed, for example, as representatives of a whole line of racial, tribal or national descent. The Rev. Aubrey St Lys in *Sybil* is 'distinguished by that beauty of noble English blood'—of 'the Norman tempered by the Saxon; the fire of conquest softened by integrity' (II. 11). Queen Victoria, 'fair and serene', has 'the blood and beauty of the Saxon' (I. 6). The two nations, rich and poor, must unite under the crown and, as in so many reformist novels, it is specifically female sympathy and love which is seen as the social balm: 'Will it be her proud destiny at length to bear relief to suffering millions, and, with that soft hand which might inspire troubadours and guerdon knights, break the last links in the chain of Saxon thraldom?' (I. 6).

Disraeli works with a broad brush and bold colours, illustrating his ideas by dramatically bringing together the opposite ends of the social spectrum as part of his political strategy. He caricatures the poor in *Sybil* and, with his use of melodrama, exploits the popular view of trade unions as objects of violence and terror. The creative energy, however, the fresh ideas and the nice, albeit snobbish social touches of Disraeli's novels contribute to the liveliness of approach and lightly ironic tone which other novelists who worked in the sub-genre often lacked.

Although *Sybil, Alton Locke* and *Mary Barton are* strongly religious novels in the sense that their polemics are rooted in the Christian social ethics of Young England Toryism, Christian Socialism and Unitarianism, nobody would classify them as 'religious fiction' in the sense of being specifically about religion. The boundaries of religious fiction are often difficult to draw, however, as many Victorian novelists reflect the religious issues of the period in their work without actually Addressing themselves to those issues. Elizabeth Gaskell's *Ruth* (1853) is included in the large Garland reprint series of Victorian 'Novels of Faith and Doubt' (1975) as a 'Novel of Dissent',[5] for the heroine, an abandoned unmarried mother, is taken in by a dissenting minister and his sister, Faith, whose religion is portrayed sympathetically in contrast to that of the Pharisaical Mr Bradshaw. Elizabeth Gaskell's main theme, however, is the broader social issue of the 'fallen woman'. *Ruth* can, therefore, also be classified as a social-problem novel. Also in the Garland series, and published in the same year as *Ruth*, is Charlotte M. Yonge's best-seller, *The Heir of Reddyffe*, listed under 'Tractarian and Anti-Tractarian Novels'. Yet Charlotte Yonge's High Church position is manifested only indirectly in the novel, whose real interest lies in the intensity of religious feeling which informs its plot. Young Sir Guy Morville, the first heir of Reddyffe to come into his inheritance in the novel, clears his name of the false charges brought against him by his cousin, Philip, who himself becomes the next heir. As a Victorian version of the 'gentil parfit knyght', his true nature is revealed in a series of heroic self-sacrifices: his rescue of sailors shipwrecked on rocks off the beach at Redclyffe (23) and of his young wife as she hangs over a precipice during their wedding tour (30), and his fitting death of a fever caught from Philip, whom he has nursed back to health in Italy (31–33). (Philip lives on to inherit Reddyffe, 'a care-worn, harassed man', 44.) The novel ran through numerous editions and reprints, largely, one suspects, because it was 'safe': the central characters are intense, upper-middle-class young people who read and talk in idyllic rural settings, and the author's moral judgements upon them are firmly based on a creed which remains unchallenged throughout.

It is therefore interesting to contrast Charlotte Yonge's use of the 'fever', a conveniently vague and yet dangerous illness contracted in many Victorian novels, with that of James Anthony Froude in his decidedly unsafe and highly controversial *The Nemesis of Faith* (1849). For although Fronde's plot also turns on the effects of a fever contracted in Italy in the last third of the novel, the circumstances and interpretation of the illness could hardly be more different. Like other religious novels of its kind, *The Nemesis of Faith* is organized around a series of spiritual crises. The hero, Markham Sutherland, becomes a sceptic, resigns his living as an Anglican clergyman and falls in love with Mrs Helen Leonard on the shores of Lake Como. During a boating trip the preoccupied couple fail to notice that Helen's little daughter Annie has got wet. They are thus indirectly responsible for her death when she develops a fever. Whereas Helen believes that this is a judgement upon her for having married a man whom she has never really loved, the shocked Markham refuses to act on her interpretation and take her away with him, seeing Annie's death as 'a punishment for the sin which he had wished to commit'.[6] (Helen enters a convent, where she dies peacefully two years later, whereas Markham dies in doubt and despair in a monastery, having been saved from suicide by the miraculous intervention of an English Roman Catholic priest who is clearly modelled on Newman.)

Unlike Charlotte Yonge's handling of the fever, Froude's is related to Markham Sutherland's earlier agonized soul-searching in which he wrestles with a more familiar mid-century problem of interpretation—that of the critical approach to Scripture and the creeds. For *The Nemesis of Faith* squarely tackles religious 'difficulties', as *Mary Barton* and *Alton Locke* tackle social problems, although the nature of Markham Sutherland's difficulties demands a quite different form to accommodate them. He describes his struggles with his own conscience over the Thirty-nine Articles, the creeds and the great nineteenth-century stumbling block of the doctrine of everlasting punishment, in a series often letters to his friend Arthur in the first section of the narrative and, after Arthur himself has described his ordination and subsequent resignation in the third-person mode, in the lengthy 'Confessions of a Sceptic' which take up the middle third of the novel. Froude's main interest is in the spiritual and intellectual torments endured by himself and other young doubters of his generation. The demands of plot and of the development of characters other than the hero are subordinated to the description of those torments.

Similarly, the spiritual life of Newman's Charles Reding in *Loss and Gain* (1848) remains the single narrow focus of the narrative throughout the novel, without generating a complex sense of relationship between the hero and his world. Unlike Markham Sutherland, however, Charles Reding defines and articulates his position on questions of doctrine by engaging in lengthy debates with other Christians—first his fellow undergraduates at Oxford and later a series of fanatics of miscellaneous persuasions,—as he takes the long and painful road from the Church of England to Rome. The greatest English Christian apologist of his time, Newman wrote most of his major works as contributions to current religious controversies. It is characteristic of him that *Loss and Gain* was written in response to another novel—Miss Elizabeth Harris's *From Oxford to Rome* (1847)—a fictionalized version of its author's own route down that road and a warning to others against following her example. Newman had already published his *Essay on the Development of Christian Doctrine* (1845), in which he explained his position in the year of his conversion to Rome. The most moving parts of *Loss and Gain*, such as the descriptions of Charles leaving Oxford (III. 3) and of his first seeing the mass celebrated (III. 10), have the intensity of autobiography. But Newman also enjoys himself in this (for him) comparatively lightweight literary genre of the novel by introducing passages of satire and broad humour into the narrative. He catches, for example, the enthusiasm and hyperbole of the undergraduate in Charles's friend Sheffield, who bursts into his room on the first day of term to announce that Oxford has 'just now a very bad inside': The report is, that some of the men have turned Romans, and they say that there are strangers going about Oxford whom no one knows anything of. Jack, who is a bit of a divine himself, says he heard the Principal say that, for certain, there were Jesuits at the bottom of it; and ... he declares he saw with his own eyes the Pope walking down High Street with the priest" (I. 14). Typically, however, this flight of fancy is merely the prelude to a discussion on the stage Charles has reached on the road to Rome. The chapter as a whole represents one more milestone on a journey which at times wearies not only the hero but also the long-suffering reader.

We have seen that Disraeli's analysis of modern English society is based on his reading of English history. Similarly, both Froude and Newman examine the spiritual life of their generation in the light of Church history. During Markham Sutherland's Tractarian phase, for example, he was 'readily induced to acknowledge that the Reformation had been the most miserable infatuation', although his 'faith in Newman' was later destroyed.[7] Following Newman's conversion and the restoration of the Roman hierarchy in England, Catholic and Protestant writers alike turned to the history of the early Church in their fiction in order to suggest the true significance of current events in England. The alternative title of Charles Kingsley's *Hypatia; or, New Foes with an Old Face* (1853) is characteristically pugnacious, as is the muscular monk in the novel, Philammon, who proves to be handy in a fight. Kingsley's anti-Catholic views on celibacy figure largely in his treatment of Philammon's exposure to the life of Alexandria, where he meets the novel's heroine, Hypatia, a pagan teacher of Greek philosophy and literature. The physicality of the persecution of the Christians in fifth-century Alexandria and of the terrible 'sports' in the theatre (22) clearly fascinated Kingsley, and the climactic martyrdom of the converted Hypatia, naked at the high altar in the church, shocked even his more sympathetic readers and critics.

This powerful novel prompted two other leading English priests to write on the martyrdom of women. In an attempt to answer Kingsley, Cardinal Wiseman initiated a Catholic Popular Library series with a novel entitled *Fabiola; or, The Church of the Catacombs* (1854), whose excesses of physical horror have prompted critics to speculate on the psychology of its author. The twelfth work in the series, Newman's *Callista: A Sketch of the Third Century* (1856), also took up Kingsley's challenge, thus anticipating the later open debate between the two men in which Newman's position was stated in the form of the *Apologia pro Vita Sua* (1864). The martyrdom of the converted Greek heroine, Callista, is treated as a miraculous event, placed in a rapidly unfolding sequence of sacraments: baptism, confirmation and the eucharist in custody (31) are followed by a public confession of her new faith (33). Her death on the rack, with limbs outstretched on a plank, at the place where slaves are buried outside the walls of the city of Sicca, suggests parallels with the crucifixion, and the novel ends with a mass for the soul of a martyr whose discarded body has lain in the sand, uncorrupted and untouched by wild beasts. *Callista* is a novel of set pieces, such as the justly famous description of the plague of locusts (15), and the development of character and plot is not sustained. In his contrast between the corrupt city with its violent mob and the cool caves in which Agellius and other converts secretly celebrate the mass, Newman conveys his spiritual vision of the world and the Church, implicitly relating a distant period of persecution when

religion was literally a matter of life and death, to the recent history of the
small Roman Catholic community in his own country.

Novelists who researched the history of the Church in order to write
about the religion of their own times were working in an age in which 'sages'
and historians also interpreted the past in relation to the present. The title of
Carlyle's *Past and Present* (1843), a work in which he contrasted medieval and
modern England, also struck the keynote of much of his other writing, while
his seminal account of *The French Revolution* (1837) provided a historical
foundation for his prophetic writings in the age of Chartism and an
'unworking aristocracy'. J. A. Froude adopted Carlyle's ideas on heroes and
hero-worship in his *History of England from the Fall of Wolsey to the Defeat of
the Spanish Armada* (1856-70), in which his highly topical anti-Catholic
sentiments found full expression. Macaulay's magisterial *History of England
from the Accession of James II* (1849–61) interpreted history as a story of
progress towards the nineteenth century—'the history of physical, of moral,
and of intellectual improvement' ('Exordium'). In Macaulay's case this other
major nineteenth-century form of extended prose narrative rivalled even
Dickens's" novels in popularity: almost 30,000 copies of the third and fourth
volumes of the *History* were sold in the first three months of publication in
1855, for which Longman paid him the unprecedented sum of £20,000. The
historical novelists of mid-century tended to be attracted to periods of
English history in which change and development were rapid and violent, as
in their own time. Ainsworth produced his *James the Second; or, The Revolution
of 1688* in 1848, the year of European revolutions and Chartism in England.
Bulwer's *Harold, the Last of the Saxons* came out in the same year.

But perhaps the most interesting historical novel written from the
perspective of the present is Kingsley's best-seller of 1855, *Westward Ho!*, a
romance of adventure and war with the dastardly Spaniards in the age of
Drake and Raleigh. Like his close friend J. A. Froude, who was already
working on the history of the period, Kingsley allowed his anti-Catholic
feeling to distort his account of England's past. In portraying the bellicose
Protestant Englishman as an imperialist with God on his side and a heroic
liberator of the victims of the Spanish Inquisition, Kingsley also sublimated
his frustrated urge to fight in the first year of the Crimean War, producing a
book which was intended to 'make others fight'.[8] His religion is central both
to his view of the war and his descriptions of the exploits of Amyas Leigh and
his crew in the West Indies and against the Spanish Armada. In a letter of
1855 he writes that the soldier 'wants a faith that he is fighting on God's side;
he wants military and corporate and national religion, and that is what I fear
he has yet to get ... That is what the Elizabethans had pp to the Armada, and

by it they conquered'.[9] In *Westward Ho!* the old sailor Salvation Yeo comes to believe that fighting the Spaniards is 'really fighting in God's battle against evil, as were the wars of Joshua or David' (16). The conflict between Amyas Leigh, the young Devonian lion, and the main Catholic characters in the novel—his cousin Eustace, a priest and therefore a superstitious liar (3, 22), and the dark, handsome Don Guzman, who lures Rose Salterne, a lovely Devon girl, into marriage—provides the structure upon which Kingsley's stirring plot is constructed. Written in only seven months, the novel proved to be a great popular success with a reading public anxious about Catholicism at home and war abroad, and who also enjoyed a good yarn. Again, the fact that *Westward Ho!* is memorable mainly for a few set pieces of exciting narrative suggests the novel's limitations. (At the end of the novel, for example, Amyas's pursuit of Don Guzman's ship after the battle of the Armada ends in the Spaniard's shipwreck and the frustrated Amyas's blinding by a bolt of lightning, 32.) Fascinating as a grossly prejudiced period piece, the novel bursts fitfully into lurid but spellbinding life.

NOTES

1. See G. M. Young, 'The Victorian Noon-Time', in *Victorian Essays*, edited by W. D. Hancock (London, 1962); Carl Dawson, *Victorian Noon: English Literature in 1850* (Baltimore and London, 1979); J. B. Priestley, *Victoria's Heyday* (London, 1972).

2. Jean-Paul Sartre, *What is Literature?*, translated by Bernard Frechtman (1950); repr. London, 1967), p. 54.

3. Sartre, p. 32.

4. Douglas Jerrold, *Mrs. Caudle's Curtain Lectures and Other Stories and Essays*, World's Classics, 122 (London, 1907), p. ix.

5. See Robert Lee Wolff, *Gains and Losses: Novels of Faith and Doubt in Victorian England* (London, 1977), p. 511.

6. J.A. Froude, *The Nemesis of Faith*, Victorian Fiction: Novels of Faith and Doubt, 68 (1849; repr. New York and London, 1975), p. 199. (The novel is not divided into numbered chapters.)

7. Froude. pp. 148–9, 158.

8. *Charles Kingsley: His Letters and Memories of his Life*, edited by Fanny Kingsley (London. 1883), p. 162.

9. *Charles Kingsley*, p. 164.

10. G.K. Chesterton, Introduction to Everyman *Edwin Drood & Master Humphrey's Clock*, quoted in Geoffrey Tillotson, *Thackeray the Novelist* (1954); repr. London and New York, 1974), p. 6.

11. Tillotson, p. 6.

12. Earlier in *Vanity* Fair Thackeray comments on novelists having 'the privilege of knowing everything' (3) and on 'the omniscience of the novelist' (15).

13. 'The Last Sketch', *Cornhill Magazine*, 1 (1860), 485–98 (p. 486).

14. 'By "principle" I mean an essence, or inner law, not as a law that is imposed by a legal authority but rather using the term as it is used in science, where we speak of the law of gravity.' M. Esther Harding, *Woman's Mysteries, Ancient and Modern: A Psychological Interpretation of the Feminine Principle as Portrayed in Myth, Story and Dreams* (1955; repr. London, 1971), p. 16. See also Barbara Hannah's Jungian study of the Brontës and Sandra M. Gilbert's and Susan Gubar's feminist study, both listed in the Brontë bibliography (see p. 254 below). Robert B. Heilman, in 'Charlotte Brontë, Reason, and the Moon', *Nineteenth-Century Fiction*, 14 (1960), 283–302, focuses on some of the passages included in my own discussion of the novel, but does not comment on the moon in relation to womanhood.

15. For discussion on *The Pilgrim's Progress* in Charlotte Brontës's novels see Michael Wheeler, *The Art of Allusion in Victorian Fiction* (London, 1979), Chapter 3, and Barry V. Quails, *The Secular Pilgrims of Victorian Fiction: The Novel as Book of Life* (Cambridge, 1982), Chapter 2. Both refer to earlier articles on the subject.

16. See Heilmann, op. cit., p. 299.

17. See also Ruth Bernard Yeazell, 'More True than Real: Jane Eyre's "Mysterious Summons'", *Nineteenth-Century Fiction*, 29 (1974), 127–43.

18. C.P. Sanger, *The Structure of Wuthering Heights*', Hogarth Essays, 19 (London, 1926), reprinted in *Wuthering Heights: An Anthology of Criticism*, compiled by Alastair Everitt (London,,1967), pp. 193–208 (p. 196).

19. 'Goethe', *Foreign Review*, 2 (1828), reprinted in *Critical and Miscellaneous Essays*. 4 vols (London, 1893), I, 172–222 (p. 192). (*OED* wrongly dates the article 1827.)

20. George Gissing, *Charles Dickens: A Critical Study* (1898; repr. New York, 1904), p. 147.

21. David Masson, *British Novelists and their Styles: Being a Critical Sketch of the History of British Prose Fiction* (Cambridge, 1859), pp. 248–59. For further comment on Masson, see pp. 6–7 above.

22. The phrase is Louis Cazamian's, in *The Social Novel in England, 1820–1850*, translated by Martin Fido (London and Boston, 1973), p. 211.

23. Compare Jane Vogel, *Allegory in Dickens*, Studies in the Humanities, 17 (Alabama, 1977), p. 3. Although Vogel's method throws up some suggestive readings of names it is often over-ingenious.

24. 'The Coming of Arthur' (1869), 410. (One of Tennyson's *Idylls of the King*.)

25. See John Butt and Kathleen Tillotson, *Dickens at Work* (London, 1957), pp. 168–71

26. 'I wander thro' each charter'd street,/Near where the charter'd Thames doth flow,/And mark in every face I meet/Marks of weakness, marks of woe.//In every cry of every Man,/ ... The mind-forg'd manacles I hear.' 'London', *Songs of Experience*

(1794). See also F.R. and Q.D. Leavis, *Dickens the Novelist* (1970; repr. Harmondsworth, 1972). pp. 282–359.

27. See H.M. Daleski, *Dickens and the Art of Analogy* (London, 1970), pp. 195, 207. See also Philip Collins. '*Little Dorrit*: the Prison and the Critics', *TLS*, 18 April 1980, pp. 445–6.

JULIA PREWITT BROWN

Class and Money

A scene in Jane Austen's *Pride and Prejudice* is typical of many scenes in nineteenth-century fiction in which a young man or woman openly discusses marriage prospects with a friend. The man is Colonel Fitzwilliam, and he explains to the heroine why he must marry for money. Brought up to lead an aristocratic life and honestly unwilling to give it up, he needs a monied marriage to maintain the expensive leisure to which he is accustomed. He cannnot afford the luxury of falling in love with a poor woman.

Colonel Fitzwilliam is an amiable character, and he is no less amiable after this admission. The heroine does not judge him morally; nor does Jane Austen, by means of narrative comment, make any apology for the seeming crassness in his situation. The reasons for this that concern us here are, first, that Jane Austen does not require us to admire him, only to admit his reality, or the truth that amiability is often quite compatible with ruthlessness; and, second, that Jane Austen could not see into the future and, therefore, predict that a generation of readers would exist as willfully obtuse about the power of class as our own. Right or wrong, this is how things stand for her characters: Class and money are the media through which they must shape their lives. Jane Austen was not interested in people who try to find themselves by going outside of society. Certainly no one succeeds in doing so even in a minor way in her novels or, for that matter, in the novels of Thackeray, Dickens, George Eliot, Charlotte Brontë, or Hardy.

From *A Reader's Guide to the Nineteenth-Century English Novel.* © 1985 by Julia Prewitt Brown.

Class and money are givens in the novels discussed in this book. They are to the novelist as the clay is to the potter, for they are not only the substance with which characters must structure their lives; they *define* character and social life. Most of the novelists discussed here would as soon set a novel outside the class structure as a potter would envision making a pot without clay.

No hero in an English novel, for example, moves in and out of society with the ease of a Huckleberry Finn. In Dickens's *Great Expectations*, Pip can only move up and down the social scale. All Huck needs to get into society is money; Pip, in contrast, needs education, manners, fine clothing, furniture, servants, the right friends, *and* money—and all of this still does not erase the stain of his origins. The society satirized along the river in *Huckleberry Finn* is a wholly seen landscape in which everything is brought into the light, whereas the society Pip encounters when he sets himself up in London is full of shade. Large areas of darkness exist, suggesting those areas of knowledge and experience that Pip can never know.

What is class? Social and economic distinctions have always existed, but I use the word here as most historians use it: to define a specifically post-Industrial Revolution, nineteenth-century phenomenon. To traditional and Marxist historians alike (if such a distinction is legitimate in historical studies today), a *class* society is set off against an *aristocratic* society as a means of understanding the transition into the modern industrial world. In Engels's terms, it was the Industrial Revolution that created a new *class*, the urban proletariat. According to this view, eighteenth-century England was an aristocracy, a hierarchy based on property and patronage, in which people took their places in a pyramidlike structure extending down from a minority of the rich and powerful at the top through ever wider and larger layers of lesser wealth to the great mass of the poor and powerless at the bottom.[1] In this largely rural society, high- and low-born were bound together by a system of agrarian economic dependency that had yet to be disrupted by industrialization on a large scale. To be sure, landed wealth had strong ties to commerce and trade (as it would later to industry), but real estate still controlled a huge percentage of all wealth. "On the eve of the industrial revolution," writes Asa Briggs, "durable national assets other than land, the oldest asset, accounted for less than one-third of the national capital of Great Britain; by 1860 their share had increased to a half."[2]

England was the first country in the world to become industrialized; from 1770 onward, the Industrial Revolution began in English cotton mills, ironworks, and coal mines. By the early nineteenth century it was in the full swing of its first phase, creating the new "class" society of the Victorians. Vertical economic conflicts arose to challenge the horizontal layers formerly joined in agrarian, economic dependency. For the first time, different economic groups or classes began to oppose each other's economic interests on a wide scale (middle-class-industrial interests vs. aristocratic-landed interests), creating the "vertical antagonism" known as "class feeling." From Austen to Hardy, this class feeling dominates the English novel.

A comparison between a novel of the eighteenth century, *Tom Jones*, and one of the nineteenth century, *Emma*, illustrates these social distinctions. The society of *Tom Jones* is still an aristocracy in which property and birth play the central roles. All the main characters are connected with the landed interests, and the major moral and aesthetic conflicts within the novel are generated from within this group. In the novels of Jane Austen, however, many characters appear from outside the world of landed interests; and these people (or their offspring) who have made their money in business challenge the traditions and assumptions of landed society. One of the most powerfully evoked characters in *Emma* is Mrs. Elton, who is associated by family with new money and trade, and whose speech, dress, and manners are frequently set off against those of the landed gentry among whom she lives. In the novel genre, it is by means of such details that vertical economic conflicts are shown to challenge the horizontal structure of the old society. Mrs. Elton's presence is disruptive because her financial and social roots are independent of traditional society. However much she thinks she needs the landed gentry to give her legitimacy, she knows unconsciously that they need her more, because she comes from that section of society that had begun producing greater and greater wealth. And in the nineteenth century, far more than ever before, all class came to be based on money.

This does not mean that everyone who is rich is a member of the upper class. But without money, people sink awfully fast, as Austen shows to be the case with Miss Bates in *Emma*. In the Victorian novel, money is the engine that takes you where you want to go. If you have money, you may not make it into the upper class in the first generation, as Dickens's Bounderby (*Hard Times*) and Thackeray's elder Osborne (*Vanity Fair*) show; usually, the first generation of new rich cannot relinquish their belief in the all-importance of money, and this makes them repellent and vulgar in the eyes of the gentry and aristocracy. But the children or grandchildren of the new rich take money for granted, like the old rich, and are therefore assimilated more easily. There are snags in the assimilation process, and Victorian novels are frequently concerned with them; but over and over again these novels tell us that, at bottom, class is the relationship that defines the flow of money. In

1835, after seeing the new industrial town of Birmingham, Tocqueville wrote that "the whole of English society is based on privileges of money," as if this state of affairs were a new one and peculiar to industrial society. Even the landed interests came to rely predominantly on money, rather than birth. As Norman Gash's *Aristocracy and People* shows, the grandest nobles derived their millions from the monopoly ownership of resources whose cash value was determined by the market—farmland, urban real estate, and coal mines. And William Pitt, Prime Minister in the last years of the eighteenth century, had argued that anyone with £20,000 a year should be given a peerage if he so wished.

The transition from an aristocratic to a class society was not a simple process; the distinction between the two kinds of society is useful mainly for the purpose of definition and should not be applied to fiction or the historical process in an oversimplified way. England in the eighteenth century was as sophisticated commercially as any country in the world, and social mobility was an integral part of the social structure. By the same token, England remained aristocratic in many ways throughout the nineteenth century until World War I. Only after that period did it attain a democracy in the sense of the word that we use today.[3]

The complexity of social change is revealed above all in the novels. In *Tom Jones*, Fielding treats the "merry England" ideal of an organic society as a nostalgic myth; the ties that supposedly bind high and low together in an aristocratic society are an hilarious illusion. At the same time, however, certain truths about that society cannot be escaped: The major comic question of the novel turns on the mystery of the hero's birth, since Fielding was aware of the precarious role that birth and the inheritance of property would play in the future of English society. Similarly, in Austen's more Victorian view, social change appears to originate with exterior economic forces; for example, characters often marry for economic reasons. But Austen also writes that marriage is "the origin of change" and shows that however strong external forces are in deciding it, it remains an original act and, therefore, a mystery.

Without forgetting, then, the complexity of class and money as they are represented in the novel, let us lay down some basic facts about them in nineteenth-century English society. How many classes were there, and of what and whom were they composed? Historians disagree in their answer to this question, but from the mid-nineteenth century to the present, it has become common to identify three classes: upper, middle, and lower; or ruling class, bourgeoisie, and working class. This distinction is most consistent with the view of class in the Victorian novel in which the major cleavages in the social system are between those who do not have to work for a living and those who do, and between those who possess some property and those who possess no property and support themselves "hand to mouth," through manual labor.

Other dividing lines—religious, political, and social—complicate this structure. The upper class was primarily Anglican, and the majority of the middle class were Dissenters.[4] In politics, the breakdown was Tory, Whig, and radical. The common associations are Tories with aristocrats and Whigs with middle-class industrialists; radicals seemed to come from all classes of society. But there were many exceptions, and party ideologies were sufficiently complicated to make this distinction too narrow.[5] Socially, the line was drawn between town and country. This distinction seemed to affect the working class more than any other. For example, country workers were far more likely to be politically conservative and members of the Church of England than city workers, who were increasingly apathetic about religion (as, partly for organizational reasons at the beginning of the century, the Church was apathetic about them) and more radical politically.

To begin at the top and at the very beginning of the century: In 1803, the upper class, or those who did not have to work for a living, comprised about 27,000 families, or 2% of the population; the middle ranks made up about 635,000 families; the lower ranks about 1,347,000 families. The upper class can be divided into three sections: the aristocracy, the gentry, and the squirarchy or class of independent gentlemen who did not have to work. The aristocracy were the great landed proprietors whose estates exceeded 10,000 acres (about 18 square miles) and who, for the most part, belonged to the peerage. With fortunes yielding an income of over £10,000 a year, this tiny yet immensely powerful group numbered from 300 to 400 families. Beneath them, the gentry was made up of the smaller landed proprietors whose estates ran from 1,000 to 10,000 acres and whose annual income ranged from £1,000 to £10,000 a year; they comprised about 3,000 families. These two sections of the upper class together—all those who owned more than 1,000 acres—owned more than two-thirds of all the land in England. Moving a step lower, the much larger group of borderline gentry and independent gentlemen had less land and income; these gentlemen and their families lived on about £700 to £1,000 a year.[6]

What do these figures mean in today's terms? Today, real income is estimated by comparing money earnings with an index of the cost of living, but there are several reasons why historians are unable to do that with absolute accuracy here. Too many details regarding both income and expenditure are unknown. Moreover, the figures listed above are based on studies made early in the nineteenth century which cannot pretend to the statistical certainty of a modern survey. Still, we have enough facts to draw some general conclusions and to see through what often seems like a veil of monetary information in nineteenth-century novels.

Until World War I, before the income taxes and inflation of this century, the English pound was worth about 5 American dollars; the pound's value remained relatively steady throughout the nineteenth century. According to the inflation figures suggested by E. H. Phelps Brown and Sheila V. Hopkins, the value of the pound has multiplied about forty-fold over the course of the nineteenth century to the present.[7] This means that a member of the real aristocracy, whose income exceeded £10,000 a year, would possess in today's terms a minimum fortune of $2 million. The gentry's income went from about $200,000 to $2 million a year, and the average gentleman needed today's equivalent of $200,000 a year to retain a place in the upper class and not work for a living.

Early in *Pride and Prejudice*, Jane Austen tells us that the income of her hero, Darcy, is £10,000 a year so that we will know just how far above Meryton, with its working lawyers and shabby gentry, Darcy really is. Known to be a member of one of the top three or four hundred families in the country, Darcy's presence at the little country ball in Meryton is equivalent to a Rockefeller attending an Elks Club dinner. Awkward as the comparison may be, we must think according to such comparisons to understand the mixture of pride, insult, and curiosity that Darcy's presence excites.

Technically, Darcy is not a member of the aristocracy, because he does not have a title, but he belongs to an ancient family and possesses family property and investments that yield the enormous income necessary to participate in aristocratic life. To qualify as an aristocrat, one had to be of titled rank, to own an estate exceeding 10,000 acres, to have enough money in revenues to live opulently, and to own a house in London to go to during the social season. Obviously there were exceptions—some ancient titles had declining fortunes—but in order to participate fully in the social life of the aristocracy, one had to have these things. The fact that Darcy marries Elizabeth Bennet, a member of the lower gentry, and befriends the landless Mr. Bingley, whose father made a fortune in business, shows that despite his ancient lineage, he is not greatly allied with the upper aristocracy. In their concern with the mobile middle ranks of society, most English novelists of the period do not explore the upper reaches of the aristocracy with the same degree of interest with which they explore classes beneath it; the aristocracy often exists in the background as the envied destination of social climbers. In

Vanity Fair, it is this highest, most frivolous stratum of society that Becky Sharp penetrates by associating herself with Lord Steyne.

Darcy's income suggests only a part of the power that a man in his position wielded. He not only had access to high political office if he wanted it; he controlled the lives and incomes of hundreds of people on his estates, many of whom had no voting power until 1832. The Reform Bill of 1832 enfranchised half of the middle class, and so many of Darcy's tenant farmers would have had the vote after that date. But until 1872, when the secret ballot was finally passed, votes were taken orally. Usually the steward or manager of the estate would accompany tenants to the voting place and remain there while he called out his preference. Consequently, the 1832 Reform Bill worked to increase the power of landlords like Darcy, since tenants usually felt impelled to vote with their landlords and votes were often sold at elections to the highest bidder.

The aristocracy, with its beautiful houses manned by up to fifty servants, its enormous annual revenues, its power in Parliament, its own constituency of tenants, and its tremendous prestige based on tradition, must be considered in all its aspects in order to appreciate the significance of property inheritance in the English novel. To inherit an estate and title was not like inheriting a mere manor house in the country to which one could retreat on holidays; it was more like inheriting a large company with majority interest and a lifetime position as chairman of the board, but with the power to decide every issue oneself. To make the analogy correct, the company would have to be in the most stable of businesses, or not as subject to the fluctuations of the market as, for example, a manufacturing concern. It would have behind it generations of capital and stable management to guarantee generations more of the same. This is the security we must contemplate when we encounter the subject of great property inheritance in the novel. To be sure, there were great families in decline and estates with huge mortgages that were put up for rent, but the most insecure aristocrat was so much more secure—socially, politically, and financially—than almost anyone below that to emphasize that insecurity would be highly misleading.

Just beneath the aristocracy were the gentry with titles of lesser significance such as Knight and Baronet or none at all. They had smaller incomes and smaller estates that were often the major residence. Their estates were much less opulent than those of the aristocracy, and manned by fewer servants (as few as five or six); only the better off had a house in town. Jane Austen writes about the gentry, focusing particularly on the way they experienced pressure from the upper-middle class to enter its ranks.

Just below the gentry lay the interesting and important stratum of "gentlemen" and their families. Since all members of the nobility were gentlemen and ladies, the singular title of "gentleman" was especially important to this untitled segment of the upper class. In Jane Austen's novels, a gentleman can be a younger son of the gentry who has not inherited an estate and who has taken holy orders (Edmund Bertram in *Mansfield Park*), or he can be the son of a man who has made a fortune in business and has been brought up as a gentleman to do nothing (Mr. Bingley in *Pride and Prejudice*). The struggling gentry in *Pride and Prejudice* are only too happy to marry their daughters to the wealthy but unlanded Mr. Bingley.

The term *lady* does not seem to have become inflated with significance until later in the century. Before then, a lady was any woman married to a gentleman. But when legislation permitted women to own their own property and gave married women the same property rights as unmarried women, many middle- and upper-class women gained the financial independence so essential to "gentle" status, and the word *lady* took on new dimension.[8] Henry James's *Portrait of a Lady* (1881) is about a young woman whose unexpected inheritance of a large fortune grants her that power of independent choice that motivates the plot of so many novels. Considered together, the title and plot of the novel suggest how essential financial independence was to the new definition of *lady*.

In the Victorian period, a gentleman required today's rough equivalent of £200,000 a year to live. Being a gentleman meant not having to work, dressing as a gentleman, and employing at least enough servants to receive and to go into society (i.e., a cook, housemaid, maid-of-all-work, and valet). The cost of clothes and servant wages was very different from the present. Until technology took over the textile industry, fine clothing was handmade and extremely expensive. In *Great Expectations*, the first allowance Pip receives for his program to become a gentleman is 20 guineas to buy clothes. This suggests, better than any statistical table, how essential clothing was to the role of gentleman, and how expensive. A guinea was a little over a pound. The 20 guineas to buy clothes—incidentally one of the few precise sums given in connection with Pip's inheritance—would be over £4,000 today. Pip's working-class surrogate father, Joe, almost faints when the lawyer displays this sum, because to him it would be about half his yearly income in blacksmith's wages.

In contrast to the cost of fine clothing, the wages of servants seem small. The labor of a man was cheaper than that of a horse. In London, where there were at least 10,000 female servants always looking for "a place," from £6 to £10 was a typical yearly wage for a maid-of-all-work, including room and board. An upper housemaid was paid £12 to £20 a year with allowances, though a lady's maid was paid only £12 to £15, probably because she had perks in the way of cast-off clothing. A cook could earn from £14 to £20 a year, and a footman £15 to £20. In very rich houses, the wages of a private chef, butler, steward, and housekeeper were higher, usually starting around £40 or £50 a year. A typical upper-class family would have a retinue of servants from the most basic workers (cook, housemaids, maids-of-all-work) to the more extravagant (valets, footmen, butlers). To convert these figures to contemporary dollars, the lowest wage of £6 would be only $1,200 today; the highest (£50) would be about $10,000, with the vast majority of servants' wages on the lower end of the scale.[9]

In a nontechnological society in which a large percentage of the working class held positions in service, the upper and lower class lived in closer quarters than either did to the middle class. This was especially true in the first half of the century; from 1850 to 1870 the number of domestic servants increased by 60%, twice the rate of increase of the population, and one that accompanied the rise of middle-class prosperity during that period. Coincidences in Dickens's early novels in which a poor person turns out to be related to a rich one have a literal analogue in the lives of many Victorians. Just as nineteenth-century maps of London show respectable areas of the city cheek by jowl with unrespectable places, Dickens shows that what were considered extremes were often adjacent. The middle class was in this sense more isolated, because the middle-class family employed fewer servants and felt less responsibility for them, whereas the aristocratic tradition of noblesse oblige compelled the aristocrat to support retired servants in their old age. The bond between the upper and lower class is suggested, in *Emma*, when the heroine makes her well-known snobbish remarks about a rising farmer:

> A young farmer ... is the very last sort of person to raise my curiosity. The yeomanry are precisely the order of people with whom I feel I can have nothing to do. A degree or two lower, and a creditable appearance might interest me; I might hope to be useful to their families in some way or other. But a farmer can need none of my help, and is therefore in one sense as much above my notice as in every other he is below it.

As Austen's novels show, there was considerable mobility and instability of class position within the lower-upper class and upper-middle class at the beginning of the century. We hear of estates changing hands in every Austen novel. Characters often drop from secure positions in the gentry to insecure ones, like the Dashwoods at the opening of *Sense and Sensibility*. In *Emma*, a governess (Miss Taylor) rises to be mistress of an estate, and a lady (Miss

Bates) drops to a barely genteel poverty. Austen's novels suggest the truth of historian Lawrence Stone's description that "a class is not a finite group of families but rather a bus or hotel, always full but always filled with different people."[10] In the early nineteenth century, the nexus of social change was to be found more in the gentry and middle class than either the working class or aristocracy. Austen shows over and over again that the apparent stability of class position is an illusion created by the slowness of change through marriage and the peculiar stability of class character, resulting from the chameleonlike adaptability of new families. Often in one generation, new families learn to dress, speak, and behave according to the customs of their new class. In *Vanity Fair*, a tradesman who makes a fortune in the tallow industry raises his son to be a gentleman and his daughter a lady; they accordingly snub him, as indeed they must if they are to secure their niche in the upper class.

With the rise of a class society, the phenomenon of snobbery, or class feeling, replaced deference. The old society had been paternalistic—that is, a hierarchical and, by definition, unequal structure held together by the reciprocal bonds of authority and deference and by clearly defined rights and duties.[11] Deference is a form of acknowledging one's place in and dependency on the old hierarchy; snobbery is a preoccupation with class distinctions resulting from increased social mobility and the necessity of those on the rise to adopt new manners and customs. Austen's novels record the increase in snobbery, although it was in the solid middle ranks that snobbery appeared to be strongest. As Thackeray professes in the *Book of Snobs* "among the respectable class, the greatest profusion of snobs is to be found," because in the ever-expanding middle ranks the greatest social mobility was present and possible.

In the domain of snob appeal, peers and Baronets were the stars of English society, viewed by the middle class with the kind of mindless awe with which Americans view celebrities today. "What high class company!" repeats Mr. Meagles in Dickens's *Little Dorrit*, in spite of the humiliations he receives at the hands of its members. The English novel is full of bourgeois parvenus who will do almost anything to consort with titled people; in *Vanity Fair*, George Osborne gladly gambles away his money to a Baronet's cardsharp son in order to be seen in his company. Streets, houses, and objects are often described solely in terms of class, as in Dickens's portrait of the "airless houses" with "enormous rents" in Grosvenor Square: "the house agent advertised it as a gentlemanly residence in the most aristocratic part of town, inhabited solely by the elite of the beau monde."

These and other examples in the nineteenth-century novel suggest that by far the most important cleavage in the social structure was that between the gentleman and the "common people." The definition of the gentleman broadened as the nineteenth century progressed, but the sense of cleavage remained strong. In the eighteenth century, birth was still the essential requirement of gentlemanly rank; if one's father was a gentleman, the other aspects of gentlemanly rank—inherited money and land, education, and manners—were sure to follow. In the course of the nineteenth century, however, the idea of the gentleman broadened to give, new-made money, education, and manners greater importance in relation to birth than they had ever had before. According to Tocqueville, the history of the gentleman concept from England to France to the United States reveals the development of democracy: "In the United States, everyone is a gentleman." (Tocqueville also claimed that the English notion of the gentleman saved England from a revolution.)

How much money did it take to *become* a gentleman? According to R.K. Webb, "the capital cost of procuring an estate which could support a gentleman's family without recourse to continuing income from the trade or profession that was left behind was perhaps thirty times the desired income."[12] It took the work of several generations, as well as prosperous marriages, to put together a fortune of £30,000, which would be the minimum sum necessary for maintaining a gentleman's family and residence on interest alone. (Emma Woodhouse's fortune in *Emma* is £30,000, roughly equivalent to a fortune of $6 million today.) What is important, however, is that in the nineteenth century, entering the gentlemanly class was finally within the grasp of those who had not been born into it.

We can see the concept of the gentleman broadening in *Emma*, when Mr. Knightley calls the yeoman-farmer, Robert Martin, a "gentleman-farmer." And we can see the power and respect that the status of gentleman was gaining as a democratic ideal when, in *Pride and Prejudice*, Elizabeth Bennet insists that she is Darcy's equal by claiming, "He is a gentleman. I am a gentleman's daughter." By 1860, a novelist could write about a blacksmith's apprentice who sets off for London to become a gentleman on the basis of money alone (*Great Expectations*). No novelist was more broadly ironic than Dickens in his treatment of the word and idea of gentleman, possibly because he was one of the few novelists of the period familiar with the working class. Pip's great social expectations turn out to be founded on a criminal's fortune. At the close of *Our Mutual Friend*, Twenlow's delicate insistence that he uses "the word *gentleman* ... in the sense in which the degree may be attained by any man," is small and touching after the immense, insoluble social problems that have preceded it.

The gentleman as social category has no real equivalent in the United States, and so Americans often have difficulty grasping its place and importance in the English imagination. In this country, as Lionel Trilling has said, it would be a little like possessing a B.A. degree, or what a B.A. used to represent, with its affirmation of social status and economic promise, and the widespread implication of inferiority regarding those who do not possess it. The B.A. degree does not mean a great deal, we think, especially if we possess one; but to be without it speaks volumes. Similarly, the untitled gentleman at the end of the eighteenth century was technically on the lowest rung of the upper class, and many were quite shabby, regarded in the way Americans view B.A. degrees from unknown colleges. To be a member of the real aristocracy would grant the kind of prestige, for example, that attending an Ivy League college does today.

The gentlemen of the early nineteenth century grew to include, besides the nobility and gentry, "the clergyman, physician and barrister, but not always the Dissenting minister, the apothecary, the attorney, or the schoolmaster; the overseas merchant, but not the inland trader; the amateur author, painter, musician, but rarely the professional."[13] In other words, one could be involved in certain kinds of work but never, of course, any kind of manual labor. Making money for the sake of supporting oneself was ungentlemanly; a paid musician was socially inferior to the musical amateur.* In the early part of the century, when Elizabeth Bennet announces that she is a gentleman's daughter and therefore eligible to marry Darcy, she means to emphasize the unassailability of her father's position as a gentleman; unlike her gentlemanly uncle in trade, her father does not work for a living at all, but lives on the revenues from his estate and investments.

How did the upper class change in the course of the century? First, as has been suggested, it received into its ranks more members of the rich middle class. Since the national income was multiplied by eight in the course of the century, inflation was relatively low, and the population rose by 400%, more people became eligible for inclusion. Toward the end of the century more businessmen were promoted to the peerage, and the percentage of landed interests in the House of Commons dropped (in 1865, three-quarters of the seats were taken up by landlords; by 1910, it had dropped to one-seventh). The lower gentry was penetrated more and more by the bourgeoisie through marriage.

The retreat of agriculture also caused a decrease in the traditional power of the aristocracy. At the end of the eighteenth century, the proportion of agricultural workers in the total labor force was two-fifths; in 1851, it was one-fifth; in 1881, it was one-eighth. Agriculture's share in the gross national product fell from 20% around 1850 to 6% around 1900. The upper class was by no means impoverished by this decline, however, since its members long held investments in industry; as noted previously, they owned resources, like coal mines, whose cash value was determined by the new economy. From 1803 to 1867, the total income of the upper class went from £33 to £180 million as a result of investment and infiltration from the rich middle class. And, until the beginning of this century, the upper class continued to occupy most positions of power and privilege in the society.

The middle ranks were distinguished at the top from the gentry not so much by lower incomes, since in many cases their incomes were higher, as by the necessity of having to work for a living.[14] Some of the great overseas merchants, officials, and judges had incomes equal to those of peers and married their children or themselves into the aristocracy. Dickens's Dombey in *Dombey and Son* is one such merchant, whose business dates back to the eighteenth century and who marries into the lower echelons of the aristocracy. The outcome of the plot, however, belies the theme of assimilation and suggests that the psychology of aristocratic life is incompatible with that of earning money. Dombey wants to live the life of an aristocrat, and so his neglected business goes to ruins.

In the early years of the nineteenth century, the greatest affluence in the middle class was to be found among freeholders and tenant farmers, but later they were overtaken by the growing number of manufacturers, merchants, and businessmen. These were the main contributors to what Disraeli called the "convulsion of prosperity" that ended in the 1870's. Their achievements in industry, commerce, and the upper ranks of administration gained on the position of agriculture with every decade. Beneath them on the economic scale were the small manufacturers, bankers, and businessmen, the old commercial professions made up of dealers in grain and yard goods, the "old professions" (i.e., the Army, Church, civil service, and law), the rising professions in medicine, law (solicitors), business (accountants, engineers), education and literary people (teachers, journalists, writers), and, at the bottom, the army of low-paid civil servants, clerks, office workers, schoolmasters, railway staff, theatre people, lunatic asylum keepers, and so on.

This economic scale does not reflect the social scale. The social hierarchy would place members of the old professions—barristers, clergymen, and service officers—on top. These positions were compatible with gentlemanly status; the younger sons of the gentry flowed into these professions, and ambitious and successful middle-class men used them as a springboard to the upper class. There was a firm prejudice against business; only gradually was it accepted as an occupation worthy of a gentleman. But even among businesses there were important distinctions: High commerce and finance ranked higher than industry because the world of industry still bore the base image of the shop.

An average middle-class income at mid-century ranged from £150 to £1,000 a year (roughly $30,000 to $200,000 today), although the very rich bourgeoisie's income could go much higher and that of the lower-middle class could sink much lower. The "middle-middle class," made up of the professions, well-off merchants, university teachers, and others, earned from £300 to £800 a year with professions heading the list. As the century progressed, the middle class increased in size and depth relative to the pyramid structure of English society. The number of middle-class families grew from 635,000 in 1803 to 1,546,300 in 1867, while the middle-class's percentage of the national income dropped from about 60% to 35%. At the top, more people shared in ruling-class levels of wealth; at the bottom, the Bob Cratchits proliferated. Victorian novels show this democratizing trend within the overall social structure, with the extremes moving toward the middle. The working class began to split into the "respectable" and the "rough" lower classes; the upper class, in turn, split between the landed classes, the professions, the old mercantile and banking bourgeoisie, and the new industrialists and entrepreneurs from the north. These "cultural frontiers," as Lawrence Stone names them, where both the upper and working classes split, were crucial boundaries in establishing the distinctly middle-class culture of the Victorians.

What characterized the middle class? First, the severe ethical style of the Victorians, with its emphasis on hard work, the home, and strict morality, was largely a middle-class phenomenon. The majority of the middle class were religious nonconformists (notably Methodists, Congregationalists, and Baptists), although there were a large number of Anglicans, too; many of the ethical preoccupations of the middle class rose out of their religious attitudes. Second, the bourgeoisie differed from the lower class in having a degree of education, if only in the form of some expertise in a nonmanual skill. Third, the average middle-class home employed servants, if only a cook and housemaids. (Only the very well off could afford to employ a valet, footmen, and butler on a yearly basis; most people of this class hired butlers and footmen for special occasions only. In the novels of Thackeray and Dickens those most desperately seeking to rise out of the middle into the upper class—Dickens's Tite Barnacles and the Veneerings—declare their ambitions by employing ostentatious footmen.) Fourth, and probably the most important distinction between the middle class and laboring poor, was that the middle-class person owned *some* property, however small, represented by stock-in-trade, livestock, tools, or the educational investment of a skill or expertise. Never dependent on any kind of manual labor, he was usually remunerated in the form of profits or salary rather than a weekly wage. There were, of course, many members of the lower-middle class who were not nearly this secure, as we can see by all the Micawbers and Bob Cratchits in Dickens's novels. Like the boundary between the middle and upper, that between the middle and lower was unstable with many members slipping downward. One of Scrooge's greatest sins in *A Christmas Carol* is that he pays a middle-class worker, his clerk, a typically lower-class weekly wage that is used up immediately to survive.

There are also many instances of upward mobility in fiction and biography that center on the cleavage between the middle and lower classes. The life of James Mill (1773–1836), the utilitarian philosopher and father of John Stuart Mill, provides an interesting example. James Mill was the son of a Scottish servant girl who recognized her son's intelligence and secured him the attention of the local gentry. They sent him to university, where he took holy orders; he was therefore likely to become either a curate or private tutor, occupations which allowed little leisure to write. Instead, he married a woman who was not of his class but slightly above him, a member of the lowest rung of the middle class. Her mother kept a lunatic asylum and could supply her daughter with a small dowry. This provided Mill with enough independence to write his first work, a history of India, which secured him a position at the East India House. Eventually, he rose to a position there equivalent to undersecretary of state. The whole story offers a kind of microcosm of English social mobility in the early years of the century, with its basis in local patronage, the rise through education and ability, and the indispensability of good luck in making a fortunate marriage. Later, James Mill's son observed that the single most important fact of the nineteenth century was that people moved out of the class into which they were born.

This brings us to the lower class of English society. As suggested earlier, some historians believe that the familiar three-part division of the class system is rather arbitrary. It has been argued that there were up to five classes, or that there were only two, or even that there were no distinguishable classes at all because of the lack of internal consistency within the different economic groups. As complex as the class system appears when studied in its economic aspect, however, there is no doubt that middle-class Victorians felt greatly divided from, and in terror of, what lay below; and that many of those who rose out of the lower into the middle class in their youth retained a sense of shame about their origins all their lives. James Mill never told his son about his parentage. Dickens never told his wife that as a child he was sent to work in a factory, even though his fiction confirms that this may have been the most disturbing experience of his life.

Comprising about two-thirds of the total population, the massive lower class was made up of artisans or skilled workers, the growing population of industrial workers, the decreasing population of agricultural workers, domestic servants, the "surplus labor" population of the unemployed poor and destitute, and finally, lunatics, paupers, vagrants, and criminals. The ways of life varied among these groups, as Dickens's novels, which feature all of them, show, but were all joined together by the same dependence on the owners of capital, the same insecure living and working circumstances, and the same low wages.

Working-class housing was often substandard and in cities and towns was so overcrowded, stinking, and filthy that it is no exaggeration to say that the worst slums of our cities today look comfortable in comparison. In Liverpool early in the century, for example, one laboring family in five lived in a cellar. Parts of Manchester housed ten people a room—before indoor plumbing and inoculation against disease were common. Since jobs were at the mercy of the market cycle, the closing of a factory meant that whole populations of workers were forced to migrate on foot to new towns. Social security did not exist. Unions were slow to become established. Wages were pitched at the lowest survival level, so that pawnbrokers' shops flourished in working-class districts. And except for the small percentage of artisans and skilled laborers at the top of the scale, there was no hope of ever escaping the grinding existence of the new working routine to which more and more laborers were subjected.

This was the industrialized working routine that, according to Engels, had four main characteristics: the intensification of the division of labor, the introduction of modern machines, the use of water and steam power, and the tendency toward concentration and centralization.. This concentration and centralization can be seen in the factory system itself and in the expansion of the great factory towns. Here is Dickens's description of the industrial town of Coketown from *Hard Times*:

> It contained several large streets still more like one another, inhabited by people equally like one another, who all went in and out at the same hours, with the same sound on the same pavements, to do the same work, and to whom every day was the same as yesterday and tomorrow, and every year the counterpart of the last and the next.

The most important division within the internal structure of the working class was between skilled and unskilled workers. The skilled worker had gone through a long apprenticeship of about seven years, as Pip does at the forge in *Great Expectations*. He usually had some education, and in the course of the century, could earn from £50 to £90 a year. Only about 15% of the work force was made up of skilled laborers. Beneath them lay the mass of semi-skilled and unskilled workers who made less than £50 a year and had little or no education; included in this group were the child-workers whose jobs made up such an important segment of the industrial economy. By 1835, children under fourteen made up about 13% of the labor force in cotton.[15] Below and beneath these people existed paupers, vagrants, and Tom-all-Alone's who barely survived on charity, and members of the underworld who lived on crime.

This bottom-level population of the unskilled and unemployed lived in the most squalid circumstances, usually in lodging houses and tenements in city slums amid the open sewers that caused repeated cholera epidemics. And when the epidemical, contagious diseases were not raging, lung disease, tuberculosis, typhus, scrofula, rickets, chronic gastritis, and countless other illnesses were. Many observers—novelists, journalists, visitors from America—commented on the sickly appearance of people in working areas.

The unemployed lived in fear of the workhouse and were at the mercy of pawnbrokers and money lenders, who could wield the threat of Debtor's Prison before anyone with a debt of over £20. They were both most tempted and most victimized by crime, and their involvement in crime often followed the fluctuations of the market cycle, as was frequently the case with women who became prostitutes only during periods of unemployment. The criminal class was palpably and visibly present in lower-class areas as can be seen in Dickens's *Oliver Twist*. Whole courtyards in London were inhabited by gangs of criminals where holes were dug through walls and ceilings so that men pursued by the police might escape.[16]

From 1803 to 1867, the population grew from just over two million to more than six million families. The huge increase in population was felt most heavily in the working class, where the number of families went from scarcely one million to over four and a half million; the number of paupers alone went from 260,000 in 1803 to over 600,000 in 1867. Dickens's novels register, for example, the increase in wandering poor people that skyrocketed in the first decades of the century. By far the largest class, the lower class controlled a comparatively small percentage of the national income: about 25% in 1803 and 40% in 1867, an increase that is 50% less than the population jump.

This jump was accompanied by high emigration from rural to urban areas, creating the new mass experience of urbanization that some historians feel was the central shock of the nineteenth century.[17] By 1851, more than half—51%—of the population lived in cities for the first time, the major increase taking place in London. By the Second Reform Bill of 1867, the majority of the urban voting population in England was made up of the working class, but it was not until 1893 that this class was sufficiently well organized politically to establish a labor party. In the course of the century, the social scale stretched and the pyramid became thinner and higher, a change that did not always benefit the lower class. There was a great increase of wealth at the top while three-quarters of all families had to share less than two-fifths of the available resources. Nevertheless, there was a leveling effect, and the society became less hierarchical.

Obviously, novelists do not view class in terms of statistics, as we have to some extent viewed it here; instead class is embodied in personal character and circumstance. It is revealed in the attitudes of different characters toward a wide range of experiences and ideas—love, sex, money, religion, the self and its possibilities. Also revealing are the particular circumstances of the characters: where they live, how they have been educated, what kind of furniture they prefer, the clothes they wear, and so on. As Michael Wood has said, realism is based on the assumption that the material world reveals. Class is therefore essential to the classic English novel, and Eliot's description of Rosamond Vincy's finery in *Middlemarch* is basically no different from Dickens's description of Maggie's rags in *Little Dorrit*. Both point to class.

Characters are individual representatives of their class; in *Emma*, Mr. Knightley is seen as an individual *and* a representative of the landed gentry at a particular moment in history. In this way social change is recorded by the novelist, and we are able to trace its course by comparing early and late fiction by the same author. The character of the great proprietor undergoes significant change from Austen's first to her last novels, in everything from how he manages his holdings and conceives of his relation to national affairs to what he does with his time at a fashionable resort. Through this figure, we see how the social structure was changing at the local level—for example, in the changing rituals attending on life at a spa such as Bath.[18] Dickens's mid-career fiction, such as *Dombey and Son*, register the end of the first phase of the Industrial Revolution in showing the shift from cotton to steel in the occupations of working-class characters. In the later novels like *Our Mutual Friend*, he shows, again by means of characters and their occupations, that the city is no longer concerned with production but with finance, and that money has taken on a systematic existence of its own.

We may echo George Eliot in saying that in the Victorian novel, since everything is based on class and money, everything is below the level of tragedy except the passionate egoism of character. In its traditional form, the English novel does not tolerate the metaphysical categories found in tragedy; the concepts of God and death are filtered through class and appear in truncated form among the props of daily existence. In Austen's novels, religion is seen in terms of its class representatives, i.e., the Tory clergymen who populate her stories. More often than not, death is the occasion for an inheritance, not a discourse on the meaning of life. This is partly what Henry James meant when he criticized one nineteenth-century novelist for being "vulgar" and overly concerned with people on the make.[19] The charge is true, and most Victorian novelists would have been amused by it; they might even have taken it as a compliment. Probably no other group of writers took more account of the limitations of their subject, or the limitations imposed on the mind, spirit, and will by life in society. In their eyes, it is James who would be vulgar, for acknowledging these limitations so secretly.

* The relation between the gentleman and the artist is a subject of George Eliot's *Daniel Deronda*, in which a gentlewoman is confident that she could triumph on the stage without giving herself much trouble. "I was sure he had too much talent to be a mere musician," says another member of the gentry about a brilliant musician.

NOTES

1. Harold Perkin, *The Origins of Modern English Society 1780–1880* (Toronto, 1972), p. 17.

2. Asa Briggs, *A Social History of England* (New York, 1983), p. 189.

3. For further discussion, see P. Mantoux, *The Industrial Revolution in the Eighteenth Century* (London, 1928; rev. ed., 1961); F. A. Hayek, ed., *Capitalism and the Historians* (London, 1954); N.J. Smelser, *Social Change and the Industrial Revolution* (London, 1959); and E.P. Thompson, *The Making of the English Working Class* (London, 1963).

4. See K.S. Inglis, *Churches and the Working Classes in Victorian England* (London, 1963).

5. See Chapter VIII on government and reform.

6. The 1803 estimates were gauged from Patrick Colquhoun's estimates of income distribution from 1803, which are explicated in Perkin, p. 20. For general information and estimates concerning income and property distribution throughout the nineteenth century, I am indebted to a variety of sources: F.M.L. Thompson, *English Landed Society in the 19th Century* (London, 1963); R.K. Webb, *Modern*

England from the 18th Century to the Present (New York and Toronto, 1968); G.E. Mingay, *The Gentry* (London, 1978); E.H. Whitman, *History of British Agriculture 1846–1914* (London, 1964); and P. Mathias, *The First Industrial Nation* (London, 1969).

7. Inflation based on charts given in E.H. Phelps Brown and Sheila V. Hopkins, "Seven Centuries of Building Wages" and "Seven Centuries of the Prices of Consumables, Compared with Builders' Wage-Rates" in *Essays in Economic History*, ed. E. M. Carus-Wilson (New York, 1966), Vol. II, pp. 168–197. To arrive at dollar figures, convert pounds into dollars by multiplying by five; allow for inflation by multiplying by forty. These calculations are, of course, very general equivalents rather than precise conversions.

A *penny* (plural, *pence*) is worth 1/240 of a pound, 1/12 of a shilling. A *shilling* is worth 1/20 of a pound, or twelve pence. A *bob* is a shilling, or five pence. A *guinea* was a British gold coin first coined for African trade, equal to £1.05. A *crown* is a British coin worth 25 pence, formerly five shillings. A *quid* is one pound sterling.

8. See Chapter VII on Marriage.

9. According to a cost-of-living source published in 1824, on £400 a year the typical family employed two maidservants, one horse, and a groom. On £700 they kept one man, three maidservants, and two horses. On £1,000 a year, they blossomed out into an establishment of three female servants, a coachman and footman, a chariot or coach, phaeton or other four-wheeled carriage, and a pair of horses. On £5,000 a year the establishment had grown to "thirteen male and nine female servants, ten horses, a coach, curricle and a Tilbury, Chaise or gig." G.M. Young, ed., *Early Victorian England* 1830–1865 (London, 1934), Vol. I, pp. 104–105.

What did all of these servants do, especially in the houses of the great? Since time- and effort-saving machinery was unknown, a large kitchen staff was necessary as well as a half-dozen women in the laundry if the family was large. One maid might be solely responsible for hand sewing, as the sewing machine was not introduced into most houses until the 1860's. One footman might be solely responsible for seeing to the candles and grates. If the family had more than one footman, they were used for a variety of tasks: to attend ladies when walking to town, to carry the family prayer books when they went to church, to disentangle horses during traffic difficulties, and so on. In the houses of the very rich, each lady had a ladies' maid, each gentleman a footman.

10. Lawrence Stone, *The Crisis of the Aristocracy*, abridged ed. (London, 1967), p. 23.

11. See David Roberts, *Paternalism in Early Victorian England* (New Jersey, 1980).

12. Webb, p. 11.

13. Perkin, p. 24.

14. ———, p. 23.

15. See Webb, p. 111.

16. The middle- and upper-class reaction to the new urban poverty and crime was to legislate, as shown in the chapter on Government and Reform; it was also to deny, as a well-known instance related to a place called Jacob's Island shows. Jacob's

Island was one of the most notorious of London slums; the open sewers that flowed under and between its decayed, doorless houses caused the cholera epidemics of 1832 and 1848. In 1850 a city alderman, Sir Peter Laurie, declared that Jacob's Island did not exist and never had existed, just as some people in this century have declared the Holocaust never existed. "I don't want to know about it; I don't want to discuss it; I won't admit it," says Dickens's Mr. Podsnap, who has come to represent the quintessential middleclass attitude.

17. At the first census of 1801 only fifteen towns had a population of over 20,000; by 1891 there were sixty-three. For further discussion of the experience of urbanization, see Steven Marcus, *Engels, Manchester and the Working Class* (New York, 1975), pp. 144–184, which includes discussion of Dickens; and Francis Sheppard, *London* 1808–1870: *The Infernal Wen* (London, 1971).

18. Compare General Tilney in *Northanger Abbey* to Sir Walter Elliot in *Persuasion*. Between these two novels, the first written around 1802 and the second in 1817, the social rituals of Bath had changed. The public ball had given way to the small dinner party in the lives of the rich. Allusions in the latter novel suggest that the gentry was drawing back in this way from the pressures of democratization. For a discussion of some of the effects of democratization on manners and speech, see my book *Jane Austen's Novels: Social Change and Literary Form* (Cambridge, Mass., 1979), p. 57. Jane Austen's disclaimer to her readers at the opening of *Northanger Abbey* refers in a general way to these changes. Because the novel was published fifteen years after it was written, Austen seems to have been worried that her readers would think she was portraying Bath inaccurately. This shows, first, how rapid the changes were and, second, how conscious Austen was of what she was doing.

19. The reference, in fact, was not to an English novelist but to Balzac; however, the criticism still applies, and was a little like the pot calling the kettle black.

CHRISTOPHER S. NASSAAR

Introduction to *The Victorians: A Major Authors Anthology*

The Victorian age was one of the most prolific in the history of English literature. In terms of poetry, non-fictional prose, the novel, and even drama (which flourished only at the end of the nineteenth century), it gave us some of the best literature the world has in its possession. The reputation of the Victorians and their literature declined sharply in the early decades of the twentieth century, as the Georgians (1911–36) insisted on defining themselves in terms of rebellion against the preceding age, but it soon recovered, and Victorian literature today is rightly valued very highly indeed. Lytton Strachey, in his *Eminent Victorians* (1918), undertook to show that the entire Victorian world was a huge hypocrisy, a facade of respectability behind which lurked all kinds of corruption and immorality. The book was vastly popular in its day, and it did prove that many great Victorians were less than ideal, but we know today that despite their shortcomings the Victorians deserve our respect, for their devotion to hard work, duty and morality brought England in a single age to a point of civilization and power it had never known before, or since. It is no exaggeration to say that, without the Victorians, our own age, whether in Britain or the United States, would hot have been possible.

From *The Victorians: A Major Authors Anthology*, ed. Christopher S. Nassaar. © 2000 by University Press of America, Inc.

THE VICTORIAN CLASS STRUCTURE

It was Queen Victoria who gave the Victorian age its name. She ruled Britain from 1837 until her death in 1901. But the Victorian period properly begins with the Reform Bill of 1832. The importance of this Bill lies in the fact that it gave voting rights to all males worth £10 or more in annual rent—in brief, it extended voting rights to the lower middle class and placed a great deal of political power in the hands of the middle classes, power which had hitherto been concentrated in the hands of the landed aristocracy. The rise of the middle classes, who were gradually taking control of England's economy, is a chief characteristic of the Victorian period.

But the aristocracy and the middle classes (they have to be referred to in the plural, since they ranged from the upper-middle to the lower-middle) constituted only about twenty percent of society; the remaining eighty percent was the lower or working class. As England industrialized in the shadow of a laissez-faire economic system, the condition of the working class in the industrial and coal-mining areas was nothing short of appalling. The apparent exaggerations in Elizabeth Barrett's poem "The Cry of the Children" (1843) and in Dickens's novel *Hard Times* (1852) are in fact fairly reliable accounts of the misery of the lower class in its struggle to earn a living. The 1840s was a period of depression in England, with much unemployment and starvation wages for those lucky enough to be employed. In 1842 the official count of paupers in England and Wales stood at 1,429,089, or approximately eighteen percent of the population. Child labor and the sixteen-hour work day were cold realities. Factory and mine conditions were horrible. The owners of mines and factories, reared in the laissez-faire mentality that unregulated working conditions ultimately benefit everyone, felt no pangs of conscience until Carlyle, horrified by what he saw around him, wrote *Past and Present* (1843), a book that had a profound effect on the rich, ultimately altering their attitude to the poor. Disraeli, who wrote a novel about factory life in England entitled *Sybil* (1845), gave it the famous subtitle *The Two Nations*, indicating the radical split between the rich and the poor.

After 1850, however, the condition of the working class began to improve as the so-called Time of Troubles was gradually replaced by a period of prosperity. A succession of Factory Acts in Parliament restricted child labor, limited working hours, and gradually improved the condition of the working class. In 1867 a second Reform Bill was passed, giving the vote to the working class. By the end of the century universal compulsory education had become a reality.

One other factor creating misery in the 1840s was the high tariffs imposed on wheat and other imported grains, known as the Corn Laws. The Corn Laws were protective, designed to shield English farmers from low-priced foreign products. The farmers did profit, but the rest of the population suffered greatly from the high price of bread. In 1845 a serious crop failure in England finally convinced the prime minister, Sir Robert Peel, to abandon protectionist measures, and in 1846 Parliament repealed the Corn Laws in favor of free trade.

THE INDUSTRIAL REVOLUTION

Dr. Thomas Arnold, Matthew Arnold's father, musing on the rapid industrialization of England during the early Victorian period, stated that "we have been living, as it were, the life of three hundred years in thirty." Thomas Babington Macaulay (1800–1859), the famous essayist, celebrated in his essays and histories in the 1850s the delightful and exhilarating progress of England, brandishing triumphantly the statistics of industrial growth. In 1897, during the Diamond Jubilee celebrating the sixtieth anniversary of Queen Victoria's reign, Mark Twain happened to be in London and was quite impressed. "Britain's history is two thousand years old," he wrote admiringly, "and yet in a good many ways the world has moved farther ahead since the Queen was born than it moved in all the rest of the two thousand put together." And indeed, by the end of the nineteenth century England had been transformed from a rural economy based on land ownership to a vast urban economy whose factories were producing and exporting at full capacity, capturing—with the help of an impressive merchant navy—markets in the far-flung corners of the world. Railways, ships, printing presses, anesthetics, telegraphs, photography and many other wonders came to dominate the scene, and the first cars began to roll out of the factories. Late Victorians, looking back, had good reason to feel proud.

And yet, there is another side to all this, detailed in part in the previous section describing the misery of the lower class. In addition, all this prosperity and material progress produced a materialistic attitude among the middle classes that most Victorian writers found repellent. Arnold's attack on the middle classes as "Philistines," the enemies of the chosen people, is a symptomatic famous example. Moreover, the machine came to be regarded as the enemy of the spiritual life, a monster to be resisted because of its terrible dehumanizing influence. It is no accident that Carlyle, in "The Everlasting No" chapter of *Sartor Resartus*, describes the materialistic universe

as "one huge, dead, immeasurable Steam-engine, rolling on, in its dead
indifference, to grind me limb from limb." Emerson, who visited England
several times in his life, wrote in *English Traits* (1856): "Mines, forges, mills,
breweries, railroads, steam-pump, steam-plow, drill of regiments, drill of
police, rule of court and shop-rule are operated to give a mechanical
regularity to all the habit and action of men. A terrible machine has possessed
itself of the ground, the air, the men and women, and hardly even thought is
free." This slavery to the machine, as Victorian writers constantly asserted,
includes all classes, for it dehumanizes human beings, forcing them to imitate
the machine and lead a regularized, routinish, machine-like existence, devoid
of creativity and originality.

The blighting of the environment was another drawback of the
industrial revolution. This is an issue that is very prominent today, but it also
existed during the Victorian period. Dickens, in *Hard Times*, presents the
industrial city of Coketown as a dark blotch polluting a beautiful natural
environment. Ruskin was deeply disturbed by the ugliness and the
destruction of natural beauty that the factories and their spread was causing.
The aesthetic movement of the 1880s and 1890s was in part a reaction
against industrialization.

THE VICTORIAN BELIEF IN PROGRESS

Despite all this, the Victorians—contrary to our nuclear age—had good
reason to believe that the world was gradually improving and that all
problems had a solution. After the defeat of Napoleon at Waterloo early in
the nineteenth century, England found itself the world's unchallenged
superpower. Gradually, London came to replace Paris as Europe's, and the
world's, most important city. When Queen Victoria came to the throne in
1837, there were approximately two million people in London; by the turn of
the century, the number had gone up to well over six million and London had
also become the world's most significant banking city. As the century moved
on, England acquired more and more colonies until a full quarter of the
earth's surface was under British rule and the English could state proudly that
the sun never set on the British Empire. Add to this the dazzling technological
progress and enormous wealth achieved during the Victorian period and the
almost uninterrupted peace it enjoyed (disturbed by the Crimean War against
Russia in 1854–56 and the Boer War in South Africa at the end of the century)
and one can see why the idea of progress took hold of the Victorian mind.
Tennyson is typical when he writes in section 106 of *In Memoriam:*

Ring out the old, ring in the new,
Ring, happy bells, across the snow:
The year is going, let him go;
Ring out the false, ring in the true.

The entire section is a Hymn to Progress that reveals an extreme optimism which few people today would be willing to share, but which was quite widespread in the Victorian period.

THE STATUS OF WOMEN

The so-called "Woman Question" was a very popular issue in Victorian times, and excited a great deal of debate. There was a widespread idea that the average weight of a man's brain is more than that of a woman's—3 1/2 lbs. to 2 lbs., 11 ozs., to be. exact—and that women therefore were intellectually inferior; thus, their place was in the home, as wives and mothers. This does not mean that women were persecuted. On the contrary, more often than not they were placed on a pedestal and worshiped. Coventry Patmore's long poem in praise of his wife, *The Angel in the House* (1854–62), was widely admired and became a best-seller. Many women enjoyed this status—Celia Brooke Chetham in George Eliot's *Middlemarch* is a good example—but others found it intolerably boring. Celia's sister Dorothea is an example from fiction. A famous real-life example is Florence Nightingale (1820–1910), who was still at home at 32 and whose mother placed intense pressures upon her not to pursue her nursing ambitions and her desire to improve the hospital treatment of patients. In 1852 she began writing a spiritual autobiography, *Cassandra*, in which she records her boredom and frustrations. Ultimately, she escaped from this stifling atmosphere and became world famous.

Boredom, however, was a privilege of middle-class and upper-class women. Among the lower classes, a full quarter of the female population worked in factories or as seamstresses or servants, and were paid very low wages. The picture of the bored, frustrated Victorian wife and mother who cannot find any outlet for her talents is largely confined to the moneyed upper classes, who were the most influential part of English society. This qualification needs to be kept in mind constantly as the "Woman Question" is explored.

Although women did not obtain the vote until 1918, their status improved considerably during the Victorian period. The classic landmark statement in their favor was John Stuart Mill's *The Subjection of Women* (1869), which argued that men and women are equal and should have equal rights and opportunities. He rejected the prevalent idea that the nature of woman is different and insisted that "what is now called the nature of women is eminently an artificial thing—the result of forced repression in some directions, unnatural stimulation in others." Mill insisted that women should be allowed to own and handle their own property, and laws were eventually passed (between 1870 and 1908) that allowed precisely that. Work opportunities for women improved as a result of feminist agitation, and I educational opportunities improved dramatically. At the beginning of Queen Victoria's reign, England's universities were closed to women. By the end of her reign they were open, and women could study even at such citadels of male conservatism as Oxford and Cambridge, although they were not allowed to earn a degree. A confident, assertive New Woman had emerged. It was left to the twentieth century, however, to continue and advance the cause of women's liberation.

THE VICTORIANS AND RELIGION

Up until the end of the eighteenth century, no one seriously questioned the idea of Christianity and it could safely be assumed that any writer, unless he clearly stated otherwise, was functioning within the Christian framework. Swift, Fielding, Pope, Dr. Johnson were all Christians. They all, in varying degrees, accepted the view that human beings were at the center of a Titanic struggle between God and Satan. In the nineteenth century, however, this world picture began to decay and change under the constant blows of new scientific discoveries, to be replaced by three different intellectual currents: Traditional Christianity, secular spirituality, and atheist materialism. The history of religion in the Victorian period is the history of the steady growth of this third current.

Religious doubt is the hallmark of the Victorian era. The astronomers were discovering a universe much vaster than had previously been thought. The geologists, led by Charles Lyell, were showing that the earth was billions upon billions of years old, that its surface had experienced very slow but dramatic changes, and that thousands of species had become extinct and were preserved only as fossil remains. This shook the faith of the early and mid-Victorians. Ruskin, a committed Christian for much of his life, wrote in 1851: "If only the Geologists would let me alone, I could do very well, but those dreadful hammers! I hear the clink of them at the end of every cadence of the Bible verses." Tennyson, whose *In Memoriam* is the representative poem of the mid-Victorian period, struggled with religious doubt spawned basically by geological discoveries. The major scientific blow, however, came in 1859, with the publication of Darwin's watershed book *The Origin of Species*, which advanced convincing proof that the various species evolved one out of the other, and that human beings by implication evolved from the lower animals. (Darwin did not make specific statements about human beings until *The Descent of Man* in 1871). Most Victorians were fundamentalist in their approach to the Bible, and accepted the story of Adam and Eve literally rather than as a symbolic tale of the initial human rebellion against God's will. Darwin's theories, by challenging the biblical story of the Creation, dealt a heavy blow to an already weakened Christian faith. They also narrowed uncomfortably the gap separating human beings from the animals. The result was a wave of atheism such as the Western world had never known before. Such major late-Victorian writers as George Eliot, Thomas Hardy, Pater and Wilde abandoned Christianity, and many educated people became convinced that science and religion are irreconcilable. A crisis of monumental proportions confronted the whole of Western civilization.

This does not mean, of course, that Christianity collapsed during the Victorian era. On the contrary, it remained quite strong, and still is. Newman, for instance, never once doubted the existence of God. His chief concern was to define his position within the Anglican Protestant church, and later to decide between Protestantism and Catholicism. Tennyson resolved his religious doubts and reaffirmed his Christian faith triumphantly in *In Memoriam*. Browning was solidly and militantly Protestant throughout his life, and Hopkins rebelled against his family and became a Jesuit Catholic priest. Both Pater and Wilde returned to Christianity, as did most of the Decadents of the 1890s. But it was apparent that Christianity was no longer the only intellectual current; it now had a bitter and powerful rival in atheist materialism, supported by scientific discoveries.

A third religious current, but one which did not attract as many followers, is secular spirituality. Many educated Victorians, unable to believe in traditional Christianity any longer but deeply religious nonetheless, accepted a spiritual view of the universe divorced from Christian belief. This trend began with the Romantics, especially Shelley and Keats, but it gathered pace in the Victorian period. Carlyle, for instance, recorded the collapse of his Christian faith in *Sartor Resartus*, confronted and rejected atheist materialism, and embraced instead a form of pantheism that regards matter as the clothes of indwelling spirit. Arnold, another non-Christian, spoke of

God as a power outside ourselves that pushes in the direction of morality. Many post-Darwinists, most notably Butler and Shaw, adopted the idea of creative evolution, that life was constantly improving and bettering itself under the influence of what Shaw called the Life Force. W. B. Yeats and Conan Doyle, at the end of the century, became ardent spiritualists, holding *séances* in dark rooms and seeking out mediums in an attempt to connect with and understand the spirit world. Spiritualism, in fact, became something of a cult in the 1890s and was the most widespread of the alternative religions. Until the end of the eighteenth century, then, Christianity was the only intellectual current. In the Victorian age, however, as in our own, a wide array of intellectual currents came into existence and the once-dominant Christian current became simply one of a bewildering number of possible choices.

THE VICTORIANS AND HUMAN NATURE

Although in Christianity unregenerate human nature is regarded as fallen and corrupt, the Romantics fostered a contrary view. Rousseau in France insisted that human beings are naturally good and that it is social institutions that corrupt them. Wordsworth spoke of "natural piety" and saw human beings in nature as spiritually pure and close to God. Keats in one of his letters wrote of "the holiness of the heart's affections." This view of human nature persisted in the Victorian period. Mill's landmark essay *On Liberty* is an excellent example. In it he attacks the Calvinists and their allies for considering human nature to be radically corrupt, and insists instead on the Greek ideal of self-development, comparing human beings to plants who need a proper atmosphere in order to blossom forth and fulfill their potential. On the whole, however, the early Victorians were concerned with the outside world, with social and political issues, and condemned Romantic self-absorption.

By mid-century, though, a clearly Romantic movement had begun to assert itself in Victorian literature and thought, and the focus began to shift once again to the world within. (It is arguable that the entire Victorian period is a continuation of Romantic literature, but this is not a question I wish to explore in this brief introduction). D.G. Rossetti (1828–82), the painter-poet, concentrated in his art and verse on blessed damozels, beautiful and very innocent-looking girls who are presented as flesh-and-blood symbols of his soul. In his later art and verse, however, his vision of the soul darkened and the siren began to dominate his work. He shifted his focus from blessed damozels to Astarte Syriaca, Lilith, Proserpine, Helen of Troy and the sirens of "The Orchard-Pit." Walter Pater, in *The Renaissance*, regarded modern human nature as largely evil and found a strange, fascinating beauty in evil. He praised Leonardo da Vinci for capturing this beauty in his paintings of the Medusa and the Mona Lisa, while Winckelmann, who tried to return to the innocence of the ancient Greeks in his art, is condemned. The final decades of the nineteenth century reveal a fascination with the dark side of the human soul. Robert Louis Stevenson published *The Strange Case of Dr. Jekyll and Mr. Hyde* (1886), in which the good Dr. Jekyll discovers a potion that allows him to release his dark, hidden impulses and change into the evil Mr. Hyde. Oscar Wilde wrote *The Picture of Dorian Gray* (1890; 1891), in which Dorian seeks to know depths of evil never before experienced by the human race, then followed it up with *Salomé*, in which Salomé is presented as a symbol of human nature, entirely evil because totally uninhibited and uncontrolled. In Wilde's *Salomé*, and in the Decadent literature of the 1890s generally, human nature is no longer white or gray but black. The mould of Pater's Mona Lisa is shattered and all purity and innocence is seen as illusion or repression. When Joseph Conrad wrote *Heart of Darkness* (1899), with its gloomy, pessimistic view of human nature, it was this background that he submitted to. In popular literature the result was Bram Stoker's classic vampire thriller *Dracula* (1897). It is possible to generalize that the drift of nineteenth-century literature and thought was towards a deepening awareness of the evil in human nature.

THE VICTORIANS AND EARNESTNESS

Oscar Wilde wrote literature that he consciously wished to be seen as the culmination of the Victorian and nineteenth-century impulses. In his dark masterpiece *Salomé* he sought to fully reverse the crumbling nineteenth-century idea that human nature is basically good. In *The Importance of Being Earnest*, his target was seriousness—both the seriousness of his own earlier works and Victorian high-seriousness in general.

For the Victorians, more than any other group or generation, were noted for their extreme earnestness. Imbued with a sense of mission and living in a country that was rapidly industrializing, colonizing the world, and achieving significant new scientific insights, the Victorians came to believe that the fundamental issues confronting the human race will be solved or decided during their era, and by them. No other age conceived of itself as an entity as the Victorians did. With this conviction came a high seriousness, a sense of responsibility, and a puritanical, ascetic attitude towards life rarely known before. Perhaps the best spokesman of this new puritanism was Carlyle, who urged the Victorians in *Sartor Resartus* to forget about happiness, which is unattainable, and to concentrate instead on duty and hard work: "*'Do the Duty which lies nearest thee,'* which thou knowest to be a Duty! Thy second Duty will already have become clearer.... Produce! Produce! ... Up! up! Whatsoever thy hand findeth to do, do it with thy whole might. Work while it is called Today; for the Night cometh, wherein no man can work."

In the same "Everlasting Yea" chapter, Carlyle exhorted the Victorians: "Close thy *Byron;* open thy *Goethe*." Byron's poetry was often morbid, a poetry of despair and introspection, or, as frequently in *Don Juan*, of gaiety and carelessness. Byron also belonged to the aristocracy, whose life-style of lazy enjoyment and hunting was much envied during the Romantic period. Carlyle rejected all this, recommending instead Goethe, whose Faust lived a life of constant struggle, achievement and progress. To be forever dissatisfied, forever working to achieve ever-higher goals, was Faust's declared creed, and Goethe broke with tradition to place him in a symbolic heaven after death—a graded heaven much like Tennyson's in *In Memoriam*, where the struggle for perfection will continue. Although there are many affinities between the Romantic period and the Victorian age, then, there is also a clear break. The aristocratic life-style yielded to a middle-class puritan code of hard work, sobriety, ascetic abstention, and a strong desire to improve the surface of the entire planet.

Along with their penchant for extreme seriousness, the Victorians gave a high priority to reputation and respectability. This was largely because the newly emergent middle class felt insecure and was afraid of slipping into the lower class. There was great insistence on a very rigid, puritanical code of sexual conduct. Young girls were expected to remain sexually innocent until marriage, and were strictly supervised. Any deviation from this rule caused great scandal. People were looked upon to behave as ladies and gentlemen at all times, and to embody a high set of values. The result was a higher moral standard than ours today, but there was also a great deal of hypocrisy and mere external conformity, as evidenced by the vast increase in the number of prostitutes in London during the Victorian period.

As the nineteenth century drew to its close, Victorian values began to wane and decay. The final decade came to be known as the "Gay Nineties," and one of its most prominent figures was Prince Edward, Queen Victoria's son and heir to the throne, whose immoral, pleasure-seeking life-style was openly condemned in many leading newspapers. Many artists and writers deliberately painted and wrote from a *fin-de-siècle* point of view. It is against this background that Wilde's *The Importance of Being Earnest* can best be understood, for its chief target is Victorian values, especially seriousness and respectability. The play turns the very word *earnest* into a pun and reduces all seriousness to the level of nonsense. Lady Bracknell is a perfect parody of Victorian respectability, as is Miss Prism, whose rigid defense of proper behavior is deflated by her sexual slips of the tongue and by the exposure of her dark secret—the loss of Jack when he was a baby! Jack and Algy are outwardly moral but both lead a secret immoral life which, when exposed, does them no real harm. Both Wilde's satanic play *Salomè* and *The Importance of Being Earnest*, each in its own way, inverts Victorian values and is *eminently fin-de-siècle*, seeking to bury an old order and herald a new. That the old order was not quite ready to be buried yet is reflected in the trials and imprisonment of Oscar Wilde in 1895.

ROBIN GILMOUR

The Novel in the Age of Equipoise:
Wilkie Collins, Trollope, George Eliot

At one point in *Our Mutual Friend* Charley Hexam, the young pupil-teacher on the make, repudiates the interest Eugene Wrayburn is taking in his sister Lizzie's education because it is a slight to his 'respectability' at a time '"when I am raising myself in the scale of society by my own exertions and Mr Headstone's aid"' (II, 6). The sense of society as a 'scale' and the prospect of 'raising' oneself on it are mid-Victorian assumptions, implying a new-found stability in the social order. In April 1865 Lord Palmerston, the then Prime Minister, gave a prizegiving speech at the South London Industrial Exhibition in which he told an artisan audience that they were fortunate to be living under a consitutional monarchy, 'and of such a monarchy an aristocracy of wealth and an aristocracy of rank are essential ingredients'. No 'impassable barriers' separated these from the rest of the nation, as in less fortunate countries, and his hearers should take comfort from the example of those who had risen from humble beginnings:

> And so I say to you—you are competitors for prizes. You may not all become Lord Chancellors or Archbishops; you may not become members of the Cabinet; but depend upon it, you will, by systematic industry, raise yourselves in the social system of your country—you will acquire honour and respect for yourselves and for your families.[1]

Both the occasion and the underlying assumptions of Palmerston's speech reveal a confidence in the stability of a hierarchical social order which would not have been felt so forcibly, if at all, 20 years earlier, and would have seemed unduly complacent 20 years later. That an aristocratic Prime Minister could speak to a predominantly working-class audience of the benefits of monarchy and aristocracy suggests how much the mood of the country had changed since the days of Chartism and the Anti-Corn-Law League. The change can be dated from the collapse of Chartism in 1848 and the orgy of national self-congratulation aroused by the Great Exhibition of 1851, and stretches for something like two decades, until the Second Reform Bill of 1867 and possibly a little later. Whether we call these the Palmerston years, or use W.L. Burn's phrase the 'Age of Equipoise', it seems very difficult, as one recent historian has said, 'not to believe in some kind of calm through at least the years 1850–65'.[2]

'Equipoise' is a useful word because it suggests a dynamic rather than static equilibrium, a balancing of forces. If the balance was underpinned in those decades by the unmistakable evidence of Britain's growing industrial prosperity and influence, then it also reflected, or so at least middle- and upper-class observers thought, the strength and adaptability of Britain's political institutions and aristocratic leadership. There was some relief mixed up in the self-congratulation, for aristocratic leadership had been under challenge in the 1840s from the industrial middle classes as much as from the Chartists. That challenge had been met, most dramatically by the repeal of the corn laws in 1846, and Palmerston was speaking here in its aftermath, in the knowledge that the order to which he belonged had, by adaptation when it mattered, consolidated its influence and prestige. His words implicitly invoke two of the concepts which modern historians have found indispensable in understanding mid-Victorian Britain, concepts particularly associated with the writings of Walter Bagehot, whose *The English Constitution* (1867) is the political classic of its time. One is the notion of 'deference', the respect traditionally paid to the squire and the duke in a country where the rights and responsibilities of landed ownership had until recently been supreme. The other is what Bagehot called 'the system of *removable inequalities*, where many people are inferior to and worse off than others, but in which each may *in theory* hope to be on a level with the highest below the throne'.[3] So Palmerston can tell the workingman to 'raise' himself in the 'social system of [his] country'; he may not become a General or an Archbishop, but upward mobility is both possible and desirable.

These ideas are very much in the air at this time, and they reflect a change in the social and intellectual climate. Samuel Smiles's *Self-Help* was published in 1859, and its author's own history illustrates the shift as well as anyone: an active radical in the 40s, Smiles came to preach a message of self-improvement essentially similar to Palmerston's in his speech. The final chapter of *Self-Help* is entitled 'Character: The True Gentleman', and the progressive democratization of the gentlemanly ideal is an important factor in the mid-Victorian balance, offering at least the promise of a moral meeting-ground beyond the divisions of class. Fitzjames Stephen noted in 1862 'a constantly increasing disposition to insist more upon the moral and less upon the social element of the word' gentleman.[4] The apocalyptic tone of Carlyle was out; he had descended to rant in *Latter-Day Pamphlets* (1850), and the hysterical 'Shooting Niagara: and after?' (1867) was widely seen as an intemperate and eccentric contribution to the political debate surrounding the Second Reform Bill. The Condition-of-England question had given way to more patient and thoughtful examination of existing institutions and their underlying principles. In addition to *The English Constitution* and Matthew Arnold's, *Culture and Anarchy* (1869), the period saw the publication of J.S. Mill's classic essay *on Liberty* (1859) and his *Considerations on Representative Government* (1861). In the developing debate about reform in the 1860s the question was no longer 'Will the social fabric survive?', but 'How has it survived these changes so well?', and 'How far and how fast should parliamentary reform go?'. A confident gradualism had taken over from earlier fears of revolution and apocalypse.

These changes in the climate of opinion are reflected in the novel. Dickens did not share the optimism of Palmerston or Samuel Smiles, but his last two completed novels deal with themes of self-improvement and class mobility in ways that suggest the topicality of the self-help ideology, as does the carpenter-hero of *Adam Bede* (1859). Similarly, the mid-Victorian *bildungsroman* is less emotionally intense than *Jane Eyre* or *Villette* but more intellectually ambitious and self-conscious, as in George Eliot's *Mill on the Floss* (1860) and Meredith's high-stepping *Ordeal of Richard Feverel* (1859). The dominant mode of mid-Victorian fiction is domestic realism, a realism grown philosophically confident in the novels of George Eliot, who in chapter 17 of *Adam Bede* gave a classic declaration of art's necessary commitment to the real:

> Paint us an angel, if you can, with a floating violet robe, and a face paled by the celestial light ... but do not impose on us any aesthetic rules which shall banish from the region of Art those old women scraping carrots with their work-worn hands, those heavy clowns taking holiday in a dingy pot-house, those rounded backs

and stupid weather-beaten faces that have bent over the spade and done the rough work of the world.... It is so needful we should remember their existence, else we may happen to leave them quite out of our religion and philosophy, and frame lofty theories which only fit a world of extremes. Therefore let Art always remind us of them; therefore let us always have men ready to give the loving pains of a life to the faithful representing of commonplace things—men who see beauty in these commonplace things, and delight in showing how kindly the light of heaven falls on them.

Such faith in the validity of realism is itself a manifestation of the confidence of the times; the belief that reality is stable and knowable and that a consensus can be reached between writer and readers about how to describe and interpret it reveals an assurance not found in, for example, Thackeray's use of the omniscient narrator, which is continually invaded by his scepticism. It was on the basis of this confident contract between writer and reader that George Eliot and Trollope set out to map the past and present respectively of English provincial life, of Middlemarch and Barchester, for this is the heyday of the provincial novel, a time when the changes in regional life wrought by the railways and industrialization were making the Victorians aware of what they were losing. A time of institutional curiosity also: Trollope's Parliamentary novels were written for a public interested in the political process itself. Their subject is the choices, adjustments, compromises and alliances that men have to make in Parliament, and the discussion of these in the society drawing-room, the gentleman's club and the country-house. Their context is the premiership of Palmerston (1855–65) whose life Trollope wrote, and the reform debates which followed it; and the writings of Bagehot and Mill. It is not to these sober, down-to-earth matters that I wish to turn first, however, but to another side of mid-Victorian fiction which must seem their antithesis, although it is as characteristic of this period as the novels of Trollope and George Eliot; and that is the so-called 'sensation novel'.

WILKIE COLLINS AND THE SENSATION NOVEL

'You know that my novels are not sensational', Trollope wrote to George Eliot in 1863. 'In Rachel Ray I have attempted to confine myself absolutely to the commonest details of commonplace life among the most ordinary people, allowing myself no incident that would be even remarkable in every day life. I have shorn my fiction of all romance.'⁵ The twin poles of mid-Victorian fiction are the realistic novel of 'commonplace life' to which Trollope aspired, and the 'sensational' novel, a vogue started by the success of Wilkie Collins's *The Woman in White* in 1860. On the face of it no two kinds of fiction could seem more different from each other than Trollope's lightly plotted comedies of manners and Collins's extravagantly plotted melodramas, and yet they shared a common concern with domestic relationships, a common devotion to the matter-of-fact in execution if not conception, and a common readership among the middle classes. A subscriber to the *Cornhill Magazine* in 1865, for example, could have followed in the same issue the instalments of Elizabeth Gaskell's *Wives and Daughters*, 'An Every-Day Story' of provincial life in the 1820s, and Wilkie Collins's dark, violent *Armadale*. The first seems almost plotless, so unobtrusively is its tale of family relationships built up, and so completely is incident subordinated to the revelation and development of character. It deals with the relations of two families in a Midlands village, the Gibsons and the Hamleys, and the unspectacular events which change their lives—remarriage, deaths, the successes and failures of children, the unlooked-for disappointments and renewals of ordinary life. When the novel does touch on sensational matter, in Osborne Hamley's secret marriage to a French nursery-maid, there is nothing sensational or melodramatic in Gaskell's treatment: the character is humanized and made the agent of the humanizing of others, by bringing a grandson to brighten the old squire's life. *Armadale* is sensational from start to finish. It has been rightly described as 'one of the most over-plotted novels in English literature',⁶ and defies brief summary, but its central action involves the friendship of two men called Allan Armadale, one 'light' and carefree and wealthy, the colourless young hero of conventional fiction, the other 'dark', thoughtful, haunted and forced to suppress his true identity by the prophecy that he will be the agent of the other's destruction, which almost comes to pass through the intervention of one of the most memorable villainesses in Victorian fiction, Lydia Gwilt. The difference between the two novels, and between the two genres, can be seen by comparing the governess figure in each book. Hyacinth Kirkpatrick, the ex-governess Mr Gibson marries, is a pretty but shallow and snobbish woman, rendered peevish by a lifetime's struggle with genteel poverty, disposed to make his home comfortable but only on her own terms: she denies him the toasted cheese he loves because "'it's such a strong-smelling, coarse kind of thing"' (11). Their relationship is a masterly study in the small, grating incompatibilities of second marriage, where each partner is too set in their ways to adjust to the other. With Lydia Gwilt in *Armadale* we move from the subtle comic art that can intimate domestic discontent through a disagreement about cheese to the broad brush of melodrama and the lurid world of laudanum drops and the poison-bottle. The red-haired Lydia is tall, beautiful and sexually attractive, with 'full, rich, and sensual' lips (III, 10) and, as Collins hissingly puts it, 'a subtle suggestiveness in her silence, and a sexual sorcery in her smile' (IV, 7). A convicted criminal, she confesses frankly to her diary how she plans to use her sexuality to trap the young heir and then murder him. The misery caused by Mrs Kirkpatrick may be altogether more probable and lifelike, but the melodramatic Miss Gwilt still communicates a convincing moral *frisson* which is a reminder of human potentialities the novel of domestic realism tended to overlook.

We have supped full with horrors since, of course, and the interest the Victorian sensation novel holds today lies less in its power to shock than in the way it shadows and subverts the sunlit world of domestic realism. In the 1860s, when Trollope was aspiring to a fiction shorn of all romance, gothic romance was making a spectacular return in novels like Collins's *Woman in White* (1859–60), *No Name* (1862), *Armadale* (1864–6), and *The Moonstone* (1868), in Mrs Henry Wood's *East Lynne* (1861), Mary Elizabeth Braddon's *Lady Audley's Secret* (1862) and *Aurora Floyd* (1863), and Charles Reade's *Hard Cash* (1863) and *Griffith Gaunt* (1865–6). Although these have features peculiar to their time, such as a preoccupation with the domestic 'crimes' of bigamy and adultery, and the presence in several of the detective police, they belong in the wider view to the strain of gothic in English fiction which the novel of manners never quite succeeded in banishing. Jane Austen's *Northanger Abbey* (1818) was only a temporary victory. Henry Tilney may rebuke Catherine Morland's suspicions that his father is a Bluebeard with a confident appeal to common sense—' " Remember the country and the age in which we live. Remember that we are English, that we are Christians.... Does our education prepare us for such atrocities? Do our laws connive at them?"' (24)—but 30 years later in *Jane Eyre* the discovery of a secretly imprisoned wife is the turning-point of the novel. Charlotte Brontë breathed new life into gothic by bringing it home from Italy to an English gentleman's country residence, and this innovation, as developed by the sensation novelists, gave a new impetus to 'the literature of horrors', in Henry James's view: 'Instead of the terrors of *Udolpho*, we were treated to the terrors of the cheerful country-house and the busy London lodgings. And there is no doubt that these were infinitely the more terrible.'[7]

'Wild and yet domestic', Dickens's comment on the opening chapters of *The Moonstone*,[8] aptly sums up the yoking together of romance and realism in the sensation novel. Scrupulously matter-of-fact in its working-out of initially improbable plot premises, the genre's speciality is the infiltration of the everyday by exotic, bizarre, or criminal secrets. Lady Audley's secret is bigamy and insanity, and the revelation that this pretty, golden-haired, model wife has murdered her first husband and is prepared to poison her second. Lady Isabel Vane in *East Lynne*, tricked into adultery by an aristocratic villain, returns after her presumed death disfigured and disguised to become the governess to her own children. Dickens's *Mystery of Edwin Drood* opens with an English cathedral town surfacing in the opium-den dreams of a respectable choir-master. *The Woman in White* is the best of the genre not because it is any less melodramatic than the others—indeed we need to stop using melodrama as a pejorative critical term in discussing these novels—but because it is more successfully constructed, and because its melodrama is convincingly integrated with characterization and setting.

Wilkie Collins (1824–89) was a protégé of Dickens who may well have influenced his master. *The Woman in White* was serialized in *All the Year Round* and anticipates the preoccupation with disguise and secrecy, with the figure of the white woman and the dead-yet-alive character, in *Great Expectations* and *Our Mutual Friend*. *The Moonstone* has long been recognized as a likely influence on *Edwin Drood*.[9] For his part Collins may well have been inspired by the Lady Dedlock plot in *Bleak House* to raise the novel-with-a-secret to the new heights of technical and psychological sophistication he achieved in *The Woman in White*. The central idea was more sensational than anything in *Bleak House*, although it had a 'factual' basis in a volume of French trials Collins picked up on a Paris bookstall. An heiress is tricked by her husband and his villainous accomplice into a private lunatic asylum, where she is substituted for a woman who resembles her—her half-sister as it turns out—and whose death leaves the heiress officially 'dead'. (The popularity of false imprisonment in these novels—it figures centrally in Reade's *Hard Cash* and *It Is Never Too Late To Mend*—is a good example of the way the sensation novelist adapted an old gothic device, the dungeon, to modern unease.) The nucleus of melodrama in *The Woman in White* is given credibility by Collins's skill in approaching and disclosing it through various different narrators. Dickens had used two narrative voices in *Bleak House*, Collins uses no fewer than ten (11 if one includes 'The Narrative of the Tombstone' recording Lady Glyde's presumed death); his stated aim was to present the story as it might unfold in a court of law, 'to trace the course of one complete series of events, by making the persons who have been most closely connected with them, at each successive stage, relate their own experience, word for word' ('Preamble'). The sometimes improbable dovetailing of narratives which this involves is offset by the way Collins varies the kind and length of his documents (diaries and letters mainly, but interspersed with the testimony of servants, a doctor, even the tombstone), and by his skill in giving each speaker an individual character and an individual voice. The effect is to throw the interest on to the way of telling as much as on to what is told.

It is this narrative self-consciousness which makes Collins an innovator, rather than his sensational material itself. Compared (say) to Mrs Henry Wood, he brought a sophisticated approach to melodrama. *East Lynne* is certainly sensational enough; it offers murder, adultery, (unwitting) bigamy, even the arrest of a corpse for debt! But the book's moral premises are the simplistic ones of popular melodrama. The hero is a middle-class paragon; the villain is the typical heartless rake; Lady Isabel's sufferings as governess to her own children and mute witness to her husband's new domestic happiness are milked for all the pathos they can yield, and more, yet they only confirm the inviolability of the code she has transgressed, and lest we miss the moral the author is at hand to supply it: 'Oh, reader, believe me! Lady—wife—mother! should you ever be tempted to abandon your home, so will you awaken! Whatever trials may be the lot of your married life ... *resolve* to bear them ... '[10] Collins is never so explicit, and rarely so unambiguous as this; without condoning the crime, he suggests that the criminal is more complex and closer to home than stage melodrama allows us to think. So *The Woman in White* offers two villains. Sir Percival Glyde is obviously the bad baronet of popular melodrama, but there is nothing obvious about Count Fosco, his accomplice. A large man, larger than life, Fosco seems the antithesis of Glyde: soft-spoken where the other is loud, gentle where he is violent, considerate towards dependents and chivalrous to women, over whom he exercises a strange power, Fosco has a quality of unpredictability one finds in the great fictional characters. Unlike Dickens's Pecksniff, whom he resembles in his vanity and florid eloquence, Fosco is given those little redeeming touches which make a character unsettling and difficult to judge—his love of pastry, his tender handling of the white mice he takes everywhere with him, the admiration for Marian Halcombe which stays his hand against her at the end. He embodies in his own person the moral relativism and denial of platitude about criminals which he expounds in a memorable scene in the boat-house at Blackwater Park: '"Crimes cause their own detection, do they? And murder will out (another moral epigram), will it? Ask Coroners who sit at inquests in large towns if that is true, Lady Glyde. Ask secretaries of life-assurance companies if that is true, Miss Halcombe. Read your own public journals"' (No. 14; II, 3).

As with the criminals, so with the two heroines in the novel: the pairing of contrasted characters establishes a totality of suggestion that is subversive of conventional norms. Laura Fairlie, later Lady Glyde, is the fair-haired heroine of romance, the Victorian ideal of woman as passive and in need of protection; her sister Marian is the antithesis of this type, as Fosco is of Glyde: she is dark-skinned, ugly, 'masculine', but also intelligent, witty, resourceful and brave. Together, and in the *ménage à trois* they form with the hero, Walter Hartwright, they suggest something of the dissociation of sensibility at the root of Victorian sexuality.[11] Marian Halcombe implicitly criticizes, even as she also complements, the sweetly spiritual ideal of womanhood the novel endorses at the level of romantic plot-making; the beautiful figure below her ugly face, the warmth and vigour of her personality, Fosco's admiration—these intimate a subterranean sexual vitality which the official image could not accommodate, to its loss.

It is Collins's feeling for the unusual in human nature that makes *The Woman in White* a classic, and rescues it from the common charge that in the sensation novel character is subordinated to plot. The novel certainly has an elaborate plot and its fair share of sensational incidents. Who can forget Walter Hartwright's first meeting with the woman in white on moonlit Hampstead Heath, or the heroine's reappearance by the side of her own gravestone? The gradual revelation of menace in the behaviour of Sir Percival and Fosco is skilfully done, too, disclosed through successive entries in Marian's diary. But this balance of psychological and sensational interest is lacking in Collins's other novels, where either the sense of menace is less, as in *The Moonstone*, or excessive plotting tends to swamp character, as in *Armadale*. The latter's over-plotting stems from his attempt to provide a working-out of Allan Armadale's prophetic dream which would keep both 'natural' and 'supernatural' explanations open, but such gestures towards the idea of Fate seem less thrilling now than the entirely terrestrial villainy of Lydia Gwilt. The prominence given to this red-haired siren in the second half of the novel, her mimicry of respectability combined with the contempt for the young hero and his sweetheart which she confides to her diary (a contempt which Collins's perfunctory handling of these characters seems to endorse), make *Armadale* the most cynical and daring of his novels, and the one which attracted the most adverse comment from contemporary reviewers.

In contrast to *Armadale* the sensationalism of *The Moonstone* is muted. There is no villainess, not even the usual unconventional heroine. One of Collins's sources was a famous contemporary crime committed within a middle-class home, the Road murder, but he softened the violence, changing murder to theft, and the bloodstains on an incriminating night-gown to paint stains.[12] In The *Moonstone* the sensation novel modulates into the detective novel, where the process of detection rather than sensational event is the chief interest of the narrative. Several elements later to become the staple of mystery and detective fiction are here brought together: a secluded country-house menaced by mysterious foreigners; a dinner-party ending in the theft of the diamond, putting the whole house-hold under suspicion; the advent of an interesting but fallible detective, Sergeant Cuff, who fails to unearth the culprit; a series of false trails followed by the least expected of denouements, in which the hero is discovered to have taken the jewel in a trance induced by opium. The story is ingenious, and ingeniously told by a number of narrators, but none of them is as memorable as Marian Halcombe or Lydia Gwilt or Count Fosco, and what they relate lacks the wildness and menace of the previous novels. Despite the Hindoo mysteries of Imperial India which open and close the novel, the air of mystery in *The Moonstone* evaporates with the elaborate explanation of the theft; such *frissons* as it has to offer are felt on the periphery rather than at the centre, in (for example) the love of the crippled servant girl, Rosanna Spearman, for Franklin Blake and her suicide in the sinister Shivering Sand.

The Moonstone may seem not quite sensational enough to sustain its length and the at times somewhat laboured joinery of its construction; and in this it is perhaps typical of the genre as a whole. The laugh that Jane Eyre hears on the third story of Thornfield Hall, 'distinct, formal mirth-less' (11), is more chilling than volumes of Miss Braddon or Mrs Henry Wood. Dickens's woman in white, Miss Havisham, touches the psychic life of a whole society; Collins's, powerful creation though she is, remains a woman in white. These comparisons are unfair, since manifestly Collins was not a Dickens or a Charlotte Brontë, and they should not be allowed to obscure the real, if limited, interest of the genre. This is twofold. 'Its primitive, troublesome vision collided sharply with that of the reigning domestic novel—which was never quite the same again', Winifred Hughes concludes in her study of the sensation novel.[13] It aired the contemporary sexual and psychological discontents of middle-class Victorian life, if only in the limited form of criminal behaviour. And by giving new and vigorous life to the element of plot in fiction, to an aesthetic which showed character at the mercy of incident and not vice versa as in the domestic novel, it provided a resource for a later novelist like Hardy, for whom that aesthetic was also a metaphysic. We shall return to this legacy of the sensation novel in the final chapter.

ANTHONY TROLLOPE

Of all the Victorian novelists, Anthony Trollope (1815–82) seems furthest from the concerns of the sensation novel. Murder is infrequent in his fiction, and when it happens, as in the murder of Mr Bonteen in *Phineas Redux*, the mystery about the murderer is quickly dispelled and attention shifts to the reactions of the man falsely accused of the murder. When he introduces an element of mystery, as in the theft of the diamonds in *The Eustace Diamonds*, it is done partly in parody of the central event of Wilkie Collins's *The Moonstone* and is made wholly subordinate to the portrayal of the adventuress-heroine, Lizzie Eustace. Although he wrote in his *Autobiography* that a good novel should be 'at the same time realistic and sensational ... and both in the highest degree' (12), it is a formula that better fits Dickens or Hardy than Trollope himself. Plot is nearly always secondary to character in his best work. Yet Trollope began his career with a novel as violent as any by Wilkie Collins or Charles Reade. *The Macdermotts of Ballycloran* (1847) contains the murder of an excise officer, a particularly gruesome account of the revenge taken on a local lawyer, in which his foot is hacked off with an axe, and the death by hanging of the central character. The book is also unsparing in its portrayal of the grinding relentlessness of poverty in rural Ireland, a highly topical subject in the 1840s. For a novelist often dismissed as a comfortable conformist, the chief merit of whose work is supposed to be, in Henry James's phrase, 'a complete appreciation of the usual', [14] this first novel is in many ways unusual—unusual in choosing a Catholic rather than Ascendancy family for its subject, and in portraying the local priest as a good man, and unusual in the quality of sympathy it brings to the characterization of Thady Macdermott in his struggles with family debt and inarticulate feelings of love for his seduced sister.

I begin with *The Macdermotts of Ballycloran* because it points to two important but often neglected facts about Trollope's work: that he was not only, or not simply, the bread-and-butter realist and mild recorder of the unspectacular everyday that his reputation, confirmed by a reading of the later chapters of the *Autobiography*, would suggest; and that he could imagine the subtle interrelations of mid-Victorian life so well because he was to some extent an outsider. It is worth remembering, when considering Trollope's portrayal of the rituals and institutions of English society, that he spent almost 16 years of his adult life in Ireland, was happy and tasted success in his Post Office career there, and wrote several of his early novels in, and two of them about, that country. Ireland, as Robert Tracy says, helped to make him an English novelist. 'When Trollope turned to novels of English life with *The Warden*, he adapted his methods of social analysis to the new subject and again wrote at least partly as an outsider.'[15] Indeed, doubly an outsider, since the *Autobiography* reveals how miserable he had been at Harrow and Winchester, where, dirty and impoverished as a result of his father's debt and his mother's neglect, he was made to feel a 'Pariah'. Trollope saw the rituals of English social life with the eye of someone who had in his youth been almost excluded from them, and he saw the great institutions of Victorian England from the perspective, initially, of an Ireland experiencing famine and unrest in the 1840s. Approaching these institutions as a partial outsider, he was able to bring to their depiction an awareness both of their stability and of the changes with which, in an age of change, they were threatened. This is especially true of the Barchester novels with which he made his reputation.

The charm of Barchester is not that it is a Never-Never Land, like the world of P.G. Wodehouse, but that it is a place threatened by, yet *coping with* change. This is surely the source of the comic reassurance offered by *Barchester Towers*. The modern world invades sleepy Barchester in the form of railways, newspapers, the new bishop from London with his low-church wife and aggressively evangelical chaplain, Obadiah Slope. In the early chapters we are made continually aware that society in Trollope, as the Victorian critic R. H. Hutton said, is 'a great web of which London is the centre, and some kind of London life for the most part the motive-power'.[16] We are firmly in the world of the 1850s. Yet the novel is ultimately reassuring because, against all the odds, the threat of change is beaten off. Mr Slope is defeated and retreats to London, and the pastoral values of rural Barsetshire, epitomized by the old squire Wilfred Thorne and his sister, win the day at the social battle of the Ullathorne Sports.

The series takes its characters from the first Barsetshire novel, *The Warden* (1855). Trollope tells in his *Autobiography* how in 1851 he had been sent to examine rural deliveries in the West of England: 'In the course of this job I visited Salisbury, and whilst wandering there on a mid-summer evening round the purlieus of the cathedral I conceived the story of *The Warden*,— from whence came that series of novels of which Barchester, with its bishops, deans, and archdeacon, was the central site' (5). It seems an idyllic moment, and it can easily lull us into forgetting that *The Warden* is an intensely topical, and even in its way partisan novel. Mr Harding is an elderly clergyman who has been appointed to the clerical sinecure of the wardenship of Hiram's Hospital, a medieval charity for old men, by his friend the bishop. A good and honest man, he never questions his right to the annual salary of £800 until a local reformer, John Bold, who also happens to be the suitor of Mr

Harding's younger daughter, makes a public issue of it. Why should the warden have £800 a year out of John Hiram's estate, while the 12 old men have each only one shilling and fourpence a day? The issue is taken up by the *Jupiter* newspaper (*The Times*) and by other reformers such as Dr Pessimist Anticant (Carlyle) and Mr Popular Sentiment (Dickens), and battle is joined between the reformers and the conservatives, led by Mr Harding's son-in-law, Archdeacon Grantly. Caught between these loud and warring factions, Mr Harding decides to resign. In words that capture the fineness and firmness of his moral scruple, Trollope writes of him that 'he was not so anxious to prove himself right, as to be so' (3).

It is a slight story, 'simply the history of an old man's conscience' Henry James called it,[17] yet in its working out deeply characteristic of Trollope and of the distinctive note he was to contribute to Victorian fiction. For in essence *The Warden* is an anti-reform novel, written at a time when the Church of England was under attack for its failure to reform itself and adjust its ways to the demands of the new industrial society. *The Times*, Trollope's *Jupiter*, was an especially persistent critic of the Established Church at this period.[18] The novel paints its picture of the charming ways of the provincial and country clergy in the shadow of the knowledge that these ways are ceasing to be relevant to the needs of Victorian England. It is this knowledge which gives the book its slight air of elegy, of special pleading for a losing cause. But it also gave Trollope his opportunity; in the bad fit between the grand view of reforming rhetoric and the intricacy of the individual case he found a subject which released his creative genius. *The Warden* is something in the nature of a personal and artistic manifesto. The thinly veiled attacks on Carlyle, Dickens and *The Times* are a declaration of a different ethic and aesthetic; against the moral imperialism of the reforming temper, in life and in letters, Trollope set the quiet-voiced realism that was to become his hallmark. What looks a clear-cut case from the newspaper office or the reformer's study proves not to be so simple on the ground in Barchester—and typically, the editor of the *Jupiter* never visits the town. The best defence of Mr Harding's sinecure is not Archdeacon Grantly 's, that he is entitled to it by law—which he may or may not be—but that he performs the duties of warden well and from the heart, providing the old men in his care with something that no salary can buy, 'that treasure so inestimable in declining years, a true and kind friend to listen to their sorrows, watch over their sickness, and administer comfort as regards this world, and the world to come' (4). This is the heart of the matter, and no theoretical settlement of rights can affect it, except for the worse, as the old men discover when Mr Harding leaves. Trollope always found the individual case more interesting than the general principle or theory, and the more individual the case the better. Hard cases may make bad law, but they make good novels, and *The Warden* is one of his best.

The theme of reform is continued and developed in *Barchester Towers* (1857), where it is given a more broadly comic treatment. The efforts of the Proudie faction to remould high-church Barchester in their low-church image touched on another topical subject because of the many low-church preferments made by Palmerston since 1855, but the *odium theologicum* inherent in the subject is skilfully avoided by Trollope, who makes the ground of contention not the differences in belief themselves but the offensiveness with which Mrs Proudie and Mr Slope go about challenging time-honoured Barchester practices. Slope's attack on music and ceremony in his cathedral sermon (I, 6), his rudeness in telling Mr Harding that 'new men' are '"carting away the useless rubbish of past centuries"' (I, 12), leave the reader in little doubt about where Trollope's sympathies lie, and the interest in the novel lies less in whether the Proudie faction will be defeated, but how. And defeated they are, but not by Archdeacon Grantly. By a delicious comic irony, the effective champions of old Barchester turn out to be the son and daughter of the absentee cleric Dr Vesey Stanhope, whose residence 'on the shores of the Lake of Como, adding to that unique collection of butterflies for which he is so famous' (I, 6) is flagrant even by pre-reform standards. His bohemian son Bertie, and beautiful crippled daughter the Signora Neroni, bring a spirit of well-bred anarchy to Barchester with which the Proudie faction cannot cope. The turning-point is the havoc they create at Mrs Proudie's reception, with Bertie first outraging the bishop with his questions ('"Is there much to do here, at Barchester?"') and then moving the recumbent signora on her sofa through Mrs Proudie's lace train—'Gathers were heard to go, stitches to crack, plaits to fly open, flounces were seen to fall, and breadths to expose themselves—a long ruin of rent lace disfigured the carpet, and still clung to the vile wheel on which the sofa moved' (I, 11).

The resistance to the incomers begun at the Proudie reception in the first volume is completed in the counterbalancing scene in the third, the comic-feudal Ullathorne Sports, the final 'battle' of the novel where Mrs Proudie is discomfited and Mr Slope humiliated. This is a doubly appropriate comic reversal—that it should happen on the occasion of Miss Thorne's absurd attempts to revive a medieval jousting tournament, and in the area of Barsetshire seemingly most ripe for Mr Slope's rubbish-cart of progress. The action of the novel thus rolls back the tide of change, moving from London to Barchester and out to pastoral Ullathorne, where the childless Miss Thorne presides over the resurrection of Barchester tradition by bringing together Mr Harding's daughter and the new high-church dean, Mr Arabin. And Arabin's desire to marry Eleanor is another reversal, since in his youth he had been influenced by John Henry Newman and had aspired to a stern and solitary apostleship, and now finds himself in early middle age longing 'for the allotted share of worldly bliss, which a wife, and children, and happy home could give him, for that usual amount of comfort which he had ventured to reject as unnecessary for him ... ' (II, 1). Arabin's discovery about himself points to what is most individual in Trollope's vision in these early novels. In an age of reform, *The Warden* and *Barchester Towers* question the moral absolutism of the reforming temper; they speak up for the comic truth that we need the 'usual amount of comfort', and that accepting the human fallibility involved in that need may be the beginning of wisdom. We should not lay claim to higher standards than we can humanly live by. This emphasis is very out of step with the high Victorian drive towards idealism and renunciation, and is a reminder of how much in Trollope has its roots in the eighteenth rather than the nineteenth century.

The six Barsetshire novels fall naturally into three pairs. The first two are concerned with the politics of the cathedral close and the conflict between old ways and new men (and women). *Doctor Thorne* (1858) and *Framley Parsonage* (1860–1) move out into the hinterland of Barsetshire and deal in more muted fashion with another conflict, that between the small gentry and their values and the larger Whig landowners, lightly underscored by the political divisions between East Barset (Tory) and West Barset (Whig). *The Small House at Allington* (1862–4) and *The Last Chronicle of Barset* (1866–7) complete the series by seeing the now familiar landscape in a more searching light, revealing the vulnerability of 'small house' values in the modern world, and the clerical poverty which coexists in Barsetshire with the prosperity of Archdeacon Grantly and his friends. Considered as a whole the six novels show how well the recurring people and scenes of the chronicle form suited Trollope's imagination; he could settle down to a particular group of characters, possess them and their world with increasing confidence and subtlety, and arrive in the course of the series at some surprising insights and conclusions.

Framley Parsonage, with illustrations by Millais, was the lead serial in the first issue of the *Cornhill Magazine:* Trollope had arrived. It has been seen by many as the pivotal novel in the Barsetshire series, but that distinction surely belongs to its successor, *The Small House at Allington*, also serialized in the *Cornhill* and illustrated by Millais. Although Trollope did not at first include it among the Chronicles of Barsetshire, and although it lacks the social range of the others and (like *Doctor Thorne*) has no clerical matter, this unhappy love-story signals an important shift in his perception of Barsetshire. *The Small House* is a Victorian *Sense and Sensibility*, the story of two sisters and their widowed mother living in the country. Both have to endure love trials, but while the elder is careful in managing her affections, Lily Dale falls deeply and, as it proves, irretrievably in love with a London civil servant, Adolphus Crosbie, becomes engaged to him, and is then betrayed as he deserts her for the attractions of rank and marriage to Lady Alexandrina De Courcy. As with Mark Roberts in *Framley*, aristocratic society proves the undoing of Crosbie, but he falls into worse than debt by succumbing to Lady Alexandrina; and the loss for Lily and her family is too painful to allow the romantic resolution which has hitherto been applied in these novels. Through this love-affair and its attendant pastoral symbolism, and in the loneliness and childlessness of nearly all the Allington characters, Trollope intimates the enfeeblement of 'small house' gentry society and its values, their vulnerability to challenge from outside. The 'spice of obstinacy about Miss Dale' (2) is handled with a psychological subtlety that is new in his work. Is Lily a 'prig', as Trollope called her (*Autobiography*, 10), for hugging her loss to her, sentimentally disinheriting herself from life by persisting in loyalty to the memory of her love for a man she comes to see is worthless? Or is she the romantic maid of constant sorrow the Victorians loved, and loved all the more (as Trollope shrewdly realized) because she will not marry her devoted suitor, Johnny Eames? Or is she a study in a proud and private temperament, living in the spirit of Emily Dickinson's lines— 'The soul selects her own society, Then shuts the door ... '? Trollope does not decide for us, and it is a measure of the artistic tact for which he does not always get credit that no two readers are likely to agree about how to interpret Lily Dale.

Lily reappears in *The Last Chronicle of Barset*, carrying her 'spice of obstinacy' and her suffering into a novel centrally concerned with the much more obstinate and more greatly suffering figure of Josiah Crawley, the perpetual curate of Hogglestock. Trollope considered this his finest novel, and Crawley is certainly his most powerful creation. Introduced in *Framley Parsonage* as a man of spiritual authority, capable of chastening the worldly-inclined Mark Roberts, but poor, proud and bitter, he comes under a cloud at the start of *The Last Chronicle*, suspected of having stolen a cheque for £20. 'He was a man who when seen could hardly be forgotten. The deep angry remonstrant eyes, the shaggy eyebrows ... the repressed indignation of the habitual frown, the long nose and large powerful mouth, the deep furrows on the cheek, and the general look of thought and suffering, all combined to

make the appearance of the man remarkable.... No one ever on seeing Mr
Crawley took him to be a happy man, or a weak man, or an ignorant man, or
a wise man' (18). For the first time in the series we see the comforts of
clerical Barchester from the other side of the fence, through the figure of an
impossible man who has been cruelly wronged, a better Hebrew scholar than
the Dean of Barchester yet still a perpetual curate on £130 a year, toiling not
in the leafy lanes of the county but among the labouring poor of bleak
Hogglestock. Trollope stops short of tragedy, but the clearing of Crawley's
name and his final acceptance into the ranks of 'gentlemen' by Archdeacon
Grantly (83) do not settle the uncomfortable questions this novel asks about
the justice of Church establishments and the worth of that comfortable
freemasonry of gentlemen which should have sustained Crawley in his hour
of need but did not. Trollope comes to these questions not through any
increased radicalism of attitude, but through the accumulated density of a
world now so thoroughly known and familiar that he can afford to surprise
us, and perhaps even himself—as he does in the magnificent scene where the
dirty and dishevelled Crawley routs Mrs Proudie in her stronghold at the
bishop's palace (18). Like Archdeacon Grantly and the Proudies, and later
Plantagenet and Glencora Palliser, Josiah Crawley is a triumph of patient
characterization. The portrait of his stubborn, painful integrity—'It's dogged
as does it' is the wisdom he learns from an old brickmaker in Hogglestock
(61)—is enriched by the perspectives provided by Lily Dale on the one hand,
continuing in her lonely decision to remain single, and on the other by the
serenity of Mr Harding, whose peaceful death at the end breathes a
tranquillity absent from Barchester now.

Plantagenet Palliser makes his first appearance, as a dry, blue book
politician, in *The Small House at Allington*, which was followed by the first of
the so-called Palliser or Parliamentary novels, *Can You Forgive Her?*
(1864–5). Trollope's political novels grew naturally out of the later
Barsetshire and are six in number, the others being *Phineas Finn* (1867–9),
The Eustace Diamonds (1871–3), *Phineas Redux* (1873–4), *The Prime Minister*
(1875–6, and *The Duke's Children* (1879–80). These are not political novels in
the sense that Disraeli's are political novels, romantic tales of young patrician
heroes grappling with their conviction of destiny in a time of falling
ministries and intellectual ferment. Trollope's are novels of a political middle
age, where the room for effective action is very limited. In keeping with his
description of himself as 'an advanced, but still a conservative liberal'
(*Autobiography*, 16), his sympathies go out to those mildly reforming
politicians in the Liberal party who are trying to hold the line between
dangerous Radicals on their own side and the tergiversations of an

unscrupulous Tory leadership desperate for office at almost any price. Plantagenet Palliser has no grand scheme for political change: his only 'cause' is decimal coinage, and that is portrayed as a ridiculous hobby-horse. It is for what he is, a public-spirited landed magnate, and not for anything that he might do, that he is important to Trollope.

'If I wrote politics for my own sake, I must put in love and intrigue, social incidents, with perhaps a dash of sport, for the sake of my readers': Trollope's definition of his task in the *Autobiography* (17) has led to a view of these novels as not really political at all, but merely novels of manners against a political background. In fact, as John Halperin demonstrates in his excellent *Trollope and Politics*, such a separation of 'love' from 'politics' is artificial: they are intertwined by what Trollope saw as the fundamental reality of life for the aspiring politician—money. Those with money, like Plantagenet Palliser, can afford to be independent and vote with their consciences; those without it must be subservient to party discipline for the pickings of office, and therefore involved in continual moral and political compromises, and in the no less compromising search for the one sure refuge in a precarious career, a wealthy wife. As Phineas Finn acknowledges at the end of *Phineas Redux*, public life is probably a 'mistake' for those without means:

> 'For a poor man I think that it is, in this country. A man of fortune may be independent; and because he has the power of independence those who are higher than he will not expect him to be subservient. A man who takes to parliamentary office for a living may live by it, but he will have but a dog's life of it.'(79)

Hence the motor of plot in the first four Palliser novels is a character's search for the partner with money. In *Can You Forgive Her?* this is the 'wild man' George Vavasor, who wants to marry his cousin Alice to use her money to get into Parliament. In the *Phineas* novels it is the 'Irish member', Phineas Finn, who is in love at different times with three eligible and influential women, and is loved in turn by two of them. In *The Eustace Diamonds* Lizzie Eustace is sought after for her money and social position by Frank Greystock and Lord Fawn, both young, poor, aspiring politicians.

Phineas is the most sympathetically conceived of these adventurers, if adventurer he can be called. An Irish Tom Jones, handsome and warmhearted, he owes his entrée to English political society to the love of Lady Laura Standish, who 'was related to almost everybody who was anybody among the high Whigs' (5). She provides him with the family rotten

borough when he loses his Irish seat, and uses her influence to get him a
government post at the Treasury. But when she marries the wealthy but dour
Scots laird Robert Kennedy, hoping thereby to have a larger say in political
life, it causes Phineas little heartache to turn his attentions to another society
lady with political connections, Violet Effingham. These amorous intrigues
run parallel to the political intrigues in a House of Commons beginning to
be engaged with the issue of parliamentary reform–the very issue which
exercised Parliament at the time of the 1867 Reform Bill debates, when
Trollope was writing the novel. There are lively portraits of the political
leaders: Disraeli can be glimpsed in Daubeny, Gladstone in Gresham, John
Bright in the radical manufacturer Turnbull; and Trollope is excellent at
portraying the party managers and hacks like Barrington Erle, who 'hated
the very name of independence in Parliament, and when he was told of any
man, that that man intended to look to measures and not to men, he
regarded that man as being both unstable as water and dishonest as the wind'
(2). Phineas is not overburdened with political convictions, but even he
squirms with pain at having to vote against his conscience on the issue of
rotten boroughs (47). He rises faster than his performance in Parliament
warrants, and falls as fast when on a visit to Ireland he commits himself to
the cause of Irish tenant-right. Again love and politics intertwine: Phineas
votes for Ireland and honesty in both, resigning from government and
marrying his hometown sweetheart, despite the tempting offer of Madame
Max Goesler's hand and fortune. His reward is to become Inspector of the
Poor Houses in Cork, a far cry from the Palace of Westminster.

Between the two *Phineas* novels fell the shadow of Trollope's bitter
experience at the Beverley election in 1868, when he came bottom of the poll
as Liberal candidate in a constituency subsequently disfranchised for bribery.
Phineas Redux is a much darker book than its predecessor. There is
disillusionment in many of the narrator's reflections, such as his observation
on Phineas's return to Parliament that he 'was again in possession of that
privilege for which he had never ceased to sigh since the moment in which
he lost it. A drunkard or a gambler may be weaned from his ways, but not a
politician' (13). The behaviour of politicians here invites the most cynical of
interpretations. The Tories take up the cause of Church Disestablishment, in
denial of all their traditions, to stay in office. A corrupt MP is acquitted in
the courts after a commission convicts him of bribery, and nobody minds
except 'some poor innocents here and there about the country who had been
induced to believe that bribery and corruption were in truth to be banished
from the purlieus of Westminster' (44). An innocent man, Phineas Finn, is
nearly convicted of murder, and emerges from his trial disillusioned with

political life: "'What does it matter who sits in Parliament? The fight goes
on just the same. The same falsehoods are acted. The same mock truths are
spoken. The same wrong reasons are given'" (68). Like *Phineas Finn*, *Phineas
Redux* ends with a resignation and a marriage. Phineas resigns his seat,
refuses Mr Gresham's offer of a Treasury post, makes the wealthy match he
has always sought; and yet this time he resigns with conviction rather than
regret, 'because the chicaneries of office had become distasteful to him' (78).
It is an important turning-point in the series.

Trollope was ambivalent about politics, revering the institution of
Parliament while increasingly deploring much that went on there. The
reverence he held on to despite deepening pessimism came to be focused in
the figure of Plantagenet Palliser, who emerges as Trollope's ideal statesman
in the later novels. He stands in relation to his uncle, the old Duke of
Omnium, who dies in *Phineas Redux*, as the Victorian gentleman to the
Regency grandee: where his uncle is idle and pleasure-loving, yet a man who
'had looked like a duke, and known how to set a high price on his own
presence' (24), Plantagenet is hard-working and abstemious, and looks like
an anxious civil servant. He is indifferent to the appurtenances of rank; he
would rather serve his country as Chancellor of the Exchequer than be Duke
of Omnium, and when he becomes Duke he prefers to live in Matching, his
country gentleman's home, than at Gatherum Castle. His growth in stature
to the noble statesman (if incompletely successful Premier) of *The Prime
Minister* is Trollope's vindication of the principle of government by
hereditary aristocracy, first set out in *Can You Forgive Her?*:

> Mr. Palliser was one of those politicians in possessing whom
> England has perhaps more reason to be proud than of any other
> of her resources, and who, as a body, give to her that exquisite
> combination of conservatism and progress which is her present
> strength and best security for the future. He could afford to learn
> to be a statesman, and had the industry wanted for such training.
> He was born in the purple, noble himself, and heir to the highest
> rank as well as one of the greatest fortunes of the country, already
> very rich, surrounded by all the temptations of luxury and
> pleasure; and yet he devoted himself to work with the grinding
> energy of a young penniless barrister labouring for a penniless
> wife, and did so without any motive more selfish than that of
> being counted in the roll of the public servants of England.... It is
> the trust which such men inspire which makes them so
> serviceable;—trust not only in their labour,—for any man rising

from the mass of the people may be equally laborious; nor yet simply in their honesty and patriotism. The confidence is given to their labour, honesty, and patriotism joined to such a personal stake in the country as gives them a weight and ballast which no politician in England can possess without it.(24)

What brings this paragon to life is Trollope's brilliant handling of his marriage to Lady Glencora. It is not portrayed as a perfectly happy marriage: in the first novel she is shown hungering for the handsome wastrel her relatives prevent her marrying, and there remain needs in her nature which her husband can never understand or satisfy. He for his part is always likely to be embarrassed by her tendency to be impulsive and indiscreet. Yet the respect that slowly grows between them, the way they complement each other's qualities so that we see depths of feeling and integrity beneath his staidness and her flightiness, make this one of the few convincing marriages in Victorian fiction. And in his typically modest way, Trollope knew the rare quality of achievement they represent: 'I do not think it probable that my name will remain among those who in the next century will be known as the writers of English prose fiction;—but if it does, that permanence of success will probably rest on the character of Plantagenet Palliser, Lady Glencora, and the Rev. Mr. Crawley' (*Autobiography*, 20).

Because they allowed his characteristic gifts most room to develop and reveal themselves, the Barsetshire and Palliser novels must be accounted his central achievement. But there are a dozen other novels as good in their own way, and one, *The Way We Live Now*, which I shall touch on in the next chapter, considered by many to be his masterpiece. If we try to define what is most characteristic in Trollope's art, we shall find ourselves talking sooner or later about three qualities in his work. First, his grasp of character: there is a good deal of conventional characterization in Trollope, inevitable in a novelist who wrote so much and relied so heavily on the romantic entanglements of love and property, but where his imagination was deeply engaged one finds an intimacy of portraiture as penetrating as anything in Victorian fiction. Second, there is the combination in his work of a mature understanding of society as a great network of institutions, rituals, codes, with an intense sympathy for the frequent loneliness of the individual within society, and especially for the exiles and misfits, those who for whatever reason have stepped beyond the accepted boundaries of their caste or social group. One thinks of Mr Crawley tramping the muddy lanes of Hogglestock, of the swindler Melmotte in his downfall in *The Way We Live Now*, or even Bishop Proudie coming to terms with the isolation his wife has created around him, and after her death 'praying that God might save him from being glad that his wife was dead' (*Last Chronicle*, 67). And finally there is his irony, a very un- Victorian irony in many ways, directed typically at the tendency—to which the Victorians were especially prone—to lay claim to higher standards of conduct than could be sustained in ordinary living. The novelist who made his name in *The Warden* with a book criticizing an importunate reformer, always retained a 'kindly but ironic perception', as Hugh Sykes Davies put it, 'of the gap between what we are, and what we ought to be, wish to be, or believe ourselves to be.'

George Eliot

George Eliot (1819–80) and Trollope were good friends, and as novelists they have much in common. Both made their reputations as chroniclers of provincial England, both were avowedly realistic in their aims (it was to George Eliot that Trollope declared his ambition to write a fiction 'shorn ... of all romance'), both held a fundamentally melioristic view of human society and history—indeed George Eliot was credited in her lifetime with coining the word 'meliorism' to define the belief that the world can be improved by human effort.[20] About each other's work they were warmly respectful, Trollope placing her novels second after Thackeray's among novelists of his day but confessing to their difficulty and lack of 'ease' (*Autobiography*, 13), George Eliot acknowledging the importance of Trollope's influence in encouraging her to write *Middlemarch*, but acquiescing in the common view of him as 'a Church of England man, clinging to whatever is, *on the whole*, and without fine distinctions, honest, lovely and of good report'.[21] But there are also many differences between them, and two in particular of far-reaching importance. George Eliot was a novelist of the past, whereas Trollope dealt almost exclusively with the present; and she was a formidable intellectual, as he was not. It could not be said of Trollope or any other Victorian novelist, what Basil Willey said of George Eliot, that his development was a 'paradigm' of the 'most decided trend' of English intellectual life in the nineteenth century, but this is certainly her distinction. 'Starting from evangelical Christianity, the curve passes through doubt to a reinterpreted Christ and a religion of humanity: beginning with God, it ends in Duty.'[22]

George Eliot came to novel-writing late, after many years on the frontier of Victorian intellectual life. The story has often been told. It begins in Coventry with the young and outwardly evangelical Mary Ann Evans reading Charles Hennell's *Inquiry Concerning the Origin of Christianity* (1838), in which she encountered, and was at once convinced by, an interpretation of the Gospels that required, in Hennell's words, 'no deviation from the known laws of nature' for their explanation, nor 'more than the operation of human motives and feelings, acted upon by the peculiar circumstances of the age and country whence the religion originated'.[23] The effect of reading Hennell was to replace in her mind the supernatural Jesus of Christianity with the natural Jesus of history, but characteristically she did not rest in this negative position. Her reading of David Friedrich Strauss's *Das Leben Jesu* (1835–6), which she translated into English as *The Life of Jesus* (1846), introduced her to a seminal work of the German 'Higher Criticism'. Strauss argued that although Jesus was not divine his life and ministry were profoundly expressive, as symbol and 'myth', of certain universal human truths, needs, and hopes. The process of reconstruction was completed when, after moving to London and becoming assitant editor of *The Westminster Review* in 1851, she read and translated Ludwig Feuerbach's *The Essence of Christianity* (1854). Feuerbach provided the ethical redirection her essentially religious nature needed. He saw religion as the projection of an entirely human need for a perfect and transcendent being: the true 'essence' of Christianity was the divinity of the human, not the humanity of the divine, and what could be rescued from the wreck of supernatural theism was a 'Religion of Humanity', founded on the bonds of feeling and sympathy between human beings. The essence of Feuerbach is summed up in George Eliot's comment: 'Heaven help us! said the old religions—the new one, from its very lack of that faith, will teach us all the more to help one another.'[24] This 'new' religion gave her an object of reverence, Humanity, and a creed, belief in the power of awakened sympathy to create fellowship, which her novels would proceed to illustrate, but also to test. She wrote in 1874 that her books 'have for their main bearing a conclusion ... without which I could not have cared to write any representation of human life—namely, that the fellowship between man and man which has been the principle of development, social and moral, is not dependent on conceptions of what is not man: and that the idea of God, so far as it has been a high spiritual influence, is the ideal of a goodness entirely human (i.e. an exaltation of the human).'[25]

'It was not science itself', Noel Annan has written, 'but science interpreted *as history*, which upset the orthodox cosmology.'[26] George Eliot understood and accepted the implications of that intellectual revolution more completely than any other English novelist of her time. Fundamental to all her writings are the notions of sequence and development, at work in the history of society, of religion, of matter. She praised one writer in a review for his 'recognition of the presence of undeviating law in the material and moral world—of that invariability of sequence which is acknowledged to be the basis of physical science, but which is still perversely ignored in our social organization, our ethics and our religion'. And in the same review of 1851 she made her first recorded reference to the founder of Positivism, Auguste Comte, and wrote that 'the teaching of positive truth is the grand means of expelling error.'[27] George Eliot was clearly a positivist of sorts, in the sense that she accepted the scientific rather than supernatural explanation of the universe, and tried in her novels to incorporate it in a progressive and affirmatory vision of human history, society and morals. But she came to positivism before she read Comte's grandiose systematization, and hers was a very English and Wordsworthian version: a faith in progress qualified by reverence for the past and a great tenderness for the human need and longing which had been expressed through, and consoled by, religious forms which could no longer be held to be supernaturally true. There is no more revealing detail in her biography than the image we have of her groaning over the translation of Strauss's *Leben Jesu*—a work that was to act like a depth-charge in the lives of many Victorian half-believers—'dissecting the beautiful story of the crucifixion', as a friend wrote, and turning for consolation to 'an ivory image of Christ on the Cross above her desk'.[28] She disliked the label 'freethinker' and soon moved away from any spirit of antagonism to dogmatic Christianity, writing in 1859: 'I have no longer any antagonism towards any faith in which human sorrow and human longing for purity have expressed themselves; on the contrary, I have a sympathy with it that predominates over all argumentative tendencies.'[29] At once intellectually advanced and emotionally conservative, striving always to reconstruct, to rescue the human truths enshrined in past forms and reconcile them with the inevitable development toward newer forms, she represents the 'conservative-reforming intellect' ('Amos Barton', 1) of her time at its most responsible.

When this has been said, however, and it is inevitably the first thing that is said about George Eliot, it must sometimes trouble the reader coming to her novels for the first time to know quite how this 'advanced' intellectual activity meets up with the nostalgic evocation of pre-Victorian village life he or she will find in, for example, *Adam Bede* or *Silas Marner*; and the same reader will look in vain in her novels for any treatment of a religious crisis comparable to her own. She left to a later generation of novelists, to Hardy and Mrs Humphry Ward, the novel of religious doubt she was uniquely qualified to write. Indeed, it is a striking feature of all her novels apart from her last, *Daniel Deronda*, that they are set in a period before the intellectual upheavals of the Victorian age. Her favoured time is around 1830, between Catholic Emancipation in 1829 and the Reform Bill of 1832, but before the rise of the Oxford Movement and the impact of geology and biblical criticism in the 1830s. The first question to be asked, then, in considering George Eliot as a Victorian novelist is why the Victorian age itself is largely absent from the subject-matter of her fiction.

Part of the answer is a combination of nostalgia for the past with a natural imaginative gravitation to the world of her childhood, but more important are the ideas of history and society set out in her review-essay of 1856, 'The Natural History of German Life'. She begins there by criticizing the unrealistic portrayal of the working classes in contemporary art and literature: 'our social novels profess to represent the people as they are, and the unreality of their representations is a grave evil'. There has been no 'natural history' of the English people comparable to the study of the German peasantry undertaken by the sociologist Heinrich von Riehl in the volumes under review. Riehl had not only observed the peasant more closely, he had brought to the exploration of peasant culture a 'thoroughly philosophical kind' of '*social-political-conservatism*':

> He sees in European society *incarnate history*, and any attempt to disengage it from its historical elements must, he believes, be simply destructive of social vitality. What has grown up historically can only die out historically, by the gradual operation of necessary laws. The external conditions which society has inherited from the past are but the manifestation of inherited internal conditions in the human beings who compose it; the internal conditions and the external are related to each other as the organism and its medium, and development can take place only by the gradual consentaneous development of both.[30]

There is much in this passage and in the review as a whole that is deeply characteristic of George Eliot, and anticipatory of her novels. Here, to reverse Professor Annan's terms, is history interpreted as science. Words like 'law', 'organism', 'medium', 'development', a phrase such as 'natural history' itself, portray the study of society as a scientific activity, and there is a strong implicit analogy throughout the review between the sociologist and the novelist. He too is a 'natural historian' exploring the '*incarnate history*' of society, perceiving 'the gradual operation of necessary laws', tracing the influence of external upon internal in individual lives. And if the novelist is a natural historian, then his medium is history and he must choose a period sufficiently distanced from the present to enable 'the gradual operation of necessary laws' to be perceived. Distance and objectivity will enable the novelist to achieve the realism of presentation which is his equivalent of the sociologist's observations, and is necessary to create the sympathetic understanding that is the moral end of art—for 'the greatest benefit we owe to the artist, whether painter, poet, or novelist, is the extension of our sympathies' (p. 270).

George Eliot's aim to write a 'natural history' of English life drove her back to the time of her own childhood and beyond, where the web of society, to use one of her favourite metaphors, could be held securely in memory. The result is a curious double perspective. 'She has walked between two epochs', Sidney Colvin said in his review of *Middlemarch*, 'upon the confines of two worlds, and has described the old in terms of the new. To the old world belong the elements of her experience, to the new world the elements of her reflection on experience'. Hence 'there is the most pointed contrast between the matter of these English tales and the manner of their telling. The matter is antiquated in our recollections, the manner seems to anticipate the future of our thoughts.'[31] This contrast between the pre-Reform Bill world she writes about and the modernity of her reflections upon it makes for a different fictional treatment of the past than in other Victorian novelists. Elizabeth Gaskell, like Thackeray also in one of his moods, is concerned with the links that bind past and present, with the continuity of memory. In novels like *Cranford* and *Cousin Phillis* she portrays the forces of change at work in the recent past that will transform the communities she writes about, and bring them into the present where she and her readers are living. In *Adam Bede*, with its 60-year time-gap, we are more aware of a disjunction between two worlds. Past relates to present by contrast and analogy—the 1832 Reform Bill in *Felix Holt* and *Middlemarch* paralleling their first readers' recent experience of the 1867 Reform Bill is another example—rather than through the threads of continuity traced by Gaskell or Thackeray. The gap between worlds is bridged but not closed by the authorial commentary, which moves, sometimes fluently, sometimes uneasily, between the different responses of irony, nostalgia and 'scientific' detachment.

Irony and nostalgia jostle on the first page of her first story, 'The Sad Fortunes of the Rev. Amos Barton' in *Scenes of Clerical Life* (1858). 'Shepperton Church was a very different-looking building five-and-twenty years ago', it begins, and the narrator goes on to confess ambivalence about the improvements that have taken place since. The 'well-regulated mind' approves, but 'imagination does a little Toryism by the sly, revelling in regret that dear, old, brown, crumbling, picturesque inefficiency is everywhere giving place to spick-and-span new-painted, new-varnished efficiency ... '. The irony tells against a too-confident faith in progress and less securely perhaps, against conservative nostalgia ('a little Toryism by the sly'). There is a double irony here, for it is the new man, the evangelical clergyman Amos Barton, who sets these improvements in motion, before his 'sad fortunes' take him away from Shepperton; and he is most in need of the tolerance of the old ways. Barton is an utterly unremarkable man, a point George Eliot makes repeatedly in the story: 'a man whose virtues were not heroic, and who had no undetected crime within his breast; who had not the slightest mystery hanging about him, but was palpably and unmistakably commonplace; who was not even in love, but had had that complaint favourably many years ago' (5). For, 'I wish to stir your sympathy with commonplace troubles—to win your tears for real sorrow: sorrow such as may live next door to you—such as walks neither in rags nor in velvet, but in very ordinary decent apparel' (7). He is plain, awkward, ill-educated, ineffective, and, like Trollope's Mr Crawley, desperately poor on a salary of £80 a year, with six children to support. The one redeeming touch in his life is his beautiful wife Milly and her love for him, and when she dies, and he has to vacate his living, he is desolate. But his sorrows create the sympathy among his parishioners that his preaching has failed to do, and they rally round him and are sorry to see him go—'his recent troubles had called out their better sympathies, and that is always a source of love. Amos failed to touch the spring of goodness by his sermons, but he touched it effectually by his sorrows; and there was now a real bond between him and his flock' (10). This simple story expresses George Eliot's 'religion of humanity' at its plainest—the human need and sympathy that were for her the Feuerbachian 'essence of Christianity'. 'Amos Barton' is not a very well-constructed work, too leisurely at the start and too rushed at the end, but it is told with a spare and compassionate realism that is strangely moving.

'Janet's Repentance' is a more ambitious story on a similar theme, also set around 1830 and concerned with an evangelical clergyman in a provincial town, but with the main elements reversed: Milby is not picturesque like Shepperton, but ignorant and backward, whereas Edgar Tryan is everything that Amos Barton is not—handsome, charismatic and a gentleman. It is a noticeably more accomplished piece of writing, better-paced and clearly focused on the central moral action of the Rev. Tryan's rescue of Janet Dempster from the despair and incipient alcoholism that her loveless marriage has brought her to. The story of Janet's conversion would edify even the most devout reader, but again the Feuerbachian message is made clear: the 'essence' of her rescue is the human love and pity shown by Tryan, working within the evangelical forms. She cannot feel the 'Divine Pity ... it kept aloof from her, it poured no balm into her wounds, it stretched out no hand to bear up her weak resolve ... ' (15). It is only when Tryan stretches out a human hand, gives of himself by confessing to his own guilty past, that the channels of feeling open: 'The tale of the Divine Pity was never yet believed from lips that were not felt to be moved by human pity' (18). All this is impressively done, and yet the spare power of 'Amos Barton' is lacking. 'Janet's Repentance' gives the air of hedging its metaphysical bets a little too calculatingly; there are too many ambiguous references to the 'Divine Presence', 'Divine sympathy', 'Infinite Love', and 'the strange light from the golden sky' which falls on Mr Tryan's hair and 'makes it look almost like an auréole' (3) indicates that we are being given a modern saint's life. It is revealing to compare the funerals that end the two books. That of Milly in 'Amos Barton' takes place 'while the Christmas snow lay thick upon the graves', and is unconsoling; they go home and 'the broad snow-reflected daylight was in all the rooms; the Vicarage again seemed part of the common working-day world, and Amos, for the first time, felt that he was alone ... ' (9). Mr Tryan is buried surrounded by intimations of immortality—it is spring, the cloudy weather clears and the sun shines, the clergyman speaks of the Resurrection and the Life, the crocuses bloom, and Janet walks 'in the presence of unseen witnesses—of the Divine love that had rescued her' (28). Given George Eliot's stated beliefs, the ending of 'Amos Barton' is not only more logical, but more honest and more moving.

These two novellas point to diverging tendencies in George Eliot's art, the one to an unadorned realism attempting the sympathetic presentation of middling characters, the other to a yearning identification with those characters who transcend the real by their exceptional gifts of sympathy and self-sacrifice. Although her philosophy committed her to the real she could not rest in it, as Trollope could; there was always a stirring beyond to more ideal forms of life, and she was intensely susceptible to the appeal of self-denying conduct. 'All self-sacrifice is good', she once wrote,[32] a statement one cannot imagine Trollope or Thackeray making. Thus her aesthetic of realism is always potentially a divided aesthetic, as U.C. Knoepflmacher says: 'Throughout her career, George Eliot's desire to be faithful to the conditions of actual existence clashed with her efforts to transcend or dignify the meanness of those conditions'.[33] The problem of fact and value inherent in literary realism is never settled in her work, and the desire to affirm value in fact keeps breaking in, either in the form of characters like Will Ladislaw in *Middlemarch*, who is made miraculously exempt from the forces of environment which bear so heavily on the others, or in the stirrings towards millenarianist romance which she surrendered to in *Daniel Deronda*. There is always an element of idealism in the realism she professed and practised. She saw no theoretical contradiction in this, following G.H. Lewes in his belief that 'Realism is ... the basis of all Art, and its antithesis is not Idealism, but Falsism.'[34] But the contradiction is there nonetheless, and it is especially apparent in her first full-length novel.

Adam Bede (1859) is a professedly realistic novel, George Eliot's attempt to do for the English countryman in fiction what Riehl had done for the German peasant in his pioneering work of sociology. But a reader looking for the English peasant as he is portrayed in her review of Riehl, with his 'slow gaze', 'heavy slouching walk', 'coarse laugh', and 'tipsy revelry' (p. 269), will soon be disappointed. *Adam Bede* is set among a respectable class of village artisans and tenant-farmers, and there is a corresponding elevation of treatment. The famous analogy with Dutch painting in chapter 17 is appropriate not because it underlines anything especially down-to-earth in George Eliot's art, but because it points to a reverent, glowing quality in her rendering of ordinary life, and to the pictorial, even picturesque, element in the early chapters. The community of Hayslope is built up almost tableau by tableau, like a series of Victorian genre-paintings—'The Workshop', 'The Preaching', 'The Rector', 'The Dairy', 'Church'. The principal characters and their idiom have a similar air of heightened typicality. The Adam Bede we meet in the opening chapter, broad of chest and straight of back, surveying his work with 'the air of a soldier standing at ease' and singing 'Awake, my soul, and with the sun/Thy daily stage of duty run ... ', is not just any workman, but the incarnation of the best attributes of the workman; he does not merely embody duty, he sings about it too, lest we miss the point. This is a special kind of realism, which rather like the *Lyrical Ballads* published the year before the novel's opening date of 1799 (and mentioned by Arthur Donnithorne in chapter 5) celebrates the moral qualities of a simple way of life in the process of describing it. Likewise, the colourful idiom of Mrs Poyser, the sharp-tongued farmer's wife, which is grounded in the discipline of farming, expresses the moral value which for George Eliot resides in the decency and worked-for plenty of the Hall Farm. So when she speaks to her Methodist niece in defence of Mr Irwine, the tolerant rector of the parish, and says of his appearance in the pulpit that

> 'it's like looking at a full crop of wheat, or a pasture with a fine dairy o' cows in it; it makes you think the world's comfortable-like. But as for such creaturs as you Methodisses run after, I'd as

soon go to look at a lot o' bare-ribbed runts on a common. Fine
folks they are to tell what's right, as look as if they's never tasted
nothing better than bacon-sword and sour-cake i' their lives.' (8)

—the association between the rector's 'comfortable' preaching and the fruits
of good husbandry is not just Mrs Poyser's characteristic way of speaking, it
also evokes a whole scheme of values in the novel. The pastoral fecundity of
the Hall Farm is a touchstone by which the angularities of Methodism, its
tendency to self-denial and even masochism, are judged. Dinah Morris has
to learn to come to terms with the natural rhythms for which Mrs Poyser is
the spokeswoman, and in doing so she has to learn some of Mr Irwine's tact
and moderation in matters of religion. It is significant that at the end she has
given up preaching and her figure is 'fuller'.

In his essay 'The Pastoral of Intellect', John Bayley has an astute
comment on the kind of characterization Adam Bede or Mrs Poyser
represent: 'It is a process, above all, of making things and people lovingly
characteristic of themselves, but the very minuteness and care in the
externalization reveals all too clearly its origins in the pictured world of
historical idea, of pondered subject.... Carpenters do not chat so as to reveal
the workings of their calling to one another ... '.[35] Lovingly characteristic of
themselves is exactly what the rustics in *Adam Bede* or *Silas Marner* are; they
express George Eliot's idea of what their relationship to their environment
should or might be, and in this, as Bayley suggests, they betray their origins
in an act of historical idealization, 'historic pastoral' he calls it. What
purports to be an exercise in realism turns out to be a realistic version of
pastoral, in which the values of a pre-Victorian, pre-industrial England are
held up for our approval and for our solace. Significantly, although the action
is placed on a symbolic turning-point, 1799, there is little sense in the body
of the novel of how society was turning on that point. The indicators of
social change are there (Methodism, the presence of an industrial town at
Stoniton) but the engine of social change is lacking; or rather the engine is
moving in reverse, bringing Methodism back from the industrial town to
blend with the unchanging countryside; just as Silas Marner's redemption is
indicated by the gradual shedding of his urban, Dissenting past, and by his
adoption of village ways—church, pipe-smoking and all. Change is present,
but only in the narrator's consciousness, as she reminds us of the passing of
'Old Leisure' (52) or tells us how irreplaceable men like Adam Bede are (19).
The imagination of *Adam Bede* is indeed doing 'a little Toryism by the sly':
its deepest impulse seems to be the wishing away of the industrial
revolution.

There is another side to the novel, however, the moral and psychological exploration of the love affair between Arthur Donnithorne and Hetty Sorrel, the squire's heir and the dairymaid, and its consequences. George Eliot speaks a good deal in her letters and narrative asides about sympathy, but there is little sympathy on hand for Hetty. As her name implies, the pretty but vain and shallow Hetty is a weed in the pastoral garden, and it hardly increases one's respect for the cosy ruralities of Hayslope to see how ruthlessly she is rooted out of the community, and how unsparing is the nemesis visited on her and Arthur. Because she is pretty and empty-headed, Hetty brings out a punitive streak in George Eliot's moralism, which is all the more jarring because of the caressing tones in which it sometimes expresses itself: 'How pretty the little puss looks in that odd dress! It would be the easiest folly in the world to fall in love with her ... ' (15), and so on. The story of Hetty and Arthur grows out of the pastoral world and its politics of deference, but Ian Gregor is surely right to see it as belonging in the end to a diferent mode, to a world of tragic destiny where, in the words of Mr Irwine, '"Consequences are unpitying. Our deeds carry their terrible consequences, quite apart from any fluctuations that went before—consequences that are hardly ever confined to ourselves."' (16)[36] It is true that Adam and Dinah are sucked into Hetty's fate, Adam through his love for her, Dinah through the comfort she brings to her cousin in the condemned cell, but these two are restored to Hayslope at the end, and the last book is given over to the restoration and celebration of the rural community in the harvest supper (53) followed by their marriage. The tragic losers are Hetty and Arthur, exiles from the pastoral world in which the teeth of fate are safely drawn and consequences are not unpitying.

With her next novel, *The Mill on the Floss* (1860), George Eliot moved beyond the static simplicities of pastoral, coming forward in time from the pre-industrial world of *Adam Bede* to the period of her own childhood and youth in the 1820s and 30s. The pastoral landscape of Dorlcote Mill, where the heroine Maggie Tulliver grows up, is seen in relation to the modern trading town of St Oggs, home of her prudent, bourgeois relations the Dodsons. The interaction between the two ways of life and the two families, the one pre-industrial, impulsive, warm, the other 'modern' and calculating, is the central subject of the novel, linking the *bildungsroman* of Maggie Tulliver to the larger forces of history and change symbolized by the River Floss. It is well known that George Eliot put a good deal of her divided feelings about her own childhood into the story of Maggie and Tom, on the one hand celebrating the Wordsworthian 'natural piety' of the deep-rooted bonds of feeling associated with place and family, on the other shrewdly exposing the male arbitrariness with which the older brother treats his emotionally hungry sister. Again, irony and nostalgia move across the gap between the narrator and the past. One readily sees why Proust should have been so moved by the recollected emotional and sensuous fullness of the opening chapters, but the 'golden gates of their childhood' which close on Maggie and Tom at the end of Book 2 close also on a scene of conflict and, for Maggie, of unfulfilled yearning. Her 'need of being loved, the strongest need in poor Maggie's nature' (I, 5), is continually thwarted by Tom and her Dodson aunts; an emotional pattern of impulsive rebellion followed by self-reproach is established in childhood and repeats itself in adulthood. The child who pushes 'poor little pink-and-white Lucy into the cow-trodden mud' (I, 10) grows into the young woman who runs—or rather drifts—off with Lucy's admirer, Stephen Guest, only to return full of remorse to ask for forgiveness. Fallible, impetuous and warm-hearted, Maggie is the most human of heroines, and also, in her way, a tragic figure in a novel which reaches for the full tragic effect. The narrator says of the spurt of jealousy that leads to Maggie pushing Lucy into the pond, that 'There were passions at war in Maggie at that moment to have made a tragedy, if tragedies were made by passion only' (I, 10); elsewhere she observes that 'Mr Tulliver had a destiny as well as Oedipus' (I, 13); and the novel ends with the drowning of Maggie and Tom.

Such intimations of tragic destiny in a novel purporting to deal with ordinary individuals in a provincial setting make *The Mill on the Floss* a work of considerable significance in the history of Victorian fiction. Broadly speaking, and with important exceptions like *Wuthering Heights*, the English novel had not hitherto been tragic in its *form*. For reasons that have to do with the novel's historical evolution from drama and epic, and its tendency to deal with the ordinary and the typical rather than the exceptional individual, it has been sceptical of the heroic (think of *Don Quixote* or *Vanity Fair*), and when it has dealt with a greatly suffering individual, like Richardson's Clarissa Harlowe, has tended to relate their suffering to a larger vision of Providence, or to an ultimately reassuring comic restoration of balance (*Adam Bede* and *The Last Chronicle of Barset* are the examples nearest to hand). The novelist's attitude to suffering has always been a little like that of the 'Old Masters' praised in W.H. Auden's *'Musée des Beaux Arts'*, who understand

> Its human position; how it take place
> While someone else is eating or opening a window or just
> walking dully along ...

The sense of other things going on deprives the tragic protagonist of the exclusive attention he receives in classical tragedy. George Eliot's innovation was to try to do justice to 'that element of tragedy which lies in the very fact of frequency' (*Middlemarch*, 20) and in ordinary living. 'The pride and obstinacy of millers, and other insignificant people, whom you pass unnoticingly on the road every day, have their tragedy too; but it is of that unwept, hidden sort, that goes on from generation to generation, and leaves no record' (*Mill*, III, 1). This involves a different, more muted kind of tragic effect. The older model of the heroic protagonist boldly confronting fate will no longer do. 'For us,' Walter Pater wrote in 1867, 'necessity is not, as of old, a sort of mythological personage without us, with whom we can do warfare. It is rather a magic web woven through and through us ... penetrating us with a network, subtler than our subtlest nerves, yet bearing in it the central forces of the world. Can art represent men and women in these bewildering toils so as to give the spirit at least an equivalent for the sense of freedom?'[37] George Eliot saw no easy answer to that question. The liberating spectacle of the Brontë heroine struggling successfully against a demeaning society gives way, in her work, to the much more evenly balanced struggle of characters like Maggie, aspiring 'above the mental level of the generation before them, to which they have been nevertheless tied by the strongest fibres of their hearts' (IV, 1). Like Pater's web, the forces of the environment are now written in the consciousness of individuals, by heredity and accumulated association, limiting their ability to break free and making that break, when it comes, a painful self-rending.

The Mill on the Floss can be seen as transitional between the old and the newer forms of tragedy. The heroic death of Maggie and Tom on the river breaks decisively with the compromise comic form of most Victorian fiction, and offers the liberation of spirit associated with traditional tragedy. But it also simplifies and even contradicts Maggie's tragic predicament at the end of the novel, which is the modern one of stalemate; she has appeared to violate communally evolved values which she herself shares, and can neither make good her escape nor repair the damage. Although it would be a misplaced emphasis to see the prudential morality of St Oggs as in any sense a 'good', the kind of tragic effect George Eliot was moving towards with Maggie Tulliver was the Hegelian conflict of valid claims discussed in her 1856 essay on 'The Antigone and Its Moral':

> [The] struggle between Antigone and Creon represents that struggle between elemental tendencies and established laws by which the outer life of man is gradually and painfully being

brought into harmony with his inward needs. Until this harmony is perfected, we shall never be able to attain a great right without also doing a wrong. Reformers, martyrs, revolutionists, are never fighting against evil only; they are also placing themselves in opposition to a good—to a valid principle which cannot be infringed without harm.[38]

So Maggie Tulliver can be seen as a 'martyr' in the conflict with the 'established laws' of her society, laws which deny her the education and the field of action open to her brother, but which are also inscribed within her, as she shows when she cannot carry through her elopement with Stephen Guest. He argues for the supremacy of the 'natural law' of instinct, she counters with an assertion of the 'sacred ties' of the past: "'If the past is not to bind us, where can duty lie? We should have no law but the inclination of the moment"' (VI, 14). The trouble with this denouement is that the elopement with the conventionally handsome Stephen bears little relationship to the terms of Maggie's dilemma, as these have been defined in the first two-thirds of the novel. A similar objection may be made to the drowning of Maggie and Tom at the end: it substitutes the pathos of death for the difficult task of repairing what seems by then an almost irreparable breach between brother and sister. We have to wait until *Middlemarch* for a novel which adequately expresses the muted modern sense of tragedy.

The first phase of George Eliot's career culminates in the short and almost flawless moral fable, *Silas Marner* (1861). This Wordsworthian story of the redemption of a lonely weaver by his love for a foundling child is, as George Eliot told her publisher, 'a sort of legendary tale'.[39] With its spinning-wheels and bags of gold and timeless English village, its sense of the mysterious 'dealings' of Providence which reward Silas with the golden-haired Eppie and leave her natural father, the local squire, childless, *Silas Marner* belongs to the mode of myth and fairy-tale. It is George Eliot's most successful pastoral novel partly because it recognizes and delights in the 'legendary' quality of pastoral and does not try to yoke it to history, as *Adam Bede* does. History, however, dominates the second phase of her career, the phase that begins with *Romola* (1862–3). This historical novel, set in a meticulously detailed Renaissance Florence, and featuring historical personages such as Savonarola and Machiavelli, is, by a familiar paradox, the least historically interesting of her novels as well as the most heavy-going, although there is a link with her more characteristic themes in Romola's development out of disillusionment into a kind of secular sainthood at the end. The experience of attempting a fully historical fiction was valuable for

George Eliot, and its fruits can be seen in the heightened historical awareness she brought to the First Reform Bill era in her next two novels. The first of these is *Felix Holt, The Radical* (1866), which contrasts the idealistic moral radicalism of Felix, a self-educated working-man, with the opportunistic political radicalism of the worldly Harold Transome, and comes down too easily but predictably (given George Eliot's own susceptibility to ethical idealism) on the side of Felix—although not without showing in the tragic figure of Mrs Transome a feeling for the complexities of human nature absent from the Felix plot. The second is *Middlemarch* (1871–2).

Middlemarch is George Eliot's masterpiece and one of the greatest of Victorian novels, if not indeed the greatest of all. This 'Study of Provincial Life', dealing with a number of interlinking characters living in a Midlands town (Coventry mostly) in the period 1829–32, is her most ambitious and successful attempt to create the impression of '*incarnate history*' she had praised in Riehl. The movement from a country or village to an urban location, and one of reasonable size, is significant and—for this reader at any rate—almost wholly a gain, since it meant a shift from the pastoral landscape of memory, with all its temptation to nostalgic idealizations, to the townscape of history. Middlemarch is a modern town of 1830, with its industry, banking system, local politicians, lawyers and doctors, a place where a 'subtle movement' of class relationships is going on, 'constantly shifting the boundaries of social intercourse, and begetting new consciousness of interdependence' (10)—a complex 'medium', then, for the explorations of the novelist as natural historian/scientist. If 'there is no private life which has not been determined by a wider public life' (*Felix Holt*, 3), what better place for examining the interaction of the two than a town in the middle of England, in the middle of the agitation surrounding the First Reform Bill, itself a middle stage in the 'march' of progress to the supposedly enlightened legislation of the Second? The historical analogy between 1832 and 1867 keeps irony and sympathy in a steady focus: the reader of 1872 is invited to look back 40 years to the genesis of the society he is living in, and any tendency he may have to condescend to these struggling and fallible characters is checked by the inescapability of change in George Eliot's universe—in 40 years time his own generation will be similarly vulnerable to the condescension of children and grandchildren.

Private life and public life are brought together by the concern so many of the characters show with reform, whether in the political, the scientific or the intellectual spheres. The Prelude suggests that the St Theresa figure of the greatly aspiring woman seeking an 'epic' life will be central, and also that her modern fate is likely to be one of failure, 'for these later-born Theresas were helped by no coherent social faith and order which could perform the function of knowledge for the ardently willing soul. Their ardour alternated between a vague ideal and the common yearning of womanhood; so that the one was disapproved as extravagance, and the other condemned as a lapse.' Thus is hinted the decline of the Christian world-vision and the special problem the modern St Theresa, Dorothea Brooke, faces in being a woman. Hers is the chief of the four plots on which *Middlemarch* is built, and in three of them the desire of characters to improve the world, or to add to the world's store of knowledge, is prominent. There is Dorothea herself, continually seeking to know how she can serve her fellow-beings, and continually checked and thwarted. There is the story of Tertius Lydgate, the young doctor with aristocratic connections, who comes to Middlemarch fired with the conviction that the medical profession might be 'the finest in the world; presenting the most perfect interchange between science and art; offering the most direct alliance between intellectual conquest and the social good' (15). Similarly concerned with intellectual conquest but, to Dorothea's dismay, indifferent to 'social good', is her husband Casaubon, the elderly pedant who has devoted his life to the search for a 'Key to All Mythologies', as Lydgate proposes to devote his to the search for the 'primitive tissue' of human physiology. Both fail, for reasons that are in differing degrees temperamental and historical. There is the story of the evangelical banker Nicholas Bulstrode, who seeks to salve his guilty conscience by doing good works in Middlemarch, in particular setting up a new fever hospital with Lydgate as the medical attendant. And fourthly there is the plot concerning the Garth family and Fred Vincy, the story of Fred's love for the plain but spirited Mary Garth, and his search for a vocation in life which she will approve. These characters, and the Rev. Camden Farebrother, who loves Mary and generously stands aside so Fred can have her, act as a foil to the greater aspirations of the others. They remind us that an honest and unselfish life is possible in Middlemarch despite the many forces in the town conspiring to reduce all its inhabitants to the same middling standard.

The main characters are forced to live in a climate of gossip. The remarkable social density of *Middlemarch* owes much to George Eliot's command of the many different voices that make up public opinion in the town. There is the 'county' view of Mrs Cadwallader, with her robust and witty attitude to Dorothea's marriage with 'our Lowick Cicero', as she calls Casaubon: '"She says, he is a great soul.—A great bladder for dried peas to rattle in!"' (6). Yet she is not allowed the last word; her placing tones are themselves placed by the larger ironic vision of the narrator, who says of Mrs

Cadwallader: 'Her life was rurally simple, quite free from secrets either foul, dangerous, or otherwise important ... ' (6). When Lydgate is introduced at Mr Brooke's dinner-party in chapter 10, it is through the conversation of Lady Chettam ('I like a medical man more on a footing with the servants') and Standish the lawyer, who have ominously lower expectations of the medical profession than Lydgate himself. The local shopkeepers, doctors and lawyers on the Infirmary board make the decision about the hospital chaplain into a virtual declaration of political and denominational allegiances, and for the first time Lydgate feels 'the hampering threadlike pressure of small social conditions, and their frustrating complexity' (18). His vote for Tyke rather than his friend Farebrother binds him to Bulstrode in the eyes of the town, with painful consequences. Lower down the social scale it is in the Green Dragon public-house that the rumours about Bulstrode's shady past start, quickly gathering to a head in the public meeting where he is asked to leave and takes the innocent Lydgate out—and down—with him (71).

The web is George Eliot's favourite metaphor for the complex interrelations of community which the narrator-scientist seeks to probe and unravel (15). So closely woven is this web that the scope for 'epic' action is very limited: Middlemarch is the most testing medium in her novels for the characteristic George Eliot idealist, a role shared by Dorothea and Lydgate. In the hopes they have conceived for their lives, both are disappointed, Dorothea because her 'spiritual grandeur' is 'ill-matched with the meanness of opportunity' open to women in this society (Prelude), and 'there is no creature whose inward being is so strong that it is not greatly determined by what lies outside it' (Finale). Lydgate's is the more tragic case because he enters the lists fully equipped, it seems, to do battle with he unreformed world of pre-Victorian medicine. The issue is more in doubt, and more dependent on 'character' than environment. So the narrator says of him, in contrast to the sentence from the Finale quoted above, It always remains true that if we had been greater, circumstance would have been less strong against us' (58). What makes his story so powerful is the intellectual grasp George Eliot brought to the imagination of his scientific ambitions, and her sense of the way these are entwined with Lydgate's masculinity. The intellectual sympathy is of itself remarkable, and many readers have sensed a resonance of affinity between George Eliot's description of Lydgate's research and her own procedure as a psychological and social anatomist:

He for his part had tossed away all cheap inventions where ignorance finds itself able and at ease: he was enamoured of that arduous invention which is the very eye of research, provisionally

framing its object and correcting it to more and more exactness
of relation; he wanted to pierce the obscurity of those minute
processes which prepare human misery and joy, those invisible
thoroughfares which are the first lurking-places of anguish,
mania, and crime, that delicate poise and transition which
determine the growth of happy or unhappy consciousness. (16)

But even more remarkable than such penetrating sympathy with intellectual
processes is the way they are incarnated in a figure who is convincingly
masculine, with powerful emotional susceptibilities and, beneath his 'spots of
commonness', great physical tenderness: 'he was an emotional creature, with
a flesh-and-blood sense of fellowship which withstood all the abstractions of
special study. He cared not only for "cases", but for John and Elizabeth,
especially Elizabeth' (15). His instinctive tenderness surfaces at two crucial
points in his story. One is the moment of his proposal to Rosamond, when
he is surprised into a declaration by the sight of her tears:

> There could have been no more complete answer than that
> silence, and Lydgate, forgetting everything else, completely
> mastered by the outrush of tenderness at the sudden belief that
> this sweet young creature depended on him for her joy, actually
> put his arms round her, folding her gently and protectingly—he
> was used to being gentle with the weak and suffering—and kissed
> each of the two large tears. This was a strange way of arriving at
> an understanding, but it was a short way. (31)

The other moment is the bitter one when Bulstrode seems to stagger when
rising from the public meeting at which he has been accused, and Lydgate
instinctively rises to help him from the room, knowing that the action will
confirm everyone's suspicion that he is in league with Bulstrode (71). In both
cases the quality in Lydgate which makes him such a fine doctor contributes
to his downfall. The logic of that downfall has been often and rightly praised,
and there is perhaps nothing in Victorian fiction—or English fiction for that
matter—to match the slow deterioration of Lydgate's marriage under the
pressure of debt and the growing sense of incompatibility between two
people who still, at some level, love each other.

'Each is a tale of matrimonial infelicity,' Henry James said of 'the
balanced contrast between the two histories' of Lydgate and Dorothea, 'but
the conditions in each are so different and the circumstances so broadly
opposed that the mind passes from one to the other with that supreme sense

of the vastness and variety of human life, under aspects apparently similar, which it belongs only to the greatest novels to produce'.[40] The critic cannot hope to demonstrate that greatness in a short space; the best he can do is to point. This critic would point, for example, to chapter 42, where Casaubon comes face to face with the prospect of his own death, and Dorothea overcomes her opposition and frustration and goes out to meet him on the dark landing. To chapter 52, where Fare-brother, himself attracted to Mary Garth, goes to plead Fred Vincy's case with her. To chapter 58, where Rosamond goes horse-riding against her husband's wishes and loses her baby, and Lydgate comes to realize the 'terrible tenacity of this mild creature' and his powerlessness over her. To chapter 74, where Mrs Bulstrode learns of her husband's disgrace, and silently renouncing the pleasure and finery of her life, puts on a 'plain black gown' and goes down to support him. To Dorothea's crisis in chapter 80, when she spends the night struggling with jealousy and disappointment at what she thinks is a love-affair between Will Ladislaw and Lydgate's wife, but resolves in the morning to silence her pain and go to help Rosamond. Most of these scenes are moments of recognition and renunciation, when a character confronts the inevitable conditions of his or her life, and is forced to renounce habit or expectation in favour of the claims of compassionate sympathy. They are sad moments, as all renunciation of energy is sad, yet also moments of subdued moral grandeur, which show the power of quite ordinary people to transcend selfishness and find meaning and value in compassion for others. To read them is rather like receiving the impression made on Dorothea after her night of crisis, when she opens the curtains to see figures moving on the road outside her gates and feels 'the largeness of the world and the manifold wakings of men to labour and endurance' (80). And lest this makes the novel seem too sombre, one would also want to point to comic scenes, such as Mr Brooke's experience on the hustings (51), and to the comic irony that plays over the portrayal of Mr Casaubon. His letter proposing marriage (5) is as good in its way as Mr Collins in *Pride and Prejudice*, and Jane Austen would not have disowned such well-turned irony as the description of Mr Brooke as a man 'of acquiescent temper, miscellaneous opinions, and uncertain vote' (1), or observation of Mr Casaubon that 'he determined to abandon himself to the stream of feeling, and perhaps was surprised to find what an exceedingly shallow rill it was ... he concluded that the poets had much exaggerated the force of masculine passion' (7)

If Henry James was right to praise the 'vastness and variety of human life' in Middlemarch, was he also right to call it 'a treasure-house of details, but ... an indifferent whole' (p. 353): Certainly the novel lacks the kind of form James himself was to aspire to, the concentration of a fully dramatized point of view, and perhaps it is none the worse for that. And almost as certainly modern criticism has woven too tight a mesh in arguing for the comprehensive unifying power of imagery, theme and structural parallelism. These elements are there, and they do unify up to a point, but there is much in the novel they do not touch. Like most of the great Victorian novels, *Middlemarch* has a redundancy of matter and life over form: that is the condition of their greatness. But it does have one important factor making for unity of tone and perspective. Like *Vanity Fair*, the novel is held together by the authority of the narrator's voice. It is this voice, by turns awkward, shrewd, arch, ironic and profound, continually mediating between the action the fictional characters are involved in and the moral life of the reader, instructing us in the difficulties and the necessity of moral conduct, asking us to feel what we know, that gives *Middlemarch* its characteristic tone of elevated pathos:

> Her finely-touched spirit still had its fine issues, though they were not widely visible. Her full nature, like that river of which Cyrus broke the strength, spent itself in channels which had no great name on the earth. But the effect of her being on those around her was incalculably diffusive: for the growing good of the world is partly dependent on unhistoric acts; and that things are not so ill with you and me as they might have been, is half owing to the number who lived faithfully a hidden life, and rest in unvisited tombs. (Finale)

These are noble words. They express 'that religious and moral sympathy with the historical life of man' which George Eliot felt to be 'the larger half of culture'.[41] That, and her sense of the ineluctability of moral consequences, was the source of her profound appeal to her contemporaries. One understands why the founders of the London Library should have made an exception for her books when some of them wanted to ban fiction from the shelves. As Walter Allen had said, 'It was on the thoroughness and cautiousness of her investigations into the problems of conduct as they face the free spirit, who must be responsible to himself in the absence of traditional and religious sanctions felt as binding, that George Eliot's great moral authority in the nineteenth century rested.'[42]

The words are sad, but is the novel they close tragic? Yes and no. There is the tragic downfall of Lydgate, but the fates of Casaubon and Bulstrode are more pathetic than tragic, and that of Dorothea, though 'unholistic' in act, is still one domestic happiness and 'fine issues'. As George Eliot told her publisher when completing the novel, there was to be 'no unredeemed tragedy in the solution of the story'.[43] In this desire to balance the tragic stress with a hope for 'the growing good of the world' she remains a novelist of her age—the age of equipoise.

Texts: Reference to Wilkie Collins's *The Woman in White* and *The Moonstone* are to the editions in the World's Classics series; those to *Armadale* are to the first book edition (1866). References to Trollope's *The Warden, Barchester Towers, Framley Parsonage, The Last Chronicle of Barset*, and *Phineas Finn* are to the editions in the Penguin English Library; other references are to editions in the World's Classics series. All references to George Eliot's novels are to the editions in the Penguin English Library.

NOTES

1. Quoted by Geoffrey Best in *Mid-Victorian Britain 1851–75* (Weidenfeld & Nicolson, 1971), pp. 234–6.

2. Best, *Mid-Victorian Britain*, p. 228. See also W.L. Burn, *The Age of Equipoise* (Allen & Unwin, 1964).

3. 'Sterne and Thackeray', in *Literary Studies* (2 vols., Dent, 1911) II, pp. 125–6.

4.. 'Gentlemen', *Cornhill Magazine* V (1862), p. 330.

5. *The Letters of Anthony Trollope*, ed. N. John Hall (2 vols., Stanford, Stanford UP, 1983) I, p. 238; letter of 18 October 1863, sending a copy of his novel *Rachel Ray* to George Eliot.

6. Winifred Hughes, *The Maniac in the Cellar: Sensation Novels of the 1860s* (Princeton, NJ, Princeton UP, 1980), p. 155.

7. 'Miss Braddon', in *Wilkie Collins: The Critcal Heritage*, ed. Norman Page (Routledge & Kegan Paul, 1974), pp. 122–3.

8. *The Letters of Charles Dickens*, ed. W. Dexter (3 vols., Nonesuch, 1938) III, p. 534; letter of 30 June 1867.

9. See Sue Lonoff, 'Charles Dickens and Wilkie Collins', *Nineteenth-Century Fiction* 35 (1980), pp. 150–70.

10. *East Lynne* (Dent, 1984), ch. 29.

11. As Harvey Peter Sucksmith suggests in his introduction to the Oxford English Novels edition of *The Woman in White* (OUP, 1975), p. xviii.

12. See Anthea Trodd, 'The Policeman and the Lady: Significant Encounters in Mid-Victorian Fiction', *Victorian Studies* 27 (1984), pp. 435–60.

13. Hughes, *Maniac in the Cellar*, p. 37.

14. *Partial Portraits* (Macmillan, 1888), pp. 100–1.

15. ' "The Unnatural Ruin": Trollope and Nineteenth-Century Irish Fiction', *Nineteenth-Century Fiction* 37 (1982–3), pp. 358–82; p. 381. Trollope lived in Ireland from 1841 to 1851, and from 1853, apart from trips abroad, until he came back to settle in England in 1859.

16. 'From Miss Austen to Mr Trollope', *Spectator*, 16 December 1882; reprinted in Donald Smalley (ed.), *Trollope: The Critical Heritage* (Routledge & Kegan Paul, 1969), p. 511.

17. *Partial Portraits*, p. 113.

18. *The Times's* campaign against clerical abuse and the Church's failure to adapt to modern conditions, and the relevance of these issues to *The Warden*, is discussed in my introduction to the Penguin edition of the novel (Harmondsworth, 1984).

19. *Trollope* (*Writers and their Work*, No. 118, Longman, 1960), p. 32.

20. See James Sully, *Pessimisim: A History and a Criticism* (Henry S. King, 1877), p. 399.

21. *The George Eliot Letters*, ed. G.S. Haight (9 vols., New Haven, Yale UP, 1954–78) IV, pp. 81–2; letter of 16 April 1863. See also M. Sadleir, *Trollope: A Commentary* (Constable, 1927), p. 367*n*.

22. *Nineteenth-Century Studies* (Harmondsworth, Penguin, 1964), p. 215.

23. Quoted by Willey, *Nineteenth-Century Studies*, p. 220.

24. *Letters* II, p. 82; letter of 22 January 1852.

25. *Letters* VI, p. 98; letter of 10 December 1874.

26. *Ideas and Beliefs of the Victorians* (Sylvan Press 1949), p. 151.

27. 'The Progress of Intellect', in *Essays of George Eliot*, ed. T. Pinney (Routledge & Kegan Paul, 1963), pp. 31, 29.

28. Walter Allen, *George Eliot* (Weidenfeld & Nicolson, 1965), p. 49.

29. *Letters* III, p. 231; letter of 6 December 1859.

30. *Essays*, pp. 270, 287.

31. *George Eliot: The Critical Heritage*, ed. David Carroll (Routledge & Kegan Paul, 1971), p. 332.

32. *Letters* I, p. 268; letter of 11 June 1848.

33. *George Eliot's Early Novels: The Limits of Realism* (Berkeley & Los Angeles, University of California Press, 1968), pp. 34–5.

34. 'Realism in Art: Recent German Fiction', *Westminster Review* 70 (1858), p. 493.

35. *Critical Essays on George Eliot*, ed. Barbara Hardy (Routledge & Kegan Paul, 1970), pp. 201, 203.

36. 'The Two Worlds of *Adam Bede*', in I. Gregor and B. Nicholas, *The Moral and the Story* (Faber, 1962), pp. 13–32.

37. 'Winkwelman', *The Renaissance* (1873; Collins, 1961), p. 218.

38. *Essays*, p. 264.
39. *Letters* III, p. 382; letter of 24 February 1861.
40. *Critical Heritage*, p. 357.

FREDERICK R. KARL

The Brontës:
The Outsider as Protagonist

Perhaps because *Wuthering Heights* (1847) is so far outside the mainstream of early Victorian fiction, readers have tended until recently to be fascinated less by the novel itself than by Heathcliff, its melodramatic protagonist. *Wuthering Heights*, however, is *more* than Heathcliff, for here we have, probably for the first time in British fiction, a view of society from a completely individual point of view, foreshadowing in its way the novels of George Eliot (in part), Conrad, Lawrence, and Joyce. In this area, Emily Brontë's departure from Jane Austen is obvious. The latter accepted her society as given and through irony strove to maintain its stability. Emily Brontë has moved to the periphery of society to delineate people who survive by passion alone, tempestuous and disordered figures who live marginal existences in which reason is subservient to violent feelings.

Heathcliff himself is symbolic of this world of anarchy; his very appearance setting him aside from the mainstream of humanity: dark-skinned like a gypsy, morose, brutish, diabolical, sullen, a kind of Byronic misanthrope with a great capacity both to love and to hate. He exists on the edge of humanity, a marginal or underground figure who becomes a personification of energy, the spirit of the moors, an antagonist of civilization. His often large-than-life qualities partake of the elements that usually go into a legendary character: unknown birth, the suggestion of demonic origin, a veritable prince of darkness in his embodiment of

From *An Age of Fiction: The Nineteenth Century British Novel.* © 1964, renewed 1992 by Frederick R. Karl.

antisocial forces. The novel becomes an operatic fable of light and dark, in which Heathcliff's dark is opposed by Catherine's light; and from this personal tension, the novel spreads into several areas of conflict from which emerges a new vision of society.

One of the difficulties with *Wuthering Heights* is that Heathcliff provides a center for the novel without becoming a "hero," in this way somewhat like Richardson's Lovelace. He is *not* admirable or sympathetic. Neither is he realistic; rather he is a figure from an unsentimental melodrama, illustrative of the author's break from both eighteenth-century realism and Scott's romanticism. The title itself refers to the atmospheric tumult that a weathering station is exposed to in stormy weather, and we recognize that passion and torment rather than rationality or rational relationships are the substance of the novel. In *Jane Eyre*, by contrast, Rochester, although similar to Heathcliff in several superficial ways, is caught in a situation that fits a more reasonable pattern, and his behavior— even his intended bigamy—is realistic within this situation. Moreover, Jane Eyre herself, while suffering torment and pain, reacts within the terms of her society, according to a realistic expectation of behavior. Heathcliff never fits; indeed, the point is that he cannot fit, that he is, like Panurge, an immaterial substance, outside the terms we usually apply to fictional characters.

Both Charlotte and Emily Brontë were obviously influenced by late eighteenth-century and Romantic poetry, and particularly by Byron's work, influences which are most apparent in their *juvenilia*, Charlotte's Angria stories and Emily's Gondal novels. Certain of the latter's themes, as well as the characters and incidents, are carried into the Yorkshire locale of *Wuthering Heights*, although the destruction of most of the Gondal Chronicles makes more definite proof impossible. Gondal (the work of both Emily and Anne) contained a moral atmosphere not unlike that of *Wuthering Heights*. As Fannie Ratchford, the long-time student of Brontë *juvenilia*, writes: "... in Emily's Gondal sin was real, paid for with Old Testament certainty in fixed wages of suffering—real suffering—and death. And Emily admitted no arbitrary force for good or evil; her Gondals were free moral agents following their own wills in accordance with circumstances." When we add a reading of Emily Brontë poetry to even a sketchy knowledge of her early work, we see that *Wuthering Heights* was no sudden miracle, nor need it have been written in collaboration with her brother Branwell, as some have strongly suggested.

Working as a parallel force in *Wuthering Heights*, as in early Browning and Meredith, are the same or similar forces that came to the surface in the so-called Spasmodic poets, especially in the feverish romanticism of Philip

James Bailey, whose *Festus* (1839)—a kind of Byronic *Faust*—was perhaps known by the Brontës. The Spasmodics, among them Sydney Dobell (later, a personal friend of Charlotte Brontë), Alexander Smith, and Richard Horne (Meredith's friend), were more concerned with violent emotions reminiscent of Elizabethan tumult than with realistic romance of the Scott variety. Their Byronic "gods" swoop through life in sublime flights of imagination, carrying all before them in their great bursts of energy and search for power. Incorporeal, unrealistic, of doubtful origin and even more doubtful direction, they parallel Heathcliff and, to some extent, Rochester. Although only *Festus* was written early enough to influence the Brontës' major work, the resemblances are plain.

Wuthering Heights, truly a novel without a hero or heroine, is episodic and loose, held together solely by the doubling of structure and character as well as by the counterpointing of themes. The structure of the inner novel— that apart from the Lockwood-Nelly Dean frame—consists of three sets of lovers: the "mythological" lovers, Heathcliff and Catherine Earnshaw; the childish lovers, young Cathy and young Linton; the healthy lovers, young Cathy and Hareton Earnshaw. This world is then counterpointed to the "normal" and loveless world of Lockwood and Nelly Dean, a ferocious, acquisitive, passionate group contrasted with the middle-class society of the narrators.

In addition to these obvious contrasts, there are the thematic conflicts implicit in the differences among the lovers themselves. Thus, on several levels, as Richard Chase has pointed out, we find schisms between Other World and This World, Savagery and Civilization, Devil and God, Matter and Spirit, Stasis and Motion; as well as those between middle-class values and the impulse to destruction, between Experience and Innocence, and, finally, between the Tale and the Frame. The novel evidently works its way out in conflict, and to trace the limits of each is to see how Emily Brontë tried to give structure to what would otherwise be an altogether rambling and loose narrative.

The Lockwood-Nelly Dean frame obviously provides a norm for the behavior of the interior characters. Without such a standard that allows judgment, Heathcliff would seem the measure of all things, rather than appearing as the spirit of male rebellion which he is. Through this relationship, Emily Brontë also secured a solid anchor in reality, so that Heathcliff, in contrast, acts unrealistically, again on the level of disobedience and freedom that the role demands. Like Richardson's Lovelace and Byron's Manfred, for example, Heathcliff is outside the world of sin and guilt; his actions, while seemingly real, become in point of fact heightened realism, a kind of surrealistic expressionism. Heathcliff strides rather than walks, fasts rather than eats, keeps vigil rather than sleeps. Just as his physical needs are obviously different from those of other men, so his life is motivated by other desires than those of normal men. His physical deprivations are, as it were, manifestations of his unconscious, obsessed as it is with the smell of revenge and the sweat of passion; to judge him within the terms of the realistic novel would be both inappropriate and misleading.

His pursuit of Catherine Earnshaw, consequently, is on a level of pure passion; lacking matter, their affair is pure spirit, pure motion. It clearly moves the two beyond the confines of this world into another one known only to them. Thus, Linton can never successfully see into Catherine's heart, for he searches with the eyes of this world, and Catherine has already been transported out of it. Furthermore, he is fixed, while she and Heathcliff are in flight. Like Milton's Satan, the latter is part of the spirit of motion. Heathcliff has flown up from the underworld into a potentially blissful union with a Catherine inexplicably denied to him by a material world which judges him unsuitable.

In working out further contrasts, Emily Brontë introduced Gothic elements to demonstrate how far removed the interior story is from the frame world of reality. Whenever Lockwood enters Heathcliff's world, he enters a domain whose substance consists of pain, melodrama, horror, and terror. From the title itself to a description of the interior of the Heights, the atmosphere is reminiscent of the Gothic novels which Jane Austen had parodied in *Northanger Abbey* fifty years before. The oft-quoted scene in which Lockwood asleep in his coffin-like oak closet, dreams of an ice-cold hand which grasps his and which he rubs back and forth on the broken pane, is full of the sadism and bizarre effects implicit in the Gothic tale. Moreover, Heathcliff himself is as melodramatic and gloomy as the typical Gothic protagonist. Nelly Dean in fitting terms describes his actions when he hears of Catherine's death:

> He dashed his head against the knotted trunk; and, lifting up his eyes, howled, not like a man, but like a savage beast being goaded to death with knives and spears. I observed several splashes of blood about the bark of the tree, and his hand and forehead were both stained; ... (p. 176, Chapter XVI).*

Nelly asks herself on occasion: "'Is he a ghoul or a vampire?'" She wonders where he came from, this male witch, and she reveals her terror, her sense of shock at this goblin who loves like neither man nor beast.

Once we note these similarities to the Gothic novel, however, we must recognize that *Wuthering Heights* looks ahead to the late works of Dickens, and to Dostoyevsky and Hardy more than it looks back to Walpole, Mrs. Radcliffe, "Monk" Lewis, or Charles Maturin. Its excesses contain a potential of realism, and its protagonist brought down by forces he cannot understand or control has become a commonplace of existential literature.

The love between Heathcliff and Catherine Earnshaw is far removed indeed from earthly considerations, for they travel in spheres unrecognized by the mortals in the novel. Like D. H. Lawrence's "sacred lovers"—Birkin and Ursula Brangwen, for example—they climb to spiritual heights, while the love of others remains merely physical. To recognize this point is to begin to understand the kind of language Emily Brontë uses when they come together. At first, seemingly melodramatic, excessively mannered and affected, it becomes a clear attempt to move beyond normal, everyday conversation. Both lovers speak from a well of passion which calls for a language different from the ordinary; and thus, as Mark Schorer has remarked, the preponderance of violent verbs, tempestuous adjectives, and charged epithets, all attempting to exalt the power of human feeling. Through language, Lockwood and Nelly as well as the reader are instructed in the nature of a grand passion.

As part of their unique love, Heathcliff and Catherine become one body and one soul: they are inseparable both in life and death. Early in the novel, Catherine tells Nelly she loves Heathcliff not because of his handsomeness but because "'He's more myself than I am. Whatever our souls are made of, his and mine are the same; and Linton's is as different as a moonbeam from lightning, or frost from fire'" (p. 92, Chapter IX). Since Catherine and Heathcliff are one, to separate them is to kill them: both literally waste away from love-longing. Having Linton's child mortally weakens Catherine, for union with anyone but Heathcliff destroys her, just as he, too, weary of a now meaningless life, dies of anguish. As lovers of medieval intensity, they live only for love. Heathcliff compares his love with Edgar Linton's: "'If he loved with all the powers of his puny being, he couldn't love as much in eighty years as I could in a day.... It is not in him to be loved like me: how can she love in him what he has not?'" (pp. 158–159, Chapter XIV). Heathcliff claims supernatural qualities, as if comparing himself to a god, a being in whom love is so fierce that it explodes into altogether new dimensions.

After Catherine's death, Heathcliff goes to her grave and uncovers her coffin, planning to embrace her and to die, if he must, in her arms. Through his over-ruling passion, Heathcliff has clear affinities with the medieval lover who "dies" for his love. In this tradition, the love is both earthly and unearthly—a real woman becomes the object of a spiritual passion; actual consummation, at least theoretically, could destroy the relationship. Characteristic of the man's feeling is a love-longing that weakens and enervates him, destroying his health and his initiative in the public world. His love occupies the whole of his time, leaving no room for other activities, for he devotes his entire life, as would a slave, to his mistress. Heathcliff's love fits into this tradition: possessed and obsessed by his attachment to Catherine Earnshaw, he becomes a slave to a grand, destructive passion.

Although Heathcliff's towering figure undoubtedly dominates the novel, neither he nor his relationship with Catherine is the whole of *Wuthering Heights*. After Catherine's death, the narrative shifts to young Cathy and young Linton, the childish lovers who are each the issue of a "bad" marriage, one that went against the laws of love. Linton is, of course, the opposite of Heathcliff: weak, effeminate, and sensitive, and, as such, the butt of his father's derision and sadism. Cathy, on the other hand, has characteristics of Heathcliff: she is untamed, tempestuous, frenetic. She is Heathcliff's daughter by temperament, as if her mother in conceiving her had imprinted Heathcliff's love upon the child. Linton is Heathcliff's burden both for having married Isabella Linton and for Catherine Earnshaw's failure to marry him. Young Linton, then, is a mockery of Heathcliff's own obsessions. More clearly than ever, we can see that the novel works on character contrasts: Heathcliff has a son approximating Edgar Linton, and Catherine has a daughter resembling Heathcliff. The roles are completely reversed: Heathcliff's sadism is now practiced by young Cathy, and Edgar Linton's compliance by young Linton.

As Richard Chase has remarked, children dominate *Wuthering Heights*; only Heathcliff and Linton become mature. Isabella is a childbride, fitting into the pattern of women who after marrying for romantic notions never grow up; Dora Spenlow of *David Copperfield* and Amelia Sedley of *Vanity Fair* are contemporary examples. Hindley is an inebriate who regresses into helpless childhood after his wife's death; then later, his son Hareton has the emotional reactions of a sullen boy, not those of a grown man. Similarly, Catherine Earnshaw dies almost a child (herself giving birth to another child), not having developed into womanhood, her love for Heathcliff retaining the fierceness and blindness of a young girl's. Then the two childish lovers themselves, young Cathy and young Linton, fit into the cycle, to be completed by the union between young Cathy and Hareton, also two very youthful and immature lovers. Their wooing, in turn, is that of two children, filled as it is with the taunts of young Cathy and the sullen affection and morose sympathy of Hareton. The latter's awkwardness and social gracelessness are an obvious throwback to young Heathcliff, although Cathy, despite her condescending manner, is capable of both compassion and decency. Once she is satisfied that she has impressed Hareton, the union can take place on an equal basis. The foundation for a healthy marriage has been laid, and Heathcliff, now lacking all energy and direction, acquiesces; for the world of children's love can no longer engage even his wrath. As Heathcliff dies, the Heights are purged, and normality returns, in the form of an acceptable love union. The novel that began with Heathcliff clawing and biting amidst the Earnshaws, and then defying Fate and Fortune in a quest to attain love, ends with a typically "healthy" Victorian denouement: a happy marriage between two childish people who nevertheless have the right instincts to bring mutal completion. The novel concludes on a note of domesticity and peaceful balance, with the children in firm control.

Except for Edgar Linton, who is peripheral to the main thrust of the narrative, Heathcliff is, then, the sole adult in a children's world, a kind of devil amidst angels. Furthermore, he is the sole active personality in the novel; everyone else is acted upon. His position as mover gives him the flexibility and mobility that make him seem a devilish giant—a huge figure from the world of injustice, of which he in turn had been a victim—moving among pygmies. Similarly, Heathcliff seems blacker than black, for his darkness (he is a Prince of Darkness) is exaggerated when contrasted with the whiteness of others. As in several Gothic novels, the deployment of images of dark and light emphasizes the theme of innocence (child) versus experience (adult), with Heathcliff's dark tones indicating him as a figure of repression. His scowl and sullenness seem to have originated in areas into which others cannot reach, a backwash of diabolism, a swamp of mental illness and physical wretchedness. Heathcliff hovers physically over the entire novel: everyone acts to please or displease him, while he acts as *he* pleases.

Emily Brontë built into the novel a "moral conscience" for Heathcliff in the form of the "frame" narrators, Lockwood and Nelly Dean, both of whom become the norm by which Heathcliff can be measured. Without the stability of the narrators, the world of *Wuthering Heights* would hardly differ from that in the youthful tales of Gondal and Angria, lacking as many of these stories did any organized sense of morality, sin, or conscience. Heathcliff would stride through the novel much as the heroes and villains of the *juvenilia*, with nothing to impede them but their own mistakes. The narrators, however, provide a society, or at least an alternative to life at the Heights.

Next to Heathcliff, Lockwood rightly seems fair and slight, a representative from the civilized world coming to grips with an undomesticated and untamed animal. His reasonableness constantly clashes with Heathcliff's tempestuousness, as much as earlier Nelly Dean's Christian precepts had clashed with the headlong paganism of Catherine Earnshaw. While both narrators are instructed in the forms of intense love, in comparison their own feelings appear ineffective and impotent. Against the violence of the tale, they provide order; against hate and sadism, they offer Christian love; against the storm, they suggest calm. Nelly Dean, in particular—her prosaic name is itself an index to her character—tries to explain the ways of God to the Devil, and is tolerated only because Heathcliff recognizes that her advice is harmless and insignificant. Her feelings and Lockwood's are transcended by the unearthly power of Heathcliff, as the latter also transcends the power to love of a typical male, Edgar Linton or Jane Austen's Darcy, for example. As a transcendent power, Heathcliff has the vigor and stature of a god (father) and a devil (father and lover); in both roles, for good or ill he sweeps all before him. Nevertheless, he has to pay the penalty for losing Catherine to Edgar Linton: he must remain wild; unlike Lovelace, he is not to be tamed by love.

Emily Brontë speculates that Heathcliff's attitudes are the result of his unsympathetic treatment in childhood. Unattractive in appearance and uncouth in temperament, he becomes the butt of the other children, particularly of Hindley Earnshaw. As a foundling, Heathcliff is an intruder upon the Earnshaw's hospitality, and he is made to suffer because of his strangeness. Unable to enter into the family, especially after the death of old Mr. Earnshaw, he chooses defiance over acquiescence. With a will toward power, he stays outside and plots revenge without regard for personal welfare or comfort. He extends his hate to all except Catherine, who reaches out her sympathy to this strange boy. Even Heathcliff's name—he is christened after a son who had died in childhood—is that of someone who partakes of another world, into which he is forced back by circumstances. Already established in his childhood is one of the basic contrasts that run through the entire novel, that between the Other World and This World.

However, can a Heathcliff be explained simply by means of a struggling, unhappy childhood? Is he not in reality closer to Hardy's Mayor of Casterbridge, Henchard—whose character is his fate—than to a naturalistic protagonist whose environment determines his nature? Like a Greek tragic figure, Heathcliff is what he is: the elements of his greatness (his will to power) contain as well as his flaw (his overweening passion), and he is unable to escape himself. What keeps Heathcliff from becoming a tragic hero is of course his ignobleness and disagreeableness; he is not sympathetic, unless we confuse his strength with virtue. Closer to a melodramatic hero than a tragic protagonist, Heathcliff nevertheless contains the immoderation and excesses of the Greek hero and gains our temporary, grudging admiration for his defiance of what will eventually doom him.

Nonetheless, the contrast between Childhood and Adulthood once established swells throughout the narrative, beginning with Heathcliff's own childhood among the Earnshaws and then extending into the second generation, in which he imposes the same harshness on young Linton, Cathy, and Hareton that was practiced on him. Particularly in his treatment of Hareton Earnshaw, Heathcliff attempts to strike back at Hindley, but here the motivation is somewhat weak, for after Catherine Linton's death, Heathcliff's virulence is not convincing. True, he rightly hates the Lintons, but his intense persecution of Hindley and then Hareton is excessive. His reduction of Hindley to a penniless and shapeless heap is part of a revenge *outside* his love for Catherine. His treatment of Hindley and Hindley's son is part of a motivation Emily Brontë cannot explain simply by his childhood; for it partakes of the self-destructive, accumulated hatred that makes Heathcliff seem a devil, or a savage from another world.

In Hareton, Heathcliff has a boy whom he systematically enslaves and whose spirit he tries to break, and yet Hareton is at least one part Heathcliff: an outcast, unwanted, sullen, uneducated, revengeful, socially inept, and in love with someone who seems unattainable. The pattern has come full circle; Heathcliff's persecution of Hareton is like the persecution of his alter ego. So strong is his spirit of destruction that he has no sympathy even for himself.

In trying to crush Hareton—for whom he retains a spark of sympathy and understanding—Heathcliff displays attitudes that find no motivation in rational thought. Therefore, to treat *Wuthering Heights* as a realistic novel is to court difficulties. Too much is uncharted and too much unaccounted for in the novel. The motivation moves upon different planes, either deep in the unconscious or else on some transcendental level which analysis cannot reach because reason is no longer a factor.

In several ways, then, *Wuthering Heights* is less a novel than a dramatic poem in which flights of imagination replace analysis, and transcendental language supplants the prose of the realistic novel. The vocabulary is an index not only to the content but to the genre itself. The language is that of the elements—Heathcliff is described as a storm, living as he does in the tumult of a tempest. The language also evokes wild animals, fire, everything that would transcend normal human relationships and raise (or lower) them to a huge abstract conflict in which Heaven and Hell themselves seem at war. Like the dramatic poem which it approximates, *Wuthering Heights* is intensely dramatic, perhaps at times melodramatic. Similarly, like a dramatic poem, *Wuthering Heights* depends less on a realistically conceived chain of events than on a certain atmosphere in which intense conflicts transpire.

If we compare (say) *Pride and Prejudice* with *Wuthering Heights*, we can readily see the differences between the "realistic" novel and the novel conceived like a dramatic or epic poem. As we have seen, Jane Austen's characters are concerned with dignity, breeding, and gentility—all the components of what we call manner; her irony is directed at those who wander ever so little from the expectations of society. Even her heroines must be redirected toward balance and judgment. Furthermore, her males—like Mr. Knightley, Colonel Brandon, even Darcy and Edmund Bertram—have the aspect and manner more of fathers than of passionate lovers, or at least of older men who are fatherly and understanding. They take the heroine into tow; they do not probe the depth of her passions.

Only thirty-five years after the publication of *Pride and Prejudice*, the picture has been radically altered. To live like Heathcliff in a perpetual heat of passion and revenge would be physically and psychologically impossible for a character who requires normal amounts of food, rest, and peace of mind. Furthermore, Heathcliff is the opposite of genteel, well-bred, and dignified. Rather than letting his reason command while his passions obey, he is obsessed by passion while his reason lags. Moreover, he hardly provides a fatherly figure—as a father, he is sadistically hateful—and he recognizes few social norms as necessary for his own or others' behavior. In the inner story of *Wuthering Heights*, there is no clear sense of a real world. Few of the daily events which make up life are apparent; none of the daily amenities are recognized. People live within different dimensions, in more heroic terms than the novel rooted in realism usually allows for. Thus the sense of swirl, of violence, of the passions of tragic drama. Up to *Wuthering Heights*—and for half a century after—the serious novel had been muted, dealing more with tones and colors than with the full breadth of emotion. Only Richardson had touched on this ground, but compared with Heathcliff, his Lovelace and Mr. B are effeminate dwarfs beside an epical figure. Not until Hardy's Henchard was there to be a major protagonist of Heathcliff's intensity and headlong drive for self-destruction.

Not only Heathcliff but also the women—Catherine Earnshaw, young Cathy, Isabella Linton—fall almost completely outside the terms of realism, for they exhibit passions which go beyond those society deems "normal." Clearly, the idea of the conventional heroine, as developed by the eighteenth-century novelists as well as by Jane Austen and Dickens, was no longer acceptable to Emily Brontë. When she wanted a conventional woman, she created Nelly Dean, who provides distance and calm from the *outside* and has little effect indeed upon her charges either as children or adults. No more than fixed and static matter herself, she has no control over the spirit and motion which characterize the other members of the Heights. Moreover, compared to their experience (their involvement in passionate life), her innocence makes her a spectator in an emotional world and precludes her chances of understanding them. She can only report and judge, and remain safely within her own world, which does not recognize the intensity of a Heathcliff or a Catherine Earnshaw.

In the story itself, she has her counterpart in Edgar Linton, and his unfortunate and unhappy life is that of a man who tries to be average in a world that defies normality. His is the measure of correct conduct, and yet rather than being a romantic hero, he is stripped of all strength, made to seem effeminate and emotionally ineffective. A virtual cripple among giants, Edgar Linton is part of a group from which only Nelly Dean is able to extricate herself. She can judge while Edgar must act, and therein lies her opportunity to save herself. Even Lockwood, despite a certain worldliness that distinguishes him from Nelly, would be smashed had he been a participant in this turbulent world. He is able to survive this world simply because he receives it in fragments; were he to have received it all at once, like Edgar, he would be staggered and crushed by forces outside his powers of understanding. As part of the frame, Lockwood and Nelly Dean, like Conrad's Marlow in *Lord Jim*, are at a safe remove from events that are enervating and destructive.

In *Wuthering Heights*, everybody shouts. The very winds which whip around the Heights are partially generated by its inhabitants; and the violence of the tumult is the fury of their expression. Gothic terror is now manifest not in ghostly figures who suffer from hallucinatory visions but in passionate people whose lives contain chaotic desires. In this respect, Heathcliff embodies Emily Brontë's vision of the male principle—a composite perhaps of her dominating father, her dissolute brother Branwell, and also of the violent Gondal and Angria characters. More a force or the naked unconscious of a man than a real being, Heathcliff is outside sin and guilt, as are the other characters in contact with him. They live as if they were original man and woman making their own terms without the dictates of a god. The world of *Wuthering Heights*, then, can be seen as a kind of anti-Paradise in which unhappiness rather than happiness is the by-product of human relationships. The arrangement of this anti-Paradise is the working of the Devil; Eve's temptation has indeed infected her progeny, and love is more an agony than a sacred feeling. By the fact that nature itself is cold and bleak life is already partially defined. The demons clash with the fair and innocent, and both are destroyed in a world that gives way completely to the anarchy and chaos of savage passion.

A Prince of Darkness, a powerful principle of blackness, a vision of maleness as it appeared to a virtually isolated authoress, Heathcliff sweeps all before him in his amoral quest for position and love in a world that has made him an outcast. Not for several years was this kind of character on a major scale to turn up in English fiction. While certain of his "underground" qualities appear in minor Dickens characters—Dolge Orlick, Steerforth, and Bradley Headstone, for example—not until the end of the century, with Hardy's Henchard, was a man to defy the universe and destroy himself by virtue of his uncontrollable passions. When a figure like Heathcliff re-enters fiction in the twentieth century, in D.H. Lawrence's novels, he smolders rather than burns; toned down, he appears as a groom or a gamekeeper or even as an animal. He still stalks passionate women, but his greatest attraction is silence instead of violence. Nevertheless, the successors of Heathcliff remain dark, either in appearance or spirit. Mysterious men, they too reject the rewards of a mechanistic world in order to enjoy the rites of passionate love.

Wuthering Heights, which was published in 1847 as having been written by an "Ellis Bell," the pseudonym Emily had already used for the publication of some of her poetry, was not well or sympathetically received. Critics accustomed to Jane Austen's realism, Scott's romanticism, and the early work of Dickens misunderstood and misinterpreted a novel that diverged so far from early Victorian conventions. Even *Vanity Fair*, is certainly less of an anomaly than *Wuthering Heights*. We remember that even *Pickwick Papers* (1837) found many admirers who thought it unfit for family reading, and that *The Ordeal of Richard Feverel* (1859) was considered the work of a wicked man. Sexuality aside, the wildness and violence of *Wuthering Heights* put off the reader, and the novel, carefully wrought as it has been discovered to be, was deemed chaotic and confused.

At about the same time Emily Brontë was writing *Wuthering Heights*, her sister Anne was about to begin *The Tenant of Wildfell Hall*, and her sister Charlotte, having completed a short novel, *The Professor*, was working on *Jane Eyre*. Although *Jane Eyre* contains several of the unconventional elements of *Wuthering Heights*, it was a great success shortly after publication; and Charlotte Brontë as "Currer Bell," gained the fame denied to both Emily and Anne. In all Charlotte wrote four novels—*The Professor* (published posthumously in 1857), *Jane Eyre* (1847), *Shirley* (1849), and *Villette* (1853)—but *Jane Eyre* was by far the most popular. On the surface, it is easy to see why *Jane Eyre* succeeded while *Wuthering Heights* failed. Like Emily, she was working with explosive material, but unlike her sister, she presented a temporized Heathcliff in the figure of Rochester and a toned-down Catherine Linton in the person of Jane. Further, while Jane is freer with her passions than the age could fully approve, nevertheless her love domesticates Rochester and leads to happiness, not to destruction.

In the Preface to her first novel, *The Professor,* Charlotte declared, like George Eliot later, that she was interested in a certain kind of "democratic realism." She talks about "real living men" and asserts that her hero "should share Adam's doom, and drain throughout life a mixed and moderate cup of enjoyment." She then admits that publishers were not interested in this kind of realism but instead would have liked "something more imaginative and poetical—something more consonant with a highly-wrought fancy, with a taste for pathos, with sentiments more tender, elevated, unworldly." She then wonders: "Men in business are usually thought to prefer the real; on trial the idea will be often found fallacious: a passionate preference for the wild, wonderful, and thrilling—the strange, startling, and harrowing—agitates divers souls that show a calm and sober surface." Accordingly, once she could not find a publisher for *The Professor,* she turned to another kind of novel in which the "imaginative" and the "poetical" were intermixed with the realistic.

It was precisely these poetical effects in *Jane Eyre* that George Henry Lewes, the critic and biographer, labeled melodramatic and objectionable.* In her answer, Charlotte Brontë repeated her remarks from the Preface to *The Professor,* claiming that Nature and Truth—her sole guides—were insufficient, that she "restrained imagination, eschewed romance, repressed excitement; over-bright colouring, too ... [she] avoided and sought to produce something which should be soft, grave, and true." In another exchange of letters, she rejected Lewes' suggestion that Jane Austen should provide a model of restraint for her. She repeated that restraint and shrewdness are not enough; one must follow one's own inspiration:

> When writers write best, or, at least, when they write most fluently, an influence seems to awaken in them, which becomes their master—which will have its own way—putting out of view all behests but its own, dictating certain words, and insisting on their being used whether vehement or measured in their nature;

new-moulding characters, giving unthought-of turns to incidents, rejecting carefully elaborated old ideas, and suddenly creating and adopting new ones.

Jane Austen, she finds, has created an "accurate daguerrotyped portrait of a commonplace face; a carefully fenced, highly cultivated garden with neat borders and delicate flowers; but no glance of a bright, vivid physiognomy, no open country, no fresh air, no blue hill, no bonny beck."

We should not expect *Jane Eyre* to hark back to Jane Austen's novels any more than *Wuthering Heights* did; rather, it looks ahead in 1847 to the next great woman novelist George Eliot, who was not to publish her first novel for another twelve years. Charlotte Brontë, in her realization that man's hopes must first be chastened by ill success, was foreshadowing George Eliot's own treatment of fortune tempered by adversity. Both authors agreed that the individual worthy of consideration would mature under adversity and that misfortune was a test of his worth. Thus, Jane Eyre does not buckle under ill treatment, but instead grows in stature as she defies persecution. Similarly, Dorothea Brooke *(Middlemarch)* matures after her first marriage and gains in sympathy and human understanding. If the "soul has strength," Charlotte Brontë was to say later in *Shirley*, "it conquers and rules thereafter."

Furthermore, her heroines determine their fortunes less by the dictates of society than by their own wishes. Their choice of mate, as well as their choice of circumstances, is based on personal feeling, regardless of what society expects. Jane Austen's heroines, we saw, had far less freedom of movement, and when they attempted to stretch their wings the author's irony brought them back. Restricted mobility, together with certain constrictions in matters of love, binds every Jane Austen heroine to an acceptable social standard. Unlike Charlotte Brontë's heroines and, later, George Eliot's, they do not pursue their husbands; instead, they wait for the man to come who recognizes their innate worth despite their superficial flaws: Elizabeth's prejudice and hasty judgment, Emma's vanity and immaturity, Fanny Price's insipidity, and Catherine Morland's foolishness. Although their passions on occasion are almost uncontrollable, Charlotte Brontë's chief heroines contain few, if any, flaws: Jane Eyre, for instance, is a model young woman, sympathetic, capable of great love and devotion, full of common sense and understanding and loyal to those who have befriended her. Even her appearance, like Fanny Price's, improves through love.

Similarly, as Jane flowers under the influence of Rochester's passion, so is he purified by the love of a good woman. In *Wuthering Heights*, it is clear that Heathcliff could have been tamed by Catherine's love had she united herself with him, for much of his violence results from her failure to defy society and marry him. The one person who could have domesticated this feral creature is unable to rise to his level of love, and by rejecting him, Catherine leaves his love free to turn into hate and revenge. Jane, on the other hand, by "taming" Rochester prevents the potential violence in him from turning into bitterness, and by providing in her steady love a prop for his passion, draws off the excess onto herself and thus neutralizes him.

Love in both novels provides a meeting ground where personal flaws can, therefore, be minimized and passions given some outlet. Heathcliff recognizes that love transcends all difficulties, including the deficiencies of his birth, but his recognition of the transcendental power of love is not sufficient to carry Catherine outside the demands of social conformity and propriety. Jane Eyre, however, is willing to sacrifice everything for love; her unwillingness to compromise herself in an affair with Rochester is more a matter of personal prudence than a submission to social demands. With this combination of daring and prudence, Jane is able to divide and conquer: Rochester is freed from his mad wife and enabled to marry her.

Clearly, then, Jane's passion is powerful and compelling, not at all the kind of controlled feeling found in a Jane Austen heroine, whose good sense forced moderation even upon her ability to love. The conflict is indeed real in Jane Eyre, for she is almost ready to succumb when Rochester pleads with her to come away:

> ... while he spoke my very conscience and reason turned traitors against me, and charged me with crime in resisting him. They spoke almost as loud as Feeling: and that clamoured wildly. 'Oh, comply!' it said. 'Think of his misery; think of his danger—look at his state when left alone; remember his headlong nature; consider the recklessness following on despair—soothe him; save him; love him; tell him you love him and will be his. Who in the world cares for *you?* or who will be injured by what you do?' (pp. 369–70).

Rochester seizes her, devouring her "with his flaming glances," but sanity, not this temporary madness, dominates Jane's decision. Rochester, however, is fully aware of her true feeling. On that topic, she is not reticent.

In a letter of 1839 to her friend Ellen Nussey, Charlotte revealed that Jane's tenacity extended to the author herself, who had turned down the marriage proposal of her friend's brother: "I felt that though I esteemed, though I had a kindly leaning towards him, because he is an amiable and well-disposed man, yet I had not, and could not have, that intense attachment which would make me willing to die for him; and, if ever I marry, it must be in that light of adoration that I will regard my husband." And in a poem, "Passion," dated December 12, 1841, she wrote: "Some have won a wild delight, / By daring wilder sorrow; / Could I gain thy love tonight, / I'd hazard death tomorrow." In a later stanza, she wrote: "No—my will shall yet control / Thy will, so high and free. / And love shall tame the haughty soul—/ yes—tenderest love for me."

The various elements of *Jane Eyre* extend back into the very substance of Charlotte Brontë's life, and, in point of fact, the novel was realized in several essential parts by 1839 or 1840, the time of the above letter and poem. In addition, *Jane Eyre*, more than any other of Charlotte's novels, finds its roots in her *juvenilia*, in the windings and unwindings of her Angria tales, as well as in her early reading. The Byronic Rochester is derived, in large part, from Arthur Augustus Adrian Wellesley, Duke of Zamorna and Emperor of Angria, around whom the young Charlotte had embroidered the heroic actions of a muscular Childe Harold. She may have come across the situation concerning the bigamous intentions of a basically good man in a story by Sheridan Le Fanu published in 1839. Rochester's mad wife derives from Lady Zenobia Ellrington, who appears in Charlotte's first love story, and who also appears, a composite of nobility and shrieking wildness, in the Angrian cycle. As Fannie Ratchford has pointed out, Bertha Mason Rochester is only partially derived from Zenobia, however; she is also found in "The Green Dwarf," Charlotte's adaptation in 1833 of Scott's Ivanhoe.*

The idea of a hidden mad wife may also have come from Mrs. Radcliffe's Gothic novel, *A Sicilian Romance* (1790).

Other Angrian figures reappear in *Jane Eyre* in one guise or another, including Rochester's ward Adèle and her mother, Céline Varens, Rochester's former mistress. Outside the Angria stories, even Helen Burns, Jane's sympathetic friend who dies of consumption, is modeled on Charlotte's sister Maria, who, also tubercular, died young and unfulfilled. The affair between Rochester and Jane follows the Angria pattern set by Zamorna and becomes a test of Jane's moral values. Unprotected by family or friends, Jane, supported only by her untried principles, must face the temptation of Rochester, just as Mina Laury in the Angrian cycle must confront a tempestuous Zamorna. But while Mina could not resist the forceful Zamorna and succumbs to his attraction, Jane honors her principles despite temporary pain.

While the love affair is obviously the most compelling section of the book, it is by no means the whole of the long novel. Not unlike the opening scenes of *David Copperfield* (to appear in two years), the early sequences of *Jane Eyre* show, among other things, the injustice of the adult world toward children. *Jane Eyre* fits loosely into the group of apprenticeship novels represented by *David Copperfield, Pendennis, Great Expectations, The Ordeal of Richard Feverel,* and in the present century by *Sons and Lovers* and *A Portrait of the Artists as a Young Man,* "loosely" because Jane herself lacks the mobility and flexibility of the typical apprenticeship hero or heroine. As a woman in a restrictive society, she can develop only within severe limitations. Her decisions must, perforce, be few, and they must also be conclusive, for within such restrictions there are few chances for her to resolve a bad choice. Like Flora in Conrad's *Chance,* Jane must make one basic decision, and this will either give her happiness or completely ruin her life. In making this choice, however, she has no other standard than the principles gained in her early apprenticeship to life. When Flora, in *Chance,* chooses Captain Anthony over her father, she makes the sole decision that leads not only to happiness but also to sanity. When Jane Eyre refuses the temptation of an elopement with Rochester—a temptation made particularly attractive by her strong love and alien position—she enters the central part of her ordeal, which must be successfully overcome before she gains her reward, a severely chastened and humbled Rochester.

Within the terms of her limited apprenticeship, Jane Eyre suffers all the indignities of her "low" position, in terms of both class and money. As in Dickens' novels of this kind, injustice consists of the stultification of one's natural feelings in the face of superior authority, be it David Copperfield with Mr. Murdstone or Sissy Jupe with Mr. Gradgrind or Pip with Miss Havisham. Although more civilized than Heathcliff, Jane appears to Mrs. Reed as Heathcliff must have appeared to the Earnshaws: undesirable, a burden, sullen, and socially backward. Clearly, she can gain self-respect and dignity only by entering a world in which she must prove herself.

The scenes with Mrs. Reed in the early pages have the same texture of sadistic cruelty that characterizes many nineteenth-century apprenticeship novels. Jane's experience in the red-room, with its overtones of Gothic terror, is indicative of her entire existence with Mrs. Reed and her spoiled, degenerate children. Charlotte Brontë helped develop the now familiar theme of the basically healthy outcast girl who is persecuted by the warped, depraved children born to privilege. Jane's hysteria in the room is a manifestation of her frustration, her only way of protest against a life that on every side restricts her development. These boundaries placed around the growing spirit—to be repeated by Dickens in Gradgrind's principles of utilitarian education and by Meredith in Sir Austin Feverel's system—are also manifest in Mr. Brocklehurst's Lowood Institution. There, every girl is an outcast, and Jane's alienation from the cruel "norm," no longer singular, does not prevent her coming to terms with herself. And although the sadism and cruelty of Mrs. Reed's are continued in the school, Jane, under the tender influence of Helen Burns, is able to achieve the mental freedom necessary for moral judgment.

Nevertheless, the repressive atmosphere of Lowood is particularly manifest in the treatment accorded Helen Burns. These scenes, as realistic as Jane's later ones with Rochester are melodramatic and wildly romantic, illustrate that non-conformity to nature leads to spiritual, and even actual, death. Mr. Brocklehurst states with all his authority: "'Yes, but we are not to conform to nature: I wish these girls to be the children of Grace....'" Jane is chastened, even by Helen Burns, for thinking too much of human love. Her friend tells her that a person has other resources which derive from God and which give strength under adversity. But Jane, while calmed by her friend's ability to rise above her immediate circumstances, must follow her heart, which leads her to seek human love and understanding, while rejecting authority and repression.

Central to the apprenticeship novel is a strong character around whom the entire narrative can be structured. This character must be of sufficient substance to sustain the weight of what is usually a lengthy narrative and also to make coherent what would otherwise be merely a string of loose episodes. In *Great Expectations*, Dickens faced this problem and successfully resolved it by severely testing Pip, who significantly changes as the novel proceeds. At all times, he has human shape and human responses. The fault in Charlotte Brontë's presentation of Jane Eyre is clearly her failure to allow change. Jane grows only chronologically, not emotionally or mentally. She is inflexibly right from the beginning; the world she defies at Mrs. Reed's is an unjust world, which she also defies at Mr. Brocklehurst's school. Later, she rejects St. John Rivers' offer of marriage, as before she rejected bondage and suppression. Her oneness of character, then, is both her strength and her fault. As a support, her singleness of purpose and knowledge of self give her moral force as well as social judgment; as a weakness, her singularity forbids the flexibility, the human flaws, and the moral confusion which are part of a truly created character. Charlotte Brontë talks a great deal about the self—especially its demands upon reason—but only rarely allows Jane to face honestly *all* aspects of it.

Jane's common sense, awareness of justice, and equity of temperament make her seem a rationalist in a world of madmen and madwomen. And it is precisely this reasonableness which defines her, despite the currents of great passion which run beneath the surface. Unlike Heathcliff, who lives only fleetingly in the reasonable world and chooses to dwell in an underground hell of passion, Jane lives by her wits without ever forgoing her deeper feelings. She is proper, relatively careful, and temperate even when her heart tells her to be abandoned. These qualities see her through a world which punishes the chaotic and chastens the disordered. Reason, qualified by a strong acceptance of Earth, marks Jane's major decisions, as later it was to mark Dorothea Brooke's choice of Will Ladislaw in *Middlemarch* and Clara Middleton's preference for Vernon Whitford in *The Egoist*. In a letter written late in his life (March 6, 1888), George Meredith revealed certain assumptions which also seem to have been those accepted by Charlotte Brontë forty years earlier. Meredith wrote:

> I have written always with the perception that there is no life but of the spirit; that the concrete is really the shadowy; yet that the way to spiritual life lies in the complete unfolding of the creature, not in the nipping of his passions. An outrage to Nature helps to extinguish his light. To the flourishing of the spirit, then, through the healthy exercise of the senses (to Mrs. J.B. Gilman, *Letters*, II, 409).

The novel becomes, in point of fact, the unfolding of Jane Eyre's spirit, from Lowood Institution, to Thornfield, to the conflict with St. John Rivers (who restricts Jane as much as had Mrs. Reed and Mr. Brocklehurst), to Jane's final reward for a sensible choice, her marriage with Rochester. The novel gains its unity more from this thematic element—the conflict between the character's quest for the life of the spirit and the forces which would thwart her—then it does from the presence of Jane herself. In this way it is unlike the typical apprenticeship novel which is usually built on episodes loosely held together by the hero's activities. Thus, *Tom Jones*, the prototype of this kind of novel, consists of a series of chapters which cohere obviously because the activities of Tom hold them together. *Jane Eyre* contains elements similar to those in *Tom Jones* and its successors, but it also rests on a more restrictive philosophical basis, the unfolding of Jane's spirit as she rebels against the repressions that society and personal relationships impose upon her.

In her quest for personal salvation, Jane communes with God and Nature; with the latter particularly she acquires strength. In episode after episode, she returns to Earth, which, as the Romantic poets had indicated, was a source of strength, a personal way to resurrection of the spirit. As Meredith was later to show in *Richard Feverel*, the rain of the storm is a form of baptism and the Earth a life-giver. As Jane wanders lost and isolated,

Charlotte Brontë comments: "Nature seemed to me benign and good; I thought she loved me, outcast as I was; and I, who from man could anticipate only mistrust, rejection, insult, clung to her with filial fondness. Tonight, at least, I would be her guest—as I was her child: my mother would lodge me without money and without price" (p. 377). Even in the recurrent reference to the great chestnut-tree, riven and black at the upper trunk but firm and strong at the base and roots, there is the intertwining connection between man and Nature: the tree is a simplified image of Jane and Rochester, seemingly split, with the sap no longer running between them, but nevertheless joined in feeling and memory, their roots also, so to speak, intermixed and inseparable.

Jane Eyre's quest for joy in a world which tries to deny her her rights derives from Charlotte Brontë's pro-feminist attitude, a continuing theme in *Shirley* (1849) and *Villette* (1853). *Shirley* is a plea for equality, justice, and status for the woman, while *Villette* in its love passages demonstrates that the woman's lack of subservience can create admiration and respect. In *Jane Eyre*, the heroine's outrage at Mrs. Reed's injustice becomes transformed into an outraged refusal to be made chattel by either Rochester, whom she loves, or St. John Rivers, whom she does not. She demands the right of choice: to choose her surroundings, occupation, friends, and mate, and to be able to reject those who would deny her this right. When these beliefs come under test, Charlotte Brontë becomes steely, and to this degree her Jane Eyre, with her deep feelings and passionate emotions, is not cousin-german to Elizabeth Bennet of *Pride and Prejudice*. It was perhaps this manifestation of masculine toughness that George Henry Lewes found disturbing in *Jane Eyre* and *Shirley*, for Charlotte Brontë answered him with some indignation:

> You will, I know, keep measuring me by some standard of what you deem becoming to my sex; where I am not what you consider graceful you will condemn me. All mouths will be open against that first chapter [of *Shirley*], and that first chapter is as true as the Bible, nor is it exceptionable. Come what will, I cannot, when I write, think always of myself and of what is elegant and charming in femininity; it is not on those terms, or with such ideas, I ever took pen in hand: and if it is only on such terms my writing will be tolerated, I shall pass away from the public and trouble it no more (November 1, 1849).

The chief area in which Jane Eyre has choice involves Rochester and St. John Rivers, both men of strong temperament who are capable of mental cruelty when their desires are thwarted. The throwback to Richardson's *Clarissa* is evident, although Clarissa's need to choose between the dissolute Lovelace and the sexually repugnant Solmes leaves her no room for maneuver. In each relationship, Jane must pass through a dark night of the soul before she can decide what to do, and in each relationship her choice involves bringing to bear a strong personal will upon an almost equally strong will. In each instance, the temptation is to give herself up to a stronger force, to Rochester's love, to St. John's sense of duty and devotion. However, like Lucy Snowe in *Villette*, Jane must return from the nadir of despair and indecision in order to assert the need for personal happiness.

The relationship that St. John Rivers offers Jane is of a completely different kind, providing a marked contrast with Rochester's. As his name implies, St. John wants to be a saint, although he forgets that most saints preserve their celibacy. However, the marriage tie he offers is almost a celibate union, based as it is on duty, sacrifice, discipline, eventual martyrdom. St. John wants a business partner, not a wife, while Jane, who has continually sought love, wants a husband, hence her offer to accompany him as a sister, a relationship which would not involve love. Jane, it is made clear, does not resist duty or sacrifice; she resists a cold union which would carry her back to the episodes with Mrs. Reed or Mr. Brocklehurst. "'He [St. John] prizes me as a soldier would a good weapon; and that is all.'"

St. John, nevertheless, retains a strong hold on her until she receives the mysterious call from Rochester, his painful voice eerily calling out for help from the hills beyond Marsh Glen. The miracle of love, as mysterious as witchcraft or superstition, is apparent, and Jane is no longer tormented by her decision. She flees to Rochester's aid, both because she loves him and because he needs help. "I [Jane] broke from St. John, who had followed, and would have detained me. It was *my* time to assume ascendancy. *My* powers were in play, and in force. I told him to forbear question or remark; I desired him to leave me: I must, and would be alone. He obeyed at once" (p. 490). Love gives her power, will, and strength. Her energies are now focused upon her own salvation as well as upon Rochester's. Unlike Catherine Earnshaw, Jane domesticates her male and makes him human.

Rochester's cruelty is a composite of frustration and desire, his previous attempt at love now mocked by a mad wife in the eaves of Thornfield and his present desires overruled by a residual propriety and gentlemanliness. His actions, accordingly, are more passionate and tempestuous than reason would dictate, and he becomes a "terrible" man when his will is circumscribed. Rochester needs the love of a good woman to cleanse him, for in marrying Bertha, he had fallen through ambition and lust into a loveless union. Although he has had several mistresses—his ward, Adèle, perhaps is his child by a French mistress—yet Jane, the first "good" woman in his life, seemingly is not to be his. The result is a volcanic passion which contrasts with the repressed but equally deep passion that corrodes St. John. A figure of storm, Rochester, like Heathcliff in this respect, has been foiled in love. And all the elements of storm that would ordinarily be dissipated in a happy union remain dammed within.

Rochester's penance for sensuality and pride is his frustration, precisely as Jane Eyre's ordeal is alienation from all societal props. But since Rochester has sinned against virtually the entire order of the universe, his penance must be substantial: his loss of sight and a hand are the measure of his debt. Once it is paid, he is a free man, free to enjoy the fruits of a normal life, purified by his relationship with Jane. In risking his life to save the servants and in trying to help his mad wife in the fire at Thornfield Hall, he becomes a Christian gentleman, coming through an ordeal that physically debilitates him while spiritually strengthening him. Rochester repents, and, unlike Heathcliff, becomes humble:

> "Divine justice pursued its course; disasters came thick on me: I was forced to pass through the valley of the shadow of death. *His* chastisements are mighty; and one smote on me which has humbled me for ever.... I began [of late] to experience remorse, repentance; the wish for reconcilement to my Maker" (p. 521).

Adversity has strengthened both Rochester and Jane; and their love, the author indicates, will be the stronger for the barriers it had to overcome. Like her contemporaries, her sister Emily partially excepted, Charlotte Brontë believed that the divine order of the universe would somehow convey happiness after it had exacted its ordeal of pain. This romantic view of love was to hold for more than twenty-five years, until late-Victorian pessimism, in Hardy and others, demonstrated that there is no guarantee of happiness and that pain is the lot of the good as well as the evil man. At this point, courtship and marriage themselves no longer held the center of the novel, and someone like Rochester becomes a Henchard struggling to regain his identity before dying.

By the time of the second edition of *Jane Eyre*, Charlotte Brontë saw that her novel had been misunderstood by a small but influential body of readers, and that some answer was necessary to defend her original intentions. Dedicating the second edition of *Jane Eyre* to Thackeray, she attacked sham and pretense in society. "Conventionality is not morality. Self-righteousness is not religion. To attack the first is not to assail the last. To pluck the mask from the face of the Pharisee, is not to lift an impious hand to the Crown of Thorns." The sentiment is curiously not unlike D. H. Lawrence's seventy-five years later. She goes on to praise Thackeray as a man who has scrutinized and exposed imposture, as "the first social regenerator of the day ... who would restore to rectitude the warped system of things." Beneath the melodrama, then, Charlotte Brontë reveals herself as a strong moralist, and her decision to attack sham by giving women their rightful place in society was to lead, later, into the novels of Meredith and George Eliot and to the plays of Shaw, several of whose themes are well within the terms set by *Jane Eyre*, *Shirley*, and *Villette*.

* All references are to the Heather Edition of the Brontës' works (London: Allan Wingate, 1949).

* In his own novel, *Ranthorpe*, published in the same year as *Jane Eyre*, Lewes eschewed "poetical effects" for stereotyped characterization, homespun philosophizing, and a personal brand of melodrama.

Scott, we recognize, was for good or ill, of special significance to Charlotte. She exhorted her friend to "... read Scott alone; all novels after his are worthless." And, "... Scott exhibits a wonderful knowledge of human nature, as well as surprising skill in embodying his perceptions so as to enable others to become participators in that knowledge." Possibly, under Scott's influence, Charlotte was tempted to write Romances rather than Novels, for his presence can be felt throughout the melodramatic and intense love affair in the middle section of *Jane Eyre*, fraught as the affair is with frenzy and danger. However, even without Scott, Charlotte would probably have reached her own conclusions, influenced as she was by late-eighteenth- and early nineteenth-century Romantic poets and by Byron in particular.

S. DIANA NEILL

London by Gaslight

The rapidly changing social conditions in England during the first few decades of the Victorian era were reflected in the changing tastes of the novel-reading public. As a result of the Industrial Revolution the face of the country altered more in the next thirty years than it had done in the previous three hundred. Coaching inns and highwaymen disappeared as the grimy railways began to wind their way across the shires and counties, linking the sombre and monotonous industrial towns.

In London the delicate rose and grey architecture of elegant Regency streets and squares gave way to the encroachments of prison-like buildings and noisome alleys where dirty and malformed children screamed at their play. Corrosive fogs poured, chill and forbidding, along the Thames.

In 1807 Winsor, a German, first illumined Pall Mall with gas and with slow inevitability the murky atmosphere of the new industrialized London was stabbed at intervals by the flaring gas-jets, caged for safety, that threw their sinister shadows across dark lanes flanked by the pitiable hovels of the poor. Canaletto's London was swallowed up in the London of Dickens, where a motley cavalcade in new, unbecoming clothes cavorted along the twisting quasi-medieval streets and passages of the old town. Down by the thriving docks amongst the gin shops a hideously squalid population struggled fiercely for existence in the free-for-all tragi-comedy of unenlightened self-interest. Like a swiftly moving tide of grey scum the

From *A Short History of the English Novel.* © 1952 by The Macmillan Company.

tenement houses of the poor began to cover the few remaining fields and meadows in the heart of the city.

These dramatic changes came during the lifetime of Charles Dickens, and his books mirror the transformation. Born in 1812—a period between Trafalgar and Waterloo—Dickens was always able to look back through a romantic haze of tears and laughter to the colour and spaciousness and the splendours of an easier way of life than the 'hard times' in which he came to manhood. Long after the coming of the railways he remembered the old coaching inns with their fine napery, blazing log fires, good and ample fare—days when there seemed to be a magic in the keen frosty air and when life assumed the wholesome benevolence of Mr. Pickwick himself. But if Dickens's heart was warmed by atavistic memories of an older semi-feudal society, his genius was quickened by the other England that was taking its place. This was the industrial England of grim cities where the poor died, worn out by hardship and despair, and where the bright hopes of youth were eclipsed by drudgery and squalor.

The social upheaval which was going on made fortunes for the successful and swept away the unfortunate. It also brought into existence a new body of middle-class readers. The Reform Act of 1832 gave a semblance of power and therefore importance to the middle class that was prospering in commerce and industry, and during the next forty years this class was to become the arbiter of literary taste, at any rate so far as the novel was concerned. On the whole it was a self-satisfied but ignorant and insular public for whom Dickens and Thackeray wrote, eager for knowledge, prejudiced, indifferent to the claims of art and imagination, sentimental and inclined to enjoy displays of moral didacticism. It liked to see virtue rewarded and vice punished and insisted on having the line between them sharply drawn. Impatient of uncertainties, it disliked having its prejudices questioned, preferring to have them confirmed.

This ever-growing reading public was neither liberal nor catholic in its tastes. In fact it was distinctly provincial. But many readers, although impatient of idleness and eccentricity, were fascinated by fashionable society while outwardly despising it and were quite ready to enjoy stories of 'high life' so long as it was discredited.

In some ways the new reading public of the Victorian age resembled those who had welcomed Defoe a hundred and fifty years earlier. Like them, they were materialistic, eager for sensation, ready to learn and voracious in their appetites. A Victorian novelist had to be able to satisfy a multiplicity of tastes; he had to be a philosopher, humorist, psychologist, artist, to mingle slapstick and sentiment. Whether his medium was realism, fantasy, farce or pathos, he must be able to grip the imagination and entertain. Without exception the Victorian novelists were masters of the art of telling a story. Their serial methods might lead to lapses and repetition and were not conducive to fine art, but the story always gripped and the reader hurried on to find out the next turn in a narrative that was rarely content with a single thread but wove a coloured web of intrigue. In such fiction climaxes were dramatic, characters boldly outlined and the atmosphere tense with excitement.

Book-selling by the middle of the century had become a major industry in which not only were large fortunes made but power exercised as well. Between 1830 and 1850 the prices of books fell sharply, and cheap miscellanies and serial pamphlets brought literature into the hands of those from whom the relatively high cost of other publications had hitherto kept it. A new race of publishers grew up alongside the older Ballantynes, Murrays and Constables, and popular writers struggled with the new men for a fair share of the profits that book-selling to the million was beginning to bring. A successful novelist like George Eliot was able to refuse an offer of ten thousand pounds for the copyright of *Romola*.

Many of these new readers had no instinctive traditions, they were unintellectual but not unintelligent; often close observers and shrewd judges of human behaviour, they were, however, without self-criticism and unable to analyse their observations. They lacked the power to discover the laws that underlay their society, but they were keenly alive to its surface variations. Apt as these readers were to substitute judgment for understanding, it was far easier to make them feel than to make them think outside their conventional patterns. This is a possible explanation of the great popularity achieved by Dickens. He shared the limitations of his public; like his readers, he was a petty bourgeois; like them he allied quickness of native wit, keen observation and sentimentality to an interest in external characteristics. Like so many of his readers, he was a man of the town, of the New London. He sprang from the swift, rootless life of the London streets. He was an average nineteenth-century cockney; but he had genius.

A certain intolerance is inseparable from the rise of a new class to power, and the earnest, serious-minded Victorian was no exception. He was anxious to improve the world in his own way; he detested frivolity and sexual licence, especially in literature; and he desired to impose his own clear-cut prejudices on letters. Certain areas of human experience were strictly excluded by a form of prudery that still awaits its final explanation, since before this time it was unknown. An unofficial censorship exercised by the circulating libraries was able to force the literature of the day to conform with middle-class standards. The public taste in fiction was virtually in the hands of Mudie, who as a writer of hymns, and with twenty-five thousand subscribers, was considered a safe arbiter and was given what now seems a fantastic monopoly of judgment. If Mrs. Oliphant is to be believed, recognition by Mudie of one of her early books seemed to her like recognition from Heaven.

Not all Victorian novelists suffered to the same extent from the restrictive censorship exercised by public opinion. Certain fields of human experience such as mystery, romance and adventure, along with humour, lay almost entirely outside its scope. But on the subject of sex the taboo was absolute. Thackeray was most affected, and his work undoubtedly impaired. Nearest in spirit to the eighteenth century he recognized his kinship with Fielding and yearned for the old freedom. The preface to *Pendennis* records his *cri du cœur*, petulant and irritable, at the repressions suffered by the writer:

> "Since the author of Tom Jones was buried no writer of fiction among us has been permitted to depict to his utmost power a man. We must drape him and give him a conventional temper. Society will not tolerate the natural in our art. Many ladies have remonstrated and subscribers left me because in the course of the story I described a young man resisting and affected by temptation. My object was to say he had passions to feel, and the manliness and generosity to overcome them. You will not hear—it is best not to know—what moves in the real world; what is the life and talk of your son."

The literary giant best fitted to feed this voracious, if inhibited, public was Charles Dickens, a sturdy individualist of no great depth of thought, but richly endowed with creative energy and showmanship. Dickens stands, by reason of the superb range of his characters, unrivalled among English novelists and invites comparison with Balzac and Dostoievski. Dickens is immortal because he is so essentially of his time.

The secret of his appeal to his own time has been stated with characteristic overemphasis by G. K. Chesterton:

> "Dickens stands first as a defiant monument to what happens when a great literary genius has a literary taste akin to that of the community. For this kinship was deep and spiritual. Dickens did not write what the people wanted. Dickens wanted what the

people wanted. And with this was connected that other fact which must never be forgotten, and which I have more than once insisted on, that Dickens and his school had a hilarious faith in democracy and thought of the service of it as a sacred priesthood. Hence there was this vital point in his popularism, that there was no condescension in it. The belief that the rabble will only read rubbish can be read between the lines of all our contemporary writers, even of those writers whose rubbish the rabble reads.... Dickens never talked down to the people. He talked up to the people. He approached the people like a deity and poured out his riches and his blood. This is what makes the immortal bond between him and the masses of man.... His power, then, lay in the fact that he expressed with an energy and brilliancy quite uncommon the things close to the common mind. But with the mere phrase the common mind, we collide with a current error. Commonness and the common mind are now generally spoken of as meaning in some manner inferiority and the inferior mind; the mind of the mere mob. But the common mind means the mind of all the artists and heroes; or else it would not be common. Plato had the common mind; Dante had the common mind; or that mind was not common. Commonness means the quality common to the saint and the sinner, to the philosopher and the fool; and it was this that Dickens grasped and developed."

Dickens did not possess the power of divining the inner workings of his age but he succeeded in reflecting from a thousand facets its temporary saliences. It was an exciting, melodramatic, warmhearted, prodigal age, and Dickens was part of it. No other novelist showed such a gift for getting inside the skins of so many characters. Everything he touched came to life beneath his hand or seemed to, although today it may appear to some that what he endowed with the magic of life was in reality a puppet show—macabre and tinselled. As the Victorian age recedes into the past it can only be evoked through literature, and the image that sprawls in the pages of Dickens is fantastic and distorted. Perhaps the origin of this distortion must be sought in certain experiences of his life, in the personal factor the irritant that produced his genius.

The first years of Dickens's childhood were spent comfortably at Portsmouth, Portsea and Chatham, where his father was a clerk in the Navy Pay Office. The boy was able to visit the theatre, to buy books and steep himself in eighteenth-century fiction both picaresque and sentimental.

Already he began to nourish day-dreams of acquiring the education of a gentleman and saw himself through the world of books becoming the heir of the centuries and moving with ease among the great ones of the past. But he was destined to have the dream rudely shattered by a turn of fortune as melodramatic as any in fiction.

His father, John Dickens, lived consistently beyond his means, got hopelessly into debt and was recalled to London. Charles, ignorant of the desperate plight of his family, followed and found them living in one of the poorest streets in Camden Town. In February 1824 his father was arrested for debt and carried off to the Marshalsea Prison. The situation of the family was serious; there was no money to buy bread and the boy was forced to pawn his precious books one by one. But worse was to come—an experience so bitter and humiliating that it continued to haunt him long after his genius had won for him a place in society denied him by his birth. His parents found a job for him in Warren's blacking factory, owned by a relative. For six months, in utter despair at the eclipse of his dreams, Dickens, still little more than a child, worked in the dirty, rat-infested old house down by the river— sticking labels on blacking bottles. To get the utmost benefit from the light that filtered through the dusty air the boys stood near the windows, where they aroused the interest of passers-by. This was the first raw impact of life on the sensitive nerves of a boy who had lived in the dream world of elegance and polite learning.

It might, with some truth, be said that Dickens never saw London. He saw only the carnival of horror that danced through his tortured imagination during this black period that brought him to the verge of despair. The nervous fits from which he suffered in his childhood reappeared and he was frequently seized with violent spasms. From a psychological viewpoint, however, worse was to follow, for the boy experienced a sense of complete betrayal by those from whom he had most right to expect protection.

His father left prison and Dickens thought this would mean his own immediate release from shame and degradation. But the family were in no hurry to take the boy away from gainful employment and he remained in the factory until his father quarrelled with the relative who owned it and the boy was removed. Even then his mother was in favour of ending the quarrel and sending the boy back. Writing to Forster, years later, he says of this:

> "I do not write resentfully or angrily; for I know how all these things have worked together to make me what I am; but I never afterwards forgot, I never shall forget, I never can forget, that my mother was warm for my being sent back."

How deeply these few months burnt themselves in his memory is seen in the following passage:

> "Until Hungerford Market was pulled down, until old Hungerford Stairs were destroyed, and the very nature of the ground changed, I never had the courage to go back to the place where my servitude began. I never saw it. I could not endure to go near it. For many years, when I came near to Robert Warren's in the Strand, I crossed over to the opposite side of the way, to avoid a certain smell of cement they put upon the blacking corks, which reminded me of what I was once. It was a very long time before I liked to go up Chandos Street. My old way home by the Borough made me cry, after my eldest child could speak."

By the time he was free to continue his education at Wellington House Academy the mischief was done. In the depths of Dickens's nature a split had occurred; a sensitive, delicate being had been plunged into experiences that could only be borne by the tough and obdurate, and the vision of a world of grim, twisted shapes, deformed, exaggerated caricatures, a world flickering with horrid images, impressed itself indelibly upon the soul of a child. It was through this window that he always saw the Victorian scene. Loving beauty, he had, in his most impressionable years, been forced into contact with the seamier side of life, with the dirt, squalor, shame and humiliation; and the resultant self-disgust and utter hopelessness were ineradicable. He had seen the sordid underworld of London, peopled by men and women diseased in mind and body, where the victims of some vast, incomprehensible system were oppressed and destroyed. He could not understand the economic fact that in the early-Victorian age the machinery of life designed to control an aristocratic, agricultural and mercantile society was incapable of being geared to industrialism.

His own adolescent sufferings were turned to good account many years later in the semi-autobiographical *David Copperfield*; but a great and universal pity for the poor and downtrodden had been awakened in him which was to provide the driving power behind his pen in book after book. It is also probable that the violence and sadism in his novels had their origin in the unresolved psychological tensions of this period, in the shock of disillusionment and in the emotional conflicts occasioned by his attitude to his parents.

His sufferings did not make him a rebel against society. He was perhaps born too soon for that. Nor is there a *fin-de-siècle* longing for escape. No ivory tower claimed him, and Dickens did not turn away from a system that seemed to crush all human aspiration towards goodness and beauty. Instead he set out to reform the system through pity and laughter, but the topical purpose effectively limited his powers as an artist.

Success came early. Dickens, like his own David Copperfield, flung himself into learning shorthand, worked in a lawyer's office (watching, remembering, and collecting 'copy'), educated himself in the British Museum Reading Room and eventually became parliamentary reporter for the *Morning Chronicle*. In 1836 he was asked by Chapman and Hall, the publishers, to write the letterpress for a set of cockney sporting prints which a popular artist, Seymour, was to illustrate. Having to rely almost entirely on imagination, for Dickens had no sporting memories or experiences, he hit upon the idea of inventing a genial, innocent and lovable old gentleman, Mr. Pickwick, who was to become world-famous as the founder of a club of harmless lunatics.

The suicide of the artist left Dickens free to pursue his own fancy, and one by one the lesser characters sprang to life and ran away with the story. In Sam Weller Dickens provided his quixotic hero with a faithful Sancho Panza, sparkling with cockney shrewdness and wit. Sam brought along his coachman father, Tony Weller, and Tony Weller was always followed by widows: "Mark my words, Sammy boy, more widows marry than single women." The vivacious Mr. Jingle kept joining the party, especially at mealtimes; and so it went on. A whole new mythology came into being, until the public could hardly wait for each new instalment. Lower middle-class life in the nineteenth century was to Dickens what the Border country had been to Scott—at once a source of inspiration and an inexhaustible storehouse of types and material.

After four or five parts of Mr. Pickwick's adventures had appeared the work suddenly sprang into popularity which each succeeding part carried higher and higher. Four hundred copies of the first part were prepared, but for the fifteenth forty thousand copies were needed. The British public took the club of harmless lunatics to its bosom, repeated what the members said, quoted them, appealed to their judgments, and found itself confirmed and strengthened. The Pickwickians had become a national institution, and 'Dickensian' humour passed into the language. Dickens's pen was, like Scott's, a fertile one. No sooner had a vein of fiction been opened up than it seemed inexhaustible. The immense vitality he poured into his books made them seem—as G. K. Chesterton has said—less like separate novels than lengths cut from the flowing and mixed substances called Dickens. In such a generous harvest there are inevitably tares among the wheat—stagey characters, slapdash work, and, to a later generation, serious lapses of taste.

Pickwick had been an essay in pure humour, a series of entertaining episodes lightly strung together. But Dickens was aware of the contrast between the atavistic memories they evoked and the cruelty and injustice in the world around him. In the novels that followed *Pickwick* he took on the familiar role of the crusader. His aim was to wring the conscience of society by playing upon its feelings and presenting scenes of harrowing misery that could be shown as the outcome of personal indifference and social callousness.

It must be remembered that what seems today the overdrawn and laboured sentimentality of his children's death-bed scenes wrung the hearts of his own contemporaries. Looking back and speaking through the mouth of David Copperfield, with complete simplicity, Dickens explained his own success and his own philosophy: "Whatever I have tried to do in life, I have tried with all my heart to do well." If heart, rather than judgment, is taken as a criterion, even the death-beds are understandable.

As a crusader for the oppressed, Dickens first attacked the stony-heartedness of organized charity. In *Oliver Twist* (1838) he showed that the Poor Law Reform Act had only strengthened institutionalism by giving authority to unkindness. In Mr. Bumble all selfish dispensers of public charity stand condemned, and in *Oliver Twist* their helpless victims find an eternal symbol. For Oliver to have become a national byword as the small boy who dared to ask for a second helping is a measure of the impact of his story on the well-fed and complacent reading public. An even worse shock was to come later, in *Bleak House*, when young Jo, typifying the utterly destitute everywhere, dies of hunger. "Dead," said Dickens, the moralizer, of his little crossing-sweeper. "Dead, Right Reverends and Wrong Reverends of every order. Dead, men and women born with Heavenly compassion in your hearts. And dying thus around us every day."

Nicholas Nickleby (1839) exposed the goings-on behind the doors of private schools. Next came *The Old Curiosity Shop* (1840), perhaps best remembered for the overstrained emotionalism of the death of Little Nell—the angel child, too good to live, a scene which provided contemporary readers with one of the highlights of fiction, but which a less sentimental age has damned to perdition. To offset the pathos of the child and her loving but wretched grandfather we have the creation of Quilp, a character impregnated with malice and wearing physical ugliness as the outward sign of spiritual repulsiveness.

A visit to America in 1842 resulted in bitter disappointment for Dickens. He had expected too much. There in a free republican State he believed he would meet with more natural goodness, equality and justice than he saw at home. Instead he found disgusting manners, a crudity that repelled him and a venality unrivalled even in Europe. *Martin Chuzzlewit* (1844) records his disillusionment. American scenes in it gave offence, but the book is memorable for its characters. Sarah Gamp ("He'd make a lovely corpse"), Tom Finch, the Franciscan Mark Tapley, and that prince of hypocrites Pecksniff, make the novel a favourite with English readers.

Dickens's peculiar power to reveal the spirit through the flesh is admirably brought out in his description of Pecksniff:

> "It has been remarked that Mr. Pecksniff was a moral man. So he was. Perhaps there never was a more moral man than Mr. Pecksniff; especially in his conversation and correspondence. It was once said of him by a homely admirer that he had a Fortunatus purse of good sentiments in his inside. In this particular he was like the girl in the fairy tale, except that if they were not actual diamonds which fell from his lips, they were the very brightest paste, and shone prodigiously. He was a most exemplary man: fuller of virtuous precept than a copy-book. Some people likened him to a direction-post, which is always telling the way to a place, and never goes there; but these were his enemies, the shadows cast by his brightness; that was all. His very throat was moral. You saw a good deal of it. You looked over a very low fence of white cravat (whereof no man had ever beheld the tie, for he fastened it behind), and there it lay, a valley between two jutting heights of collar, serene and whiskerless before you. It seemed to say, on the part of Mr. Pecksniff, 'There is no deception, ladies and gentlemen, all is peace, a holy calm pervades me.' So did his hair, just grizzled with an iron grey which was all brushed off his forehead, and stood bolt upright, or slightly drooped in kindred action with his heavy eyelids. So did his person, which was sleek though free from corpulency. So did his manner, which was soft and oily. In a word, even his plain black suit, and state of widower, and dangling double eyeglass, all tended to the same purpose, and cried aloud, 'Behold the moral Pecksniff.'"

By 1850 Dickens had added to his output the Christmas Tales including *A Christmas Carol* (1843), *Dombey and Son* (1848) and *David Copperfield* (1849–50). The first of these is Dickens's touchstone. It is a miracle play. The little cripple, Tiny Tim, is not a real little boy like David, puzzled, loving and trying to learn his way about the world. He is youth and innocence personified, just as Scrooge typifies the lovelessness of the miser. In the warm glow of the Christmas spirit, ugliness and evil vanish, and Scrooge is transformed by the all-pervading benevolence and goodwill in the very air about him. It may seem a far cry from Dickens to Shelley, but there is something in common between the lyrical epilogue to *Prometheus Unbound* where a universe is filled with radiant harmony by the triumph of love and the transformed heart of the crabbed Scrooge giving renewed hope to the little cripple, Tiny Tim.

The earlier novels had been constructed to no very definite plan. They are mostly picaresque, the hero acting as the connecting link between one episode and the next. In *Dombey and Son* there is a central theme. It is not so much the sombre figure of Mr. Dombey who holds the story together, as the cold pride of Mr. Dombey—destroying the lives of those with whom he comes in contact. There is considerable poetic imagination and truth in the scene in the desolate house, where Dombey is left alone, the muddy footmarks which symbolize his own path through life, as he has trampled on the affection of his daughter, Flo, in revenge for the loss of his son, Paul.

Of *David Copperfield* Dickens wrote: "I like this one the best," and the novel may be regarded as a veiled autobiography. In the chapters covering David Copperfield's childhood Dickens showed an imaginative understanding of the child's point of view that was new in literature. The bewilderment of a little boy, at the mercy of adult decisions and their unpredictable whims, is described with a tenderness which must have surprised families where well-brought-up children were locked in dark cupboards for the slightest display of 'naughtiness'.

Bleak House, which followed in 1853, is a tragedy which, in tragic intensity, far surpasses the gloomy history of Mr. Dombey. Suggested by the celebrated proceedings arising from the estate of one William Jennings, who died in 1798, leaving property at Birmingham worth many millions, the case of Jarndyce and Jarndyce is a commentary, at once tragic and satiric, on the abuses of the old courts of Chancery, the delays and costs of which brought misery and ruin on its suitors. The plot is intricately woven, and the central theme so skilfully used, that every episode and every character has something to contribute to the inexorable chain of events leading towards the exposure of Lady Dedlock. But surpassing this is the force of symbolism in the novel. In fact in this sombre story of hearts worn to despair and minds driven to madness by the inscrutable injustice and infinite delays of the Law there is much to recall the world of Dostoievsky, while the powerful intensity with which symbol and plot are fused is reminiscent of Kafka.

From the physical fog that blots out the city Dickens passes to the dreadful nights of spiritual darkness that is at its thickest and most terrible in the workings of a system of Law that has lost touch with human needs.

> "Fog everywhere. Fog up the river, where it flows among green aits and meadows; fog down the river, where it rolls defiled among the tiers of shipping, and the waterside pollutions of a great (and dirty) city. Fog on the Essexmarshes, fog on the Kentish heights. Fog creeping into the cabooses of the collier-brigs; fog lying out in the yards, and hovering in the rigging of great ships; fog dropping on the gunwales of barges and small boats....
>
> "Gas looming through the fog in divers places in the streets, much as the sun may, from the spongy fields, be seen to loom by husbandmen and ploughboy. Most of the shops lighted two hours before their time—as the gas seems to know, for it has a haggard and unwilling look.
>
> "The raw afternoon is rawest, and the dense fog is densest and the muddy streets are muddiest, near that leaden-headed old corporation: Temple Bar. And hard by Temple Bar, in Lincoln's Inn Hall, at the very heart of the fog, sits the Lord High Chancellor in his High Court of Chancery. Never can there come fog too thick, never can there come mud and mire too deep, to assort with the groping and floundering condition which this High Court of Chancery, most pestilent of hoary sinners, holds, this day, in the sight of heaven and earth."

Through the fog of frustration and throughout the book the two Wards in Chancery, and others connected with them, grope their way. Poor little Miss Flite has already lost her reason, and gradually it becomes clear that as Richard Carstone's golden optimism wavers towards despair, he too will be driven mad, or rather that he will escape into madness from an unbearable agony of uncertainty. For

> "This is the Court of Chancery; which has its decaying houses and its blighted land in every shire; which has its worn-out lunatic in every madhouse, and its dead in every churchyard; which has its ruined suitor, with his slipshod heels and threadbare dress, borrowing and begging through the round of every man's acquaintance; which gives to monied might, the means of

wearying out the right; which so exhausts finances, patience, courage, hope; so overthrows the brain and breaks the heart; that there is not an honourable man among its practitioners who would not give—who does not often give—the warning, 'Suffer any wrong that can be done you rather than come here!'"

Dickens the social reformer tilted at the vast, apathetic and incomprehensible web woven by a legal system that had lost touch with reality; but the story seems to have taken possession of him and far surpasses the original purpose. It also inspired him to the creation of some of his best characters. Dickens, often so unsuccessful with the delineation of educated men and women, has several in this book who are more or less convincing. The best of all is Sir Leicester Dedlock—ludicrous, stiff and inarticulate, but in his utter moral integrity by no means a caricature of the English ruling classes. The suave lawyer Tulkinghorn and the shy philanthropist Mr. Jarndyce are both rather more than types. There are a host of interesting minor characters, among whom may be mentioned Harold Skimpole, drawn from Leigh Hunt, who disguises his complete selfishness under a guise of childish irresponsibility. The irascible yet generous Boythorn, with his canary, is drawn from Walter Savage Landor.

Dickens's powers of characterization were limited. Apart from the obviously stagey and melodramatic figures, he is apt to carry the reader away by sheer quantitative achievement. On closer analysis many of his immortal creations turn out to be not real persons, but brilliantly sketched personifications of vices and virtues, reminiscent of the 'humours' of Ben Jonson. In *Bleak House,* however, even a minor character like Mrs. Bagnet is not just a soldier's wife; she is Mrs. Bagnet and nobody else. Sometimes it is hard to differentiate. Mrs. Jellyby might be a type—the kind of woman who neglects her home in order to work for a mission to Borrioboola-Gha; but again Dickens's intense powers of observation and love of detail come in to save her. She is unique as the slatternly housewife whose curtains were skewered back with forks!

In *Hard Times* (1854), a novel instinct with power, he returned to the attack on the industrial evils of his day, epitomizing in Coketown all industrial towns and in the Gradgrinds and the Bounderbys showing up the inhuman representatives of the system of enlightened self-interest that had only theory to recommend it.

The target in *Little Dorrit* (1857) is the unreformed Civil Service, with its nepotism and its injustices. Here the dice are loaded against the Circumlocution Offices and the human Barnacles who make the system work but whose selfishness and indifference destroy the soul in the society they serve.

With *A Tale of Two Cities* (1859) Dickens returned to the historical novel, a genre which he had already essayed in *Barnaby Rudge*, a story of the Gordon Riots. His limitations are soon disclosed when he strays outside the magic London circle in which he conjured up his fantastic rout. His attitude to the French Revolution suggests the fundamental dualism at the root of Dickens's political convictions, which made him, for instance, although a radical, an opponent of the Chartists because he hated physical violence. "The aristocrats deserved all they got, but the passion engendered in the people by the misery and starvation replaced one set of oppressors by another." His sympathies were with the suffering, but he feared violence, for it stirred in him deep-rooted emotional complexes that had their origin in his adolescence and had never been resolved.

To the last phase of Dickens's literary career belongs *Great Expectations* (1861), a work regarded by many critics as his best. The story of the benevolent convict, young Pip, the proud Estella and the tragically eccentric Miss Havisham is well told, while the description of the Great Salt Marsh where Pip first meets the convict creates an atmosphere of cold horror that challenges comparison with Hardy's study of Egdon Heath in *The Return of the Native*.

Three years later came *Our Mutual Friend* (1864), a mellow and charming book, noteworthy for the interesting character of the schoolmaster, Bradley Headstone, the first murderer in Dickens to exhibit any complexity of character. And he is the first to present himself as a member of respectable Victorian society. The novel contains a dreadful and convincing picture of the double life led by Bradley Headstone as he goes about his duties as a schoolmaster after he has decided to murder Eugene, for whom the woman he loves has manifested a preference.

At the time of his premature death in 1870 Dickens was working on what might be called a psychological thriller, *The Mystery of Edwin Drood*. Eastern influences which were beginning to affect literature are seen in the character of Jasper Drood, the opium-smoker, Kali-worshipper, and choirmaster and precentor of Cloisterham Cathedral. This is one of Dickens's more complex character studies, and may contain much unconscious self-analysis. Perhaps Dickens comes near to revealing the split in his own personality in emphasizing Jasper's two states of consciousness that never clash, but each of which pursues its separate course as though it were continuous instead of broken.

The murderer, Drood, has lived all his life in an atmosphere of sanctity, worshipping the Christian God, singing hymns and directing the devotions of others, but his other self has surrendered to the enchantment of evil, embodied in an alien civilization, drugs, and hallucinations. Oddly enough, Dickens had spent his life writing novels full of goodwill, sentiment, high spirits and kindliness, but the most vivid experiences related in them were all inspired by evil, violence, malignity, cruelty. It has been suggested that Dickens himself was perhaps caught between two classes of society as the choirmaster between two civilizations, and in both cases the conflict resulted in a strong impulse to destroy. Dickens the artist sublimated his evil passions in the nerve-torturing scenes of sadism he depicted; Drood committed murder.

All his life Dickens drove himself hard—perhaps too hard. At the height of his fame he was not only writing and editing, but also giving dramatic readings from his books in both England and America. These brought, him money and also a certain emotional satisfaction. In the idolatrous applause of a vast audience, throbbing with excitement as he threw all his considerable histrionic skill into making them see the death of Bill Sykes or the murder of Nancy, Dickens found the anodyne he needed to soothe past hurts that time had hidden but not healed.

His death was sudden and dramatic. On 9 June, 1870, he had put in a long day on *Edwin Drood*, when he had a stroke while he was eating dinner. He got up from the table in his stunned condition and said he must go to London; then he fell to the floor and never recovered consciousness. He died the next afternoon.

Perhaps Dickens's major contribution to literature, that which gives him his rank among the giants, was his discovery of new sources of humour. Like Smollett, the greatest literary influence on him, he saw the humour of funny faces. A child who was asleep in a room in which Dickens was writing later recalled how, waking up suddenly, she saw the novelist make faces at himself in the looking-glass and then return to his desk and continue his work.

He was delighted, too, by the humour of odd tricks of speech, like the jerky, machine-gunning staccato conversation of Mr. Jingle, and the ungrammatical circumlocutions of the uneducated in sentences from which they can only extricate themselves by means of more and more relative clauses. He went far beyond Smollett in the supreme sophistication which can see childish fun in the contrariness of inanimate objects. The 'veskitt' button that won't button was something new in English literature—it suggests something of the Russian Gogol. Dickens exploited to the full the absurdity of the apt or ludicrously unsuitable name, and he loved to mock the humour of the professional outlook—the overriding egotism which makes an undertaker say that a beautiful funeral is something to "reconcile us to the world we live in".

A clue to Dickens's gift of portraiture is to be found in his confession that he used to console himself for his small troubles when a boy by impersonating his favourite characters in the novels he read.

> "I have been Tom Jones (a child's Tom Jones, a harmless creature) for a week together. I have sustained my own idea of Roderick Random for a month at a stretch.... I have seen Tom Pipes go climbing up the church steeple; I have watched Strap with a knapsack on his back, stopping to rest himself upon the wicket-gate and I know that Commodore Trunnion held that club with Mr. Pickle in the parlour of our little village alehouse."

Dickens's approach to character was that of the actor, not that of the philosopher or the psychologist. The actor who is a fine artist. He observed from the outside, he built up character boldly and swiftly, catching the salient features, and his cut-and-thrust method triumphed because it resulted in something unforgettably vivid. Life was always surprising him and forcing him to keep in a state of constant excitement about it. Dickens did not need the co-operation of the reader, he only wanted his delighted approval. Nothing is suggested; everything is clearly presented. It is as if Dickens caught life grimacing and clicked the shutter—the result is both ludicrous and lifelike.

Genius he had in plenty, but it was untutored, and the restless fertility in contriving situations and inventing characters was never pruned by concern for form. Dickens added little to the development of the novel; it remained in his hands what it had been in the eighteenth century, a picaresque tale with a moral bias or the happy blending of drama and narration. Perhaps the author was less intrusive than formerly and the marshalling of climaxes undertaken at more breathless speed, but Dickens discloses no conscious artistic purpose—he is quite indifferent to the medium he uses.

Apart from his supreme value as an entertainer in fiction Dickens earned the gratitude of posterity for awakening the social conscience. In an age marred by callousness and complacency Dickens never lost faith in fundamental human goodness. Although he could see with clear eyes the stronger impersonal evil created by society, he continued to believe in the kindly fatherhood of God and in the triumphant power of love. Organization, whether political, charitable or religious, he rejected; the law killed, and spirit and systems, no matter how efficient, were no substitutes for the warm human relationships that were based on man's responsibility for his fellows. In his ideal of spontaneous benevolence flowing from some inexhaustible fountain of human goodness Dickens saw the great solvent of the grief and misery that poisoned life around him.

Dickens is the Victorian age in fiction, or a large part of it. He shared its faults of taste, its love of melodrama, its exuberant vitality, its belief in the sharp division of humanity into sheep and goats. He shared, too, the innate optimism of the period. His novels, humour apart, are morality plays in which the good angels win the battle for the soul of man, which is just what the majority of the Victorians were sure they would.

Thackeray, who was Dickens's contemporary and great rival for popular favour, lacked alike his weakness and his genius. Much that Dickens hungered after—culture, social position, breeding—was his by right, and he had a great gift for writing dialogue, a strong sense of irony, and a style "easy and sympathetic, carved in slow soft curves". Rather unkindly, Thackeray has been called the "apostle of mediocrity", although this might be regarded as a tribute to his masterly naturalism in fiction. He recognized Dickens's skill in narration, which made his own seem flat and unexciting.

> "Boz tells a good palpable story. I know the tune I am piping is a very mild one … only a homely story…. Yet look you, one is bound to speak the truth as far as one knows it, whether one mounts a cap and bells or a shovel hat."

Thackeray was less interested in the great upheavals of the age than in the manners and morals of the *beau monde* around him: "Yes," he says in effect, "this is Vanity Fair; not a moral place certainly, nor a merry one, though very noisy."

As a so-called moralist, William Makepeace Thackeray came into his stride slowly. Born in India in 1811, he was educated at Charterhouse, and Trinity College, Cambridge. Finding that academic distinction had less appeal than a butterfly existence on the Continent, he left the University after one year, and moved to Coblenz and Weimar. For a time he considered taking up a study of law, but found the training "one of the most cold-blooded prejudiced pieces of invention that ever man was slave to".

An inheritance of eight hundred pounds a year enabled him to bid farewell to the law and he set off for Paris. There he read widely, studied the language and revelled in the freedom and excitement provided by the gayest city in the world. Bubbling over with kindness and good humour—he was just twenty-one—his powers of enjoyment at their height, Thackeray plunged into the sparkling whirlpool, and found life good. It was apparently too good to last. Some unlucky speculations by his stepfather, Major Carmichael Smythe—later to be immortalized as Colonel Newcombe— accounted for the loss of the young man's fortune as well as his own, and Thackeray was forced to face the unpleasant necessity of earning a living.

His first efforts met with no success. Under a Dickensian prodigality of *noms de plume*—Yellowplush, Titmarsh, Gahagan, Fitzboodle—he began to contribute articles and stories, often illustrated by himself, to periodicals. His fortunes reached their nadir in 1835 and he was so self-distrustful that he lay on a sofa reading endless novels, and declaring, "If in another six months I can do no better I will go out and hang myself."

He was roused from this *Oblomov* mood and provoked into a more sustained effort by disgust at a contemporary taste for crime novels in which the hero was a glamourized villain. Moved by sentimental pity for the victims of an unjustly harsh penal code, certain writers of fiction had begun to champion the criminal against society. Among examples of this dangerous tendency to condone the brutalities of the criminal while attacking the harshness of the penal code were Lytton's *Paul Clifford* and *Eugene Aram*.

When Harrison Ainsworth joined the 'gallows' school with *Rookwood* (1834) and *Jack Sheppard* (1840), combining much spurious sentimental rhetoric with echoes of the Gothic terror, Thackeray brought up bigger guns with *Barry Lyndon* (1844), in which the hero, gambler, villain and bully, describes his own baseness with blatant self-complacency. The irony implicit throughout is also explained in footnotes, but the subject remains unrelievedly painful. The book is chiefly interesting for the character-drawing. Barry Lyndon is drawn in the round, and is far more than a Jonsonian humour. He is not just a monster of vice. He may throw a carving-knife about, but he feels the action needs justification: "I was drunk, as anyone could see."

After further literary ventures and a spell in Paris as foreign correspondent for the newspapers his father launched so optimistically and so vainly, Thackeray wrote *Vanity Fair*, a book that brought him immediate fame and established him high among the great Victorians.

Here at last was an authentic picture of the upper middle classes who lived in the big new Bloomsbury squares, presented with clear-sighted realism and sparkling irony. Society in the eighteen forties was becoming fluid owing to the influx of wealth. The new fortunes made in the City, in India and in industry, were storming the old social fortresses. Everyone wanted to get in, but the only assured passports were birth and wealth. *Vanity*

Fair is the story of a woman who had neither. Instead Becky Sharp had brilliant green eyes, a ruthless determination to get on in life, a hard, calculating mind, no kindliness or humour, but unfailing good temper. Infinitely more gifted than the fortunate ones around her, the poor pupil from Miss Pinkerton's Academy demanded her share of the prizes of life. Becky's bohemian nature is fascinated by the flashing magnificence of the social scene. In her imagination she has a right to wealth and position; but the princess *de jure* is only the governess *de facto*.

Becky Sharp was something new in fiction. Since Defoe's Roxana the novel had known only the colourless conventional heroines of romance or the repulsive caricatures that Smollett perfected. Here was an adventuress with the world as her oyster, a study in instinctive trickery, inherent duplicity and the supple energy of the eternal feminine—the adventuress who scandalized and conquered her world. Becky, by her marriage to Rawdon Crawley, scaled the social ladder and rose to dizzy heights of social distinction; but the ladder was a magic one and could withdraw itself at will. At the first breath of disapproval it vanished, for society extends little tolerance or protection to those whose right to its patronage does not rest on an accepted foundation.

It is noticeable that Thackeray gives his pet characters good entrances. Becky is first seen flinging Johnson's Dictionary out of the carriage window as she leaves Miss Pinkerton's Academy for ever. Beside her glowing personality the true heroine, Amelia, seems, then and throughout the book, a dull and colourless foil. She is tender, sentimental, stupid and loving—all feminine characteristics Thackeray greatly admired—along with "adorable purity", maternal love, lack of self-confidence, an angelic ignorance of men's ways and a proper touch of female jealousy. Such asides to the reader as "If the women did not make idols of us, and if they saw us as we see each other, would life be bearable, or could society go on?" tend to date him. There had been many Amelias before, but Becky, the indefatigable, scandalous little Becky, was a creation that owed nothing to literature but a good deal to life.

Contrasting the two women, Thackeray brings out the realistic philosophy of human nature and the fallacies behind too sharp a distinction between sheep and goats. The good are often blind, powerless and foolish, while the unscrupulous are full of passionate intensity, but extremely able. It is, however, when he sees conventional morality and the ritual of society confronted by the weakness of the flesh that the perceptions of Thackeray become luminous and his pen moves with deadly precision. Here lies the source of his incisive irony that delighted to reveal a truth so often ignored by Victorian moralists. Lust and cowardice are the targets for his keenest shafts. Men, he maintained, were rarely heroes, and when they were it was through chance rather than by design. This point of view gives significance to his version of the battle of Waterloo in *Vanity Fair*. Ignoring the heroics of the battlefield, he concentrates on the confused, panic-stricken civilians in Brussels. Under the impact of fear all the unseen undercurrents of self-love are forced to the surface. Becky, who has kept her horses, can thus take an exquisite revenge on Lady Bareacres, who has humiliated her socially, by refusing her ladyship the horses so essential for her flight. The horses again are used to reveal the selfish cowardice of Joe Sedley. He is willing to buy them and fly, leaving his sister with no protector.

> "What good can I do her, suppose—suppose the enemy arrive? They'll spare the women, but my man tells me that they have taken an oath to give no quarter to the men—the dastardly cowards."

Thackeray derives much of his realism from his discipline. He tends to avoid over-dramatic climaxes, observing that life has a fondness for understatement and undertones. Impending tragedy is often averted by unimportant trifles or precipitated into insignificance by an elusive nuance. Herein lies the great difference in style between Dickens, who loves to marshal his characters to some overwhelming climax, and Thackeray. To gain the measure of this difference it is only necessary to imagine how Dickens would have handled Rawdon Crawley's discovery of Becky and Lord Steyne.

Thackeray's next novel, *Pendennis* (1848–50), is autobiographical, with Charterhouse somewhat idealized as Greyfriars. Among many amusing characters in the story is Captain Shandon, the editor of the *Pall Mall Gazette*, who drafts his first prospectus in the Fleet.

Henry Esmond (1852) is a historical novel, and to some the best in the language. Written in a style of easy urbanity, it evokes the age of Queen Anne—the world of Swift, Steele, Harley and Bolingbroke, the world of the dastardly Mohocks, the notorious Lord Mohun and his most distinguished victim, the Duke of Hamilton. The story, concerned with an eccentric Catholic family, loyal to the Stuarts, is presented against a contemporary background of political and religious bigotry. In Beatrix Esmond, with her dazzling beauty and tone-deafness to all emotion, Thackeray drew another of the vampire women of whom he disapproved in principle but whose fascinations inspired his greatest creative efforts. Ill-fortune overtakes them in the end, but there is no blame for the leopard who "follows leopard law".

Compared with Beatrix the virtuous and unblemished Lady Castlewood is boring and insipid, although she has awakened in her creator an obvious tenderness. Esmond, melancholy languishing on his eyelashes, and full of pathetic resignation, is surely the least vital hero in fiction. The last scenes, written with white-hot irony, show Beatrix, impelled by vanity, ruining the Stuart cause for which her brother has risked his life.

The Newcomes (1853–5) contributed to fiction in the person of Colonel Newcome an idealized portrait of Thackeray's stepfather, a simple-minded gentleman, guided through life solely by the sentiments of duty and honour. A generation able to thrill to the snowflakes that attended the death of Little Nell was equally touched by the pathos of the Colonel's death-bed. 'Adsum' passed into the language of devotional sentimentality.

Thackeray's last novel, The Virginians (1859), relates the fortunes of the descendants of Colonel Henry Esmond, and in particular of his daughter Rachel, who married a Warrington (ancestor of the friend of Pendennis) and survived him as owner of an estate in Virginia. The book contains a vivid account of the rakish and unprincipled society of the day and introduces Wolfe and Washington. The later part deals with the American War of Independence.

Thackeray died in 1863 at the relatively early age of fifty-two, worn out by his efforts. Love of extravagant living and a laudable desire to provide generously for his daughters led him, in spite of his temperamental lethargy, to force up his income to the ten-thousand-pounds-a-year level. To this end he undertook lecture tours in England and America. In both countries he was a great success. Fashionable society attended his lectures and echoed his opinions. In one lecture he damned Swift so effectually that a disrelish for the greatest English satirist became a hallmark of good taste for a generation. Yet, strangely enough, Thackeray had much in common with Swift; perhaps he feared the terrible consequences of looking at life too long and too steadily without the comforting assurances of illusion.

Among novelists a high place must be assigned to Thackeray in spite of his indifference to form and his lack of intensity. In his work he rejected the complicated plot used by Dickens, allowing his story—usually spread out over a period of several years—to develop through the actions and speech of his characters. The characters themselves are plausible, no distressing sense of caricature mars their naturalness, but their innermost thoughts are not revealed, for Thackeray failed to develop a technique of self-anaylsis. He makes up for this to some extent by his subtle use of dialogue. Like Jane Austen, he is a master of eloquent reticence, and he can give a double edge to the most seemingly harmless comment. Sentiment he portrays with far greater delicacy than Dickens; he avoids the charge of vulgarity so often brought against his contemporary, and if he is compelled to describe the sordid—as in the account of Becky's fall into the demi-monde of cheap Continental hotels—he does it with ironic detachment.

Thackeray's strength as a novelist lies in his power to persuade the reader that the play of action in a novel rises straight out of character, so that the course of events has the inevitability of life. Like Tolstoy, he can express a sense of life larger than that which is confined within the story. Just as he, the author, can draw aside his chair and speak to the reader, so do his characters appear to have a life of their own outside the limits of their appearances in the story. This sense of reality is aided by the trick of letting the same character appear in several novels.

His weaknesses spring from the limitations imposed on him by the age in which he lived and from which he consciously suffered. His insight into the workings of human nature was profound but satiric, and for its full expression required an atmosphere of freedom. But this freedom was precisely what he lacked and, in consequence, a conflict developed between Thackeray's creative inspiration and the Victorian age. The Victorian age triumphed, with the result that the novelist was compelled to be false to his own genius. Thackeray's artistic perception of characters and situations was, within his range, infallible, but the power to set down what he saw was cramped by a somewhat pharisaical moral code. That he submitted so readily to his age is the measure of his weakness.

Chief among the minor contemporaries of Dickens and Thackeray were Anthony Trollope, Charles Kingsley, Mrs. Gaskell, Charles Reade and Wilkie Collins.

Trollope (1815–82) is a Victorian novelist whose writings have enjoyed a considerable revival in the twentieth century. He is a garrulous male Jane Austen, as satisfied with society, and blandly unaware of the storms and stresses introduced by Darwin and Marx, as she of the distress occasioned by the French Revolution and the Napoleonic wars.

Trollope, educated at Harrow and Winchester, succeeded (thanks to an unexacting examination system) in establishing himself in the Post Office, and was sent, in connection with his duties, to Ireland as a travelling inspector. As a writer he might be described as an industrious Philistine who quickly acquired a routine that enabled him to write at any time and anywhere. Much of his literary work was done while he was travelling about the countryside. Irish life interested him and contemporary Irish affairs provided material for his early novels, *The Macdermots of Ballycloran* (1847) and *The Kellys and the O'Kellys* (1848). *Castle Richmond* (1860) records the famine in 1846–7, of which he had been an eye-witness.

The almost idolatrous admiration of Trollope in the nineteen thirties and forties was not, however, inspired by the Irish novels but by his perfect studies of English clerical life, *The Warden* (1855), *Barchester Towers* (1857), *Doctor Thorne* (1859) and *The Last Chronicle of Barset* (1867). These novels reflect the cathedral world that is peculiarly English, a world of seeming calm, a "twilight of gray Gothic things" that yet seethes with intrigue below the surface. The idea of these stories is said to have come to him in the shadow of Salisbury Close while he was meditating on some contemporary scandal concerning a misappropriation of church funds. Suddenly he had a glimpse of a world within a world, outwardly placid, with dignity unruffled, but, in point of fact, tense and grim, stiff with *amour propre*, where attack and counter-attack were launched with quixotic enthusiasm and an unchristian lack of charity.

The time was ripe for the 'Anglican' novel. Hunting parsons and comfortable pluralists, whose cellars were frequently dearer to them than their libraries, had long been threatened by the Wesley movement, which spread dramatically in the nineteenth century. By the eighteen fifties new forces were attacking the Church from without and feuds were disintegrating it from within. Rome, Calvin and the scientists were alike menacing the Anglican order. No easy way of restoring lost prestige offered itself; older dignitaries resented the new men whose reforming zeal and anxiety to achieve success at any price led them to treat the Church as merchandise. No writer, not even Dickens, was as sensitive as Trollope to the idiom, idiosyncrasies and snobbery of the clerical profession. He possessed a microscopic eye for their idiosyncrasies. But what interested him were not the fiercely contested points of doctrine that were dividing the age, but individuals. Few writers have caught the faint, musty flavour of cathedral town personalities as well as he.

The masterpiece of the series is undoubtedly *Barchester Towers*, which is rich in finely conceived characters: the gentle and innocent Mr. Harding; the superb and slightly unapproachable Dr. Grantley, his son-in-law; the odious and insufferable Slope, so justly punished for his interfering perfidy by having to turn Methodist in order to marry a rich widow; the pathetic and faintly ridiculous curate, Quiverful, and his fierce, maternal wife: all are beyond criticism as ecclesiastical 'types'. But Trollope surpassed himself in the creation of the Bishop's wife—the She-Bishop, Mrs. Proudie. She belongs to the realm of high comedy; like Barchester itself she is at once temporal and eternal. The scene when she is discomfited by her arch-enemy, Mr. Slope, and the Bishop, milder than any worm, turns at last and asserts himself, is among the great moments in the history of the Comic Spirit.

Certain emotions—pride, arrogance, spite and envy—Trollope understood supremely well and presented in fiction with quiet authenticity. Their appearance in the lives of those whose business it was to have banished them provided a rich store of satiric material for his pen. But Trollope was no thinker: he did not criticize the world he depicted; he could never have seen in the Church of England of his day the 'musical banks', beautiful but useless, that Samuel Butler saw and satirized. Keenly observant and passionately interested in individuals, Trollope imposes on them an uncomplex and unified organization. He identified himself with the nineteenth century governing class, and reflected it admiringly. All that was tranquil in Victorian England preened itself in the pages of Trollope; class loyalties, class tolerance and class distinction he accepted unquestioningly, for him the pillars of society were still the country gentry and the Church. Like Jane Austen, he was a snob, but perhaps he showed just a shade more understanding of curates.

Charles Kingsley (1819–75), whose popularity has waned in the last few decades, was inspired to protest against the domestic insipidities—or so they seemed to him—of Anthony Trollope. He wanted in the novel stirring episodes, varied excitement and a past that seemed richer in colour than the drab futilities of contemporary Victorian cathedral towns.

In *Hypatia* (1853) his subject is Alexandria in the time of the Goths, and in *Westward Ho!* (1855) the Elizabethan age of the seadogs—Drake and Hawkins and the *Golden Hind*.

In *Alton Locke* (1850), the biography of a converted Chartist, he exposes conditions in the sweated tailoring trade. Kingsley, like Dickens, had been impressed by Carlyle's attacks on the economics of the Manchester school. He accepted industrialism and, as a good Victorian, he believed in progress; but he wanted it to be Christian progress. Fired with reforming zeal, Kingsley crusaded against dishonest traders, sweated industries, hypocritical creators of slums and disease, and the eternal enemies of social hygiene. Today he is remembered less for his historic novels and for his books of social propaganda, *Yeast* and *Alton Locke*, than for his immortal fantasy *The Water Babies*. In this political fairy story about a dirty little chimney sweep, who dies, and goes to a dream-like afterworld under the sea, Kingsley carried on the massed onslaught of the reformers against the evils of industrialism.

Charles Reade (1814–84)—the novelist with a notebook—added documentation to the novel as a weapon for the social reformer. He investigated prisons, and studied tool-making, the law business, banking, even life between the decks on an ocean steamer. He also found out what life was like for Australian gold-diggers. He describes his methods of gathering material in *A Terrible Temptation*. The results of his experience and his reading were poured into his novels; and when he turned from the present to the past he remained faithful to the habit of minute and detailed realism. Reade was an admirable story-teller. Novels such as *Peg Woffington* (1853), *Hard Cash* (1863), *Griffith Gaunt* (1866), an exciting story of adventure with an anti-Catholic bias, and *Foul Play* (1869), a good example of Reade's narrative power, are still of some interest.

His masterpiece, however, *The Cloister and the Hearth* (1861), is a historical romance. The story, which is laid in the fifteenth century, was inspired by the author's reading of the *Colloquies* and the *Life of Erasmus*, and writings of Froissart and Luther. Vivid scenes in monasteries, taverns and palaces characterize this stirring tale of Renascence Europe on the eve of the Reformation, and of the father of Erasmus, who became a Dominican friar on hearing a false account of the death of the mother of his child. In spite of the blue book accuracy there is not a trace of true objectivity in *The Cloister and the Hearth*, for prejudice and Victorian earnestness made him turn the story into an attack on the hated Catholic Church and its enforced celibacy of the clergy.

Mrs. Gaskell (1810–65), best known as the author of *Cranford* and as the biographer of Charlotte Brontë, joined the social crusaders by describing conditions, as she had seen them in Manchester, in *Mary Barton* (1848) and *North and South* (1855). *Cranford*, often read and loved as a charming and idyllic period piece, shows the repercussion of Big Business on two small-town sisters. A bank fails, and they are ruined, though obliged by the conventions of the day to keep the flag of gentility proudly flying. Miss Matty, burning two candles alternately, so that any chance visitor will assume that she can afford to burn two at once, has been clearly observed and recorded as a victim of revolution.

As a counterblast against the socialist and radical tendencies of the time Disraeli in his later novels set forth a new political doctrine—the young England policy of the enlightened Tory democrats. A sturdy supporter of feudal responsibility, Disraeli feared the consequences of Liberal individualism, which seemed to be destroying social harmony and replacing it by the harsh creed of class warfare. Poverty and discontent, the reverse side of economic progress and industrialism, were threatening to endanger public order. The novel with a purpose had long been popular and now it began to grapple with the fundamental problems at issue.

In *Captain Popanilla* Disraeli had tilted at the commercial middle class; twenty years later he saw them endangering unity and breaking down, by their *laissez-faire* system, the bonds which had formerly bound all classes to one another. The Whig aristocracy was egoistic and without trust, the energetic middle class solely absorbed in the pursuit of wealth. The men of reason, cold-blooded sophists, deceiving theorists, economists, utilitarians, had succeeded in separating class from class and destroying solidarity. Left to itself and uninspired by a lofty morality or sense of social justice, industry was becoming a juggernaut crushing beneath its unyielding mechanism all hopes of a good life and common culture. *Coningsby* (1844), *Sybil* (1845) and *Tancred* (1847) set out the political doctrine which should renew the inspiration of the Christian ages from the fountains of the East.

To his old gift for satire Disraeli added an emotional fervour that found characteristic expression in *Sybil* when he denounced the system that was dividing England into two nations animated by a mutual hatred that threatened to replace their common patriotism.

> "'Two nations between whom there is no intercourse and no sympathy; who are as ignorant of each other's habits, thoughts and feelings, as if they were dwellers in different zones, or inhabitants of different planets; who are formed by a different breeding, are fed by a different food, are ordered by different manners, and are not governed by the same laws.'
>
> 'You speak of ... ' said Egremont, hesitatingly.
> 'The Rich and the Poor.'"

Had Disraeli not given his life to statesmanship, his reputation as a novelist might well have fared better than it has. His work is still fresh and vigorous and the passing of time has shown that his insight into the domestic and social problems created by liberalism was little short of prophetic.

With so many writers ministering to their love of didacticism Victorian readers still turned sometimes in their hours of ease from scarifying pictures of social unrest to the far more scarifying mystery thrillers of Wilkie Collins, the first English novelist to deal with the detection of crime.

Thanks to the habit of bringing out novels as serials, in shilling numbers, this form of literature was reaching an enormous new body of readers which had hitherto been out of its reach. Like the audience of a country town suddenly visited by a troupe of actors, they were untrained in the conventions of the new art to which they were introduced. The public in the new industrial towns did not ask for sermons on the conditions around them; they wanted melodrama—the more sensational the better—to help them escape from their own drab lives. They wanted to be stimulated and excited, but they would have turned in scorn from the tinsel romance that thrilled Isabella Thorpe and her friends. Wilkie Collins, with an admirable grasp of the market, brought Gothicism up to date. His famous formula for a successful novel was, "Make 'em laugh; make 'em cry; make 'em wait." In *The Woman in White* (1860) he whirled his theatrical characters through a fantastic plot, broken by a series of climaxes preceded by breathtaking suspense, seeking and finding the depths of depravity below the apparently prosy surface of middle-class life.

The Woman in White opens in Hampstead, but having invented a crime too subtly ingenious for an Englishman, the author invents an Italian Count to commit it. Criminal psychology had advanced since the days of Mrs.Radcliffe and Maturin. Readers were more knowing, and Collins endows his villain with a Falstaffian physique, on the ground that it is hard to believe a fat man malevolent. He further disarms the suspicions of English readers by stressing the Count's devotion to pet animals. To make him even more acceptable his creator endows him with his own tastes. Thus Fosco is credited with a knowledge of the arts, a fondness for opera; he is a gourmand and a cosmopolitan critic of English ways. The resultant virtuoso in the art of forgery and deception, with his cool audacity and subtle insight into human nature, may be a monster, but he is fascinating enough to pass in good society. Count Fosco has a long chain of descendants in modern fiction.

In *The Moonstone* (1868), a novel which had an undoubted influence on Dickens in *The Murder of Edwin Drood*, Collins exploited with advantage popular interest in the East. The story is far simpler in structure than *The Woman in White* and it has no characters to compare with Count Fosco in power and cunning, but the atmosphere is charged with a haunting sense of mystery and fear. A man under the influence of drugs takes a jewel, stolen long before from the head of an Indian idol, and unknowingly conceals it. The situation is complicated by the mysterious appearance of three Brahmins, who have come to England in search of their treasure. Sergeant Cuff, the first detective in English fiction, figures in the story. Collins is a skilful narrator, and the recent revival of interest in his work may be a tribute to his power, one little exercised by contemporary writers.

Later in the century Collins was followed by another exponent of the detective thriller, Sir Arthur Conan Doyle, who will always be remembered for his creation of the amateur detective Sherlock Holmes and his foil Dr. Watson, whose adventures were embodied in a cycle of stories which first appeared in 1891.

The busy, strenuous years of ever-expanding British prosperity saw novels pour from the presses in a turbulent spate of mediocrity with here and there something good tossed up on the bank and rescued from oblivion.

Among these were George Borrow's admirable wind-on-the-heath gypsy tale *Lavengro* (1851) and *The Romany Rye* (1857), full of country lore, in which the reader could escape from industrialism into a remote underworld as exotic in its own way as the Far East.

Growing interest in adolescence and education led Thomas Hughes in the mid-century to write *Tom Brown's Schooldays* (1857), the story of an ordinary schoolboy at Rugby in the great days when Dr. Arnold was creating the modern Public School.

After the success enjoyed by Sir Walter Scott the historical novel never went out of favour and in the eighteen thirties Scott's mantle fell on the elegant shoulders of Edward Bulwer, Lord Lytton, a writer of somewhat romantic tastes. His best-known historical novel is *The Last Days of Pompeii* (1834), a stirring technicolor version of the volcanic eruption that destroyed Pompeii. Bulwer's versatility is shown in his creation of the 'fashionable' novel—the butt of Disraeli and Thackeray—at the beginning of his career with *Pelham* (1828) and in the Utopian fantasy *The Coming Race*, which was published in 1871. In this romance of the future the author describes his visit to a subterranean race that in distant ages took refuge from inundations in the bowels of the earth. Owing to the discovery of *Vril*, a form of energy embodying all the natural forces, this race has reached a high degree of civilization and scientific achievement. Their country is a Utopia in which there is neither crime nor war, neither poverty nor sensuality. Their women are physically stronger than their men, and it is the women who choose their spouses. This idealized study of a matriarch society is used to attack the principle of democracy based on numbers—a system that, according to Bulwer Lytton, leads to rivalry, misery and degradation.

If by his 'fashionable' novels Lytton influenced that feminine literary phenomenon 'Ouida', *The Coming Race* was not without its effect on Samuel Butler and H. G. Wells.

At this point in the history of the novel selection becomes increasingly difficult unless the strictest canons of excellence are employed. A high standard of technical competence is common enough as the novel develops and becomes the most popular literary form. But few English writers before the time of Henry James considered the novel as an art form or concerned themselves at all with its implications and possibilities. Although popular, the novel had not yet been assigned a lofty position in the literary hierarchy. Serious writers did not regard it in the same light as poetry or the drama. The novel was a form of entertainment, and well-brought-up children were taught not to read novels before luncheon. An educated Victorian reader idled away an evening with a novel when he did not feel equal to reading something more important—history, for example, or poetry.

But changes in its status begin to appear; they are the work of writers who brought to the novel a poetic intensity of feeling and a passionate seriousness.

J. HILLIS MILLER

Time and Intersubjectivity

Our Mutual Friend (1864–1865), or the last *Chronicle of Barset* (1866–1867), or *Middle-march* (1871–1872), or *The Mayor of Casterbridge* (1886), is, like any other work of literature, made exclusively of words. In this sense it may be said to designate an imaginary or mental world. The words of a novel objectify the mind of an author and make that mind available to others. An analogy may be found for this in everyday life. The hidden consciousness of each person we meet is incarnated in his body, in his gestures, his facial expression, his speech. This presence in the world opens the other person to our spontaneous and unreflecting comprehension. The writing of a novel is also a gesture, and this is its primary reality. It brings into visibility what its author is. A man is what he does, and this is as true for the writing of a novel as for any other action. Every page of *Oliver Twist* (1837–1839), or *David Copperfield* (1849–1850), expresses something more than any theme or story or dramatization of character. It expresses the unique quality of Dickens' mind. The fact that a novel is made of words means that it is also a form of consciousness. The reading or criticism of Victorian fiction is therefore, like any other reading or criticism, to be defined as consciousness of the consciousness of another. Through the act of reading the reader tries to identify himself with another mind and to reexperience from the inside the feelings and thoughts of that mind. Reading a novel is a form of intersubjectivity.

From *The Form of Victorian Fiction*. © 1968 by the University of Notre Dame Press, Notre Dame, Indiana.

A novel, however, differs from many other forms of literature, lyric poetry for instance, in that the mind which its words express is not a single meditating or perceiving consciousness, not a solitary mind exploring itself or exploring its relations to objects outside itself—trees, flowers, mountains, and clouds. A novel is a structure of interpenetrating minds, the mind of the narrator as he beholds or enters into the characters, the minds of the characters as they behold or know one another. Not isolated consciousness, not consciousness at grips with natural objects, not consciousness face to face with God in meditation, but consciousness of the consciousness of others— this is the primary focus of fiction. The novelist's assumptions, often unstated ones, about the ways one mind can interact with other minds determine the form his novel takes.

Point of view, for example, is a special case of the consciousness of the consciousness of others, perhaps the most important case, since it embraces the whole novel. The narrator, as much recent criticism has assumed, is a role the novelist plays, an invented personality who is often granted within the looking-glass world of the novel certain unique powers, powers of ubiquity in space and time, powers of direct access to other minds. The basic mode of narration in Victorian fiction is neither dialogue nor internal monologue, but indirect discourse, that mode of language in which a man plays the role of a narrator who relives from within the thoughts and feelings of a character and registers these in his own language, or in a mixture of the character's language and his own language. Indirect discourse is therefore continuously and necessarily ironical, however mild or attenuated this irony may be. The juxtaposition in indirect discourse of two minds, that of the narrator and that of the character, is, one might say, irony writ large. An exploitation of the fact that one can in language imagine oneself as having direct access to another mind makes Victorian fiction possible. A Victorian novel is therefore a version of the dramatic monologue, a version in which the monologuist superimposes his own voice, judgment, and mind on those of the character. As a version of the dramatic monologue the novel may be seen as an extension of that commitment to the playing of roles through sympathetic identification which is an important factor in romanticism. There is an unbroken continuity from Keats's extension of his negative capability from urns and nightingales to people ("I am with Achilles shouting in the Trenches," he said in a letter[1]), to Browning's elaborate exploration in his dramatic monologues of what Charles du Bos called his power of "the introspection of others,"[2] to the structure of related minds in *Middlemarch* or *The Return of the Native* (1878). There are always at least two persons present in a monologue by Browning, the speaker and Browning himself, though critics have since the days of the first Browning Society been arguing about the way in which the poet is present in "Bishop Blougram's Apology" or "Mr. Sludge, 'the Medium.'" Often, as in the two monologues cited, there is a third person present too, a listener, so that a dramatic monologue by Browning is an embryo novel, as Henry James saw when he spoke of "The Novel in *The Ring and the Book*."[3] In the same way an epistolary novel might be defined as a series of dramatic monologues, each addressed by one character to another. The novel in letters is a simplified version of the form any novel takes[4] In all these cases the writer plays the role of a narrator who can enter into the lives of other people and speak for the inner quality of those lives. Victorian fiction grows out of earlier forms of intersubjectivity in literature and is itself a form of intersubjectivity.

The narrator of a novel comes into existence in an act in which the novelist plays the role of a role-player. The character is a mask outside a mask. The characters in the novel, on the other hand, are unconscious of the narrator's knowledge of them. Nevertheless, they in their turn live their lives in terms of their relations to others. In most Victorian novels there is relatively little detached self-consciousness, the self-consciousness of a single person becoming aware of himself in separation from other people. In Victorian novels, for the most part, the characters are aware of themselves in terms of their relations to others. The integrity of the selfhood of each person depends neither on reaching the deep buried self by a descent into the mind in solitary meditation, nor on a contemplation of rocks, trees, and daffodils, nor on confrontation of a deity who is the ultimate foundation of the self. In most Victorian novels the protagonist comes to know himself and to fulfill himself by way of other people. A characteristic personage in a Victorian novel could not say, "I think, therefore I am," but rather, if he could ever be imagined to express himself so abstractly, "I am related to others, therefore I am," or, "I know myself through my relations to others," or, "I am conscious of myself as conscious of others." Much of the language of most Victorian novels is used to express the narrator's awareness of the characters in their awareness of themselves in relation to other people. A Victorian novel may most inclusively be defined as a structure of interpenetrating minds. Therefore, analysis of work by the major Victorian novelists depends on discriminating definition of the forms of interpersonal relations in any given novel or group of novels.

2

The mode of existence of a group of related minds is fundamentally temporal. This does not mean that one should not think of these relations as generating a space, the interior space created by the words of the novel. It is inevitable that the reader should think of the field brought into existence by tensions between minds as a space and that he should use terms like proximity and distance, exteriority and interpenetration, superimposition and juxtaposition, continuity and discontinuity, to express the way at any one moment in a novel the narrator is related to the characters and the characters to one another. Moreover, the landscape of a novel—houses, gardens, roads, hills, and rivers—constitutes an interior space polarized by the tensions between the characters and expressing those tensions.

Nevertheless, time is a more important dimension of fiction than space. A novel is a temporal rhythm made up of the movement of the minds of the narrator and his characters in their dance of approach and withdrawal, love and hate, convergence and divergence, merger and division. The structure of a novel is a musical design made up of the constantly changing interplay between mind and mind which constitutes the action. Any given passage in a novel is a moment in that perpetually ongoing movement and draws its meaning from its multiple temporal relations to what comes before and after, just as in music a given note or chord has meaning only in relation to what precedes and follows.

The time of a novel is polyrhythmic. This results because each of the characters has his own time, as does the narrator. Each stands in a different relation to the present of the action as it passes, and each has his own temporal structure of recollection and anticipation. In any given passage in a novel these various temporal rhythms overlap or interact like the waves within waves in a great breaker making for the shore. The dramatic action of a novel is the temporal pattern made of the sequence of interactions between minds, each with its own temporal flow, as they move toward some equilibrium or dispersal of their relationships.

Comprehension of all the novels by a single novelist may perhaps best be obtained not by a comparison of motifs, situations, or characters from novel to novel, but by a comparison of the melodies created in the various novels by the interweaving of the minds of the characters. Through juxtaposition of these melodies a temporal pattern fundamental to the novelist in question may be identified.

3

A passage in Thomas Hardy's *A Pair of Blue Eyes* (1872–1873), will show how temporal perspectives determine form and meaning in Victorian fiction. This text is a good example of the way a multiplicity of times is interwoven in the texture of a novel. Human beings have in daily life such an extraordinary ability to sustain several simultaneous rhythms of time that the temporal complexity of a given passage in a novel is easily taken for granted. It may be detected by an effort of analysis which stands back from the passage and interrogates it for its temporal structure. The present moment in our reading of a novel is never enclosed in itself, nor is it just expanded by a single structure of temporal "ecstasies" like that analyzed by Martin Heidegger in *Sein und Zeit*. Heidegger's description of a movement toward a future from which the past arises as a "has-been" and is made present may be the basis for all temporal structures in a novel,[5] but in a typical passage in fiction there may usually be distinguished a number of different times superimposed at various distances from one another with that atmosphere between them which Marcel Proust calls "the poetry of memory."[6]

The passage in *A Pair of Blue Eyes* comes at a dramatic moment for three of the protagonists. Elfride Swancourt has already caused the death of one lover and is now in the process of betraying a second lover, Stephen Smith, in order to confirm her hold on a third lover, Henry Knight, once Stephen's best friend. To keep Knight she must deny that she has ever known Stephen, deny that she ever promised to marry him, deny that she once nearly carried that promise out. The betrayal comes in the instant of a look, a look of secret recognition which passes between Elfride and Stephen as her new lover helps her mount her horse:

> Her old lover still looked on at the performance as he leant over the gate a dozen yards off. Once in the saddle, and having a firm grip of the reins, she turned her head as if by a resistless fascination, and for the first time since that memorable parting on the moor outside St. Launce's after the passionate attempt at marriage with him, Elfride looked in the face of the young man she first had loved. He was the youth who had called her his inseparable wife many a time, and whom she had even addressed as her husband. Their eyes met. Measurement of life should be proportioned rather to the intensity of the experience than to its

actual length. Their glance, but a moment chronologically, was a season in their history. To Elfride the intense agony of reproach in Stephen's eye was a nail piercing her heart with a deadliness no words can describe. With a spasmodic effort she withdrew her eyes, urged on the horse, and in the chaos of perturbed memories was oblivious of any presence beside her. The deed of deception was complete.[7]

Many different times are present in the experience of the reader of this passage. There is his own time of reading, the sequence of moments which passes as he reads the words and of which he has at least a partial awareness. To read a novel is in one sense to be carried out of the real world and transported into an imaginary world generated by the words, but the reader never loses altogether his awareness of the clock time which passes as he reads and of the situation in the real world which that passage of time determines. The reader also has a more or less explicit awareness of the time when the author wrote the words. He knows a man named Thomas Hardy sat one day at his desk and wrote down these words out of his head and on the paper before him. He is also likely to know something of the facts of Hardy's life and to have heard that *A Pair of Blue Eyes* bears a relation to Hardy's courtship of his first wife, Emma Lavinia Gifford, and perhaps a relation also to his earlier love for Tryphena Sparks.[8] Hardy wrote *A Pair of Blue Eyes* not in a pure ascent into the realm of imagination, but by means of a transformation of an earlier time in his life which must have been more or less vividly present to him as he wrote. The writing of the novel was an attempt to come to terms with that past by moving toward a satisfactory change of it into a fiction.

The chief means of that transformation is the creation of the voice and viewpoint of the narrator. The storyteller has his own time, a time very different from the doubling of past in a present reaching toward its completed change into a fiction which is Hardy's experience as he writes down the words. The narrator, it needs hardly be said, is not the real Hardy. He is a voice Hardy invented to tell the story for him; or, to put this another way, the narrator is a personality created by the tempo, diction, and tone of the words Hardy chose to put down on paper. Hardy's narrator, in this passage in *A Pair of Blue Eyes*, as throughout his fiction, stands outside the events of the novel in the sense of existing at a time when they have all passed. He looks back on the action after it is over or down on it from a height which is outside of time altogether. He has ubiquity in time and space and knows everything there is to know within that all-embracing span. Moreover, from his point of view the events of the story are real events which he describes not as they were for Hardy (imaginary, fictive), but as if they had a substantial existence independent of the narrator's knowledge of them.

Although the narrator is to the world of the novel as we are to the real world around us in the sense of not doubting its reality, he has a superhuman power of memory and clairvoyance. He can put himself at will within the minds and feelings of any of the characters at any time in their lives. He tells any one moment of the story in terms of a full knowledge of all that happened prior to that moment and after it. The omniscient narrator is the most important constitutive convention for the form of Victorian fiction, the convention easiest to take for granted, and the convention which is the oddest of all, the one requiring the most analysis and explanation.

Time of the reader, time of the author, time of the narrator—already I have identified three superimposed temporal rhythms in the passage. In addition there are the times of the various characters present in the scene, a different one for each character. Hardy has the good novelist's ability to single out in imagination two or three people from the vast multitude of possible characters and to concentrate not on their isolated awareness of themselves (Hardy's characters rarely have such self-consciousness), but on their awareness of themselves as aware of one another. This awareness dwells in time, and each character's consciousness of the others has its temporal dimensions. In this passage, for example, Elfride and Stephen are aware of the way she has a few moments before, during their visit to the family tomb of the Luxellians, refused to recognize him. They are also conscious, as Hardy makes explicit, of all the earlier episodes of their courtship, episodes which have taken up most of the novel to this point.

One of the extraordinary things about fiction is the small amount of notation which is necessary to give the reader a knowledge of the temporal depths in the characters' minds. Part of the reason for this is the existence of a similar depth in the reader's relation to the novel. The reader is at any point aware not only of the words he is now reading, but also of the words he has already read. He has a more or less confused and indistinct, but nonetheless effective, memory of all those other passages, and this enters strongly into his response to any passage he now reads. He has a confused anticipation of future passages, even at a first reading, partly because of hints about the future dropped along the way by the narrator, who knows, of course, all that has not yet happened. What the reader remembers, in *A Pair of Blue Eyes* as in most Victorian fiction, is the narrator's earlier presentation of the characters' moments of awareness of other people, for this is what occupies most of the novel. The reader remembers the earlier experiences of the characters and the characters are shown as having this memory themselves, so that two kinds of memory, each with its own proper structure and quality, are super-imposed. In the passage from *A Pair of Blue Eyes* the reader does not have to be reminded by the narrator of the last time Elfride and Stephen met, nor does he need to have reconstituted for him a generalized memory of all their past relations, since most of the novel has been made up of language which has been creating a vicarious memory in the reader to match the living memories of the characters.

The central event of the passage from *A Pair of Blue Eyes* is a look, one of those looks so frequent in Hardy's fiction, in this case a look which identifies the present moment of the relation between Stephen and Elfride as the betrayal of their past allegiance and therefore as forming an instant more important than most instants, a "season in their history," a turning point in its development. In addition there is the consciousness of Knight watching this look without comprehending it or seeing the temporal depths which enter into it. The interaction between these three minds is a good example of the relationship between persons which is characteristic of Victorian fiction. Far from being cut off from other people and seeing them from the outside as objects, Hardy's characters, like those of other Victorian novelists, often have a perfect intuition of the other person's heart. The Victorian novelists assume that each person lives within a field generated by the presence of other people. This field gives a man access to the minds of others, though that access may for one reason or another be barred. In this passage Stephen's eye expresses to Elfride an intense agony of reproach. His body and its gestures incarnate his subjective state and make it visible to her, although Knight does not see the agony of reproach in Stephen's eye at all.

At the same time as the reader is presented with this incomplete overlapping of three consciousnesses, he is also presented the separate quality of Elfride's mind, the chaos of perturbed memories which fully occupies her attention as she rides away from Stephen and which makes her oblivious of Knight and the surrounding scene. In this passage at least five different temporal rhythms can be distinguished: the reader's time, the novelist's time, the narrator's time, the time of the intersubjective field created by the various degrees of understanding which the characters have of one another, and the private time of one of the characters. Taken together they make up the modulating chord of intersubjective relations poised momentarily in this particular text, but ultimately including the whole novel, its author, and its reader.

This passage, like any other text in *A Pair of Blue Eyes*, constitutes itself while it is read as a present around which the rest of the novel organizes itself in a unified temporal structure holding past and future in the open as integral aspects of the present. Time is the fundamental dimension of fictional form not because the novel represents the "stream of consciousness," the "flux of experience," or "life as a process." These terms, like so many phrases current in the criticism of fiction, are implicitly spatial; they assume that time is a linear sequence, so that life is a movement along a preexistent road or river, past and future lying spread out before and behind like beads on a string, all moments side by side and of the same nature, extending infinitely in either direction. In fact, however, time is a constituent dimension of fiction because, as the passage from *A Pair of Blue Eyes* suggests, novels excel in expressing the temporality of the present as a reaching toward a future which will contain a reassimilation of the past. The novel is by nature an open form. In various ways it represents human existence as standing outside itself, as reaching toward an as yet unpossessed totality which will complete it and draw the circle of life closed. This "standing outside itself," this "reaching toward," are basic characteristics of human temporality. Any conception of fiction as having the closed perfection of spatialized form will tend to falsify the ways in which a novel may represent the temporality of the present as generated from a movement toward a finite future which will repossess the past. In the passage from *A Pair of Blue Eyes* there are many different related temporal rhythms, but each may be seen as another version of this presence of a present which lives and moves in the yearnings of its incompletions. Elfride, for example, goes toward a future love affair with Knight which will be lived according to her perturbed memories of her past with Stephen. The intersubjective tensions in this passage, as in so many other texts in Victorian fiction, are established by a reaching out of each person toward another who will, he thinks, bring to perfection his as yet unfulfilled selfhood. This dissatisfaction is the motive energy of love for Hardy, for Trollope, for George Eliot, for Thackeray. It is one of the most important ways man can experience his temporality.

The narrator's time, the novelist's time, and the reader's time have the same structure as Elfride's. The narrator stands in that future which possesses in potentiality the completed past, but he moves back through that past trying to bring it up to the future as a present actualized in words. The novelist seeks to comprehend his own past existence by moving away from it into an imaginary future which his story continuously generates, in one version of the hermeneutical circle of interpretation. The reader in his attempt to understand the novel is caught in another form of the temporal circle of interpretation, reaching toward a perfected understanding of the whole which is never attained, but which is presupposed as already existing in any partial explication.[9] To approach a novel by way of the reader, the author, the narrator, the characters individually, or the characters in their relation to one another is to encounter in each case a new example of the structure of temporality which provides the generative energy of fictional form. The criticism of fiction depends on exact discrimination of the versions of this structure operative in any given novel, no less than on discrimination of patterns of intersubjectivity.

4

Thackeray's *The History of Henry Esmond, Esq.* (1852) offers an opportunity to explore further the implications of temporal form in Victorian fiction.[10] In this novel Thackeray uses one of the conventional modes of the Victorian novel as a means of self- exploration. In this case the convention is that of the autobiographical novel, with its roots in the confessional form going back through Rousseau and Montaigne to St. Augustine. The novel is a good demonstration of the fact that an autobiographical narration, like an impersonal one, exists as a structure of overlapping times, interpenetrating minds, and interweavings of imaginary and real. Thackeray's sophistication about the alternative possibilities of style and point of view leads him to manipulate strategically the fact that the narrator of an autobiographical novel is an assumed voice and personality. *Henry Esmond* has probably a better claim even than *Pendennis* (1848–1850), to be called the most personal of Thackeray's novels, the one in which he most completely projects his sense of his own life and destiny. In *Henry Esmond*, Thackeray attempts more or less deliberately to confront his own life by the indirect means of playing the role of an invented character. Nevertheless, it is also true that Thackeray remains conscious of the difference between himself and Esmond and keeps a distance and power of judging which is present explicitly in his statements about Esmond and implicitly in the form the novel takes.

Thackeray was in Esmond embodying and dismissing a false attitude in himself rather than yielding to the temptation to justify himself or to live out in a fantasy of wish-fulfillment the life he thought he deserved. "The hero" of *Henry Esmond*, Thackeray wrote to his mother, "is as stately as Sir Charles Grandison ... a handsome likeness of an ugly son of yours."[11] "As stately as Grandison"—surely this suggests Thackeray's perspective on Esmond's self-righteous pomposity, as does the phrase "handsome likeness" the way Esmond is too good to be true, certainly too good to be a true likeness of Thackeray himself. Elsewhere he called Esmond a "bore" (III [1946], 72), and he told Anthony Trollope that the fact no one reads *Esmond* ought not to be surprising: "After all, *Esmond* was a prig."[12] Thackeray never speaks directly within the novel for his own view of Esmond, since Esmond has all the talking to himself, or almost all. Thackeray's judgment is present, however, in the way Esmond unintentionally gives the reader information which makes it possible to understand him better than he understands himself. Thackeray's view is also present covertly in the way the preface by Esmond's daughter Rachel, the only part of the text not written by Esmond himself, invites the reader, in spite of its filial piety toward Henry Esmond, to remember that the body of the text is Esmond's subjective reconstruction of his life, not an objective account by an unbiased narrator.

The structure of overlapping times in *Henry Esmond* is something like that of *A Pair of Blue Eyes*, but there are added complexities, and time is more explicitly a part of the theme. In *Henry Esmond* Thackeray attempts to come to terms with his own life by playing the role of the old Henry Esmond, now happily married to the first Rachel, living in Virginia, and as his life draws to a close sitting safe in his armchair writing the story of his own life, turning back in memory to his youthful adventures and playing in his turn the role of the young Henry Esmond, speaking of his younger self throughout in the third person. The aging Esmond can see his young self from a safe distance as another man, as a "he." The basic mode of discourse in *Henry Esmond* is a doubling of minds which is the analogue in the autobiographical or confessional novel of the doubling in the more usual Victorian novel by which an omniscient narrator, standing at a time after the events of the story are over, re-creates by indirect discourse the inner experience of the protagonists. In *Henry Esmond* the reader is constantly given two interpenetrating minds, that of the young Henry oriented in infatuated desire toward the future and that of the old Henry, sagely disillusioned about all but himself, and oriented in musing reminiscence toward the past. The novel is generated out of the interaction of these two consciousnesses. Surrounding this double role-playing, or latent behind it as a ghostly presence, is Thackeray himself. As Gordon Ray has shown, Thackeray's relations to his mother and to Jane Brookfield are the generative source of the feelings and events of the story. In writing "the last eight chapters of the first book of *Esmond* and the first two chapters of the second," says Ray, Thackeray "again lived through the whole course of the Brookfield affair and made it a part of his novel."[13]

Reality and the imaginary are, however, related in yet another way in *Henry Esmond*. It is, after all, a historical novel and contains descriptions of actual events and people—England's wars in the late seventeenth and early eighteenth centuries, Addison, Steele, Swift, Marlborough, the Pretender, and so on. As in all historical fiction, the reader is constantly moving back and forth between his sense that the novel is a faithful mirroring of history and his recognition that a historical novel can never be history but is a fictional transposition of history into the realm of the imaginary. If the style, and in the first edition the typography, of *Henry Esmond* are meant to recall eighteenth-century diction, syntax, and bookmaking, nineteenth-century styles and attitudes continuously interpose, as for example in the way the novel expresses not so much a mid-eighteenth-century view of history as the nineteenth-century Whig view which Thackeray had encountered in the first two volumes of Macaulay's *History of England* (1848).

Three times and three attitudes are constantly superimposed in the language of the novel: 1852, the time of writing; the time of Esmond's old age, when he is supposed to be composing his memoirs; and the late seventeenth and early eighteenth centuries, when the events narrated are supposed to have taken place. There are places in the novel when this superimposition of times is even further complicated, as when the old Esmond remembers returning in middle life to Castlewood and recalling his childhood there. The text here is a memory within a memory. Moreover, it provides the occasion for the novel's most explicit clue to the placement of the narrator: "How well all things were remembered!" says Henry. " ... We forget nothing. The memory sleeps, but wakens again; I often think how it shall be when, after the last sleep of death, the *réveillée* shall arouse us for ever, and the past in one flash of self-consciousness rush back, like the soul revivified."[14]

The novel is that *réveillée*, a flash of self-consciousness which resurrects, after its temporary sleep in the depths of memory, all Esmond's past in an instantaneous panoramic vision of the whole. The point of view of the novel is not just that of an old man "at the close of his life," who "sits and recalls in tranquillity the happy and busy scenes of it" (I. 7. 73). The narrator is a man so close to death, possessing so perfect a memory of his life and so clarified a judgment of it, that it is as if he had already moved outside of time. He is like a revivified soul looking back from the detachment of eternity on the outstretched span of his life. One evidence for this is the way Esmond talks of the last day or the last hour of his life as if it had already happened. From the point of view of the place where he stands, the end of his life as much as its beginning has become part of the past: "To the very last hour of his life, Esmond remembered the lady as she then spoke and looked ... " (I. 1. 6); "Esmond could repeat, to his last day, some of the doggerel lines in which his muse bewailed his pretty lass ... " (I. 9. 92).[15]

Henry Esmond is punctuated by references to memory which call attention to the fact that everything in the novel is seen through a gentle haze of reminiscence, at once distant and close, vivid and softened by time, as in Esmond's remark that his vision of the angry Rachel, after he has brought home the smallpox, standing with "the taper lighting up her marble face, her scarlet lip quivering, and her shining golden hair" ... "remained for ever fixed upon his memory" (I. 8.88). In another place he exclaims: "How those trivial incidents and words, the landscape and sunshine, and the group of people smiling and talking, remain fixed on the memory!" (I. 1. 9). The law of this remembering is given in those texts which affirm the total presence of the past in the eternal moment of the narrator's memory: "Her words as she spoke struck the chords of all his memory, and the whole of his boyhood and youth passed within him" (II. 1. 180). Or: " ... such a past is always present to a man; such a passion once felt forms a part of his whole being, and cannot be separated from it.... Parting and forgetting! What faithful heart can do these? Our great thoughts, our great affections, the Truths of our life, never leave us. Surely, they cannot separate from our consciousness; shall follow it whithersoever that shall go; and are of their nature divine and immortal" (III. 6. 422–423).

Esmond, however, is here talking of his infatuation with Beatrix. He is talking about it from the perspective of a time long after that infatuation is over, a time when he no longer loves Beatrix and can view his foolish fascination with detached objectivity, as well as relive it with its first intensity. It is immortally part of him and yet no longer identical with him. This doubleness is the fundamental structuring principle of *Henry Esmond*. The old Esmond relives the young Esmond's worship first of Rachel and then of Beatrix from a point of view which sees their folly in the perspective of a godlike detachment from all passion. He relives them as forever passed. Here the implications of omniscient narration in Victorian fiction are given an explicitly theological definition. To remember everything and see everything clearly, as Esmond thinks he does, is to see everything from the perspective of those portals of death within which the aged Esmond stands. Esmond is like a god or like a risen soul, "divine and immortal," or at least he assumes that he is. He claims to be outside the uncertainties of time, no longer living as an incomplete self yearning toward a future union with the woman he loves, but in full possession of himself by way of a full possession of all the times of his life. He looks back on those times, so he thinks, with a perfect extratemporal perspective on them. He sees their truth with unclouded lucidity of vision.

In chapter four I shall attempt to show that Esmond unwittingly gives the reader the information necessary to put in question his claim to possess godlike knowledge of his own life and godlike superiority to other people. For Thackeray, as for George Eliot or for Thomas Hardy, no man or woman can be a god for another. The complexity of *Henry Esmond* lies in the fact that it presents this indirectly, through the autobiography of a man who discovers that no other person can be worthy of his worship but who fails to apply this discovery to himself. Esmond sets himself up in solemn fatuity as a god worthy of the worship of others. This theme is dramatized with admirable subtlety in the temporal structure of the novel. If no man or woman can be a god to another person, then no man can claim to have a panoramic vision of the whole temporal course of his life. In questioning Esmond's insight into the meaning of his own life, the novel also questions the convention of fiction which supposes that an individual narrator can see things like a transcendent god or like an epic bard who sings under the guidance of some heavenly muse. For Thackeray, as for the other major Victorian novelists, man remains within time and cannot escape from it by spatializing it. Omniscience is possible only to a narrator who is a collective mind rising from the living together of men and women in a community. In *Henry Esmond*, as in *A Pair of Blue Eyes* and in many other Victorian novels, temporal form and the exploration of interpersonal relations are so closely intertwined that one may be said to be the embodiment of the other. If this is so, the critic may be justified in speaking of time and intersubjectivity as the fundamental formative principles of Victorian fiction.

Notes

1. *The Letters of John Keats:* 1814–1821, ed. Hyder Edward Rollins, I (Cambridge, Mass., 1958), 404. The context extends Keats's statement: "According to my state of mind I am with Achilles shouting in the Trenches or with Theocritus in the Vales of Sicily. Or I throw my whole being into Troilus...."

2. "*Pauline* de Browning: Extraits d'un Cours inédit," *Etudes anglaises*, VII, 2 (April 1954), 164: "Tintrospection d'autrui."

3. *Notes on Novelists* (New York, 1914), pp. 385–411.

4. For an excellent discussion of the implications of form in the epistolary novel, see Jean Rousset, "Une Forme littéraire: le roman par lettres," *Forme et signification: Essais sur les structures littéraires de Corneille à Claudel* (Paris, 1962), pp. 65–108.

5. See Martin Heidegger, *Sein und Zeit*, 10th edition (Tübingen, 1963), p. 326: "Die Gewesenheit entspringt der Zukunft, so zwar, dass die gewesene (besser gewesende) Zukunft die Gegenwart aus sich entlässt. Dies dergestalt als gewesend-gegenwärtigende Zukunft einheitliche Phänomen nennen wir die *Zeitlichkeit*." For a translation see Martin Heidegger, *Being and Time*, trans. John Macquarrie and

Edward Robinson (London, 1962), p. 374: "The character of 'having been' arises from the future, and in such a way that the future which 'has been' (or better, which 'is in the process of having been') releases from itself the Present. This phenomenon has the unity of a future which makes present in the process of having been; we designate it as *'temporality.'*"

6. "En Mémoire des églises assassinées," *Pastiches et mélanges*, 33rd edition (Paris, 1937), p. 108: " ... la résistante douceur de cette atmosphère interposée qui a l'étendue même de notre vie et qui est toute la poésie de la mémoire." For a discussion of the concept of polyrhythmic time see Gaston Bachelard, *La Dialectique de la durée* (Paris, 1936), especially chapters 6 through 8.

7. *A Pair of Blue Eyes, The Writings of Thomas Hardy in Prose and Verse*, Anniversary Edition, x (New York and London: Harper & Brothers, [1920]), Ch. 27, pp. 302–303.

8. See Carl J. Weber, *Hardy of Wessex: His Life and Literary Career* (New York, 1965), pp. 75–88, and for a somewhat exaggerated account of the place of Tryphena Sparks in Hardy's life, see Lois Deacon and Terry Coleman, *Providence and Mr. Hardy* (London, 1966).

9. See Martin Heidegger, p. 152: "Alle Auslegung, die Verständnis beistellen soll, muss schon das Auszulegende verstanden haben." ("Any interpretation which is to contribute understanding, must already have understood what is to be interpreted," trans. Macquarrie and Robinson, p. 194). For a discussion of this idea in Heidegger's theory of interpretation, see Paul de Man, "New criticism et nouvelle critique," *Preuves*, no. 188 (Octobre 1966), 34–35, and see also, for a discussion of the opposition between linear time and polyrhythmic or hermeneutical time, Paul de Man, "Georg Lukács' *Theory of the Novel*," *Modern Language Notes*, LXXXI, 5 (December 1966), 533–534.

10. See Henri A. Talon, "Time and Memory in Thackeray's *Henry Esmond*," *The Review of English Studies*, N. S., XIII, 50 (May 1962), 147–156.

11. *The Letters and Private Papers of William Makepeace Thackeray*, ed. Gordon N. Ray, II (Cambridge, Mass., 1945), 815.

12. Anthony Trollope, *Thackeray* (New York: Harper & Brothers, n. d.), p. 121.

13. Gordon N. Ray, *Thackeray: The Age of Wisdom: 1847–1863* (New York: McGraw-Hill, 1958), p. 181. See pp. 180–188, and also Gordon N. Ray, *The Buried Life: A Study of the Relation between Thackeray's Fiction and His Personal History* (Cambridge, Mass., 1952), for full discussions of the connection between *Henry Esmond* and Thackeray's "longing passion unfulfilled" for Jane Brookfield.

14. *The History of Henry Esmond, Esq.*, *The Works of William Makepeace Thackeray*, The Centenary Biographical Edition, x (London: Smith, Elder, 1911), Bk. III, Ch. 7, p. 435.

15. Henri Talon, in citing these texts, justly observes that Esmond talks of himself "as if he were already dead" (p. 150).

ELAINE SHOWALTER

Feminine Heroines:
Charlotte Brontë and George Eliot

Women beginning their literary careers in the 1840s were seeking heroines—both professional role-models and fictional ideals—who could combine strength and intelligence with feminine tenderness, tact, and domestic expertise. At the same time, they perceived themselves and their fictional heroines as innovators who would provide role-models for future generations. As Geraldine Jewsbury explained to Jane Carlyle:

> We are indications of a development of womanhood which is not yet recognized. It has, so far, no ready-made channels to run in. But still we have looked and tried, and found that the present rules for women will not hold us,—that something better and stronger is needed.... There are women to come after us, who will approach nearer the fullness of the measure of the stature of a woman's nature. I regard myself as a mere faint indication, a rudiment of the idea, of certain higher qualities and possibilities that are in women.[1]

The feminine novelists needed intimacy with other women both for inspiration and for sympathetic friendship, but they were much less likely than male novelists to have personal contact with other professional writers. They took advantage of such opportunities as came their way: they

---

From *A Literature of Their Own: British Women Novelists from Brontë to Lessing*. © 1977 by Princeton University Press.

corresponded with each other, sought each other out, and occasionally, like Dinah Craik and Elizabeth Lynn Linton, encouraged younger female disciples. Jewsbury had a sister who wrote poetry, and found more sisterly support in her passionate friendship with Jane Carlyle; the Brontë sisters supported each other. Most women of this generation, however, depended upon literature and the circulating library to provide the sense of connectedness; fictional heroines had to take the place of sisters and friends. Ellen Moers sees this purposeful reading as one of the special professional characteristics of literary women:

> Male writers could study their craft in university or coffee house, group themselves into movements or coteries, search out predecessors for guidance or patronage, collaborate or fight with their contemporaries. But women through most of the 19th century were barred from the universities, isolated in their own homes, chaperoned in travel, painfully restricted in friendship. The normal literary life was closed to them. Without it, they studied with a special closeness the works written by their own sex, and relied on a sense of easy, almost rude familiarity with the women who wrote them.[2]

That the feminine novelists learned to make use of the past and draw confidence from the example of their predecessors does not mean that they simply became adoring disciples. Women novelists of an older generation, such as Hannah More, Maria Edgeworth, and even Jane Austen, were too didactic for a younger group of aspiring professionals. Feminine novelists often believed the popular stereotypes of the old-maid authoress. Elizabeth Barrett, for example, had been warned by Mary Russell Mitford that all "literary ladies were ugly. 'I have never met one in my life,' she wrote, 'that might not have served for a scarecrow to keep the birds from the cherries.'" Thus, meeting Lady Dacre in 1838, Barrett expected "a *woman of the masculine gender*, with her genius very prominent in eccentricity of manner and sentiments," and was astounded to find instead someone with "as much gentleness and womanlyness as if she could be content with being loved."[3]

Jane Austen was an early favorite of male critics, recommended, like a priggish elder sister, to unruly siblings and apprentices. G.H. Lewes recommended Austen to Charlotte Brontë in 1848, but Brontë rejected her as being elegant and confined, "a carefully-fenced, highly-cultivated garden, with neat borders and delicate flowers."[4] Brontë herself did not wish to submit to pruning and miniaturization. By 1853 Austen's name had become a byword for female literary restraint, as is demonstrated by the protest of a critic for the *Christian Remembrancer*: "'A writer of the school of Miss Austen' is a much-abused phrase, applied now-a-days by critics who, it is charitable to suppose, have never read Miss Austen's works, to any female writer who composes dull stories without incident, full of level conversation, and concerned with characters of middle life."[5]

Works of female rebels were more inspiring than those of the docile Jane Austen. George Sand's novels of passion were eagerly read (twelve were translated into English in the 1840s). Sand, with her trousers and her lovers, became the counter-culture heroine of many feminine writers. It was Sand whose life suggested how women writers might develop. In an awkward and desperately sincere sonnet, published in 1844 and quoted often throughout the century, Elizabeth Barrett addressed Sand as a tremulous amalgam of genius and true womanhood:

> True genius, but true woman! dost deny
> Thy woman's nature with a manly scorn,
> And break away the gauds and armlets worn
> By weaker women in captivity?
> Ah, vain denial! that revolted cry
> Is sobbed in by a woman's voice forlorn!—
> Thy woman's hair, my sister, all unshorn
> Floats back dishevelled strength in agony,
> Disproving thy man's name: and while before
> The world thou burnest in a poet-fire,
> We see thy woman-heart beat evermore
> Through the large flame. Beat purer, heart, and higher,
> Till God unsex thee on the heavenly shore
> Where unincarnate spirits purely aspire!

Sand became a heroine, not because she had transcended femininity, but because she was involved in the turbulence of womanly suffering. The sonnet's title, "To George Sand: A Recognition," emphasized the feminine writer's need to respond to the "woman-heart" revealing itself in the "poet-fire." The "weaker women in captivity" could recognize the sister behind the man's name.

The feminine writers were thus looking for two kinds of heroines. They wanted inspiring professional role-models; but they also wanted romantic heroines, a sisterhood of shared passion and suffering, women who sobbed and struggled and rebelled. It was very difficult for the Victorians to believe that both qualities could be embodied in the same woman. The simplest resolution would have been find the role-model in life, the heroine in literature, but it did not work out that easily. The tendency of critics, instead, was to polarize the female literary tradition into what we can call the Austen and the Sand lines, and to see subsequent women writers as daughters of Jane or daughters of George.

In rejecting Austen and deciding instead to write about "what throbs fast and full, though hidden, what the blood rushes through, what is the unseen seat of life,"[6] Charlotte Brontë had chosen a volcanic literature of the body as well as of the heart, a sexual and often supernatural world. She was thus seen as the romantic, the spontaneous artist who "pours forth her feelings ... without premeditation."[7] George Eliot was seen as the opposite: a writer and a woman in the Austen tradition, studied, intellectual, cultivated. In her reviews of the silly lady novelists, Eliot defined her own professional ideal, the "really cultured woman," who

> is all the simpler and the less obtrusive for her knowledge ... she does not make it a pedestal from which she flatters herself that she commands a complete view of men and things, but makes it a point of observation from which to form a right estimate of herself. She neither spouts poetry nor quotes Cicero on slight provocation.... She does not write books to confound philosophers, perhaps because she is able to write books that delight them. In conversation she is the least formidable of women, because she understands you, without wanting to make you aware that you *can't* understand her.[8]

As Eliot's disparagement (in her *Letters*) of Dinah Mulock, Margaret Oliphant, and Mary Braddon shows, the cultured woman, while never engaged in overt competition with men, was very much in competition with other women.

By 1860 the Austen-Sand lines had incorporated Brontë and Eliot, so that any woman who published a book could expect to find herself compared to one or the other extreme. Brontë and Eliot themselves were invariably matched with Sand and Austen, with some variation from book to book. It was not until the end of the century that critics pointed out the steady intellectual development in Eliot, and it is only very recently that attention has been paid to the pre-meditated structure and controlled imagery in Brontë's novels. The complacent manner in which the *Saturday Review* tried to reduce George Eliot's originality to an Austen-Brontë hybrid was typical of the Victorian effort to put a woman novelist in her place, in all senses:

> We may think ourselves very fortunate to have a third female novelist not inferior to Miss Austen and Miss Brontë; and it so happens that there is much in the works of this new author that reminds us of these two wellknown novelists without anything like copying. George Eliot has a minuteness of painting and a certain archness of style that are quite after the manner of Miss Austen, while the wide scope of her remarks, and her delight in depicting strong and wayward feelings show that she belongs to the generation of Currer Bell.[9]

As Charlotte Brontë and George Eliot increasingly came to dominate their period and to represent the models against which other women novelists were measured, they too became the objects of both feminine adulation and resentment. Feminine novelists could not evade rivalry with Brontë and Eliot, as male novelists could, by restricting them to the women's league. In a letter to Blackwood's pleading the case of her new novel, Mrs. Linton inevitably compared it to *Jane Eyre* and *Adam Bede;* she insisted that it was "not a weaker book than any of these." (It was rejected.)[10] For twenty years, Mrs. Oliphant, who was also published by Blackwood's, had to negotiate subjects in terms of what Eliot was writing (for example, to drop a biography of Savonarola lest it follow too closely on *Romola*) and to hear annoying comparisons of *Salem Chapel* and *Adam Bede.*[11] Oliphant was, however, one of the first to note that *Jane Eyre* had changed the direction of the female tradition: "Perhaps no other writer of her time has impressed her mark so clearly on contemporary literature, or drawn so many followers onto her own peculiar path."[12] Oliphant saw herself as less passionate than Brontë, but also (a source of self-congratulation) as less feminine: "I have had far more experience and, I think, a fuller conception of life. I have learned to take perhaps more a man's view of mortal affairs."[13] Nonetheless, self-esteem was precariously maintained in the shadow of these colossal figures, and those less successful often wondered whether they must forever be content to follow haltingly on Brontë's peculiar path, or build a cottage on the Eliot estate.

Even before the Gaskell biography, contemporaries such as Jane Carlyle and Harriet Martineau had been intrigued by Brontë. In *The Life of Charlotte Brontë*, Gaskell helped create the myth of the novelist as tragic heroine, a myth for which readers had been prepared by *Jane Eyre*. The

Brontë legend rapidly took on the psychic properties of a cult, complete with pilgrimages to Haworth and relics of the three sisters. Women novelists like Elizabeth Sewell found the biography a personal document, "intensely, painfully interesting."[14] In America, too, the *Life* became the treasured book of thousands of women.[15] A kind of spiritual identification with the Brontës went so far that in 1872 Harriet Beecher Stowe claimed to have managed a two-hour conversation with Charlotte in a gossipy seance, a "weird & Brontëish" chat, she proudly confided to George Eliot, in which Charlotte had given "a most striking analysis" of Emily.[16] As late as the 1890s, the society novelist Mrs. L. B. Walford liked to show visiting journalists the tea set she had purchased from the Brontë parsonage, and today the London department store Harrods carries an excellent line of Brontë cake and an unlikely Brontë liqueur.

George Eliot was a much more formidable figure. Feminine novelists were compulsively drawn to compare themselves to both Brontë and Eliot, but Brontë exemplified in every sense the bonds of sisterly affection. Eliot was reserved, inaccessible, and opaque. In her maturity she violated the values of sisterly communion in the female subculture by avoiding close friendships with other women writers. She had even violated the essential rule of respectability, and not only gotten away with it but also made a sanctuary of exile. She made a great deal of money and worked under the best of circumstances, with Lewes as her business manager, with an attentive and generous publisher, and eventually with an adoring young husband. Her female contemporaries never faltered in their praise of her books, but they felt excluded from, and envious of, her world. Her very superiority depressed them.

But criticism of the Eliot legend was one of the ways in which feminine novelists were attempting to define themselves. Mrs. Oliphant's *Autobiography* was an unusual experiment in introspection occasioned by the Cross biography of Eliot: "I have been tempted to begin writing by George Eliot's life.... I wonder if I am a little envious of her? I always avoid considering formally what my own mind is worth. I have never had any theory on the subject."[17] In *My Literary Life*, Eliza Lynn Linton acidly recalled her early meeting *chez* John Chapman with Marian Evans, who "held her hands and arms kangaroo fashion; was badly dressed; had an unwashed, unbrushed, unkempt look altogether; and ... assumed a tone of superiority over me which I was not then aware was warranted by her undoubted leadership. From first to last she put up my mental bristles." Linton thought of herself as forthright and spontaneous, the sort of woman who is loved for her faults. She was made to feel uncomfortably inadequate by the novelist: "She was so consciously 'George Eliot'—so interpenetrated head and heel, inside and out, with the sense of her importance as the great novelist and profound thinker of her generation, as to make her society a little overwhelming, leaving on baser creatures the impression of having been rolled very flat indeed."[18] Eliot also attracted worshipful disciples, but though Mary Cholmondeley, sitting down to her chapter in Shropshire in the 1890s, "raised her eyes in humility and fidelity to George Eliot,"[19] most nineteenth-century women novelists seem to have found her a troubling and demoralizing competitor, one who had created an image of the woman artist they could never equal, one who had been "kept ... in a mental greenhouse and taken care of," while they staggered "alone and unaided, through cloud and darkness."[20] Their sense of professional inferiority frequently exploded into hostility; Alice James asserted: "She makes upon me the impression ... of mildew, or some morbid growth."[21]

George Mandeville's Husband, a forgotten novel written in 1894, throws some light on the jealousies, animosities, and ambitions that underlay women novelists' response to George Eliot. The author, Elizabeth Robins, was an American actress living in England, a feminist who wrote several successful novels, acted in Ibsen's first London productions, and later became a chief propagandist for the militant suffragettes of the W.S.P.U. Yet *George Mandeville's Husband*, which she published under a pseudonym, is a denunciation of pseudointellectual women novelists and a satire on George Eliot. "George Mandeville" resembles George Eliot in name only; she is a pretentious second-rater who sacrifices her husband and daughter for the adulation of a bunch of cranks and hacks. Her husband avenges himself by turning the daughter into a Victorian Angel. He maintains that he would rather his daughter "scrubbed floors than wrote books," but as he describes the busy little nest he envisions for her he realizes "with a sudden and unusual emotion ... that the dozen womanly things he vouchsafed to her did not altogether satisfy the imagination even of this woman-child." Such moments of doubt, however, are rare; throughout the book Wilbraham denounces professional women—most viciously, George Eliot.

When his daughter mentions George Eliot in evidence of women's abilities, Wilbraham responds with an abusive monolog:

> Yes, yes, all women say George Eliot, and think the argument unanswerable. As if to instance one woman (who, by the way, was three parts man) did more than expose the poverty of their position.... She was abnormal.... Read her letters and diaries. When you grow up, study her life—not as it was commonly

reported, but as it *was:* She was a poor burdened creature, fitter
to be pitied than blazoned abroad as example and excuse.

His daughter caves in immediately and concedes, "George Eliot *looks* awful.
Her picture frightens me!"

It would be interesting to know how the novel was received in 1894.
Robins seems to empathize with George Mandeville's ambitions, and she
hints that Wilbraham's suffocating love, rather than the mother's neglect,
destroys the daughter. Yet the attack on George Eliot is full of passionate
conviction. In one authorial interruption, Robins generalizes about the
experience of a woman writer in her day:

> Who shall not say there was no element of courage and of
> steadfast strength in the woman who, year in, year out, sat
> chained to her writing-table, ceaselessly commemorating the
> futile and inept, leaving behind her day by day upon that
> sacrificial altar some fragment of youth and health, some shred of
> hope, some dead illusion. To sit down daily to the task of being
> George Eliot, and to rise up "the average lady-novelist" to the
> end, must, even if only dimly comprehended, be a soul-tragedy of
> no mean proportion.[22]

Eliot's example was as inescapable as it was inimitable. Robins' own
prose in this passage is an unconscious imitation of Eliot's style, as George
Bernard Shaw warned her.[23] The Eliot mystique of majestic, cerebral, and
ultimately sibylline detachment influenced both the prose and the
professional styles of the next generation. Mrs. Humphry Ward, Mary
Cholmondeley, and "John Oliver Hobbes" (Pearl Craigie) continued to act
the Eliot role long after it had become an anachronism. The seriousness that
seemed regal in Eliot looked pretentious and foolish in Mrs. Craigie and
Mrs. Ward; and an irreverent group of critics (including Max Beerbohm)
caricatured the solemnity that won Ward the nickname "Ma-Hump."

Feminine novelists had been persuaded that Eliot represented their
highest evolutionary stage, but in the early twentieth century a new female
aestheticism saw possibilities that liberated them from her legend. Dorothy
Richardson discarded Eliot's example simply because she thought that Eliot
wrote "like a man."[24] Most of the feminist novelists, however, detected a
more complicated personality behind the literature than had the Victorians.
Craigie, who wrote an essay on Eliot for the Encyclopedia Britannica, saw in
the famous intellectual restraint a heroic struggle rather than a stony

indifference. For her, Eliot's moral greatness came from "her infinite capacity for mental suffering and her need of human support," so disciplined and elevated that the novels were "wholly without morbidity in any disguise."[25]

Appropriately, an essay written by Virginia Woolf in 1919 helped restore Eliot to her rightful position after a period of Victorian and Edwardian backlash. In this extremely sympathetic piece, Woolf concedes all the flaws in the novels, but finds in the heroines Eliot's hard-won triumph over her own self-mistrust, and her fidelity to female experience:

> The ancient consciousness of woman, charged with suffering and sensibility, and for so many ages dumb, seems in them [Eliot's heroines] to have brimmed and overflowed and uttered a demand for something—they scarcely knew what—for something that is perhaps incompatible with the facts of human existence.... For her, too, the burden and the complexity of womanhood were not enough; she must reach beyond the sanctuary and pluck for herself the strange bright fruits of art and knowledge. Clasping them as few women have ever clasped them, she would not renounce her own inheritance—the difference of view, the difference of standard—nor accept an inappropriate reward.[26]

In this essay a woman critic was able for the first time to reconcile the two sides of the George Eliot legend, to bring suffering and sensibility into relation with art and knowledge. Victorian women writers, when they contemplated George Eliot, had felt somehow betrayed. They thought she had rejected them because she had avoided intimacy; they thought she had despised them because she had held them to a rigorous standard. They could not equal her, and they could see no way around her. It was not until the generation of the 1890s had dramatically—even sensationally—redefined the role of the woman writer that Virginia Woolf could look back and see in George Eliot, not a rival, but a heroine.

The legends attached to Brontë and Eliot in their lives were reversed in the heroines of their novels. Brontë's Jane Eyre is the heroine of fulfillment; Eliot's Maggie Tulliver is the heroine of renunciation. Together *Jane Eyre* and *The Mill on the Floss* are full and powerful descriptions of growing up as a female in Victorian England. Both contain a few explicit feminist passages, but they are classic feminine novels. They realistically describe an extraordinary range of women's physical and social experiences, but also suggest experiences through the accumulation of images and symbols. Of the two novels, *Jane Eyre*, published thirteen years earlier, is by far the more experimental and original; the significance of Brontë's use of structure, language, and female symbolism has been misread and underrated by male-oriented twentieth-century criticism, and is only now beginning to be fully understood and appreciated. Although both novels deal with the same subject, defined by Q. D. Leavis as "the moral and emotional growth of a passionate, badly managed child into a woman,"[27] the heroine Jane Eyre achieves as full and healthy a womanhood as the feminine novelists could have imagined; the gifted and lovable Maggie Tulliver represses her anger and creativity, and develops a neurotic, self-destructive personality. The formal differences in the two novels, between Brontë's freewheeling, almost surrealistic expression of her heroine's inner life, and Eliot's much more conventional, naturalistic, and self-conscious narrative, suggest in themselves the differences in the novelists' approaches to feminine fictions of release and control.

In *Jane Eyre*, Brontë attempts to depict a complete female identity, and she expresses her heroine's consciousness through an extraordinary range of narrative devices. Psychological development and the dramas of the inner life are represented in dreams, hallucinations, visions, surrealistic paintings, and masquerades; the sexual experiences of the female body are expressed spatially through elaborate and rhythmically recurring images of rooms and houses. Jane's growth is further structured through a pattern of literary, biblical, and mythological allusion. Brontë's most profound innovation, however, is the division of the Victorian female psyche into its extreme components of mind and body, which she externalizes as two characters, Helen Burns and Bertha Mason. Both Helen and Bertha function at realistic levels in the narrative and present implied and explicit connections to Victorian sexual ideology, but they also operate in an archetypal dimension of the story. Brontë gives us not one but three faces of Jane, and she resolves her heroine's psychic dilemma by literally and metaphorically destroying the two polar personalities to make way for the full strength and development of the central consciousness, for the integration of the spirit and the body. Thus *Jane Eyre* anticipates and indeed formulates the deadly combat between the Angel in the House and the devil in the flesh that is evident in the fiction of Virginia Woolf, Doris Lessing, Muriel Spark, and other twentieth-century British women novelists.

The novel opens at Gateshead, with Jane's transition from the passivity and genderlessness of childhood into a turbulent puberty. This emotional menarche is clearly suggested, despite the fact that Jane is only ten years old, by the accumulation of incident and detail on the psychic level. "I can never get away from Gateshead till I am a woman," she tells Mr. Lloyd;[28] and, having passed through the gate, she has evidently entered upon womanhood by the end of chapter 4. Her adolescence is marked first by her sudden and unprecedented revolt against the Reeds, a self-assertiveness that incurs severe punishment and ostracism, but also wins her freedom from the family. It is also colored by her pervasive awareness of the "animal" aspects of her being—her body, with its unfeminine needs and appetites, and her passions, especially rage. From the undifferentiated awareness of her "physical inferiority" to the Reed children, Jane becomes minutely conscious both of the "disgusting and ugly"[29] physical sadism of John Reed, and of her own warm blood and glittering eyes. The famous scene of violence with which the novel begins, John Reed's assault on Jane and her passionate counterattack, associates the moment of rebellion and autonomy with bloodletting and incarceration in the densely symbolic red-room.

It is thus as if the mysterious crime for which the Reeds were punishing Jane were the crime of growing up. The red-room to which Jane is sentenced by Mrs. Reed for her display of anger and passion is a paradigm of female inner space:

> The red-room was a spare chamber, very seldom slept in.... A bed supported on massive pillars of mahogany hung with curtains of deep red damask, stood out like a tabernacle in the centre, the two large windows, with their blinds almost drawn down, were half shrouded in festoons and falls of similar drapery; the carpet was red; the table at the foot of the bed was covered with a crimson cloth.... This room was chill, because it seldom had a fire; it was silent, because remote from the nursery and kitchens; solemn, because it was known to be so seldom entered. The housemaid alone came here on Saturdays, to wipe from the mirrors and the furniture a week's quiet dust; and Mrs. Reed herself, at far intervals, visited it to review the contents of a certain secret drawer in the wardrobe, where were stored divers parchments, her jewel-casket, and a miniature of her deceased husband.[30]

With its deadly and bloody connotations, its Freudian wealth of secret compartments, wardrobes, drawers, and jewel chest, the red-room has strong associations with the adult female body; Mrs. Reed, of course, is a widow in her prime. Jane's ritual imprisonment here, and the subsequent episodes of ostracism at Gateshead, where she is forbidden to eat, play, or socialize with other members of the family, is an adolescent rite of passage that has curious anthropological affinities to the menarchal ceremonies of Eskimo or South Sea Island tribes. The passage into womanhood stresses the lethal and fleshly aspects of adult female sexuality. The "mad cat," the "bad animal" (as John Reed calls Jane),[31] who is shut up and punished will reappear later in the novel as the totally animalistic, maddened, and brutalized Bertha Mason; *her* secret chamber is simply another red-room at the top of another house.

The obsession with the "animal" appetites and manifestations of the body, and the extreme revulsion from female sexuality are also articulated through one of the submerged literary allusions in the text to *Gulliver's Travels*. This book has been one of Jane's favorites, but after her experience in the red-room it becomes an ominous and portentous fable; Gulliver seems no longer a canny adventurer, but "a most desolate wanderer in most dread and dangerous regions,"[32] a pilgrim in the adult world like herself. Like Gulliver, Jane moves from the nursery world of Lilliput to an encounter with the threatening and Brobdingnagian Reverend Brocklehurst ("What a face he had, now that is was almost on a level with mine! what a great nose! and what a mouth! and what large, prominent teeth!"),[33] and an increasing Calvinist awareness of the "vile body" that leads to the climatic encounter with Bertha, the female Yahoo in her foul den.

A strain of intense female sexual fantasy and eroticism runs through the first four chapters of the novel and contributes to their extraordinary and thrilling immediacy. The scene in the red-room unmistakably echoes the flagellation ceremonies of Victorian pornography. As in whipping scenes in *The Pearl* and other underground Victorian erotica, the *mise-en-scène* is a remote chamber with a voluptuous decor, and the struggling victim is carried by female servants. Jane is threatened with a bondage made more titillating because the bonds are to be a maid's garters: "'If you don't sit still, you must be tied down,' said Bessie. 'Miss Abbot, lend me your garters; she would break mine directly.' Miss Abbot turned to divest a stout leg of the necessary ligature. This preparation for bonds, and the additional ignominy it inferred, took a little of the excitement out of me." This threatened chastisement of the flesh, although not actually carried out in the red-room scene, is a motif that links Jane with Helen Burns, who submissively accepts a flogging at Lowood School from a teacher named Miss Seatcherd. Jane herself, we learn later, has been flogged on the "neck" in Mrs. Reed's bedroom.[34]

Whipping girls to subdue the unruly flesh and the rebellious spirit was a routine punishment for the Victorians, as well as a potent sexual fantasy; as late as the 1870s the *Englishwoman's Domestic Magazine* conducted an enthusiastic correspondence column on the correct way to carry out the procedure: It is interesting here to note that sexual discipline is administered to women by other women, as agents for men. Bessie (Jane's favorite servant) and Miss Abbot, acting on behalf of Mrs. Reed, who in turn is avenging her son, lock Jane up; at Lowood the kindly Miss Temple starves the girls because "she has to answer to Mr. Brocklehurst for all she does";[35] at Thornfield Grace Poole is hired by Rochester as Bertha's jailor. Thus the feminine heroine grows up in a world without female solidarity, where women in fact police each other on behalf of patriarchal tyranny. There is sporadic sisterhood and kindness between the women in this world, and Jane finds it ultimately at Marsh End with Diana and Mary Rivers; but on the whole these women are helpless to aid each other, even if they want to.

Lowood School, where Jane is sent by her aunt, is the penitentiary for which the red-room was the tribunal. Like Lowick, Casaubon's home in *Middlemarch*, Lowood represents sexual diminishment and repression. In this pseudoconvent, Jane undergoes a prolonged sensual discipline. Here the girls are systematically "starved" (in Yorkshire dialect the word means "frozen" as well as "hungry"), and deprived of all sensory gratification. Clad in stiff brown dresses, which "gave an air of oddity even to the prettiest," and shorn of their hair, the last sign of their femininity, the girls of Lowood are instructed in the chastity they will need for their future lives as poor teachers and governesses. Brocklehurst proclaims that his mission "is to mortify in these girls the lusts of the flesh."[36]

As an institution, Lowood disciplines its inmates by attempting to destroy their individuality at the same time that it punishes and starves their sexuality. Distinctions between the little girls and the "great girls," the preadolescents and the young women, are obliterated by the uniform all are forced to wear. The purpose of Brocklehurst in starving the "vile bodies" is to create the intensely spiritualized creature the Victorians idealized as the Angel in the House. Virtually sexless, this creature, as Alexander Welsh provocatively suggests in *The City of Dickens*, is in fact the Angel of Death, who has mystical powers of intercession in the supernatural order, and whose separation from the body is the projection of the Victorian terror of the physical reminders of birth and mortality.[37]

The Angel of Lowood is Helen Burns, the perfect victim and the representation of the feminine spirit in its most disembodied form. Helen is a tribute to the Lowood system: pious, intellectual, indifferent to her material surroundings, resigned to the abuse of her body, and, inevitably, consumptive. She is one extreme aspect of Jane's personality, for Jane too is tempted by the world of the spirit and the intellect, and has a strong streak of masochism. Helen is the woman who would make a perfect bride for St.

John Rivers; she is his female counterpart. But although Helen, with "the aspect of an angel," inspires Jane to transcend the body and its passions, Jane, rebellious on her "pedestal of infamy" in the classroom, resists the force of spiritual institutionalization, as she will later resist the physical institutionalization of marriage with Rochester.[38] Ultimately, it is Helen's death that provides the climax of the Lowood experience. She dies in Jane's arms, and Jane achieves a kind of victory: the harsh regime of Lowood is modified, its torments palliated. Like Bertha Mason, Helen is sacrificed to make way for Jane's fuller freedom.

The "animal" aspects of womanhood, which have been severely repressed during Jane's sojourn at Lowood, reassert themselves when, at eighteen, she goes as governess to Thornfield Hall. Bertha Mason, who is confined to, and who *is*, the "third story" of Thornfield, is the incarnation of the flesh, of female sexuality in its most irredeemably bestial and terrifying form. Brontë's treatment of the myth of the Mad Wife is brilliantly comprehensive and reverberative, and rich with historical, medical, and sociological implications, as well as with psychological force.

Bertha's origins in folk history and literature are interesting in themselves. There are numerous literary precedents in the Gothic novel, particularly Mrs. Radcliffe's *Sicilian Romance*, for mysterious captives; the situation, in fact, is repeated to the point of appearing archetypal. Other explanations for Bertha depend upon real case histories that Brontë had encountered. Mrs. Gaskell mentions one in her *Life of Charlotte Brontë*; Q. D. Leavis refers to another, a Yorkshire legend about North Lees Hall Farm, where a mad wife had allegedly been incarcerated. Indeed, there were several Yorkshire houses with legends of imprisoned madwomen: Wycollar Hall, near Colne, and Norton Conyers, which had a chamber called "the madwoman's room."[39] The legends themselves express a cultural attitude toward female passion as a potentially dangerous force that must be punished and confined. In the novel, Bertha is described as "the foul German spectre—the vampyre," "a demon," "a hag," "an Indian Messalina," and "a witch." Each of these is a traditional figure of female deviance with its own history in folklore. The vampire, who sucked men's blood (as Bertha does when she stabs her brother), and the witch, who visited men by night and rode them to exhaustion, were the products of elemental fears of women. H. R. Hays suggests that in England the "basic charge against the witch as a night demon and seducer springs clearly from the experiences of a repressed and celibate male clergy," that is, from erotic dreams accompanied by nocturnal emissions.[40]

Brontë herself, alluding to the latest developments in Victorian psychiatric theory, attributed Bertha's behavior to "moral madness."[41]

Opposed to the eighteenth-century belief that insanity meant deranged reason, the concept of "moral insanity," introduced by James Cowles Pritchard in 1835, held madness to be "a morbid perversion of the natural feelings, affections, inclinations, temper, habits, moral dispositions, and natural impulses, without any remarkable disorder or defect of the intellect, or knowing and reasoning faculties, and particularly without any insane illusion or hallucination."[42] Women were thought to be more susceptible than men to such disorders and could even inherit them. Sexual appetite was considered one of the chief symptoms of moral insanity in women; it was subject to severe sanctions and was regarded as abnormal or pathological. Dr. William Acton, author of the standard textbook on *The Functions and Disorders of the Reproductive Organs* (1857) admitted that he had occasionally seen cases in the divorce courts of "women who have sexual desires so strong that they surpass those of men." Acton also acknowledged "the existence of sexual excitement terminating even in nymphomania, a form of insanity which those accustomed to visit lunatic asylums must be fully conversant with; but, with these sad exceptions, there can be no doubt that sexual feeling in the female is in the majority of cases in abeyance."[43]

The periodicity of Bertha's attacks suggests a connection to the menstrual cycle, which many Victorian physicians understood as a system for the control of female sexuality. Bertha has "lucid intervals of days—sometimes weeks," and her attack on Jane comes when the moon is "blood-red and half overcast."[44] "In God's infinite wisdom," a London physician wrote in 1844, "might not this monthly discharge be ordained for the purpose of controlling woman's violent sexual passions ... by unloading the uterine vessels ... so as to prevent the promiscuous intercourse which would prove destructive to the purest ... interests of civil life?"[45] As Carroll Smith-Rosenberg points out, the image of the "maniacal and destructive woman" closely parallels that of the sexually powerful woman: "Menstruation, 19th century physicians worried, could drive some women temporarily insane; menstruating women might go berserk, destroying furniture, attacking family and strangers alike ... Those 'unfortunate women' subject to such excessive menstrual influence," one doctor suggested, "should for their own good and that of society be incarcerated for the length of their menstrual years."[46]

In precise contrast to the angelic Helen, Bertha is big, as big as Rochester, corpulent, florid, and violent. When Jane sees her in the chamber on the third story, she is almost subhuman:

In the deep shade, at the farther end of the room, a figure ran backwards and forwards. What it was, whether beast or human being, one could not, at first sight tell; it grovelled, seemingly, on all fours; it snatched and growled like some strange wild animal; but it was covered with clothing, and a quantity of dark, grizzled hair, wild as a mane, hid its head and face.[47]

Like Gulliver observing the Yahoos, Jane is pushed almost to the brink of breakdown by her recognition of aspects of herself in this "clothed hyena." Much of Bertha's dehumanization, Rochester's account makes clear, is the result of her confinement, not its cause. After ten years of imprisonment, Bertha has become a caged beast. Given the lunacy laws in England, incidentally, Rochester has kept the dowry for which he married her, but cannot file for divorce even in the ecclesiastical courts. Rochester's complicity in the destruction of his wife's spirit is indicated in Jane's recognition of the third story's resemblance to a corridor in "Blue-beard's castle," in Rochester's accounts of his sexual exploitation of Bertha, Céline, Giacinta, and Clara, and in Jane's uneasy awareness that his smile "was such as a sultan might ... bestow on a slave."[48]

Madness is explicitly associated with female sexual passion, with the body, with the fiery emotions Jane admits to feeling for Rochester. In trying to persuade her to become his mistress, Rochester argues that Jane is a special case: "If you were mad," he asks, "do you think I should hate you?" "I do indeed, sir," Jane replies; and she is surely correct.[49] Thus it becomes inevitable that Bertha's death, the purging of the lusts of the flesh, must precede and successful union between Rochester and Jane. When they finally marry, they have become equals, not only because Rochester, in losing his hand and his sight, has learned how it feels to be helpless and how to accept help, but also because Jane, in destroying the dark passion of her own psyche, has become truly her "own mistress."[50]

The influence of *Jane Eyre* on Victorian heroines was felt to have been revolutionary. The post-Jane heroine, according to the periodicals, was plain, rebellious, and passionate; she was likely to be a governess, and she usually was the narrator of her own story. Jane, Maggie Tulliver, Mrs. Gaskell's Mary Barton and Margaret Hale (in *North and South*), Mrs. Oliphant's *Miss Marjoribanks*, and even Miss Yonge's Ethel May (in *The Daisy Chain* and its sequels) were more intellectual and more self-defining than the sweet and submissive heroines favored by Bulwer-Lytton, Thackeray, and Dickens. Some reviewers applauded the change; *Bentley's Quarterly Review*, for example, found Bulwer-Lytton's "conception of female excellence" rather old-fashioned by 1859, since the "august band of female novelists has ... set up counter ideals ... women who can stand alone, reason, lead, instruct, command; female characters wrought out with such power that they take hold on men's minds."[51]

There were many others who were alarmed by the drive to self-fulfillment Jane exhibited; *The Spectator* in April 1860 deplored the "pale, clever, and sharp-spoken young woman" who had become the fashion; the *Saturday Review* pretended resignation to the dominance of "glorified governesses in fiction," who, like the poor, would be always with them, since literature had "grown to be a woman's occupation."[52] Even the *Westminster Review* wished for an end to the reign of "the daughters direct of Miss Jane Eyre.... Of these heroine governesses one can only wish that England may have more of them and the circulating libraries less."[53] On a more personal note, Walter Bagehot objected that women novelists, out of jealousy for their heroines, made them unattractive: "Possibly none of the frauds which are now so much the topic of common remark are so irritating, as that to which the purchaser of a novel is a victim on finding that he has only to peruse a narrative of the conduct and sentiments of an ugly lady."[54]

Twentieth-century women novelists have frequently rewritten the story of Jane Eyre with endings Brontë could not have projected. In Jean Rhys' *Wide Sargasso Sea*, Brontë's novel is sympathetically retold from the perspective of an oppressed and betrayed Bertha Mason. Rhys emphasizes the racial aspect of Bertha's Creole background; Bertha comes to represent the native, the heart of darkness, the Other. In Doris Lessing's *The Four-Gated City* (1969), the heroine is housekeeper to a seductive man, whom she falls in love with; he too, it turns out, has a mad wife, who lives in the basement. The distance between the Brontë attic, which rationalizes lust in the mind, and the Lessing basement, which accepts the dark mystery of the body, is one measure of the development of the female tradition. More profoundly, at the end of the novel Lessing's heroine liberates the mad wife, and together they leave and take an apartment. Can we imagine an ending to *Jane Eyre* in which Jane and Bertha leave Rochester and go off together? Obviously such a conclusion would be unthinkable. Such possibilities and such solutions are beyond the boundaries of the feminine novel. Jane's marriage to Rochester is essentially a union of equals, but in feminine fiction men and women become equals by submitting to mutual limitation, not by allowing each other mutual growth.

George Eliot admired *Jane Eyre*, although she protested against Jane's refusal to become Rochester's mistress: "All self-sacrifice is good, but one would like it to be in a somewhat nobler cause than a diabolical law which chains a man body and soul to a putrefying carcase."[55] What Eliot was unable to understand in Brontë's fiction was the difference between self-sacrifice and self-assertion. Jane Eyre suffers in running away from Rochester, but she acts out of the instinct of self-preservation: "*I care for myself. The more solitary, the more friendless, the more unsustained I am, the more I will respect myself.*"[56] For Jane Eyre, action is a step toward independence; even if it begins as escape, it is ultimately directed toward a new goal. For George Eliot, believing that "all self-sacrifice is good," renunciation becomes a virtue in itself. *The Mill on the Floss* (1860) sympathetically analyzes the unfulfilled longings of an intelligent young woman in a narrow and oppressive society, but nonetheless elevates suffering into a female career.

There are many similarities between *Jane Eyre* and *The Mill on the Floss* that reflect the themes and techniques of the feminine novelists. Ellen Moers has pointed out that the Red Deeps, where Maggie meets Philip Wakem, are "a real geography of sexual indulgence—a woman's private terrain";[57] this terrain is Eliot's equivalent of the red-room, an adolescent female space in which sexual longing and dread are mingled. Like Brontë, Eliot uses folklore to provide metaphors for the deviant woman. As a little girl, Maggie is fascinated by the stories of witchcraft in Defoe's *History of the Devil*: "That old woman in the water's a witch—they've put her in to find out whether she's a witch or no, and if she swims she's a witch, and if she's drowned—and killed, you know—she's innocent, and not a witch, but only a poor silly old woman. But what good would it do her then, you know, when she was drowned?"[58] Like Jane, Maggie has the option of angelic innocence, which leads to death, or "witchlike" self-preservation, which leads to social rejection. Another important metaphor for Maggie is the gypsy queen, a fantasy that Eliot realistically and humorously undercuts. The myth of the gypsy camp, which Eliot along with Brontë and other Victorian novelists adapted from romantic poetry and painting, stands for an escape from the zero-sum game of Victorian social codes, at the price of such amenities of civilization as tea, books, and groceries. Maggie's contact with this world, briefer, more disillusioning, and more humiliating than Jane's experiments with rebellion, is instructive. The Bertha in Maggie, the alter ego, the semi-criminal double, who is violent and sexual, has no real part to play in the novel. She is clearly a childish fantasy of Maggie's, fleeting, silly, and quickly repressed.

Brontë locates the conflict between passion and repression within Jane, and represents it as Helen vs. Bertha (as well as St. John vs. Rochester); Eliot represents the conflict primarily as a sexual difference, as Maggie vs. Tom. Eliot's original title for the novel (she was calling it "Sister Maggie" until January 1860) and the title of the first book ("Boy and Girl") highlight the relationship of Maggie and Tom, and the conceptualization of feminine passion and masculine repression that are the extremes of sex-role conditioning. One Victorian critic, Richard Simpson, observed about Eliot that "the antithesis of passion and duty figures itself to her mind as a kind of sexual distinction; so that if woman could be defecated [*sic*] from all male fibres, she would be all passion, as man, purged of all feminine qualities, would be all hard duty." Tom Tulliver is an instance of a male nearly pure; the purest form of woman is "a being with black hair and large dark eyes ... a mass of yearnings, passions, and feelings,"[50] in short, Maggie.

Eliot goes to some pains to show how the differences in expectations, education, and daily treatment by the family form Maggie and Tom. Tom's life is not easy, any more than Maggie's is, but the disciplines to which he is called are lighter for him to assume because they are basically in accordance with his personality. The qualities that denote Tom's mind—will, self-control, self-righteousness, narrowness of imagination, and a disposition to dominate and to blame others, all the traits of the authoritarian personality—Eliot sees as masculine, and the correlatives of status and self-esteem. Tom is never so "susceptible," never so much "like a girl," as when he is made to feel stupid at school.[60] If there is any single aspect of sexual differentiation that Eliot points to as significant, it is this difference in self-esteem that depends upon the approbation of the family and social circle. Tom learns when very young not to doubt himself, while Maggie, to the end of her life, is self-doubting and unassertive. Maggie's self-esteem is pitifully dependent on Tom's love, and she will sacrifice any legitimate claim of her own personality to avoid rejection by him.[61]

Unlike Tom Tulliver, Stephen Guest, and Lucy Deane, Maggie Tulliver and Philip Wakem are insecure in their sexual identity, and this insecurity is one of the shared emotions that brings them together. Because he is a cripple, Philip has led a girl's life; he has been barred from sports and swordplay and ultimately forced to be "perfectly quiescent," as immobilized as Maggie herself. It is a commonplace in feminine fiction for the sensitive man to be represented as maimed; Linton Heathcliff in *Wuthering Heights*, Phineas Fletcher in Dinah Craik's *John Halifax, Gentleman*, Charlie Edmondstone in Charlotte Yonge's *The Heir of Redclyffe*, and even such late versions as Colin Cravan in Frances Hodgson Burnett's *The Secret Garden* all suggest that men condemned to lifelong feminine roles display the personality traits of frustrated women. Philip, for example, has enough empathy to penetrate Maggie's mournful resignation, but he also has a "peevish susceptibility," compounded of "nervous irritation" and the "heart-bitterness produced by the sense of his deformity."[62]

Because he shares many of Maggie's dilemmas, Philip is uniquely qualified to analyze them for her and for the reader. Maggie is unable to channel her passionate energy into productive work, to yoke her pride, ambition, and intelligence into a single effective force, as Tom does, and she therefore must find some strategy for subduing her own nature and securing Tom's approval. Her tactics, as Philip perceives, are escapist and renunciatory. In most conflicts Maggie cannot face the truth about her own feelings and has to persuade herself that other people are making her do things. In her clandestine meetings with Philip in the Red Deeps, she is vaguely aware that he is sexually unattractive, and that she is becoming entrapped in an exploitative and oppressive relationship; but rather than admitting these feelings and accepting the responsibility of acting upon them, she allows the meetings to be discovered and passively accompanies Tom to a showdown with Philip. It is clear that Tom, although he is brutal and even sadistic, speaks truthfully to Philip, and that in accusing Philip of taking advantage of his sister's loneliness he is acting out some of Maggie's anger and aggression. At the end of the scene Maggie is "conscious of a certain dim background of relief in the forced separation from Philip,"[63] but she deceives herself into believing that she is simply relieved to be free of concealment. When Maggie *does* feel sexually attracted to a man, she has no vocabulary for her emotions and must define her physical excitement as "love"; she must pretend that Stephen Guest has kidnapped her and that she is helplessly drifting away, when it is obvious that they are colluding in the elopement. Even after her awakening in the boat, when she makes the decision to resist Stephen, Maggie cannot move toward a purposeful construction of her life.

Whereas Jane Eyre, in a roughly similar impasse, runs away to start an independent life, Maggie is perversely drawn to destroy all her opportunities for renewal: to refuse the job in another town, to plead compulsively for Tom's forgiveness, to remain in the oppressive network of the family and the community, waiting hopelessly for them to validate her existence. Pain and self-abnegation become the all-absorbing experiences of her life: "life stretched before her as one act of penitence, and all she craved, as she dwelt on her future lot, was something to guarantee her from more falling."[64]

"You are not resigned," Philip warns Maggie. "You are only trying to stupefy yourself."[65] Jane Eyre lets the torrent of pain pour over her; "'I came into deep waters,'" she quotes from Scripture; "'the floods overflowed me,'"[66] Maggie never penetrates to the depths of her own pain; she diverts all her energy into escape and self-stupefaction. The ultimate flood is lethal, it seems, because the heart's need has been dammed up for so long.

Eliot's metaphor for Maggie's evasion of responsibility is opium. Her personal credo, expressed in a letter to Barbara Bodichon, was "to *do without opium*, and live through all our pain with conscious, clear-eyed endurance"— not, one notes, resistance.[67] Maggie, however, struggles to "dull her sensibilities," to subdue her longing, to transcend the volcanic Brontëan anger and hatred that could "flow out over her affections and conscience like a lava stream."[68] Philip serenades her appropriately with an aria from *La Somnambula*

The submerged image of the opiate in *The Mill on the Floss*, one that Eliot uses more explicitly in some other novels, reflects the world of Victorian feminine turmoil. Physicians reported that many women were driven to real opium and opium derivatives by the hopeless monotony and restriction of their lives. Headache remedies, patent medicines and sleeping-draughts, nostrums to which many women were addicted, contained high percentages of alcohol and opium. In 1857 one physician wrote: "Many women would pass the most indifferent night.... The chagrins of life would prey too severely; regrets and disappointments and painful reminiscents would visit them too acutely did they not deaden the poignancy of suffering, actual or remembered, by the 'drowsy syrups.'"[69] In 1871 another doctor related the causes of female drug addiction to the female role in a passage that might easily describe Maggie in St. Oggs: "Doomed, often, to a life of disappointment, and it may be, of physical and mental inaction, and in the smaller and more remote towns, not unfrequently, to utter seclusion, deprived of all wholesome social diversion, it is not strange that nervous depression, with all its concomitant evils, should sometimes follow—opium being discreetly selected as the safest and most agreeable remedy."[70]

Florence Nightingale, a member of Eliot's generation, diagnosed the narcissism, depression, addictiveness, and inertia of Victorian women as suppressed anger and lack of real work in the world: "If ever women come into contact with sickness, with poverty, and crime in masses, how the practical reality of life revives them! They are exhausted, like those who live on opium or on novels, all their lives—exhausted with feelings which lead to no action."[71] Maggie's fictional heroines, too, are losers, dark sufferers like Scott's Minna and Rebecca, for whom all endings are unhappy.

The Victorians were bothered by Maggie Tulliver's lack of moral balance rather than by her passivity; they wondered what sort of example she might be to "the hundreds of clever girls, born of uncongenial parents."[72] But the problems of Eliot's passive, self-destructive heroine seem much more persistent in women's literature than those of Brontë's rebel. Maggie is the progenitor of a heroine who identifies passivity and renunciation with womanhood, who finds it easier, more natural, and in a mystical way more satisfying, to destroy herself than to live in a world without opium or fantasy, where she must fight to survive. This heroine, like Maggie, has moments of illumination, awakenings to an unendurable reality; but she quickly finds a way to go back to sleep; even death is preferable to the pain of growth. Kate Chopin's *The Awakening* (1899) and Edith Wharton's *The House of Mirth* (1905) both deal with the futile struggle for consciousness. Chopin's Edna Pontellier thinks "it is better to wake up after all, even to suffer, rather than to remain a dupe to illusions all one's life"; but when her lover abandons her she drowns herself.[73] Wharton's Lily Bart wakes courageously to the "winter light" in a narrow room, but she too is unable to adjust to a life of work and adult responsibility. Emotions and ideas that she has never been educated to understand rush in on her, and in the end she takes a lethal overdose of chloral, enjoying "the gradual cessation of the inner throb."[74]

In Margaret Drabble's *The Waterfall* (1969), the twentieth-century heroine, despite all the new sciences of introspection, is as much a victim of her emotions, as little in control of her life, as is Maggie Tulliver. Drabble's novel, with its Victorian images of floods and cascades, ironically comments on the continuity of the female tradition:

> These fictional heroines, how they haunt me. Maggie Tulliver had a cousin called Lucy, as I have, and like me she fell in love with her cousin's man. She drifted off down the river with him, abandoning herself to the water, but in the end she lost him. She let him go. Nobly she regained her ruined honor, and, ah, we admire her for it, all that superego gathered together in a last effort to prove that she loved the brother more than the man.
>
> She should have ... well, what should she not have done? Since Freud we guess dimly at our own passions, stripped of hope, abandoned forever to that relentless current. It gets us in the end; sticks, twigs, dry leaves, paper cartons, cigarette ends, orange peels, flower petals, silver fishes. Maggie Tulliver never slept with her man. She did all the damage there was to be done to Lucy, to herself, to the two men who loved her, and then, like a woman of another age, she refrained. In this age what is to be done? We drown in the first chapter.[75]

NOTES

1. Quoted by Virginia Woolf in "Geraldine and Jane" *The Second Common Reader*, New York, 1960, p. 129.

2. Ellen Moers, "Women's Lit: Profession and Tradition," *Columbia Forum*, I (Fall 1972): 27–28.

3. *Elizabeth Barrett to Miss Mitford*, ed. Betty Miller, London, 1954, pp. vii, 29–30.

4. Quoted in Gaskell, *Life of Charlotte Brontë*, London, 1919, p. 282.

5. Quoted in Kathleen Tillotson, *Novels of the Eighteen-Forties*, London, 1956, p. 144.

6. Letter of 1850, quoted in Q.D. Leavis, introduction to *Jane Eyre*, Penguin edition, Harmondsworth, 1966, p. 10.

7. "The Mill on the Floss" *Westminster Review* LXXIV (1860), in *George Eliot: The Critical Heritage*, ed. David Carroll, New York, 1971, p. 139.

8. "Silly Novels by Lady Novelists," in *Essays of George Eliot*, ed. Thomas Pinney, New York, 1963, p. 317.

9. *Saturday Review* IX (April 14, 1860): 470.

10. See Vineta Colby, *The Singular Anomaly: Women Novelists of the Nineteenth Century*, New York, 1970, p. 29.

11. See *Autobiography and Letters of Mrs. M.O.W. Oliphant*, ed. Mrs. Harry Coghill, New York, 1899, pp. 185–186, 187–188, 190.

12. "Modern Novelists—Great and Small," *Blackwood's* LXXVII (1855): 568.

13. Oliphant, *Autobiography*, p. 67.

14. *The Autobiography of Elizabeth M. Sewall*, ed. Eleanor L. Sewell,. London, 1907, p. 160.

15. See Barbara Bodichon, *An American Diary 1857-58*, ed. Joseph W. Reed, Jr., Middletown, Connecticut, 1972.

16. *The George Eliot Letters*, V, ed. Gordon S. Haight, New Haven, 1955. pp. 280–281. Eliot was skeptical.

17. Oliphant, *Autobiography*, p. 4.

18. *My Literary Life*, London, 1899, p. 99.

19. Percy Lubbock, *Mary Cholmondeley: A Sketch from Memory*, London, 1928, p. 49.

20. Oliphant, *Autobiography*, p. 5; Dinah Mulock, "The Mill on the Floss," *MacMillan's* III (1861), in *George Eliot: The Critical Heritage*, p. 157.

21. *The Diary of Alice James*, ed. Leon Edel, New York, 1934, P. 41.

22. "C.E. Raimond," *George Mandeville's Husband*, London, 1894. pp. 42, 61, 57–58, 62–63.

23. Letter of February 13, 1899, in G.B. Shaw, *Collected Letters 1898-1910*, ed. Dan H. Laurence, New York, 1965, p. 77.

24. *Dawn's Left Hand*, in *Pilgrimage*, IV, New York, 1967, p. 240.

25. Quoted in Colby, *Singular Anomoly*, p. 22.

26. "George Eliot," *The Common Reader*, London, 1925, p. 217.

27. Introduction to *Jane Eyre*, p. 28.

28. Ch. 3, p. 56. Page references are to the Penguin edition, Harmondsworth, 1966; I have also indicated chapters.

29. Ch. 1, p. 42.

30. Ch. 2, pp. 45–46.

31. Ch. 2, p. 44; ch. 1, p. 41.

32. Ch. 3, p. 53.

33. Ch. 4, p. 64.

34. Ch. 2, p. 44. For a discussion of Victorian flagellation literature see Steven Marcus. "A Child is Being Beaten," in *The Other Victorians*, New York, 1966, pp. 252–65. Marcus is dealing with male sexual fantasies, however. In their edition of *Jane Eyre*, Jane Jack and Margaret Smith note that the word "neck" "used sometimes to be used with a wider signification than now, for a woman's breast or (as here) shoulders. There is an element of the Victorian euphemism about it." *Jane Eyre*, London, 1969, p. 586, n. 61. For a recent discussion of Victorian corporal punishment of girls, see Mary S. Hartman, "Child-Abuse and Self-Abuse: Two Victorian Cases," *History of Childhood Quarterly* (Fall 1974): 240–241.

35. Ch. 5, p. 82.

36. Ch. 5, p. 79; ch. 7, p. 96.

37. *The City of Dickens*, London, 1971, pp. 155–160, 222–225. Welsh suggests that Jane herself has Angelic qualities; but the novel emphasizes her unwillingness to accept the role; when Brocklehurst tells her about the child who emulates the angels by learning psalms, Jane replies, "Psalms are not interesting" (ch. 4, p. 65). As a young woman, she tells Rochester emphatically, "I am not an angel ... and I will not be one till I die: I will be myself" (ch. 24, p. 288).

38. Ch. 7, p. 99.

39. Introduction to *Jane Eyre*, p. 19. H. F. Chorley, reviewing *Jane Eyre* in the *Athenaeum* in 1847, also knew of a possible source. See Miriam Allott, *The Brontës: The Critical Heritage*, London, 1974, p. 72.

40. *The Dangerous Sex: The Myth of Feminine Evil*, New York, 1964, p. 152.

41. Letter to W. S. Williams, January 4, 1848, in Shorter, *The Brontës: Life and Letters*, I, London, 1908, p. 383.

42. Eric T. Carlson and Norman Dain, "The Meaning of Moral Insanity," *Bulletin of the History of Medicine* XXXVI (1962): *131*. See also "Moral Insanity," in Vieda Skultans, *Madness and Morals: Ideas on Insanity in the Nineteenth Century*, London, 1975, pp. 180–200.

43. Quoted in Marcus, *The Other Victorians*, p. 31.

44. Ch. 27, p. 336; ch. 25, p. 304.

45. George Robert Rowe, *On Some of the Most Important Disorders of Women*, London, 1844, pp. 27–28, quoted in Carroll Smith-Rosenberg, "Puberty to Menopause: The Cycle of Femininity in Nineteenth-Century America," *Feminist Studies* I (1973): 25.

46. Edward Tilt, *The Change of Life*, New York, 1882, p. 13, quoted in Smith-Rosenberg "Puberty to Menopause," 25. See also Skultans, *Madness and Morals*, pp. 223–240.

47. Ch. 26, p. 321.

48. Ch. 11, p. 138; ch. 24, p. 297.

49. Ch. 27. pp. 328–329.

50. Ch. 37, p. 459.

51. "Novels by Sir Edward Bulwer Lytton," I (1859): 91–92. See also Margaret Oliphant, "Charles Dickens," *Blackwood's* LXXVII (1855): 465: "Mr. Thackeray and His Novels," *Blackwood's* LXXVII (1855), 95; and comments by Dinah Craik on a novel she read for Macmillan's in 1860: "When Mr. C. has to do with boys & men he does them capital—but his women are *not* women exactly—airy ideals—not flesh & blood." Berg Collection, New York Public Library.

52. "The Mill on the Floss," *The Spectator*, April 7, 1860: 331; "Women's Heroines," *Saturday Review*, 1867: 261.

53. *Westminster Review*, n.s. XIII (1858): 297–298.

54. "The Waverley Novels," *Literary Studies*, II, London, 1879, p. 167.

55. Gordon S. Haight, *George Eliot: A Biography*, New York, 1968. p. 65.

56. *Jane Eyre*, ch. 27, p. 344.

57. "Women's Lit," 34.

58. *The Mill on the Floss*, ed. Gordon S. Haight, Boston, 1961, I, ch. 3, pp. 16–17.

59. "George Eliot's Novels," *Home and Foreign Review* III (1863), in *George Eliot: The Critical Heritage*, p. 239.

60. *Mill on the Floss*, p. 126. Blackwood wrote her that "Tom's life at Stelling's is perfect. It is perfectly wonderful how you have been able to realise the boy's feelings. Men will read it like reminiscences of what they themselves felt—suffered" (*George Eliot Letters*, III, p. 263).

61. For an extremely interesting Horneyan analysis of Maggie's defensive strategies, see Bernard J. Paris, "The Inner Conflicts of Maggie Tulliver," *A Psychological Approach to Fiction*, Bloomington, 1974.

62. *Mill on the Floss*, II, ch. 4, p. 148.

63. Ibid., V, ch. 6, p. 305.

64. Ibid., VII, ch. 2, p. 430.

65. Ibid., V, ch. 3, p. 286.

66. *Jane Eyre*, ch. 26, p. 324.

67. Letter of December 26, 1860, *George Eliot Letters*, III, p. 366.

68. *Mill on the Floss*, IV, ch. 3, p. 252.

69. Dr. Robert Dick, *The Connexion of Health and Beauty*, London, 1857, quoted in Patricia Branca, *The Silent Sisterhood*, Pittsburgh, 1975, p. 149. See also Barbara Hardy, "The Image of the Opiate in George Eliot's Novels," *Notes and Queries* (November 1957): 487–490.

70. Dr. F. E. Oliver, "The Use and Abuse of Opium," quoted by John S. Haller, Jr., and Robin M. Haller, *The Physician and Sexuality in Victorian America*, Urbana, 1974, p. 279.

71. "Cassandra," in Ray Strachey, *The Cause*, Port Washington, N.Y., 1969, p. 407.

72. Dinah Craik, "The Mill on the Floss," *Macmillan's* III (1861), in *George Eliot: The Critical Heritage*, p. 157.

73. *The Awakening*, in *Complete Works of Kate Chopin*, II, ed. Per Seyersted, Baton Rouge, 1969, p. 996.

74. *The House of Mirth*, New York, 1962, ch. 13, p. 375.

75. *The Waterfall*, New York, 1969, p. 184.

JEFF NUNOKAWA

Sexuality
in the Victorian Novel

VICTORIAN NOVELS AND THE HISTORY OF SEXUAL DESIRE

A history of sexual desire?[1] Are not the intimate intensities of mind and body
that go by that name as insulated from the mass and massive public events
that we commonly call history as hunger or pain? Is not the heart filled with
passion always the same old story, a drama whose costume may vary from
period to period, but whose script remains essentially unchanged? But while
much that we experience as sexual desire seems a largely immutable
condition of human (and perhaps not just human) existence, the scope and
shape of the meanings that we attach to this experience are decided by a
complex of historical forces, not least of which, for those of us who live in its
aftermath, is the Victorian novel itself. Thus, for example, the great
expectation, usually observed in the breach, that sexual bonds will culminate
in marriage, or its contemporary cognate, the Permanent Relationship, finds
its most eloquent propagations in what one of their critics calls "our books,"[2]
the novels whose promise of romance we know by heart as surely as we have
forgotten the details of their plots. If we continue to acknowledge, typically
in the privacy of our own disappointments, as universal truth a vision of
sexual desire as the engine and origin of a partnership at least lifelong, this is
in no small part because of the sentimental education we receive from the
Victorian novel and its afterlife in more recent narrative forms. If, against

---

From *The Cambridge Companion to the Victorian Novel*, ed. Deirdre David. © 2001 by Cambridge
University Press.

often overwhelming evidence to the contrary, we persist in perceiving the halo of "happily ever after" light up the object of our sexual affections, that is in no small part because books like *Jane Eyre* (1847) and *Middlemarch* (1872) have taught us so well to do so.

The question that we will take up here is not whether or where there is sexuality in the Victorian novel: generations of readers, including those who were present at their creation, have routinely detected all kinds of erotic energy even in the household words with which Dickens and Thackeray entertained the whole family in the middle of the century, not to mention the tales of outlaw passion with which Hardy or Wilde scandalized even mature audiences at the end. Sexual desires are everywhere in the Victorian novel, either as an explicit topic or as a subterranean force close enough to the surface that it may as well be.[3] This chapter aims to consider not whether or where sexual desire is admitted in the Victorian novel, but rather how it is described and organized when it is; not whether the characters who inhabit the Victorian novel are allowed erotic passion, but rather how they, and through them we, are trained to define and discipline it. Taking a cue from the most influential investigations of sexuality conducted over the past century and a half, the method of this chapter will be the individual case study: we will trace the career of erotic desire in five more or less familiar novels written at the heart of the Victorian period: *Jane Eyre* (Charlotte Brontë); *The Tenant of Wildfell Hall* (Anne Brontë, 1848); *Vanity Fair* (William Thackeray, 1848); *Adam Bede* (George Eliot, 1859), and *Our Mutual Friend* (Charles Dickens, 1865). To cast these texts as exemplary is by no means to claim that they comprehend the character of sexuality in the Victorian novel, but rather to suggest the dense network of cultural cause and effect that surround the formation of desires that often feel as simple as the pangs of hunger.

For those familiar with the course of Victorian fiction, a decision to end a survey of its erotics at 1865, rather than to take up works that inhabited and indeed helped to ignite the climate of sexual controversy that characterized the later part of the nineteenth century will seem odd, even perverse. Why not an investigation of *Tess of the D'Urbervilles* (1891) or *The Picture of Dorian Gray* (1891), whose ostentatious fin-de-siècle erotics would seem to make them eligible, indeed perhaps inevitable subjects for an essay on sexuality in the Victorian novel? I want to suggest though that many of the central strains in the history of sexual desire that are dramatized in the works of Hardy, Gissing, Wilde, and for the matter Proust and Freud, strains of desire which help to define the way we live now, are predicted in the writings of the mid-Victorians scrutinized here. Thus, for example, the sense conveyed so fully in Hardy that erotic attraction, and in particular male heterosexual desire, has the destructive force and the aura of inevitability that we attach to a natural disaster or an industrial revolution, finds a crucial antecedent in the works of the texts taken up in this chapter. Or to mention another, more devious example, the effort that Wilde describes in his famous novel to immortalize homosexual desire in the portrait of the young man who incites it, may be read as an effort to reverse a mid-Victorian tendency, eloquently apparent in a work like *Jane Eyre*. Brontë's attraction, one which makes way for those that end in matrimony and family values. (It hardly seems necessary to remark, by the way, the enduring potence of this trend in an era when a health crisis has worked to encourage the proclivity of our culture to perceive the homosexual as little more than a picture of what must die young.)[4] As with everything else human, when it comes to sex, the past is prelude.

ANNE BRONTË AND THE DISCIPLINING OF DESIRE

Even the many who have never read the novel are more than familiar with the warning that *The Tenant of Wildfell Hall* delivers about the hazards of passion unchecked by judgment, the catastrophe that results when our assessment of someone is clouded by our desire for him; the often sounded "warn[ing] ... against ... fixing [our] affections where approbation d[oes] not go before, and where reason and judgement with[o]ld their sanctions."[5] Also those who have never read *The Tenant of Wildfell Hall* will be able to guess that the admonition issued early and often in the novel—"[f]irst study; then approve; then love" (*Wildfell Hall*, 150) —falls on deaf ears: after all, who, apart from someone who has a reason to know it already, could take such advice seriously? Certainly not the novel's young protagonist, to whom this warning is addressed, Helen Huntingdon, who can hardly hear her guardian's exhortations across the gulf that separates those who feel sexual "fascinations" from those who seem to have forgotten how. Like more recent admonitions to just say no, that guardian's exhortation pays no heed to the power of the attraction that it would simply subordinate to "reason and judgment."

At first glance, the distance between the guardian's cold perspective and the girl's passionate eye could not seem greater: while her aunt appears to inhabit a bloodless universe where the "attractions" of the "handsomest" are "nothing ... Principle is the first thing; after all; and next to that, good sense, respectability, and moderate wealth" (150)—the girl herself belongs to a world where there is nothing else: "he is always in my thoughts and dreams. In all my employments, whatever I do, or see, or hear, has an ultimate reference to him"(168). But the difference between these estimates of attraction is smaller than it seems, since in her very condemnation of "the snares and wiles of the tempter," the guardian gives the devil his due; her anxious warning grimly acknowledges as all but irresistible the allure which her niece more happily admits:

> "Helen," said she, with reproachful gravity... "I know many ... that have ... through carelessness ... been wretched victims of deceit; and some, through weakness, have fallen into snares and temptations terrible to relate."
>
> "Well, I shall be neither careless nor weak."
>
> "Remember Peter, Helen! Don't boast, but watch. Keep a guard over your eyes and ears as the inlets of your heart, and over your lips as the outlet, lest they betray you in a moment of unwariness. Receive, coldly and dispassionately, every attention, till you have ascertained and duly considered the worth of the aspirant; and let your affections be consequent upon approbation alone. First study; then approve; then love. Let your eyes be blind to all external attractions, your ears deaf to all the fascinations of flattery and light discourse—These are nothing—and worse than nothing—snares and wiles of the tempter, to lure the thoughtless to their own destruction."   (150)

The vigilance urged in this passage extends beyond wariness about "external attractions" to include as well wariness about the attraction *to* them; beyond the fascinating suitor to include as well the senses and affections that he targets: "Keep a guard over your eyes and ears as the inlets of your heart;" "let your affections be consequent upon approbation alone." And even so, what power of vigilance, no matter how broad its scope, could possibly withstand a temptation as insinuating as the one Helen's guardian fears? How to resist an enemy whose fascinations are as hard to avoid as the weariness that comes as surely as the sun sets, the weariness that overtakes even the most zealous apostle, who, at the moment of truth, despite his best intentions, cannot stay awake to save his soul?

Sexual temptation is as hard to withstand as the need to sleep, or as the thrill of what is forbidden: common sense tells us that the siege mentality the guardian elaborates ends up giving aid to the enemy. Everyone knows that the best fan for the flame of desire is prohibition, and that an eye ever keen for any sign of what has been prohibited does nothing so much as to illuminate and expand its allure. This irony informs Michel Foucault's influential *History of Sexuality*, whose subject is the spirit of surveillance that we hear in *The Tenant of Wildfell Hall*, a spirit which, taking as its point of departure the tactics and sense of seriousness attached to religious confession, articulates itself in modern methods and institutions of supervision (for example, what was called sexology in the nineteenth century and psychoanalysis in the twentieth), established to monitor and categorize sexual desire and practice. If, on one hand, the conviction that our sexual desires and the way we respond to them are matters of the utmost importance (crucial both to the management of society, as well as to the destiny and definition of the individual who inhabits it), justifies the networks of surveillance that Foucault considers a crucial version of modern political power, then these forms of supervision themselves function to promote the very centrality of sexuality which gives them their reason for being in the first place. According to the reciprocal development that Foucault traces, the institutions established to monitor sexuality are not merely reactions to the recognition of its central significance, they themselves help to make it so significant.

But there is another, more immediate explanation for the empire of the erotic that reigns in *The Tenant of Wildfell Hall*. If the power of sexual desire is amplified by the force of surveillance arrayed against it and because of it, this power is secured in the first place by the absence of competing attractions. The alternative that the aunt offers in place of the excitement of sexual love is hardly very enticing: "Here the conversation ended, for at this juncture my uncle's voice was heard from his chamber, loudly calling upon my aunt to come to bed. He was in a bad humour that night; for his gout was worse" (*Wildfell Hall*, 167). Who would choose to lie in such a bed, rather than the one that Helen makes for herself with the handsome reprobate she marries? Who would have the will power sufficient to withstand the temptation of unsafe sex when the alternative is a sensible marriage such as the one that Helen's guardian suffers, the passionless partnership whose terms are spelled out by the mother of another character in the novel?: "I'm sure your poor, dear father was as good a husband as ever lived, and after the first six months or so were over, I should as soon as expected him to fly, as to put himself out of his way to pleasure me. He always said I was a good wife, and did my duty; and he always did his—bless him!—he was steady and punctual, seldom found fault without a reason, and always did justice to my good dinners, and hardly ever spoiled my cookery by delay—and that's as much as any woman can expect of any man" (79).

The dullness of such a marriage has a name in Brontë's novel: that name is duty. "He always said I was a good wife, and did my duty; and he always did his." According to the terms of marriage set out here, a woman can hope for nothing other than doing her duty to a husband who can look forward to nothing other than the prospect of performing his to her in turn. This marriage contract reflects the bleak climate of obligation that prevails generally in *The Tenant of Wildfell Hall*, starting on its first page, in which the novel's hero describes the sacrifice of his own desires to satisfy the demands of his father:

> My father ... was a ... farmer ... and I, by his express desire, succeeded him in the same quiet occupation, not very willingly ... He exhorted me, with his dying breath, to continue in the good old way, to follow his steps, and those of his father before him, and let my highest ambition be, to walk honestly through the world, looking neither to the right hand nor to the left, and to transmit the paternal acres to my children in at least as flourishing a condition as he left them to me.   (35)

The specific form that duty, or imposed obligation, takes in this passage—the protagonist's occupation—sounds like what Marx in his early manuscripts calls alienated labor: "the alienation of the worker ... means ... that it exists outside him ... as something alien to him."[6] While Marx is describing a form of work quite opposed to the occupation of a "gentleman farmer," in either case, no matter how diversely, what one must do is severed from what one wants to do. For a school of thought that Marx founded, the spirit of alienation expands beyond the zone of labor where it begins to take hold in the culture more generally.[7] We may hear a symptom of this dissemination when praise of a husband sounds like the memory of a fair employer: "he seldom found fault without a reason"; or like a recommendation of a good worker: "he was steady and punctual." And whether or not the dutiful marriage takes its form from the workplace, its "steady and punctual" subject is certainly fit for it. He is ready in particular for the "steady and punctual" work required by the capitalist system whose "triumph" is, in one historian's phrase, "the major theme"[8] of the era in which Brontë wrote.

For those who inhabit the dull world of duty that Brontë surveys, the excitement of sexual desire is the only thrill in town. In a world like this, there is no counterweight to love: nothing can check its power since nothing can compete with its luster. But if desire cannot be displaced by another interest, it must nevertheless be contained. Accordingly, the novel seeks not to annul the fascination of sexual desire—how could this be possible when nothing can hold a candle to it?—but rather to discipline it. If the novel is powerless to extinguish the erotic drive, it can nevertheless inculcate the inclination to defer its indulgence.

This inclination is encouraged by the assurance the novel delivers that the denial of sexual desire is indeed only its deferral. The hard renunciation prescribed by and for the characters who appear in *Wildfell Hall* is softened by the faith that one will have in the future what one must relinquish for the present. For those who inhabit the novel, this faith is founded explicitly on a familiar religious belief in a paradise that comes at the end of their lives: "We shall meet in heaven. Let us think of that" (409). For its readers, though, such faith is implicitly conducted by the no less familiar ending of the novel itself. The miracle at the end, the union of two lovers who had given up all hope of ever being together in this life, is routine enough in, and then beyond the Victorian novel, that it can come as no surprise to anyone. It is routine enough to take up tenancy within its reader as the unspoken article of faith by means of which the work of mourning is silently annexed by its opposite, an article of faith felt in the buried hope that we will have again the lost lover at the moment we have given him up for good.

The blessings of its happy ending are cast beyond the last pages of Anne Brontë's novel into the culture of capitalism where it is inscribed. Like a religion that justifies those who are enriched by the profits of the capitalist system,[9] or one that counsels resignation to those who labor to produce them, the secular scripture of desire promulgated by novels like *The Tenant of Wildfell Hall* promotes a faith that renders more tenable the sacrifices of desire exacted by that system. In the novel's closing scene of lovers together at last, an icon is born to ease the daily labor of renunciation exacted from the worker who must leave her own wishes at the door of the factory or office; in the closing scene of lovers together at last, an image arises that lights the path away from the pleasures that we want by the promise that we can return to them.

THE PASSIONS AND THE INTERESTS IN *VANITY FAIR*

The strain of sexual desire entertained in Brontë's novel takes place outside the sphere of the economy; it takes form as an impulse whose suspension is demanded by a capitalist regime sufficiently established by the middle of the nineteenth century to count as a principle of reality, a regime which depends upon and demands steady, punctual labor, or at least the habit of pulling out of bed and showing up to work on time. Elsewhere though, as in Thackeray's famous novel, the trouble with desire is not how little it has to do with economic values, but rather how much. *Vanity Fair* records the contamination of the cool motives associated with the marketplace by the heat of a passion that will pay any price, no matter how inflated, to have what it wants, a passion too blind to see the price it pays will not secure the prize in any case, a passion Thackeray and others identify as the essential style of sexual love.

A passion which puts those who are touched by it in the most embarrassing positions: for anyone who has read the novel, the spectacle of Jos Sedley at Vauxhall, drunk enough to make his move on Becky Sharp, clings like the memory of a personal humiliation: "'Stop, my dearest, diddle-diddle-darling,' shouted Jos, now as bold as a lion, and clasping Miss Rebecca round the waist. Rebecca started, but she could not get away her hand."[10] His death, probably by the same hand near the end of the novel merely literalizes the mortification he suffers for it near the beginning. And while Jos Sedley, "that fat *gourmand*," (*Vanity Fair*, 93) furnishes the broadest target for the "barbed shaft of love," no one is exempt from it: "[Rawdon Crawley] raved about [Becky] in uncouth convulsions. The barbed shaft of love had penetrated his dull hide" (173). "'I'll make your fortune,' she said; and Delilah patted Samson's cheek" (204).

Finally freed from its embrace, *Vanity Fair's* most long suffering fool of love, George Dobbin, sums up its damages:

> I know what your heart is capable of ... it can't feel such an attachment as mine deserves to mate with, and such as I would have from a woman more generous than you. No, you are not worthy of the love which I have devoted to you. I knew all along the prize I had set my life on was not worth the having; that I was a fool, with fond fancies too, bartering away my all of truth and ardour against your little feeble remnant of love. I will bargain no more: I withdraw. (776)

Whether it be the virulent strain signified by the fever of "uncouth convulsions" caused by Becky or the lighter but finally no less debilitating mutation that takes the shape of "fond fancies" prompted by Amelia, the problem with desire is a failure at the bottom line: simply put, love is a bad bargain; the return that it offers is no match for the investment it requires. More exactly, the problem with desire that *Vanity Fair* diagnoses is a failure to consider the price. It is only when he is cured of his passion that the lover can figure out that the cake is not worth the candle: only then, can he perform the simple arithmetic which reveals that the cost of Amelia is not worth the price that he must pay for her. Like a sign of returning health after a long illness, Dobbin's inclination to perform such calculations announces that the force of his desire for the woman he has loved throughout the novel has finally dissipated.

The disaster of desire fans out from the privacy of bedrooms and closets, and spills into the broader avenues of society in the novel. Thus, the "passion" for gambling that possesses the denizens of *Vanity Fair*: "the mania for play was so widely spread, that the public gambling-rooms did not suffice for the general ardour, and gambling went on in private houses as much as if there had been no public means for gratifying the passion" (430). If the "general ardour" for getting money breaks into the private houses where the transactions of sexual passion are usually conducted, Thackeray's very rendering of the drive for money as a form of passion describes the opposite movement: it leaves no doubt that erotic drives have already left their private domains, and come to electrify the current of greed.

Like the sexual desire that it comes to duplicate, the love of money is an impulse powerful enough to prompt irrational expenditures; it is powerful enough to overwhelm the inclination to balance the cost of an investment against the benefit that results; powerful enough to overwhelm the capacity to know when expenditure is wasteful because it is powerless to secure the object of desire. Thus, the problem with the drive for money in *Vanity Fair* is not that it is too much engrossed in the cool rational calculations of the marketplace, but that it has become too little so. It is not that the gambler is too greedy, but rather that his desire for gain overwhelms his capacity to secure it: like the lover who fails to recognize a bad bargain when he sees it, the gambler fastened to the roulette wheel or card table is too ardent to consider his chances carefully enough to quit while he is ahead.

Its infection by the forces of sexual passion disables what an important tradition of political theory regards as the signal virtue attached to the profit motive. In *The Passions and the Interests: Political Arguments for Capitalism Before its Triumph*, Albert O. Hirschman traces in the writings of figures such as Hume, Montesquieu and Dr. Johnson a line of thought which praises the motive of moneymaking as a calm desire that works to counteract passions such as anger and lust.[11] While by the lights of this tradition, the economic interest in acquisition opposes other, less governable passions, in Thackeray's novel this interest has been overtaken by the impulses that it is supposed to contain. The result is the general ardour of *Vanity Fair*, an overheated passion or a quiet delusion that debases, impoverishes or destroys everyone it touches.

But while economic interest cannot be relied upon to contain the vicissitudes of desire in *Vanity Fair*, the novel counts on desire to absorb the rule of interest sufficiently well to regulate itself. If the extinction of Dobbin's desire for Amelia is the condition that enables him to see her clearly in the end as a poor purchase, it is also the effect of that calculation; if the heat of passion has deranged the rationality of economic interest, the

rationality of economic interest in turn casts its cooling light upon the heat
of passion. The calmness that prevails at the end of the novel, the quiet
afterglow that succeeds the intensity of desire, is the achievement of a sexual
subject who has taken to heart the lessons of an economic principle that has
ceased to prevail in the precincts of a stock exchange as much given over to
the general ardor as the compulsive gambler or the drunken lover. It is the
achievement of a sexual subject who has taken to heart an economic principle
which is now nowhere else in sight.

JANE EYRE: HOMOSEXUALITY AS HISTORY

The cases we have examined so far allow us to recognize two kinds of history
written by the Victorian novel. If, as I suggested at the outset, the Victorian
novel helps to make the history of our sexuality, spelling out the plots by
which we define and thus experience its pleasures and hazards and showing
us our unconscious inheritance of their history, such stories are no less made
by history. The dramas of desire staged by the Victorian novel are enacted
against the epic backdrop that Eric Hobsbawm calls the "global triumph of
capitalism ... the major theme of history in the decades after 1848.'12
Sometimes what Anne Brontë calls "the frenzy of ardour" is posed by the
novel as a threat and an exception to a dull sense of duty allied with the
common sense of capitalism; sometimes this frenzy appears to merge with
economic interests, as it does in *Vanity Fair*: in either case, though, whether
sexual passion is defined by its distance from the economic interests at the
heart of the capitalist system or by its closeness to them, the specter of
market society everywhere haunts the scenes of desire that everywhere haunt
the Victorian novel.

But if the sexual desire featured in the Victorian novel is always part of
a broader social history that it absorbs and disseminates, it also has a history
all its own. Novels like *David Copperfield* (1850) and *Jane Eyre* tell a story of
sexual education whose hero is prepared for mature love by the youthful
infatuations he experiences on his way there, a story as familiar as the
reassurance that a species of sexuality whose enduring power to alarm is "just
a phase." In the history of desire written by the Victorian novel, various
forms of homoerotic passion make a brief but crucial appearance; the sexual
education conducted by the Victorian novel includes a typically forgotten
course of homoerotic enthusiasm which teaches heterosexuality its lessons.
Such education is not confined to the novel. The particular course we will
audit takes place in *Jane Eyre*, but its cognates range from the homosexual

desires that psychoanalytic theory casts as the prolegomena to heterosexuality, to the famous predisposition of a sophisticated song writer whose best-known lesson in love teaches the greater glory of the birds and the bees.

Jane Eyre, though, warms the heart with a story of man and wife which could not be less like the cool festal glamour imagined by the Cole Porter song, where good looks are as prerequisite as evening clothes. Plain Jane progresses to the heights of a metaphysical romance where looks do not matter, or matter only because to love them requires the insight to see past them. He was not easy on the eyes, Jane Eyre declares upon first meeting Rochester, and that was just as well, for, of course, she was not much to look at herself: "I had a theoretical reverence and homage for beauty, elegance, gallantry, fascination; but had I met those qualities incarnate in masculine shape, I should know instinctively that they neither had nor could have sympathy with anything in me, and should have shunned them as one would fire, lightning, or anything else that is bright but antipathetic."[13]

The raised voice of a "Mighty Spirit" that manages to rouse a lover miles out of earshot is only the most ostentatiously metaphysical feat of an affair of heart and soul that everywhere surpasses the boundaries of the body. No less wonderful, only more familiar than the transcendent powers of love recorded in *Wuthering Heights*, desire in *Jane Eyre* shows its genius by choosing an object with little to show for itself. A devotion maniacal enough to reject the impediments of mortality is no more miraculous than the passion inspired by a woman who is not "pretty" and a man who is not "handsome" (*Jane Eyre*, 163); a romance high enough to rise above death has nothing over an earthbound one that flourishes in the face of homeliness or harshness. Phrenology, not astrology, is the conceit that guides this courtship; Rochester and Jane Eyre find each other's signs not in the stars, but in bodily forms rendered immaterial by their reading.

If the object of desire in *Jane Eyre* is not the body, neither is it strictly the soul; it is rather a figure found passing from the province of the first to the second. What is admired here is not what is already abstract, but what becomes so: Jane cherishes Rochester neither by adoring nor by ignoring his formidable physique, but by tracking its sublimation; before her loving eyes, his rough features are ignited into a trinity of metaphysical forces "more than beautiful": "Most true it is that 'beauty is in the eyes of the gazer.' My master's colourless, olive face, square, massive brow, broad and jetty eyebrows, deep eyes, firm, grim mouth—all energy, decision, will—were not beautiful, according to rule; but they were more than beautiful to me" (203–4). For his part, Rochester returns the abstracting tribute of this regard; rejecting the "gazelle eyes" of "the Grand Turk's seraglio," his passion is reserved instead for the "something glad" he detects in the "glance" of the most ordinary of English girls; for the "becoming air" he witnesses her become: "Although you are not pretty any more than I am handsome, yet a puzzled air becomes you" (163).

Like the penchant for flogging from which some public schoolboys never seemed to recover, Jane's taste for the disincarnated begins at school; her longing for the metaphysical is defined by the original objects of her desire, Maria Temple and Helen Burns. Their bodies, unlike the too solid flesh of the hated John Reed, "dingy and unwholesome skin; thick lineaments in a spacious visage, heavy limbs and large extremities" (41), are forever disappearing: "she looked tall, fair, and shapely; brown eyes with a benignant light in their irids, and a fine penciling of long lashes round;" "on each of her temples her hair a very dark brown, was clustered in round curls ... Let the reader add, to complete the picture, refined features; a complexion, if pale, clear; and a stately air and carriage, and he will have, at least as clearly as words can give it, a correct idea of the exterior of Miss Temple—Maria Temple, as I afterward saw the name written in a Prayer Book entrusted to me to carry to church" (79–80). As Jane enumerates Maria Temple's qualities, the lady, or at least her body, vanishes; the eclipse that begins as the parts of her body give way to a transparent aspect and an abstract disposition, becomes total when Maria Temple becomes a name; the "steps" that Jane's "organ of veneration" "trace" with "admiring awe" go all the way, in the course of this passage, from the sphere of the body to the pages of a book.

For Jane Eyre, and for us as well, such translations of the body are less the dismissal of sexual excitement than the source of it. We would be hard pressed to deny the erotic value of the "interest" that Rochester's features hold for Jane Eyre, at the moment they are stripped of the garments of the body, "an interest, and influence that quite mastered me—that took my feelings from my own power and fettered them in his" (204), even without Freud's suggestion that sexual excitement starts in the swerve away from bodily needs; even without the more common sense view that sex really gets started when it gets into the head.[14]

As it does when, alone at night with Maria Temple, and the girl she loves even more, Jane's "organ of veneration expand[s]" beyond all limit as she watches "powers within [Helen Burns]" arise from "her own unique mind" to displace her frail body:

they shone in the liquid lustre of her eyes, which had suddenly acquired a beauty more singular than that of Miss Temple's—a beauty neither of fine colour nor long eyelash, not pencilled brow, but of meaning ... of radiance. Then her soul sat on her lips, and language flowed, from what source I cannot tell; has a girl of fourteen a heart large enough, vigorous enough to hold the swelling spring of pure full, fervid eloquence ... my organ of veneration expand[ed] at every sounding line.

(*Jane Eyre*, 104–5)

A compulsion to repeat stations the sublime object of Jane's first love as the model for subsequent ones. If Jane speaks less and less during the course of the novel of the teacher and the classmate she adored, she has nonetheless taken them in as the definition of what is to be loved; if she puts away the objects of her schoolyard passion with other childish things, she finds them again in the body of a man made fabulous by its change into "energy, decision, will."

But while the object of Jane Eyre's homosexual enthusiasm survives as the ghostly paradigm for her heterosexual passion, the course of disembodiment that defines this figure ensures that it survives *only* as such. For the path of sublimation trodden by Helen Burns is another name for the drive towards death; her eloquence another name for her epitaph. A rumor of morbidity encrypted in the graveness of Maria Temple's countenance and her mention in a book of prayers, is substantiated by Helen Burns's headlong progress to the grave. When she speaks of "the time when we shall put off our cumbrous flesh, and only the spark of the spirit will remain" (91), she speaks for herself; the look that Jane would die for: "What a smile! I remember it now, and I know that it was the effluence of fine intellect, of true courage; it lit up her marked lineaments, her thin face, her sunken gray eye, like a reflection from the aspect of an angel"—is the look of one near death, the glance of a "passing martyr, imparting strength in transit" (99).

This drive towards death is determined by a Victorian pattern legislated in and beyond *Jane Eyre*, a pattern that ensures that all passion leads, one way or another, to Church; a pattern which ensures that all passion leads either to the altar, where Jane and Rochester are finally married, or to the graveyard where Helen Burns is buried. The thought that Rochester will marry another woman, and the subsequent discovery that he already has, is death for Jane: "I am not talking to you now through the medium of mortal flesh," she remarks to Rochester at the moment when she believes he will marry someone other than herself, "it is my spirit that addresses your spirit; just as if both had passed through the grave." "I can but die," she declares later, at the end of her suicidal flight from the man she loves after the revelation that he is already married, and her rejection of his proposal that she live as his mistress.

Such melodramatic sentiments, surprising from a heroine whose speech is normally as plain as her face, conform to a law of desire inscribed in more books than *Jane Eyre*. A law with two clauses: where the telos of the marriage plot falters in and beyond the Brontë novel, that of the death drive takes over; when passions are accidently or constitutionally prevented from reaching the altar, they come instead to the bleakest of houses. Barred at the nuptial door, those taken up by such passions must cross a different bar, the one that an unmarried missionary nears at the close of *Jane Eyre*: "St. John is unmarried: he will never marry now ... The last letter I received from him ... anticipated his sure reward ... 'My Master,' he says, 'has forewarned me' ... he announces more distinctly, 'Surely I come quickly!' and ... I more eagerly respond, 'Amen; even so, come"' (477).

Extramarital passions may be less heated than those that confirm St. John Rivers's bachelor status, but they always tend to the same conclusion. When Jane and Helen finally sleep together, they do so in a deathbed: "Miss Temple had found me laid in [the] little crib; my face against Helen Burns's shoulder, my arms round her neck. I was asleep, and Helen was dead" (114). And with this, Jane has learned all she can from the girl she loves, who dies defining the criterion for desire; the tutor who, like a "martyr in transit," takes the hit not only for herself, but for her partner in passion, as well. For Jane is only asleep; she will arise and go now to put what she has learned into practice: the transubtantiated body of the man she finally marries is the ghost of the girl who dies because she can't marry Jane herself. "Her grave is in Brocklebridge Churchyard: for fifteen years after her death it was only covered by a grassy mound; but now a gray marble tablet inscribed with her name, and the word '*Resurgam*"' (114).

SEXUALITY AND SOLITUDE IN *ADAM BEDE*

With *Adam Bede* we return to the relation between sexuality and its social context, at first to notice a basic aspect of that relation, overlooked in the socio-economic genealogies of sexual desire that we sought to assemble through *The Tenant of Wildfell Hall and Vanity Fair*: namely that in one simple sense, there is no relation between them at all. None, that is, except for mutual exclusion: when it comes down to it, sexual desire and sexual intercourse in and beyond *Adam Bede* typically takes place behind the closed doors or secret hideaways of private houses or fantasies; when it comes down to it, sexual intercourse is usually conducted only in the absence of broader society, usually only when those who are not involved directly with the lovers have been removed from sight, or mind, or both. Except for those whose particular passions involve public venues, or those whose straitened circumstances offer them no other, sex is generally a private affair.

"They were alone together for the first time. What an overpowering presence that first privacy is!"[15] You do not have to know Adam Bede to know this story: the scene alone, the scene in which two people find themselves alone, provides all the cue that is required to surmise what is about to happen here. (Eliot's readers will have an additional advantage figuring out the erotic dimensions of this scene: her novels are filled with situations like this, situations in which the pressure of potential sexual intercourse between two people arises solely from the fact that they are alone together.) You do have to know Adam Bede to know that the sexual encounter that is about to take place between Arthur Donnithorne and Hetty Sorrel "alone together" destroys their relations with everyone else in the book. Only those who have read the novel can be aware that as a result of what takes place here, Arthur loses his best friend—Adam Bede will soon happen upon this scene, and things will never be the same between the two men; only those who have read the novel will know that, as a result of their affair, Arthur Donnithorne and Hetty Sorrel are forced away from the community that had been their home. (No wonder that, "for the rest of his life," Adam Bede "remembered" the moment before he discovers his best friend with the woman he wanted to marry "as a man remembers his last glimpse of the home where his youth was passed, before the road turned, and he saw it no more" [*Adam Bede*, 341]; no wonder, since so much exile arises from the scene he is about to encounter of "two figures ... with clasped hands ... about to kiss" [342].)

But if you have to read *Adam Bede* to glean all the ways that the intercourse between Arthur and Hetty drives them apart from other people, the most basic one is as familiar as the lock on the bedroom door, or the lie that is told to conceal what goes on behind it. You do not have to read *Adam Bede* to recognize the most anti-social element of sexuality in the world of the novel, since it is the same in our own: "The candid Arthur had brought himself into a position in which successful lying was his only hope" (344–5); "Arthur was in the wretched position of an open generous man, who has committed an error which makes deception seem necessary;" "Arthur had impressed on Hetty that it would be fatal to betray, by word or look, that there had been the least intimacy between them." The couple keep their secret as long as they can, and so does the narrator, who declines to reveal it even to the reader, whom she elsewhere flatters with special access to the inside story. No one else knows how far things have gone between Arthur, and Hetty until the scandal of the pregnancy makes it impossible to hide it any longer.

And then there is another zone of sexual privacy in Eliot's novel even more isolated than the spot in the forest where Hetty and Arthur meet, a zone that escapes detection altogether, a realm of desire that cannot be exposed because it cannot be communicated. We hear of it when the narrator joins the rakish squire as he stops his tour of a family farm to admire "a distractingly pretty girl of seventeen,"

> standing on little pattens and rounding her dimpled arm to lift a pound of butter out of the scale.
>
> Hetty blushed a deep rose-colour when Captain Donnithorne entered the dairy and spoke to her; but it was not at all a distressed blush, for it was inwreathed with smiles and dimples ... [she] tossed and patted her pound of butter with quite a self-possessed, coquettish air, slyly conscious that no turn of her head was lost.
>
> There are various orders of beauty, causing men to make fools of themselves in various styles, from the desperate to the sheepish; but there is one order of beauty which seems made to turn the heads not only of men, but of all intelligent mammals, even of women. It is a beauty like that of kittens, or very small downy ducks making gentle rippling noises with their soft bills, or babies just beginning to toddle and to engage in conscious mischief—a beauty with which you can never be angry, but that you feel ready to crush for inability to comprehend the state of mind into which it throws you, Hetty Sorrel's was that sort of beauty. Her aunt, Mrs. Poyser, who professed to despise all personal attractions and intended to be the severest of mentors, continually gazed at Hetty's charms by the sly, fascinated in spite of herself ...   (89–95)

As it comes to rest in this passage with "a beauty like that of kittens, or very small downy ducks ... or babies just beginning to toddle," the sexual luster that is concentrated on "a distractingly pretty girl of seventeen," is dispersed, but it is hardly canceled. While the universal attraction that dominates this scene drifts from the particular species of sexual desire (male, heterosexual) where it originates in this passage, it is hardly detached from sexual desire altogether. Like the girl who arouses it, "slyly conscious that no turn of her head was lost," the force of attraction that turns every head, "not only of men, but of all intelligent mammals, even of women" is animated by an erotic element as hard to deny as it is to define: "Her aunt ... continually gazed at Hetty's charms by the sly, fascinated in spite of herself."

Even if she could do so herself, how could we take the dimensions of sexual desire in Mrs. Poyser's sly, fascinated gaze? The universal attraction for Hetty Sorrel is paradoxically quite private:

> It is of little use for me to tell you that Hetty's cheek was like a rose petal, that dimples played about her pouting lips, that her large dark eyes hid a soft roguishness under their long lashes ... of little use, unless you have seen a woman who affected you as Hetty affected her beholders, for otherwise, though you might conjure up the image of a lovely woman, she would not in the least resemble that distracting kitten-like maiden.   (128)

Those who know her will recognize that the doubt that Eliot's narrator expresses here about her ability to convey the experience of someone else is as fugitive as any of her moods. Elsewhere she could hardly be more at home with the task of communicating the inmost impulses of others; elsewhere she is sufficiently certain of her qualifications for this task, that she mounts a virtual science out of sympathy. Here, though, all of that confidence is lost in a sense of the distance between self and other—how can I describe the experience of someone else to you unless you have had the experience yourself?; how, therefore is communication possible unless it is redundant, and therefore not really communication at all?—here, when it comes to conveying how "Hetty affected her beholders."

More than a barrier that defines one limit of sympathy, the case of sexual attraction provokes a recognition of those limits more generally:

> I might mention all the divine charms of a bright spring day, but if you had never in your life utterly forgotten yourself in straining your eyes after a mounting lark, or in wandering through the still lanes when the fresh-opened blossoms filled them with a sacred, silent beauty ... what would be the use of my descriptive catalogue?   (128)

Like a universal attraction that descends from a particular one, the general problem of other minds that Eliot invokes when she connects her inability to convey the attraction of Hetty Sorrel to her inability to convey the pleasures of a spring morning begins with the specific case of sexual desire, the specific case whose details are never quite worked out of the abstract principle which arises from it: "I could never make you know what I meant by a bright spring day. Hetty's was a springtide beauty; it was the beauty of young frisking things, round-limbed, gambolling, circumventing you by a false air of innocence" (128).

The solitude of the desiring subject in Eliot's novel makes her a stranger to the society that Foucault studies, and that we have touched upon before in this chapter, a society of supervision where the powers of discernment convene first of all on sexuality; a society of surveillance in which sex is "*the* secret" that must be known, and moreover a secret that can be known: "What is peculiar to modern societies, in fact, is not that they consigned sex to a shadow existence, but that they dedicated themselves to speaking of it *ad infinitum*, while exploiting it as *the* secret."[16] A fascination for "a distractingly pretty girl of seventeen," a sly attraction that must remain private, not because it is culturally unacceptable but rather because it is simply incommunicable, defeats, as if by the force of a natural fact, the intrusions of "modern societies" committed to and even constituted by the task of putting sex in view by putting it into "discourse."

But if the loneliness of Eliot's sexual subject liberates her from one aspect of modern society, it is only to inscribe her in another. If this illegible character resists a social power that consists of seeing over and through its subject, she is quite fit for the climate of alienation that Durkheim and Weber called modern society, an urban and capitalist society where anonymous, or nearly anonymous associations have replaced personal attachments. Such relations, Georg Simmel remarks, require minimal knowledge about the other party: "The modern merchant who enters business with another; the scholar who together with another embarks upon an investigation; the leader of a political party who makes an agreement with the leader of another party … all these know … only exactly *that* and no more about their partner which they *have* to know for the sake of the relationship they wish to enter."[17]

Hetty Sorrel, towards the end of the novel, venturing to the city with the secret of her pregnancy, is a model citizen of this society. "'Ah it's plain enough what sort of business it is,'" says the wife of the landlord at the inn where she stays. But what is plain to her, apart from the broadest sense that Hetty has been done wrong by the man she loves, is only the aspect of the girl that is relevant to another sort of business, the sort that she and the landlord have to conduct with her:

"She's not a common flaunting dratchell, I can see that. She looks like a respectable country girl, and she comes from a good way off, to judge by her tongue. She talks something like that ostler we had that come from the north: he was as honest a fellow as we ever had about the house—they're all honest folks in the north."

(Adam Bede, 423)

Glimpsed in this exchange is the brave new world of modern society, one where the mysterious subject of sexuality, frightened and lonely perhaps, but with her secret still intact, could not be more at home.

OUR MUTUAL FRIEND AND THE EROTICS OF DOWNWARD MOBILITY

Far from the madding crowd in Eliot's novel, a man sees no social difference between himself and the woman he wants: "While Arthur gazed into Hetty's dark beseeching eyes, it made no difference to him what sort of English she spoke; and even if hoops and powder had been in fashion, he would very likely not have been sensible just then that Hetty wanted signs of high breeding" (178). Stationed at the heart of society in Dickens's novel, a man sees little else: "so hard to touch, so hard to turn!" the hero laments in *Our Mutual Friend*, as he gazes from his lowly station at the haughty goddess he adores, "[a]nd yet so pretty, so pretty!".[18]

And yet? Would it not be more candid for the passion-struck John Harmon to say *and thus* so pretty? For it is not just that sexual desire leaves intact the sense of social distinction that separates its subject and object in *Our Mutual Friend*, rather sexual desire requires it. How would it be possible to disentangle John Harmon's fascination with the "scornful" Bella from the cuts he suffers at her hands? His longing, if not his love for her, is only whetted when she reminds him that they are separated by a social gulf as great as any; his longing, if not his love for Bella is only made vivid by the sight of "the proud face with the downcast eyes, and ... the quick breathing as it stirred the fall of bright brown hair over the beautiful neck" *(Our Mutual Friend*, 432).

We have reasons to suspect a strain of sexual desire here that inverts the more familiar Victorian privileged male taste for lower-class girls or boys. More exactly, we have reasons to suspect that John Harmon is excited by Bella's social altitude, less as a thing in itself than by how low it makes him feel by comparison; reason to suspect that whatever his announced motives for doing so, the situation that John Harmon goes to extraordinary lengths to set up for himself in the novel—designated by his father's will to inherit his vast fortune and to marry Bella Wilfer, he instead shams his own death, disguises himself as a penniless stranger named John Rokesmith, takes lodgings at the

Wilfer's house and a secretarial position with the couple who have inherited his fortune and brought Bella to live with them "upon equal terms" (257)—is tailor-made for a sexual taste that, submitting to the taxonomical spirit of nineteenth-century sexology, we could call "class masochism."

We may suspect that the sense of abjection with which Bella leaves him is the very point of his elaborate exercise in declassment; we may suspect that the eager hand he lends her in putting him down is animated by the pleasure of pain: "He went down to his room, and buried John Harmon many additional fathoms deep ... And so busy [was] he all night, piling and piling weights upon weights of earth above John Harmon's grave ... [until he] lay buried under a whole Alpine range; and still the Sexton Rokesmith accumulated mountains over him, lightening his labour with the dirge, 'Cover him, crush him, keep him down!'" (435) (Signs of a sexual taste for class denigration surface all over Dickens's novels, as when the brokenhearted Pip recalls the origin of his socio-economic discomfort in *Great Expectations:* "Truly it was impossible to dissociate her presence from all those wretched hankerings after money and gentility."[19] The girl he desires is entangled less with the desire to get money and gentility than with the sense of wanting it, with "wretched hankerings after" these things rather than the determination to get them.)

The suspicion that Harmon's desire for Bella is caught up with the sense of abjection that she provides for him is confirmed rather than contradicted by the satisfaction of that desire in the honeymoon household where the Harmons and the Boffins finally dwell together. Confirmed, because this is the end of his desire in both senses of the term: the wedded bliss finally achieved by John and Bella Harmon may be more joyful, but it is no less erotically impoverished than the passionless marriage advocated by Helen Huntingdon's grim guardian or the frightening domesticity projected by Bella's sadly ridiculous parents. If, as Nancy Armstrong declares in *Desire and Domestic Fiction,* class differences in the eighteenth- and nineteenth-century novel "are ... represented as a struggle between the sexes that can be completely resolved in terms of the sexual contract,"[20] this resolution, at least in the Dickens novel, comes at the cost of the sexual element in the sexual contract. Too busy playing house, "Bella, putting her hair back with both hands, as if she were making the most business-like arrangements ... enter[ing] the [domestic] affairs of the day" *(Our Mutual Friend,* 749), has no time now to let her hair down long enough for her former role as class sadist.

We need only weigh the difference between John Harmon's fantasy of social abjection and Lizzie Hexam's fantasy of social ascent to sense what will probably be obvious anyway, that the category of class masochism in *Our*

Mutual Friend is a species of male sexuality:

> "I wonder if anybody has ... captivated ... [Mr Wrayburn], Lizzie!"
>
> "It is very likely."
>
> "It is very likely? I wonder who!"
>
> "Is it not very likely that some lady has been taken by him, and that he may love her dearly?"
>
> "Perhaps. I do not know. What would you think of him, Lizzie, if you were a lady?"
>
> "I a lady!" she repeated, laughing. "Such a fancy!"
>
> "Yes. But say: just as a fancy, and for instance."
>
> "I a lady! I, a poor girl who used to row poor father on the river."   (401)

Thus an irony as common as the greener grass on the other side: while the desires of the entitled man are bound up with a hankering to be taken down the class ladder, the desires of the river dredger's daughter are condensed in a dream of upward mobility. And if the difference between the desires of John Harmon and Lizzie Hexam seems only a matter of class rather than sex, consider that the most virulent strain of social masochism recorded in the novel appears well below the upper reaches of the novel's social anatomy, in a man who dwells at the bottom edge of respectability:

> Bradley Headstone, in his decent black coat and waistcoat, and decent white shirt ... He was never seen in any other dress, and yet there was a certain stiffness in his manner of wearing this, as if there were a want of adaptation between him and it recalling some mechanics in their holiday clothes. He had acquired mechanically a great store of teacher's knowledge ... From his early childhood up, his mind had been a place of mechanical stowage. The arrangement of his wholesale warehouse, so that it might be always ready to meet the demands of retail dealers—history here, geography there, astronomy to the right, political economy to the left ... had imparted to his countenance a look of care.   (266–7)

The drive for social improvement that engrosses Bradley Headstone, whose threadbare respectability requires infinite pains to sustain, illuminates by contrast the downward trajectory of his sexual compulsion. Consider his anguished declaration to Lizzie:

I love you. What other men may mean when they use that
expression, I cannot tell; what I mean is, that I am under the
influence of some tremendous attraction which I have resisted in
vain, and which overmasters me. You could draw me to fire, you
could draw me to water, you could draw me to the gallows, you
could draw me to any death, you could draw me to anything I
have most avoided, you could draw me to any exposure and
disgrace.   (454–5)

Headstone's "tremendous attraction" pulls him to a hideous death, but also
to the social ruin at least as bad as that in the book of the anxious *arriviste*
"who had toiled hard to get what [he] had won, and ... had to hold it now that
it was gotten" (267). Drawn on by his "tremendous attraction," Bradley
Headstone falls not only to the bottom of the river, "under the ooze and
scum" (874), but, no less horribly, to the bottom of the social order.

And the downward pull of Bradley Headstone's attraction manages to
defeat the drive upward that is also confided there. In her study of the social
intercourse between men routed through the channel of a common desire for
the same woman, Eve Kosofsky Sedgwick remarks that "the link of rivalry
between himself and Eugene Wrayburn," his upper-crust competitor, is the
closest that Bradley Headstone comes to "patriarchal power," and, we might
add, the cultural capital that his rival possesses in abundance.[21] But, as
Sedgwick suggests, this is a miss as good as a mile—there is no way that the
downtrodden schoolteacher can keep up with his entitled competitor, who
amuses himself by inciting and frustrating Headstone's hunger to emulate
him: "I tempt him on, all over London ... Sometimes I walk; sometimes, I
proceed in cabs, draining the pocket of the schoolmaster, who then follows in
cabs ... [I] tempt the school master to follow" (*Our Mutual Friend*, 606).

The gulf made vivid by Bradley Headstone's humiliation by a man who
can afford things that he cannot may seem less a matter of masochism than
the simple fact of class difference. But if Bradley Headstone is set up by the
social order to lose the race for Lizzie Hexam from the start, he also appears
to relish his loss. Like John Harmon, Headstone goes to considerable trouble
to arrange a drama in which he stars as Social Inferiority:

"You think me of no more value than the dirt under your feet,"
said Bradley to Eugene, speaking in a carefully weighed and
measured tone, or he could not have spoken at all.

"I assure you, Schoolmaster," replied Eugene, "I do not think
about you."

"That's not true," returned the other; "you know better."

"That's coarse," Eugene retorted, "but you *don't* know better."

"Mr. Wrayburn, at least I know very well that it would be idle to set myself against you in insolent words or overbearing manners. That lad who has just gone out could put you to shame in half-a-dozen branches of knowledge in half an hour, but you can throw him aside like an inferior. You can do as much by me, I have no doubt, beforehand."

"Possibly," remarked Eugene.   (344)

And the downward direction of Bradley Headstone's sexual drive is more than a matter of its practical effects in the novel; more even than its entanglement with a taste for social denigration. It is not just that his desire drives him downward on the social scale, or, like his upper-class counterpart John Harmon, that he desires to be so driven; it is also that his desire is socially inferior in its very nature:

He held as straight a course for [Lizzie's house] as the wisdom of his ancestors, exemplified in the construction of the intervening streets, would let him, and walked with a bent head hammering at one fixed idea. It had been an immovable idea since he first set eyes upon her. It seemed to him as if all that he could ... restrain in himself he had restrained, and the time had come—in a rush, in a moment—when the power of self-command had departed from him. Love at first sight is a trite expression quite sufficiently discussed; enough that in certain smouldering natures like this man's, that passion leaps into a blaze, and makes such head as fire does in a rage of wind, when other passions, but for its mastery, could be held in chains.   (396)

The passion that is released in this "smouldering nature," the passion embodied in "a bent head hammering at one fixed idea," takes the form of labor—not the respectable occupation of the schoolteacher, but rather the labor of the blacksmith or the factory worker, the work that is done by those whose unchaining Marx saw as the start of a conflagration that would bring down the socio-economic order.

But if the return of the repressed in Bradley Headstone raises briefly the specter of revolution, it works as well to contain another kind of threat to society, a threat posed not by smouldering masses who seek to incinerate it, but rather by climbers who seek to enter it. They are everywhere in the novel. The dogged efforts of Bradley Headstone at respectability are matched by the delirious machinations of those who seek to enter a higher society: "Mr. and Mrs. Veneering were bran-new people in a bran-new house in a bran-new quarter of London. Everything about the Veneerings was spick and span new. All their furniture was new, all their friends were new, all their servants were new, their plate was new, their carriage was new, their harness was new, their horses were new, their pictures were new" (48). And such machinations are matched by virtually everyone else in the social gulf between Headstone and the Veneerings.

The clamor of improvement heard everywhere in *Our Mutual Friend* that originates in a capitalist economy providing unprecedented opportunities for class ascent, at least to some Victorians, is the social unrest that the class-defined and defining character of Bradley Headstone's sexuality helps to contain. It is in the context of a drive for upward mobility as incessant in the world of *Our Mutual Friend* as sexual desire itself that we can most fully understand Dickens's defense of traditional class distinctions, a defense that Franco Moretti describes: "Dickens succeeds in keeping alive the taxonomical rigidity of 'traditional-feudal' thought even after the erosion of its material bases ... What marks the vast majority of Dickensian characters is, after all, the very same impossibility to 'escape from oneself which in *Tom Jones* was the result of one's 'trade', and in Dickens, who is writing about a socially more fluid world, is connected to something strictly personal."[22]

And what could be more strictly personal than sexual passion? What better way to secure a wavering sense of someone's social rank than by translating it into the intimate idiom of his desire? The class position from which Bradley Headstone seeks to rise haunts his very efforts to do so, in "the stiffness of manner" that makes him in "respectable" dress like a "mechanic" in his "holiday clothes"; in the stiffness of mind that makes his exertions to transcend that position only a sublimated version of the labor that defines that position in the first place. But the ghost of the mechanic returns most fully in the passions that a "respectable" man cannot deny forever, the passion that sets him on a "course" set out for him by "his ancestors," "with a bent head hammering at one fixed idea." And here we return to the sexuality in the Victorian novel that has concerned us all along, the propagations of passion through which the forces of history make themselves felt.

Notes

1. Those familiar with it will recognize that the phrase that begins and the thought that informs this paragraph are drawn from Michel Foucault's *History of Sexuality: An Introduction—Volume 1*, trans. Robert Hurley (New York: Random House, 1978).

2. Franco Moretti, "Kindergarten," *Signs Taken for Wonders*, trans. Susan Fischer, David Forgacs, David Miller (London: Verso, 1983), 181.

3. Although to phrase it this way is to risk obscuring how significant the particular forms of indirection are in determining the course and character of sexual desire in and beyond the Victorian novel. For an exemplary recent consideration of this question, see William A. Cohen, *Sex Scandal: The Private Parts of Victorian Fiction* (Durham, NC: Duke University Press, 1996).

4. On the definition of the homosexual as a form of desire and then later a mode of identity associated with early extinction in the Victorian period and beyond, see Jeff Nunokawa, "In *Memoriam* and the Extinction of the Homosexual," ELH 58.2 (1991), 427–38; "All The Sad Young Men: AIDS and the Work of Mourning," in Diana Fuss, ed., *Inside/Out: Lesbian Theories, Gay Theories* (New York: Routledge, 1992). On Wilde's efforts to invert this trend, see Jeff Nunokawa, "The Importance of Being Bored: The Dividends of Ennui in *The Picture of Dorian Gray*" in Eve Kosofsky Sedgwick, ed., *Novel Gazing: Queer Readings in Fiction* (Durham, NC: Duke University Press, 1997), 151–66.

5. Anne Brontë *The Tenant of Wildfell Hall*, ed. G. D. Hargreaves (1848; London: Penguin, 1979), 165. All subsequent citations of the novel refer to this edition.

6. Karl Marx, *Economic and Philosophic Manuscripts of 1844*, trans. Martin Mulligan (Amherst, NY: Prometheus Books, 1988), 72.

7. See, for example, Georg Lukács, "Reification and the Consciousness of the Proletariat" in *History and Class Consciousness*, trans. Rodney Livingston (Cambridge, MA: The MIT Press, 1971), 83–222; Henri Lefebvre, *Critique of Everyday Life*, trans. John Moore (New York: Verso Press, 1991); Herbert Marcuse, *Eros and Civilization: A Philosophical Inquiry into Freud* (Boston: Beacon Press, 1955).

8. E.J. Hobsbawm, *The Age of Capital, 1848–1875* (New York: Scribner, 1975), xiii.

9. Max Weber, *The Protestant Ethic and The Spirit of Capitalism*, Introduction by Randall Collins; trans. Talcott Parsons (Los Angeles: Roxbury Publishing Company, 1996).

10. William Makepeace Thackeray, *Vanity Fair*, ed. J.I.M. Stewart (1848; London: Penguin, 1985), 93. All subsequent citations of the novel refer to this edition.

11. Albert O Hirschman, *The Passions and the Interests: Political Arguments for Capitalism Before Its Triumph* (Princeton: Princeton University Press, 1977).

12. Hobsbawm, *The Age of Capital*, xvii.

13. Charlotte Brontë, *Jane Eyre*, ed. Q.D. Leavis (1847; New York: Penguin, 1966). All subsequent citations refer to this edition.

14. Sigmund Freud, "Three Contributions to the Theory of Sex," *The Basic Writings of Sigmund Freud* (New York: Random House, 1938), 553–629.

15. George Eliot, *Adam Bede*, ed. Stephen Gill (1859; London: Penguin, 1980), 176. All subsequent citations of the novel refer to this edition.

16. Foucault, *History of Sexuality*, 35.

17. Georg Simmel, *The Sociology of Georg Simmel*, trans. and ed. Kurt Wolff (New York: The Free Press, 1950), 319.

18. Charles Dickens, *Our Mutual Friend*, ed. Stephen Gill (1865; London: Penguin, 1971), 257. All subsequent citations of the novel refer to this edition.

19. Charles Dickens, *Great Expectations*, ed. Angus Calder (1860; London: Penguin, 1985), 257.

20. Nancy Armstrong, *Desire and Domestic Fiction: A Political History of the Novel* (New York: Oxford University Press, 1987), 49.

21. Eve Kosofsky Sedgwick, *Between Men: English Literature and Male Homosocial Desire* (New York: Columbia University Press, 1985), 168.

22. Franco Moretti, "The Conspiracy of the Innocents," *The Way of the World: The* Bildungsroman *in European Culture*, trans Albert Sbragia (London: Verso, 1987), 193.

JOHN R. REED

George Meredith, Samuel Butler, Thomas Hardy, and Theodore Watts-Dunton

Discursive secular writers on the subject of the will offered a widening range of opinion in the latter half of the nineteenth century as science introduced new avenues for examining man's self, his nature, and his freedom. Chief among these new avenues was the broad theory (or set of theories) covered by the term "evolution," reviewed in chapter 7 of the study. The present chapter looks at some representative novelists who incorporated new thinking about human nature in a wide range of attitudes reflected in the manner of their narrations.

George Meredith believed in free will and progress. Balancing a trust in reason with a respect for intuition and imagination, he located freedom in the latter with its power of liberation through language, especially metaphor. For Meredith, to learn to read life was to imagine it into being. Life was art and narration. But to the artist of art and of life alike, conquest of self was the first step toward reading the text of life correctly. Samuel Butler had less faith in reason, more in the unconscious motive powers. He proposed his own theory of evolution, in which heredity severely limited human freedom. His method was to shock his readers into awareness. Shock was, in his theory, the one way out of a simple and rigorous determinism. For Thomas Hardy, the human power for imagining life as a story was a prominent source of human misery, because most people aspire to circumstances that the conditions of natural life will not permit. They do not realize that they project false stories

From *Victorian Will*. © 1989 by John R. Reed.

from their own unexamined desires. Hardy's narrative method suggests that the only safe place for fictions is in art. Finally, Theodore Watts-Dunton's *Aylwin* contains a hodgepodge of many of the contending attitudes toward free will and the prison of circumstance prevalent at the end of the century and cavalierly offers the conclusion that man is free in a wonderful, mysterious, and inexplicable world. All of these writers reflect the growing complexity of views about the free will versus determinism dispute, and their narrative strategies indicate conscious or unconscious efforts to render philosophical assumptions in appropriate vehicles.

Three important writers of the late nineteenth century rejected theism and were unwilling to retain the Christian structure of morality. The philosophical assumptions underlying their novels provide an instructive gradation. George Meredith was frankly optimistic, progressive, and vitalistic; Samuel Butler was more guarded and even sardonic but nonetheless generally inclined to accept an evolutionary and progressive design for humanity; and Thomas Hardy, while claiming to be a meliorist, generally pictured man as an incompetent antagonist against fate, whose few successes were brief and limited.

Meredith was a champion of idealist progressive evolution, believing that man was a creature lodged in matter but constituted of spirit, itself connected with the Earth Spirit or Spirit of Life, an idea he derived from Goethe's writings and that he shared with other writers of the period, notably his friend Swinburne.[1] Positive in his anticipation of man's future, he placed great value on comedy as a means of assisting human improvement. For civilized communities in particular, Meredith believed that comedy was the true specific of social ills because it had as its chief target human egoism. So long as egoism is useful to society and the nation the imps of comedy forebear, but in a place like England in the late nineteenth century, where great valor is seldom required, idle egoism is open game.[2]

Game is what Meredith calls comedy, and games and gamelike activities (for example, the chase or hunt) abound in a novel like *The Egoist* (1879) to illustrate that the rules by which men live may be viewed as play and thus under his control. Even the laws of nature may be realigned to suit human designs. What else is technical progress? Meredith had as little faith in science as he did in religion. "We have little to learn of apes," he said, offering art as the true means of educating mankind (Meredith, *Egoist*, 4). Art, too, is gamelike. Meredith's artist sets his own rules within the general necessity of language and its communicating function, then makes his created world live, not by playing the part of a detached providence but by entering and informing the very being and substance of his characters and their world. His method for achieving this union is to submerge author and characters in a bath of language that, in calling attention to itself, presumably distracts the reader from the barriers that *telling* normally constructs. Robert M. Adams notes the antistory function of the willow pattern allusion underlying the narrative of *The Egoist*, the abandonment of an authoritative moral voice in the novel and the absence of other expected devices. "Poetic justice simply doesn't happen in the book; virtue doesn't get much rewarded, vice is hardly punished. Apart from divine providence, it doesn't look as if the author believes in that other special dispensation of the Victorian novelist, bilateral symmetry."[3] Meredith is not as innovative as Adams makes him sound, for Thackeray had anticipated him in many ways. Both employed narrative methods that presented man as neither trapped nor driven by a necessary scheme of God, fate, or causal invariance but as confined by his own petrified desires. Comedy could dissolve these "mind-forged manacles" and allow man his freedom once more and also keep him on his guard against the process of ossification. Like Shelley's Prometheus confronting a tyrannical Zeus, Meredith believed that man would be able to throw off the dominion of false ideas once he realized that their force rests in his own submission to them. Walter Wright says that "putting man in some outer region of the spiritual universe or making him a deterministic creature was contradictory to Meredith's belief in the significance of individual spirituality. At the same time, he believed that the individual mind reached its highest form only when in intimate concord with nature and when self-forgetfully participating in a community of ideas. It was a function of literature to illustrate this truth and to show how affinity of human minds was to be achieved."[4]

Meredith was not content merely to create characters and set them moving in a plot. Language itself had to test the rules by which information was communicated. Though man's freedom was not unlimited, it was ample and growing. If man's ideas were to expand and increase that freedom, the medium by which those ideas were transmitted would have to change as well. We cannot examine the many devices that Meredith used to effect his purpose, but a glance at one or two might make the point.

Though he had a good deal of faith in exposition and allowed himself many opportunities to lecture his readers, Meredith had much greater confidence in metaphor.[5] Gillian Beer says of *Beauchamp's Career* (1875) that Meredith used metaphor to show his characters waking to imaginative life.[6] Beer believes that it is with this novel that Meredith achieves his distinctive style. Whether or not that is so, Meredith had long experimented with metaphoric and other stylistic variations and considered himself an innovator with language.[7] In much of his fiction, for example, he used certain basic image patterns to carry moral values. Thus clothed/unclothed frequently suggests truth/disguise, and mountain/lowland suggests spiritual ascent as opposed to sensuous indulgence. Meredith customarily used organic metaphors to develop positive associations and often selected other metaphorical patterns for the significance of their vehicles. In the opening chapter of *Beauchamp's Career*, Meredith characterized the British fear of invasion with a series of metaphorical forms from personifications of Panic, the Press, the Government, and the People, to a complex analogy of a squire who has been frightened by a Robin Hood figure into vowing an investment in self-protection. At the end of this long passage, Meredith seems to dismiss his similitudes in favor of direct statement. "Similes are all very well in their way. None can be sufficient in this case without levelling a finger at the taxpayer—nay directly mentioning him."[8] Meredith could have told us directly that the invasion panic was contrived by government and effected through the press in order to frighten taxpayers into financing military improvements. His verbal fireworks seem gratuitous, since their main purpose is to provide an introduction for the hero of his novel. When Meredith does introduce Neville Beauchamp a paragraph later, he relates him to the substance, but not the tropes, of the elaborate disquisition on panic. "Young Mr. Beauchamp at that period of the panic had not the slightest feeling for the taxpayer. He was therefore unable to penetrate the mystery of our roundabout way of enlivening him." (Meredith, *Career*, 6). Beauchamp does not have the subtle, metaphoric, and intuitive intellect necessary—along with reason—to grasp an issue so volatile and so complex. Thus he remains perplexed about the threatened conflict. His rudimentary solution is to address a letter to the French Guard personally taking up their challenge. Of course he is absurd, but he is absurd because he cannot understand that human motives and actions are not overt and logical, and that though intimately interwoven, human lives are affiliated by largely inexpressible feelings, not matured ideas. Meredith's metaphorical language demonstrates this point, then opposes to it Beauchamp's bare, literal, and vulnerable mind.

Beauchamp's great fault is that he lacks a subtle enough intelligence; he is not adept at fathoming the unexpressed. He has "not the faculty of reading inside men"; he "has no *bend* in him" (Meredith, *Career*, 355, 437). He wants life to be simple, direct and rational, though his own spoiled romances might have shown him how false such a hope is. Meredith ironically uses a coagulation of metaphors to describe Beauchamp's obsession with a single idea. Such an obsession, he says, "is at once a devouring dragon, and an intractable steam-force; it is a tyrant that has eaten up a senate, and a prophet with a message. Inspired of solitariness and gigantic size, it claims divine origin. The world can have no peace for it" (Meredith, *Career*, 355). In a novel about political controversy and the struggle of a young man to achieve heroic ends, these metaphors, the steam engine aside perhaps, are extremely fitting.

Dedicated to reason, Beauchamp is inadequately appreciative of other modes of understanding, but he is educable. He learns patience himself and recommends it to others (Meredith, *Career*, 510). In the novel's last chapter, entitled "The Last of Neville Beauchamp," Lady Romfrey looks upon the young man not as one who has failed but "as one in mid career, in mid forest, who, by force of character, advancing in self-conquest, strikes his impress right and left around him, because of his aim at stars" (Meredith, *Career*, 515). Beauchamp achieves only half the necessary education before his early death, but his career compares favorably with others who lack his willingness to challenge accepted conditions, especially his early love Renée, whose chief liability is "her sense of submission to destiny" (Meredith, *Career*, 57). Beauchamp does not achieve the full freedom and self-comprehension that Meredith would wish for men, but he learns Dr. Shrapnel's lesson that "the victory over the world, as over nature, is over self" (Meredith, *Career*, 401). His death attempting to save another life is an emblematic proof of that.

Metaphor is for Meredith a means to help his readers experience the consciousness of his characters and a marking device of values. But metaphor also provides the organic filaments that weave his narratives together in imitation of the binding power of the Spirit of Life, filaments sometimes almost invisible but operative nonetheless. Between his reference to the English taxpayer and his presentation of Beauchamp's naivete in the first chapter of *Beauchamp's Career*, Meredith offers a striking image of his own role as story teller. He says that he will paint "what is, not what I imagine." Immediate experience, its politics, and the ideas of men will be his themes which he will keep "at blood-heat, and myself calm as a statue of Memnon in prostrate Egypt! He sits there waiting for the sunlight; I here, and readier to be musical than you think. I can at any rate be impartial; and do but fix your eyes on the sunlight striking him and swallowing the day in rounding him, and you have an image of the passive receptivity of shine and shade I hold it good to aim at, if at the same time I may keep my characters at blood heat" (Meredith, *Career*, 6). Meredith asserts his artistic self-command while ironically identifying his role as essentially passive, an identification not to be trusted, as the immediately succeeding metaphor of himself as warrior or hunter suggests. His apparent immobility is belied in his power to create, to be "musical." Moreover, Meredith cloaks himself with the mystery and authority of magic and the supernatural by appropriating the Memnon allusion.[9] Metaphors of magic and wizardry recur throughout the novel, interlacing the mundane with the mystery of creativity. Lamenting that he can not write simple tales of mystery and adventure, Meredith says his narrative manner is "like a Rhone island in the summer drought, stony, unattractive and difficult between two forceful streams of the unreal and the over-real which delight mankind—honour to the conjurers!" (Meredith, *Career*, 461). But if he is statuesque, stony, and difficult, he still sings, and what he sings is change. If Beauchamp never becomes a singing Memnon, at least he escapes what Lord Romfrey calls the national scourge of being "a statue turned out by an English chisel" (Meredith, *Career*, 514). Statues, like novels, are memorial works of art, but if they do not "sing" with the sunrise of each succeeding generation, there are mere museum pieces or urban decorations. Beauchamp does not achieve Meredith's aims, but he has proven his freedom from the stultification of changeless obedience to tradition.

Meredith had dealt with incomplete careers before. *The Ordeal of Richard Feverel* (1859) introduced a young hero with such natural gifts and such inherently positive impulses that his success in self-fulfillment should be easy. Unfortunately, his father takes charge of his education and systematically unsuits the young man for the life he must face. Even this early novel is supported by a tissue of metaphors supporting the central notion that human impulses must be guided, not balked, that self-control, not theoretical compulsion leads to healthy adult activity.[10] Sir Austen's misguided system leads Richard into error that causes the early death of his wife, Lucy, and his own psychic shipwreck. Lady Blandish charges Sir Austen with a double-sided crime in destroying the prospects of these two promising young people. In his arrogance "he wished to take Providence out of God's hands" by substituting his own concept of Science. Looking on the wrecked young lives, Lady Blandish says, "I shall hate the name of Science till the day I die."[11]

Meredith trusted neither religion nor science as dogmatic systems. He sympathized with spontaneity and naturalness and made these sympathies evident in his novel, though spicing them with irony in the chapter that describes the blossoming love of Richard and Lucy. "Away with Systems! Away with a corrupt world! Let us breathe the air of the Enchanted Island!" he begins, then presents the young lovers as inhabitants of a prelapsarian garden. "They have outflown Philosophy. Their Instinct has shot beyond the ken of Science. Imperiously they know we were made for Eden: and would you gainsay them who are outside the Gates, and argue from the Fall?"

(Meredith, *Ordeal*, 192,194). This enchanted world will have its own disastrous Fall when Richard's father usurps providential authority.

The Ordeal of Richard Feverel is not a tightly constructed narrative. Meredith did not aim at tightly constructed narratives, wanting his novels to convey the same sense of natural unpredictability and potential for development that he saw as a part of life. Gillian Beer has made this point succinctly.

> Meredith's open discussion of technique within his novels is a part of his belief in free will. This belief expresses itself in a number of ways: he gives character pre-eminence over shapeliness of plot; he flouts the analogues and expectations he has built up in the reader; he exploits comedy (with its emphasis on the accountability of individuals) and he invokes the comic spirit, which insists on observation rather than involvement from reader and narrator alike. He seeks our free assent to the implications of what he shows rather than a passing emotional submission to fiction. (Beer, 38–39)

She adds that, though Meredith may discuss his techniques and comment on the events and characters of his novels, he "never suggests that he is in command of the fate of his characters or that he can alter the direction of the story. By his narrative interventions he breaks the illusion that there is one absolute way of rendering the world: the interventions complicate what may appear simple" (Beer, 39). Meredith avoided careful plotting because he recognized that plots were akin to fatalism, and he was not a fatalist. As we have seen, these narrative preferences were already a part of the tradition of English fiction when Meredith began to write.

Meredith's first novel gave an indication of his tendency to liberate characters from plot. He called it *The Shaving of Shagpat: An Arabian Entertainment* (1855), and, as George Eliot remarked, its narrative combined the episodic quality of Eastern fiction with the intellectual aspirations of Western literature.[12] This allegorical fantasy embodied Meredith's moral aspirations; in it, the ordinary citizen Shibli Bagarag learns to "master the event"; that is, take command of himself and hence of the world around him. "Shagpat represents the pretentions of the modern social system, and Shibli Bagarag is the naive young reformer tested and toughened by a series of perils and temptations that represent the chief forces of worldliness and self-indulgence."[13] Unlike so many of Meredith's central figures, Shibli is entirely successful in his effort.

Harry Richmond, for example, must face a world as challenging as, if more forgiving than, those of Richard Feverel and Neville Beauchamp. As he finishes telling his own story, Harry admits that he is still "subject to the relapses of a not perfectly right nature, as I perceived when glancing back at my thought of 'An odd series of accidents!' Which was but a disguised fashion of attributing to Providence the particular concern in my fortunes: an impiety and a folly!" [14] It is Austen Feverel's offense more prominently developed. *The Adventures of Harry Richmond* (1871) is largely about the folly of assuming a providential design, in Richmond Roy's case, special providence. But to be free, men must strip away all illusions of fate and destiny and take the responsibility of their lives upon themselves. The husband in *Modern Love*(1862) refuses the cowardly displacement of responsibility for his situation on others.

> I am not one of those miserable males
> Who sniff at vice, and daring not to snap
> Do therefore hope for heaven. I take the hap
> Of all my deeds. The wind that fills my sails
> Propels; but I am helmsman. Am I wrecked,
> I know the devil has sufficient weight
> To bear: I lay it not on him, or fate.
> Besides, he's damned. That man I do suspect
> A coward, who would burden the poor deuce
> With what ensues from his own slipperiness.[15]

Meredith wanted no blaming of the devil, or God, and so renounced providential control and urged his readers to accept the blood heat of his creations as their own, while he provided the music of their story as naturally and as magically as the statue of Memnon when the morning sun strikes upon it.

Sometimes Meredith's themes and methods come together in a particularly happy manner, as in his finest novel, *The Egoist*. A major concern of the novel is liberation, in particular, Clara Middleton's release from her engagement to Sir Willoughby Patterne. As she begins to feel the discomfort of being treated like one of Willoughby's possessions, she craves liberty, blaming "herself and him, and the world he abused, and destiny into the bargain" (Meredith, *Egoist*, 51). At first, mental liberty is her immediate need; "She asked for some little, only some little, free play of mind in a house that seemed to wear, as it were, a cap of iron" (Meredith, *Egoist*, 67). But before long she is yearning for a Perseus to rescue her, a comrade or lover

(Meredith, *Egoist*, 85). However, she gradually learns that to free herself she must educate herself to the use of her free will. She can do this by learning to read the world and herself.[16] In one of his notebooks, Meredith advised himself, "The book of our common humanity lies in our own bosoms / To know ourselves is more a matter of will than of insight" (Beer, quoting Meredith's notebook, 109).

Willoughby exclaims to Clara, "You have me, you have me like an open book, you, and only you!" (Meredith, *Egoist*, 52). Unfortunately for Willoughby, it is true that Clara shares with other captives "that power to read their tyrant" (Meredith, *Egoist*, 120). Though she has a moment of doubt that she has "misread" Willoughby, she soon revives confidence in her assessment of him and does not give way to the editing of herself that the narrator describes as woman's usual protective behavior.

> Maidens are commonly reduced to read the masters of their destinies by their instincts; and when these have been edged by over-activity, they must hoodwink their maidenliness to suffer themselves to read: and then they must dupe their minds, else men would soon see they were gifted to discern. Total ignorance being their pledge of purity to men, they have to expunge the writing of their perceptives on the tablets of the brain: they have to know not when they do know. The instinct of seeking to know, crossed by the task of blotting knowledge out, creates that conflict of the natural with the artificial creature to which their ultimately-revealed double-face, complained of by ever-dissatisfied men, is owing. (Meredith, *Egoist*, 170)

In planning her escape from Willoughby, Clara feels driven by necessity and appalled that this act will transform her into a legible object. "She was one of the creatures who are written about" (Meredith, *Egoist*, 126). Even Clara's father, understandably for a scholar, sees her as a text. "She has no history," he reassures Willoughby. "You are the first heading of the chapter" (Meredith, *Egoist*, 161). But she is not the legible tale either of them can inscribe or read. "There was no reading of her or the mystery" of her changed mood for Willoughby (Meredith, *Egoist*, 119).

Willoughby is doubly disqualified for interpreting Clara. To begin with, he assumes that "Providence, otherwise the discriminating dispensation of the good things of life," has arranged everything to suit him (Meredith, *Egoist*, 243; also 91, 370, 236). Complicating this false assumption about how the story lines of existence are actually disposed is Willoughby's reservoir of usable texts. Willoughby's lexicon of tender language and his expectations about story derive from his "favourite reading ..., popular romances" (Meredith, *Egoist*, 187). He even believes that his education in these romances has given him a predictive power (Meredith, *Egoist*, 196). He must suffer the bitter irony later, when he has lost Clara and fallen back upon the faded and toughened Laetitia Dale, of being told that Society is in his debt for a "lovely romance" (Meredith, *Egoist*, 398). By this time, Willoughby has "learnt to read the world," and is not happy with the information it provides (Meredith, *Egoist*, 399). He knows too late that he has concocted a parody of his Providential Romance.

But if Willoughby's reading expectations falsely cast him as the hero of a splendid romance, he cannot help belittling Vernon Whitford's sordid history of love. Vernon married his landlord's daughter, who proved disreputable before her early death. "The story's a proof that romantic spirits do not furnish the most romantic history," Willoughby intones to Clara (Meredith, *Egoist*, 319). But Clara has already fallen under the spell of Vernon's alpine imagery for freedom, and when Meredith's novel ends, these two find themselves the proud owners of the happy ending originally designated as Willoughby's property. This outcome is possible, however, only because Clara decides to follow some stern advice from Vernon at a crisis in her life. Like Savonarola in *Romola*, Vernon meets his heroine in flight from her unwanted lover and the life he promises and advises her to return and face her situation. The London train leaves without her. "She had acted of her free will: she could say that." Returning to Patterne Hall, Clara is downcast. "She could have accused Vernon of a treacherous cunning for imposing it on her free will to decide her fate" (Meredith, *Egoist*, 229, 232). But it is precisely this act of free will that allows for the happy conclusion to her story. The tyrant Willoughby who seemed the master of his fate ends up the captive, betrayed by his egotism, whereas his dependents are liberated through their capacity to read themselves and others not as preinscribed texts but as mysterious elements of a narrative in the process of unfolding.

Bondage, confinement, and restraint of all kinds preoccupy Meredith's writing and are closely associated with his preoccupation with clothes, masking, and disguise. Meredith drives his narratives insistently toward disclosure and release, through a narrative method of indirection, elision, and withheld information. In a sense, Meredith throws the responsibility for liberation on the characters themselves and upon the readers. Characters often enslave themselves by accepting rules set down by others. We have already noted this fault in Renée, Beauchamp's early love. Sometimes characters believe themselves to be free but are subtly imprisoned by their own errors, as with Sir Willoughby Patterne or the central figures of *The Tragic Comedians* (1880). The seventeen-year-old Clotilde von Rudiger is enchanted by Alvan, a promising young politician. Both mistake her originality for independence and courage and their tragedy follows from the discovery that she lacks the fortitude to throw off the shackles of social and class convention. Alvan has flaws of his own. He does not realize that he gradually commits himself to codes that he does not endorse. He makes such concessions when trying to gain acceptance by Clotilde's family and in the management of his political career. The narrator summarizes concisely: "Ceasing to be a social rebel, he conceived himself as a recognized dignitary, and he passed under the bondage of that position."[17] Any man who makes Respectability his Zeus must look to his liver.

One of Meredith's most elaborate and serious examinations of self-liberation is *Diana of the Crossways* (1885). Early in the novel we are made aware of Diana's yearning for "the glittering fields of freedom."[18] Her escape from her husband's control is the first manifestation of this freedom, a liberty she fears to lose by returning to him or by being caught by any other man. But Diana has not fully learned the lesson that "by closely reading herself ... she gathered an increasing knowledge of our human constitution, and stored matter for the brain" (Meredith, *Diana*, 113). She has yet to accept the injunction of her beloved friend Emma who tells her that we may be happy if we "but keep passion sober, a trotter in harness" (Meredith, *Diana*, 180). Like other characters in the novel, especially Sir Lukin Dunstane, she cannot abandon notions of providence, destiny, and fate. She is particularly willing to accept Percy Dacier's trust in fortune when he pleads with her to run away with him. "Fortune is blind," he says. "She may be kind to us. The blindness of Fortune is her one merit, and fools accuse her of it, and they profit by it! I fear we all of us have our own turn of folly: we throw the stake for good luck" (Meredith, *Diana*, 238). Like Eliot's unwise characters who willingly gamble because they assume a world governed by chance, Diana accepts this world view and its argument in a moment of weakness. Preparing for flight with Dacier, Diana "thought of herself as another person, whom she observed, not counselling her because it was a creature visibly pushed by the Fates" (Meredith, *Diana*, 241). At this moment her faithful admirer Thomas Redford appears, calling Diana to Emma's sickbed. Something stronger than fate intervenes, though Diana continues to feel that "hand resembling the palpable interposition of Fate had swept" her and Dacier apart (Meredith, *Diana*, 246). But the fates are mere excuses that men make for their own confusion and lack of command, as Meredith suggests ironically when the consequences of Diana's revelation to the press about the prime minister's impending change of policy about the Corn Laws become apparent. "She heard also of heavy failures and convulsions in the City of London, quite unconscious that the Fates, or agents of the Providence she invoked to precipitate the catastrophe, were then beginning cavernously their performance of the part of villain in Diana's history" (Meredith, *Diana* 258). When Emma Dunstane comments to Redworth on the irony of fate that has affected Diana's life, he replies heatedly.

> "Upon my word," he burst out, "I should like to write a book of Fables, showing how donkeys get into grinding harness, and dogs lose their bones, and fools have their sconces cracked, and all run jabbering of the irony of Fate, to escape the annoyance of tracing the causes. And what are they? Nine times out of ten, plain want of patience, or some debt for indulgence. There's subject:—let some one write, Fables in illustration of the irony of Fate: and I'll undertake to tack-on my grandmother's maxims for a moral to each of 'em. We prate of that irony when we slink away from the lesson—the rod we conjure. And you to talk of Fate! It's the seed we sow, individually or collectively." (Meredith, *Diana*, 356)

Diana herself finally accepts this truth and in coolly assessing her own errors remarks, "Ah! let never Necessity draw the bow of our weakness: it is the soul that is winged to its perdition" (Meredith, *Diana*, 360). She learns self-mastery, as her meeting with Dacier and his new bride shows. She discovers the "laws of life" and confidently submits to marriage again, realizing that with Redworth it need not be a form of bondage.

Diana spends a good part of her time in disguise because she feels it necessary to play a role. Acting images abound in this novel. But Diana has another form of disguise. "Metaphors were her refuge. Metaphorically she could allow her mind to distinguish the struggle she was undergoing, sinking under it. The banished of Eden had to put on metaphors, and the common use of them has helped largely to civilize us" (Meredith, *Diana*, 231). In a fallen world, roles and metaphors are necessary to communicate sentiments not acceptable as naked fact. But if Diana cloaks herself in protective metaphors, in this novel and all of his others Meredith himself employed metaphor precisely to unclothe illusions by calling attention to the habits of language that create them. Something similar happens with the rich complex of allusions imbedded in the title of this novel.[19] This Diana is neither goddess nor witch but a woman who needs to discover the laws of nature by which she may control her own life and find happiness. Meredith is subversive in his use of the metaphor and resistant to literary convention as well. Refusing the role of theatrical stage manager demanded by his English audience that calls for a tidy nuptial chapter, Meredith says, "Rogues and a policeman, or a hurried change of front of all the actors, are not a part of our slow machinery" (Meredith, *Diana*, 371). Meredith is not, like Thackeray, a puppet master calling attention to the puppet nature of his creations but has the same aim of permitting his characters to achieve their own freedom. Thackeray distracted his readers to free his characters; Meredith makes the opposite choice of intimacy.

Meredith's last novel, *The Amazing Marriage* (1895), simplifies the themes of freedom and bondage. Carinthia, the book's heroine, represents individual integrity, "I hate anything that robs me of my will," she says.[20] And nothing does. Her main contest is with Lord Fleetwood, who himself has a determined but "shifty will" (Meredith, *Marriage*, 254). Smitten by Carinthia, he fears subjection to her. He recognizes her strength of will and fears that she will appropriate the masculine role. Still, he proposes to her and feels honor-bound to marry her. He thinks of her as a witch who has entrapped him but admits that Carinthia has not duped him; "he had done it for himself—acted on by a particular agency" (Meredith, *Marriage*, 197). Though she must suffer, Carinthia retains her integrity and independence much as Aminta does in related circumstances in *Lord Ormont and His Aminta* (1894). She remains secure in her belief in her own freedom, she feels that she shapes her own destiny. By contrast, Lord Fleetwood feels his life dogged by the fates. Moreover, like other unattractive figures in this novel, he is a gambler. Such slaves of fortune, Meredith explains, are "feverish worshippers of the phantasmal deity called the Present; a god reigning over the Past, appreciable only in the Future; whose whiff of actual being is composed of the embryo idea of the union of these two periods." This sort of character counts on luck, but the Black Goddess of gambling corrupts as it enslaves her devotees. "Their faith as to sowing and reaping has gone; and so has their capacity to see the actual as it is" (Meredith, *Marriage*, 112). In a world of change, all causal relations are called in question. Free will loses significance except as a random act. But for Meredith, strength of will is strength of purpose too, and only those who believe themselves free to alter events can have a settled purpose that is not renunciation and submission.

For Meredith, as for other novelists in nineteenth-century England, gambling served as a metaphor for chance. But he believed the correct attitude toward life was to view it as orderly, not random; as subject to certain laws, not directed by capricious fates. Eliot placed her faith in the invariable law of consequence and trusted in a steady advance of human intellect and moral strength. Meredith, without examining such complicated issues as first causes and scientific determinism, asserted that men, and perhaps more particularly women, were capable of controlling their own lives. The metaphor for that control was art. Like Clara Middleton, women and men must learn to read the world and themselves so that they may participate in the ongoing narrative. They would not look to a providential author to make their stories for them. Unlike most novelists of his time, Meredith attempted to leave control in the hands of his characters, though ironically, his elaborate style led many readers to suppose that he was dominating rather than liberating them. Meredith's philosophy abandoned dualism between matter and spirit, and his literary method sought a comparable erasure of the boundary between idea and its medium, language.[21] Language was to idea as blood was to spirit through the medium of brain. Text was the word made flesh.

Meredith rather easily overlooked many difficult issues that prevented other non-Christian writers from so bracingly and whole-heartedly endorsing freedom of the will. We have already had a taste of Samuel Butler's more dour views as they appeared in his expository works, but those views bear upon his fictional methods as well. Not only was Butler aware of the logical difficulties in definitely asserting belief in free will or determinism, he was astonishingly clever in toying with these beliefs. *Erewhon* (1872) is a satire with serpentine developments on many of the ideas with which we are concerned. Much of this satire depends upon elaborate reversal, hence the Erewhonians do not perceive a pocket watch as evidence of creator, according to Paley's analogy but regard it as the "designer of himself and of the universe; or as at any rate one of the great first causes of all things."[22] Similarly, for Erewhonians, progress means preventing the evolution of machines, which they perceive as a competing species (Butler, *Erewhon*, 81–2). Other sly reversals in which the Erewhonians punish ill health as a crime and worship ideals instead of an anthropomorphic God also have their obvious bite. A more surprising reversal has to do with the Erewhonian mythology of the unborn who live in a pleasant preterrestrial spiritual state. Only the most foolish of them choose to die in that world in order to be born into ours. The unborn are warned of the risks of such a passage, for example the possibility of being born to wicked, foolish, or unsympathetic parents. Their perception of human freedom is interestingly skewed. Advisors warn the unborn: "if you go into the world you will have free will; that you will be obliged to have it; that there is no escaping it; that you will be fettered to it during your whole life, and must on every occasion do that which on the whole seems best to you at any given time, no matter whether you are right or wrong in choosing it." They add that heredity and environment will bias the nature of such choices and will most likely incline to misery, after which they conclude: "Reflect on this, and remember that should the ill come upon you, you will have yourself to thank, for it is your own choice to be born, and there is no compulsion in the matter" (Butler, *Erewhon*, 186–87).

Man, in this view, has a free will that does not differ at all from determinist impulse except that the creature is free to choose birth, something denied to humans, who presume that everything afterward is free. Learning about the evolutionary threat to humans posed by machinery, the narrator develops an analogy that demonstrates how very like determinism the Erewhonian view of free will is. Responding to the charge that machines cannot evolve because they lack a will, he argues that "a man is the resultant and exponent of all the forces that have been brought to bear upon him, whether before his birth or afterwards. His action at any moment depends solely upon his constitution, and on the intensity and direction of the various agencies to which he is, and has been, subjected. Some of these will counteract each other; but as he is by nature, and as he has been acted on, and is now acted on from without, so will he do, as certainly and regularly as though he were a machine" (Butler, *Erewhon*, 245).

Other Erewhonian theories are Butler's own notions carried to extremes. Some Erewhonians propose that animals, because they so resemble man, also have rights; these proponents argue in favor of vegetarianism until another subtle argument demonstrates that plants are intelligent as well, perhaps even superior. They feed themselves, protect themselves and know what they want as much as any human embryo does. "The rose-seed did what it now does in the persons of its ancestors—to whom it has been so linked as to be able to remember what those ancestors did when they were placed as the rose-seed now is. Each stage of development brings back the recollection of the course taken in the preceding stage, and the development has been so often repeated, that all doubt—and with all doubt, all consciousness of action—is suspended" (Butler, *Erewhon*, 278). This pattern is, of course, the same scheme that Butler would later advance seriously in *Life and Habit* and other works.[23]

Butler's skills in *Erewhon* are only partly novelistic. It might be more accurate to call him a fabulist here. His narrator, an amateur writer, recognizes the difficulty, admitting, "I should never come to an end were I to keep to a strictly narrative form, and detail the infinite absurdities with which I daily come in contact" (Butler, *Erewhon*, 105). The first six or seven chapters, however, constitute a smooth narrative much in the manner of travel and adventure literature of the time. But reader expectations are set up for a reversal when the tale shifts suddenly into an expository form containing other narratives and texts within it. In a crude and unpolished way, the form of Butler's narrative reflects its import, though it would be rash to claim much more than this, especially since Butler himself mocks the purpose of his narrative by having his narrator present it as a fund-raiser to finance a missionary trip back to Erewhon.

The Way of All Flesh (1872–84; published 1903) is a novel and a carefully considered one, and its form follows the pattern implied in Butler's philosophical theories, though the novel itself rarely takes up the touchy issue of free will and determinism directly. Butler's concept of heredity is central to the novel, which rehearses in the history of the Pontifex family, the ideas set forth in Life and Habit (1878) and elsewhere. Heredity is another name for the memory of matter, and just as cells or rose-seeds "remember" earlier cells and rose-seeds, so humans carry an unconscious memory of their progenitors. Ernest Pontifex carries the "information" of preceding generations, information that is released through trauma. His grandfather was a creative, impulsive, constructive man. Ernest's father was a priggish, unimaginative man. Ernest outgrows the cowardice instilled in him by his immediate family and, through a series of fortunate disasters, discovers qualities more like those of his grandfather, though his form of creativity— writing—is less practical and not immediately effective. Peter Morton explains that Ernest is passive because survival for him requires camouflage, not conflict. "For in each Lamarckian generation each person bodies forth the total experience of his forebears and even of the totality of life itself; for he is in truth frighteningly free, almost in the existential sense of being forced to raise himself by his own moral bootstraps."[24] Elsewhere, Morton says that Butler "is profoundly optimistic about the individual's freedom to choose a destiny and melioristic in his attitude to the family organism" (Morton 175). But I suspect that this is too positive an assertion of Butler's position. After all, most of mankind goes about its business entrapped, like Theobald and Christina Pontifex, in one or another set of prohibitions. They create their own images of sin and doom and then learn to fear them. Ernest, though he does break out of this pattern, scarcely exerts a determined will in the process. His disasters come from his impulse to imitate others—as with his zeal for the College of Spiritual Pathology that ultimately leads to his arrest for accosting a young woman and his loss of money to an embezzling friend. Ernest's good fortune results mainly from luck in the form of his Aunt Alethea and his godfather, Overton, the narrator of the novel.[25]

Other Victorian novelists—Eliot and Meredith are notable examples— deplored the dependence on lucky chance exhibited by their weaker characters, but Butler saw chance as an inevitable part of life. Biological inheritance itself is a throw of the dice. After that, luck is predictable. Early in the novel, Butler made his position clear.

> Fortune, we are told, is a blind and fickle foster-mother, who showers her gifts at random upon her nurslings. But we do her a grave injustice if we believe such an accusation. Trace a man's career from his cradle to his grave and mark how Fortune has treated him. You will find that when he is once dead she can for the most part be vindicated from the charge of any but very superficial fickleness. Her blindness is the merest fable; she can espy her favorites long before they are born.[26]

Butler satirizes human dependency in Theobald Pontifex's courtship. Ernest's father earns his university fellowship, is ordained, and takes a place with Mr. Allaby, the rector of Crampsford, who has five unwed daughters. As soon as they have met Theobald, the girls quarrel over which is to become his wife. Mr. Allaby recommends gambling as a solution and the next chapter opens with "the Miss Allabys in the eldest Miss Allaby's bedroom playing at cards, with Theobald for the stakes" (Butler, *Flesh*, 52). Christina wins, and, though Theobald is not the man she hoped for, she accepts the challenge and snares him. Theobald has very little control of this most important decision.

Once luck and external circumstance have had their play, the individual possesses sufficient freedom to react to events and is more likely to do so if some shock frees him from the bondage of convention. "Every change is a shock," the narrator explains; "every shock is *pro tanto* death. What we call death is only a shock great enough to destroy your power to recognize a past and a present as resembling one another" (Butler, *Flesh*, 283). After a series of such shocks, Ernest decides to abandon the respectability associated with his past and begin again at the bottom. This pattern is repeated in full at least one more time. Gradually Ernest becomes self-confident enough in handling his "inheritance" to deserve the financial inheritance left to him by his aunt and supervised by Overton.

Theobald, seeing himself as representative of paternal authority, demanded complete obedience of his children, insisting that the "first signs of self-will must be carefully looked for, and plucked up by the roots at once before they had time to grow" (Butler, *Flesh*, 106). But what is a weed to Theobald is a flowering plant to Butler. For example, he insists on the value of pleasure. In *Erewhon* this notion was expressed by the Erewhonians punishing their citizens for bad health. We owe it to ourselves, Butler says, to follow our wills. We should not deny but indulge ourselves. "All animals, except man, know that the principal business of life is to enjoy it—and they do enjoy it as much as man and other circumstances will allow. He has spent his life best who has enjoyed it most; God will take care that we do not enjoy it any more than is good for us" (Butler, *Flesh*, 98).

It is in this clear turning away from the traditional Christian pattern of self-denial, self-control, and self-sacrifice that Butler offers his own radical pattern of freedom. Most champions of freedom had hitherto agreed to the need for self-suppression in one form or another. True freedom came only through the reining in of wildness. But Butler had less confidence than Meredith in man's conscious powers and more explicitly sided with those who argued for a subtler, secret motive force. "I fancy," he writes early in the novel, "that there is some truth in the view which is being put forward nowadays, that it is our less conscious thoughts and our less conscious actions which mainly mold our lives and the lives of those who spring from us" (Butler, *Flesh*, 27).

The Way of All Flesh does not depart from the pattern of the late nineteenth-century English novel in appearance, but it embodies assumptions that make it something of a sport. Like all of Butler's works, from *Erewhon* and *Luck or Cunning* to *The Authoress of the Odyssey*, *The Way of All Flesh* aims to violate expectations, to educate by means of a salubrious shock. His novel employs standard narrative means, but his narrative, in effect, goes nowhere. At the end of the novel, Ernest, his main character, has achieved nothing special. He has earned his right to survive through luck and a little cunning. Characters are set forth as though they have comprehensible motives, though our narrator regularly suggests that men's motives cannot be known, not even by themselves. Ultimately, this example of novelistic art, conventionally expected to present a history of development, an endorsement of social structure, and a moral, offers none of these. Instead it presents the embodiment of a thesis. The novel itself is the flesh of Butler's theory by which that theory can be known, and because Butler believed that intellectual schemes were relative and idiosyncratic, the embodiment of his theory becomes the transcription of his self, something he admits openly.

> Every man's work, whether it be literature or music or pictures or architecture or anything else, is always a portrait of himself, and the more he tries to conceal himself the more clearly will his character appear in spite of him. I may very likely be condemning myself, all the time that I am writing this book, for I know that whether I like it or no I am portraying myself more surely than I

am portraying any of the characters whom I set before the reader.
(Butler, *Flesh*, 74–75)

Man is free for Butler but free to utilize only what luck (heredity and
circumstance) and cunning (his decisions prompted by unconscious
impulses) have provided. He must suffer and grow, though beside him a
benevolent force may be waiting to reward him for bungling into self-
awareness. Like the novelist who sets out to tell a tale and must work with
language and personal experience, the free man writes the text that was
encoded in him long ago.

So much has been written about tragedy, fate, and chance in Hardy's
fiction that I need not devote as much time to Hardy as he would otherwise
deserve here. It is clear from his poetry, especially *The Dynasts*, that Hardy
had a secure, if not entirely coherent, philosophy encompassing the notion
of will. To some degree he simply secularized the Christian view while
draining it of its high valuation on self-sacrifice. Human will is a part of the
Immanent Will—a power more positively viewed by Swinburne and
Meredith as the Life or Earth Force—that energizes the universe.
Supposedly unaware of Von Hartmann's writings, Hardy assumed that he
was innovative in suggesting that the Unconscious Will was "becoming
conscious with the flux of time."[27] Otherwise, the Immanent Will was very
like an unconscious or thoughtless deity, a characterization that appears
comically in several of Hardy's poems, such as "God-Forgotten," "God's
Education," and "God's Funeral." Instead of asserting the traditional view
that man discovers his unity through the spark of intelligence or soul within
himself, Hardy reversed the process and made the unconscious will capable
of acquiring the consciousness already evident in man. Moreover, whereas
the good Christian discovered his freedom in submitting his will to God's,
Hardy's individual was freest when least exposed to the notice of the forces
that impel life. Nonetheless, as J. Hillis Miller has noted, man still remained
only a part of the Great Will.

> Even when the individual will acts with the paradoxical
> freedom of a self-acting finger it is still no more than a portion of
> the universal Will. As a result, the more powerfully a man wills or
> desires, the more surely he becomes the puppet of an all-shaping
> energy, and the quicker he encompasses his own destruction. As
> soon as he engages himself in life he joins a vast streaming
> movement urging him on toward death and the failure of his
> desires.[28]

Bert Hornback says that, for Schopenhauer, "though man '*acts* with strict necessity,' he '*exists* and is what [he] is by virtue of [his] *freedom*.' In Hardy, this freedom is the freedom of character, of what the dramatist deals with as being. The necessity is the moral necessity of consequence, an 'incessant impulse' which shows itself dramatically in patterns of intense coincidental recurrence in the lives of free men."[29] Coincidence, Hornback continues, is the artistic device Hardy uses to reveal the moral drama in the lives and situations that he constructs. In this, Hardy would then resemble Eliot in her unabashed use of coincidence to regulate and unite the various story lines her characters follow. Peter Morton, approaching *Tess of the d'Urbervilles* with inheritance theory in mind, concludes that the novel asserts a rigid determinism and a total pessimism, with its numerous coincidences reinforcing a sense of character as fate (Morton, 206).[30]

Hardy may be read in many ways, the emphasis on freedom or its lack varying with the reader. Nor can Hardy himself be trusted entirely in what he said about his philosophical notions. Hardy did not consider himself a philosopher and often denied that he held settled views.[31] Nonetheless, he did make broad assertions helpful for anyone trying to understand his art, which is what interested him most. Hardy said that nonrationality was the principle of the universe, thus excluding any theistic assumptions (Florence Hardy, *Later Years*, 90). He dismissed both chance and purpose as the guides of human life, asserting the primacy of necessity (Florence Hardy, *Later Years*, 128). Life to him was an interlocking web, all things merging into one another.[32] In referring to his "prematurely afflicted century," Hardy looked down the future hoping that whatever transpired for the human race, pain for it and its companion animals would be kept to a minimum by "loving-kindness, operating through scientific knowledge, and actuated by the modicum of free will conjecturally possessed by organic life when the mighty necessitating forces—unconscious or other—that have 'the balancing of the clouds', happen to be in equilibrium, which may or may not be often."[33]

Hardy expressed these general views and felt free to judge the philosophies of others, but he never presumed to render a consistent philosophy in his own writing.[34] He said that his works of art offered not a system of philosophy but provisional impressions, and I believe that we must accept this demurrer (Florence Hardy, *Later Years*, 175).[35] Hardy wanted his art to intensify the expression of things (Florence Hardy, *Early Years*, 231). This intensification inevitably involved the distorting and shaping of circumstances, and since Hardy also believed that art was the expression of idiosyncrasy, such shaping inevitably mirrored the artist's nature (Florence Hardy, *Early Years*, 294). Hardy went so far as to declare that each individual artist discovers a new the design of nature, implying that the design is peculiar to his own method of perceiving, not abiding in nature itself (Florence Hardy, *Early Years*, 198).[36]

In a very intelligent and adventurous essay on *Tess of the d'Urbervilles*, Charlotte Thompson, beginning with the assumption that Hardy believed that the mind has the power to alter the material world, demonstrates how words become things in the novel, how ideas receive literal form.[37] Although the narrator can manipulate language, he is not entirely in command of the world he describes. Thompson's reading reinforces Hardy's own assertion that transformations in the natural world take place through an interpreting mind mediating between the realms of substance and idea largely by means of simile. F. D. Maurice and others had argued the case for the embodiment of ideas in matter on the model of the incarnation of Christ.[38] And Meredith self-consciously complicated language, forcing his readers to recognize just how difficult the process of converting ideas into substance was. Hardy stressed how language often entraps and occasionally frees human beings, how traditions embodied in language hold the human spirit in fee.

Tess of the d'Urbervilles is founded on the bitter irony that a foolishly proud attempt to recover the inheritance of a family name leads, by way of the false possessor of that name, to a much older, natural, and painful inheritance. The superficial significance of a name is trivial in comparison with genetic inheritance. Moreover, the Durbeyfields are degenerate in name and character from their notable forebears. Tess's trump card is not her d'Urberville blood, but her face.[39] She is attractive not because of her history but because of what she is and maybe. Her characteristic mode of thought is future directed. Only as her sufferings accumulate does she feel the weight of the past. Though intelligent, Tess is moved primarily by emotion and imagination, and it is partly her failure to control these traits of her nature that brings about her misfortune. Hardy takes pains to indicate how much Tess is a victim of her imagination. After her fall, when she goes out walking alone at night, she is hypersensitive to her surroundings. "At times her whimsical fancy would intensify natural processes around her till they seemed a part of her own story. Rather they became a part of it; for the world is only a psychological phenomenon, and what they seemed they were" (Hardy, *Tess*, 72). Tess also suffers from the imagined disapproval of her companions, though the narrator specifically indicates that her associates are sympathetic rather than hostile. Her misery is "founded on an illusion. She was not an existence, an experience, a passion, a structure of sensations, to anybody but herself. To all humankind besides Tess was only a passing thought." Tess has broken a social law but not one recognized among the harvesters nor, for that matter by her own instincts. "Most of the misery had been generated by her conventional aspect, and not by her innate sensations" (Hardy, *Tess*, 77).

The law that does matter is the "irresistible law" that draws Tess and Angel together, the same "cruel Nature's law" that makes the other milkmaids feverish with desire (Hardy, *Tess*, 109 and 124). And Tess is much closer to this law than Angel is, for he lives largely in his mind, a dupe to the illusions generated there. Tess cannot see the world simply as it is; instead it becomes a scheme of values, of gifts and debts. When Angel declares that he has taken a marriage license not requiring Church publication of the banns, Tess is relieved, but fears "this good fortune may be scourged out of me afterwards by a lot of ill" (Hardy, *Tess*, 173). Ill follows partly because Tess tries to repay the debt to fate, first by leaving a note for Angel explaining her situation and later by confessing to him on their bridal night. She feels that it "was wicked of her to take all without paying. She would pay to the uttermost farthing; she would tell, there and then" (Hardy, *Tess*, 188). But the oral version of Tess's history creates an important change between the newlyweds; "the complexion even of external things seemed to suffer transmutation as her announcement progressed.... And yet nothing had changed since the moments when he had been kissing her; or rather, nothing in the substance of things. But the essence of things had changed" (Hardy, *Tess*, 190–91). We shape the world subjectively and then live with the consequences. For Hardy, the imagination that Romantics heralded for its capacity to fashion a pattern or story for existence, becomes dangerous in the way Mary Shelley had suggested because it can construct a story remote from the real incidents of life. It is even worse if the story is beyond the individual's control. Unlike her mother, for whom Tess's marital misfortune is like a crop failure, "a thing which had come upon them irrespective of desert or folly; a chance external impingement to be borne with; not a lesson," Tess sees intent, almost narrative purpose in events. "How unexpected were the attacks of destiny!" she thinks when she learns that her parents doubt her story of being married (Hardy, *Tess*, 215–16). This placing herself at the center of a "story" in which forces beyond her control direct her destiny occasions much of Tess's suffering. The same, on a different level, is true of Angel too.

Hardy did not condemn his characters for their poetic fancies but simply showed how out of keeping such high-minded poetry was with daily life. Tess insists upon justice operating in her universe; she believes she has moral debts to pay. As Hardy sees it, this and her idealism make her virtuous. He argued that, despite her failings, Tess maintains an innate purity, though her outward purity left her with the murder of Alec. "I regarded her then as being in the hands of circumstances, not normally responsible, a mere corpse drifting with a current to her end."[40]

Joseph Warren Beach described Hardy as a determinist rather than a fatalist. Both types, he explained, agree on the helplessness of the individual will against the will in things. "Only the determinist conceives the will in things as the sum of natural forces with which we have to cope, whereas the fatalist tends to a more religious interpretation of that will as truly and literally a *will*, an arbitrary power, a personal force like our own. Sometimes Mr. Hardy allows his characters the bitter comfort of that personal interpretation."[41] Actually, Hardy may be described as a determinist writer of fatalists' tales, his characters' sufferings often arising from their confusion of the two attitudes. Though fatalism may be their bitter comfort, it is also the source of their pain.

No narrative intrusion summarizes the philosophical structure of Hardy's fictional universe. So dependent is that structure upon individual perception that the novelist can only illustrate how characters create their worlds and suffer the consequences. But Hardy knew how significant the shaping power of the artist is, how important that that shaping power should appear to be esthetic and not an imitation of providence.[42] In his early fiction Hardy was apparently less concerned with art finished according to a coherent esthetic creed than with simple success as a writer. His invitation of suggestions on what he should write and his ready yielding to editorial alterations of his texts indicate that trade considerations were dominant in his early works. But from the beginning, Hardy was fascinated by the mechanics of consequence. Bathsheba Everdene impulsively sends a valentine to Boldwood as a joke, unaware of the possible consequences of her act. The valentine excites Boldwood's love and initiates a sequence of events leading to tragedy. Boldwood cannot conceive a lack of serious motivation behind the valentine. "The vast difference between starting a train of events, and directing into a particular groove a series already started, is rarely apparent to the person confounded by the issue," Hardy coolly remarks.[43]

Dale Kramer sees Bathsheba's act as a "directionless act of free will" and Boldwood as caught up "in a chain of events consequent upon his own unintentional act of free will."[44] For Kramer's purpose of showing the tragic pattern developing in the narrative this description is adequate, but it seems doubtful that "free will" is exactly the word to use for what Hardy depicts. Impulsiveness depends upon character traits inherited or bred; the nature of the consequences that follow from impulsive acts depends upon circumstance. Gabriel Oak, a man careful to control his impulses, is nonetheless unfortunate, but he responds to his misfortune calmly with "that indifference to fate which, though it often makes a villain of a man, is the basis of his sublimity when it does not" (Hardy, *Crowd*, 46).

Hardy explained that in *Two on a Tower* he attempted "to set the emotional history of two infinitesimal lives against the stupendous background of the stellar universe and to impart to readers the sentiment that of these contrasting magnitudes the smaller might be the greater to them as men."[45] This was also the mature Hardy's central objective, as the insignificance of human life was his constant theme. *The Return of the Native* is a forthright embodiment of this view. Speaking in his own voice, the narrator describes Clym Yeobright's face as "the typical countenance of the future," recording a new attitude toward existence, "the view of life as a thing to be put up with, replacing the zest for existence which was so intense in early civilizations." Long centuries of disillusion have instructed man. "That old-fashioned revelling in the general situation grows less and less possible as we uncover the defects of natural laws and see the quandary that man is in by their operation."[46] Clym has returned to Egdon Heath discontented with his life in fashionable but superficial Paris and hoping to improve the educational circumstances of the country population. He feels a deep kinship with the Heath, a kinship subtly reinforced by the resemblance between his face and the face of Egdon Heath. "It was at present a place perfectly accordant with man's nature—neither ghastly, hateful, nor ugly; neither commonplace, unmeaning, nor tame; but, like man, slighted and enduring; and withal singularly colossal and mysterious in its swarthy monotony. As with some persons who have long lived apart, solitude seemed to look out of its countenance. It had a lonely face, suggesting tragical possibilities" (Hardy, *Return*, 4). The enemy of the Heath is civilization, yet civilization is what Clym wishes to bring to it. He thus inadvertently betrays the Heath despite his kinship to it because he wants it to be other and "better" than it is. Clym's is an aspiration of the mind, prompted by selfless generosity, but based upon a fundamental illusion according to the "laws" of Hardy's novel. Eustacia Vye is the conscious antagonist of the Heath. She considers herself "above" the Heath and its denizens and longs to escape, craving the very civilization that is opposed to all that the Heath represents.

Eustacia is proud of her power, which has a magical quality in her own eyes. Johnny Nunsuch tending her fire is a "little slave" who "seemed a mere automaton, galvinized into moving and speaking by the wayward Eustacia's will." He resembles a statue magically animated by Albertus Magnus (Hardy, *Return*, 47). Eustacia compares her power to summon Damon Wildeve to the Witch of Endor's summoning of Samuel (Hardy, *Return*, 52). She is rebellious but directs her resentment "less against human beings than against certain creatures of her mind, the chief of these being Destiny" (Hardy, *Return*, 56). She is dangerous because having "lost the godlike conceit that we may do what we will," she has not "acquired a homely zest for doing what we can" (Hardy, *Return*, 57). Such a condition may lend grandeur to a character but also betokens mischief. Eustacia's allusions suggest that she views herself heroically, placing the blame for her misfortune on a consciously hostile force. She thinks herself worthy of a Saul or Bonaparte yet finds herself linked to two inferior men. "'How I have tried and tried to be a splendid woman, and how destiny has been against me! ... I do not deserve my lot!' she cried in a frenzy of bitter revolt. 'O, the cruelty of putting me into this ill-conceived world! I was capable of much; but I have been injured and blighted and crushed by things beyond my control! O, how hard it is of Heaven to devise such tortures for me, who have done no harm to Heaven at all'" (Hardy, *Return*, 236).

Like Tess Durbeyfield, Eustacia makes herself the chief character in a drama. Her attitude is pagan, projecting a fate so interested in her life that it actively thwarts her ambitions. She wishes to rise above the level of the Heath and is boldly associated with the Rainbarrow and other elevated places. But she comes to rest at the lowest point available, in the depths of the pond, as does Wildeve, her male counterpart, who also aspires to a fortune far above what the Heath can offer. What life teaches man above all else is the folly of aspiring on the basis of vain illusions. Here again the Heath is instructive. Just after Clym and Eustacia agree to marry, Clym looks out at the Heath. "There was something in its oppressive horizontality which too much reminded him of the arena of life; it gave him a sense of bare equality with, and no superiority to, a single living thing under the sun" (Hardy, *Return*, 164). Later, forced by his impaired vision to work as a furze cutter on the Heath, Clym begins to understand the lesson of its horizontality. He tells Eustacia that he could rage against the fates like Prometheus, but "the more I see of life the more do I perceive that there is nothing particularly great in its greatest walks and therefore nothing particularly small in mine of furzecutting" (Hardy, *Return*, 199).

Furze growing ruggedly close to the ground provides a model for human existence, whereas the fir trees by Clym's cottage signify the danger of aspiring. This clump of trees thrusts up so high it appears "as a black spot in the air above the crown of the hill." After her walk to Clym's house, Mrs. Yeobright rests beneath these trees and notices that they are "singularly battered, rude, and wild." Forgetting her own "storm broken and exhausted state," she observes in detail how the weather has splintered, lopped, distorted, blasted, and split the trees. Even with no wind blowing, the trees keep up "a perpetual moan" (Hardy, *Return*, 217). They are a monitory emblem of the suffering that comes to those who try to rise above the natural conditions around them. Heights symbolize danger in other novels as well—a tower with an observatory in it that leads to an unwise romance in *Two on a Tower*, a church tower that collapses, an emblem of the collapse of Henry Knight's unrealistic idealism about the woman he loves in *A Pair of Blue Eyes*, and elsewhere, as in *The Mayor of Casterbridge or Jude the Obscure*, the aspiring to a metaphorically "higher" social condition.[47] Perhaps one of the saddest instances is Tess's elevation to the ritual stones at Stonehenge because of her parents' yen for a possible rise in their social condition.

Hardy does not condemn ambition but cautions that it is often based upon illusions about oneself and the world, upon interpretations of the world that are shaped by one's own emotional and intellectual cravings. The Heath is an antidote to such fancies, and Thomasin, the embodiment of a sensible approach to life.

> To her there were not, as to Eustacia, demons in the air, and malice in every bush and bough. The drops which lashed her face were not scorpions, but prosy rain; Egdon in the mass was no monster whatever, but impersonal open ground. Her fears of the place were rational, her dislikes of its worst moods reasonable. At this time it was in her view a windy, wet place, in which a person might experience much discomfort, lose the path without care, and possibly catch cold. (Hardy, *Return*, 283)

In *The Mayor of Casterbridge* (1886), Hardy provided two contrasting types of character, one almost certainly doomed, the other capable of some satisfaction in life; one struggling to assert himself, the other content to hold her own against destiny. Michael Henchard is a man of great vigor whose failing is to allow his temper to affect his judgment.[48] His misfortunes generally follow from his own errors—very notably his wilful sale of his wife and child when under the influence of drink. Henchard is volcanic and aggressive. Contrasting him with the Jacob-like, patient, and humble Donald Farfrae, the narrator says that the latter's success was probably not due to luck. "Character is Fate, said Novalis, and Farfrae's character was just the reverse of Henchard's, who might not inaptly be described as Faust has been described—as a vehemently gloomy being who had quitted the ways of vulgar men without light to guide him on a better way" (Hardy, *Mayor*, 88).[49] Henchard's misery stems from his own actions and from his obstinate impulse to locate the source of his trouble outside himself. "Henchard, like all his kind, was superstitious, and he could not help thinking that the concatenation of events this evening had produced was the scheme of some sinister intelligence bent on punishing him. Yet they had developed naturally" (Hardy, *Mayor*, 96–97). By the time Henchard learns the lesson of his sufferings, he lacks the zest to engage the struggle of life again. The "ingenious machinery contrived by the Gods for reducing human possibilities of amelioration to a minimum" has fashioned life this way (Hardy, *Mayor*, 244).

Elizabeth-Jane's career follows a different pattern. She has intelligence and good looks, but what serves her best is a certain cast of temperament. "Like all people who have known rough times, light-heartedness seemed to her too irrational and inconsequent to be indulged in except as a reckless dram now and then." She has a healthy fear of destiny common to thoughtful people who have suffered. Because she expects little, what comes to her seems much—a serene married life wherein she can instruct others in the secret "of making limited opportunities endurable" (Hardy, *Mayor*, 255).

Most critical attention has correctly focused on Henchard; after all, the novel specifically singles him out and provokes additional curiosity by its subtitle, "A Story of a Man of Character." As we have seen in part 1, character in Hardy's day was understood to include strength of will. Hardy demonstrates how faulty this kind of character may be when it is unreflective. Henchard has a strong character, but Hardy scarcely could have meant to recommend that character as a moral model. From his selling his wife to his violence toward Farfrae, Henchard is a forceful but not an admirable character. Literary allusions indicate a tragic dimension to Henchard's life, but they are so complex and even contradictory that they must be sifted carefully. As Frederick R. Karl has indicated, in *The Mayor of Casterbridge* "Greek tragedy now serves modern sensibilities, and its external determinism is now internalized and seen as of man's own making" (Hardy, *Mayor*, 383). But this novel is not only about tragedy. Hardy was right to insist that he should not facilely be labeled a pessimist. He wrote to William Archer that he was not a pessimist. "On the contrary, my practical philosophy is distinctly meliorist. What are my books but one plea against 'man's inhumanity to man'—to woman—and to the lower animals? ... Whatever may be the inherent good or evil of life, it is certain that men make it much worse than it need be. When we have got rid of a thousand remediable ills, it will be time enough to determine whether the ill that is irremediable outweighs the good."[50] Elizabeth-Jane's modest but real achievement of content is an example. She has no illusions and cannot therefore easily be led into folly. She will not forge the links of her own chain of evil destiny.

Jude the Obscure (1895) offers little hope of contentment and less grandeur of tragedy. Suffering and frustration in this book are relentless. Many of its thematic lines come together in the sequence of Father Time's murder of his siblings and his own suicide. Sue Bridehead reacts bitterly. "There is something external to us which says, 'You shan't.'"[51] As a young woman, Sue saw existence as a melody or dream with a First Cause working somnambulistically. She felt then "that at the framing of the terrestrial conditions there seemed never to have been contemplated such a development of emotional perceptiveness among the creatures subject to those conditions as that reached by thinking and educated humanity. But affliction makes opposing forces loom anthropomorphous; and those ideas were now exchanged for a sense of Jude and herself fleeing from a persecutor" (Hardy, *Jude*, 270). This rendering is similar to Mary Shelley's description of selfish imagination begetting a destiny that returns to haunt it. If the imagination is the agent and proof of man's free will projecting his freedom into the future, then that freedom is a kind of curse because it makes possible an agony of frustration by creating unrealizable dreams.

Both Jude and Sue picture themselves as figures in mental landscapes that they have created. Jude's improbable dream of achieving a university degree and Sue's pagan enthusiasm for a life of intellectual and emotional independence both overlook the liabilities within themselves and the social inertia ranged against them. They persist, from the highest motives, in making decisions that invariably put them at odds with the general community. In addition, they have not understood their own most elementary impulses of sexuality and comradeship, and worst of all they have fabricated false images of one another. Ironically their initial false images become the real ones, the two lovers changing places and remaining as remote from one another as they were at the start. Surely circumstance is hard on Jude and Sue, but they themselves have oiled the ingenious machinery that will crush them.

Hardy seems to have remained undecided about just what freedom meant to human beings. In "The Profitable Reading of Fiction," he said that the novels having the best effect on a healthy mind show character and environment combining to work out individual destiny, but he did not explain precisely what character was and whether it was entirely shaped by a force such as inheritance.[52] Roy Morrell suggests a parallel with the Existential philosophy of Sartre, arguing that the lack of causal psychological back grounds in Hardy's people "is a measure of their freedom." They are determined by environment but only temporarily.[53] As J. T. Laird asserts, Morrell is surely right to emphasize the role of choice in Hardy's narratives, but I believe that he exaggerates the degree of "freedom" these characters enjoy.[54] Henchard's sometimes perverse choices are conscious but determined by ungovernable impulses beneath his conscious mind, yet Morrell singles him out as one who could have done otherwise.[55] Hardy's poetry frequently illustrates the ironic consequences of "wrong" choices, though it does not suggest that "right" choices were possible, or, in a long perspective, "better." Perhaps Laird's position is safest. Hardy does not offer a world of "complete natural determinism," but certain attitudes are linked— at the inactive range, passivity, fatalism and the life of nature, at the active range, precipitancy and recklessness. Thus Hardy isolates a limited ground for sane achievement. His "championing of will and its concomitants, foresight, alertness, and dependability, is accompanied by a healthy respect for stoicism."[56] What was clear to Hardy was that man's gifts of intelligence and sensibility were out of keeping with the forces of nature. In a variation of Mary Shelley's message in *Frankenstein*, Hardy indicates that man's highest qualities are doomed to frustration because they are based upon illusions of purpose and order that cannot be proven to exist. If man is free, his freedom consists in imagining an illusory world. Those characters who make no attempt to bend the "laws" of nature or society to their needs—like Thomasin and Elizabeth-Jane—discover that it is possible to live in accommodation with the forces around them.

Just as man shapes his destiny through the fictions he creates, Hardy shapes his fiction by making destinies obviously contrived. He believed from his earliest attempts at fiction that unusual incidents were necessary to gain a reader's interest. He used coincidence, sometimes improbable coincidence purposely to show the shaping power of the narrator, to indicate how incidents with no special significance in themselves—a note slipped accidentally under a carpet, a Furmity woman reappearing at an inconvenient time—resemble malign gestures of fate only because human beings have made decisions and created illusions that charge these events with an ultimately specious significance. Love itself is one of the most damaging illusions, and most of Hardy's stories turn on the workings of human passion.[57]

Like other novelists we have examined, Hardy insisted that his characters shaped their own destinies.[58] Michael Millgate writes of *The Mayor of Casterbridge*, where Elizabeth-Jane serves as onlooker and reader representative, that it is "almost as though Hardy shrank from the responsibilities of omniscience, from the necessity for moral judgments and firm intellectual commitments, and found a certain security in adopting— usually quite inconsistently and on a scene-to-scene basis—the limited but essentially human perspectives available to particular characters."[59] But

Hardy is most faithful to his own view when muting the role of the narrator, just as a writer like Collins could best embody his views in multiple narrative, where the author need not assert any definitive opinion. The great power of Hardy's narratives is in the contrast between the stories his characters shape for themselves and the one that Hardy is shaping for them. Marlene Springer has suggested that, through his elaborate use of allusion, Hardy "requires of his readers that they bring to his novels an imaginative effort, that they read as connoisseurs."[60] Just as Meredith used difficult metaphorical language to compel his readers to engage in the imaginative act which he saw as the apex of human freedom—the liberation of the creative mind—Hardy sought to compel his readers, by his use of allusion and other narrative devices, to recognize how easily the patchwork heritage of human intelligence could provide images and ideals dangerous when taken seriously and applied to life. Eustacia Vye likens herself to the Witch of Endor, believing she is an exalted and powerful person. The narrator likens her to numerous avatars but consciously mixes his classical, biblical, and popular dramatic references, thus demonstrating his own power of enlarging Eustacia's character. But he immediately shrinks that character back to its proper dimension when he asks simply, "Why did a woman of this sort live on Egdon Heath?" (Hardy, *Return*, 54). It is instructive when a novelist enhances character by allusion but dangerous when a character does the same; as when Sue Bridehead pictures herself as a pagan antagonist of Christian civilization. The artist employs his allusions in a narrative under his control; the living being (or the character figuring that being) has no such control and cannot depend upon the operational effectiveness of such allusions and other fancies.

Hardy's generally unobtrusive narrator does not seem to be shaping the events of his story, but it is *his* fiction that will prevail, not those of his characters. Behind the strange circumstances of his stories there is a design, but it is that of the author's self-conscious fiction, that is, his art. The characters who take such fictions for realities see themselves as actors in a story created by powers who scheme out their destinies, but in thus believing in a design behind their own projections they lose the very power of their will by investing all of its energy in an illusion. The artist does not mimic providence; instead, providence merely resembles a faulty artist. In fact, there is neither artist nor artistry beyond the realm of human fictions. The freedom of man's will rests only in his power to create fictions, and only in art is it possible to indulge this gift without suffering the unpredictable consequences such fiction making engenders. Hardy the artist assumed not the role of providential creator but of representative humanity utilizing its fictionalizing power to illustrate the very dangers that power entails.

Perhaps a fitting way to bring this section to a close is by discussing a novel that, while looking back to the marvels of Romanticism, incorporated many of the issues familiar to late-Victorian writers. Theodore Watts-Dunton's *Aylwin* (1898) was a surprising best-seller, exploiting certain late-century fascinations—as with gypsies and Wales—and promoting a renewed nature worship that Watts-Dunton himself wrote of elsewhere as the Renascence of Wonder. The novel is not well made. It was composed over a number of years and never did mend its seams appropriately. The basic plot is simple—Henry Aylwin, the narrator, falls in love with Winifred Wynne but is separated from her by the death of her father, who has violated the tomb of Aylwin's father and presumably suffered his curse. This incident drives Winifred into a hysterical madness and she disappears. The remainder of the story is Henry's account of his efforts to recover her.

Henry's chief contest is between his desire and the frustrations of circumstance. This theme is stated early in the novel when Henry recounts how, upon departing for Cambridge, he thought of all that he intended to do for Winifred though fate itself should say no. "I did not know then, as I know now," he reflects, "how weak is human will enmeshed in that web of Circumstance that has been a-weaving since the beginning of the world."[61] Annoyed by the superstitions of his ancestors both Romany and English (his father's first wife was a gypsy), Henry turns instead to "the wonderful revelations of modern science, my attitude towards superstition—towards all supernaturalism—oscillated between anger and simple contempt" (Watts-Dunton, *Aylwin*, 45). And yet he is snared in a world where Christian mystical belief and gypsy superstition bedevil him. His father's curse is effective; the fateful sign that guides Winifred in her madness proves actual, not merely a figment of her distorted mind. Henry is angered to find his own logical mind yielding to superstitious interpretations of events. His dilemma is typified by two paintings and the world views they present. On the one hand is the mystical painting "Faith and Love" by Wilderspin, a disciple of Henry's father; on the other is Cyril Aylwin's caricature of this painting. The first represents Isis unveiled as a joyful maiden flanked by Faith and Love, a symbol of "the true cosmology" of Henry's father and is the opposite of "that base Darwinian cosmogony which Carlyle spits at, and the great and good John Ruskin scorns," Wilderspin explains (Watts-Dunton, *Aylwin*, 189). The cynical Cyril's mockery of this painting uses the lower-class, crude, and vulgar Mrs. Gudgeon as model for an Isis grinning beneath a veil held by two figures, one resembling Darwin, the other Wilderspin. She is the Goddess of the Joke, Cyril explains, "who, when she had the chance of making a rational and common-sense universe, preferred amusing herself with flamingoes, dromedaries, ring-tailed monkeys, and men" (Watts-Dunton, *Aylwin*, 245). This contrast is intensified by the fact that Winifred, supposed to be Mrs. Gudgeon's daughter, is the model for Wilderspin's Isis. Two widely opposite types of women stand for two views of the world. The conflicting values expressed in the two paintings spill over into life, for when Henry discovers that Winifred was the model for Wilderspin's painting, Mrs. Gudgeon, her opposite, tells him that Winifred has died and been buried in a pauper's grave. The Goddess of the Joke announces the triumph of nihilistic philosophy. Henry collapses in agony. "And there at the feet of the awful jesting hag, Circumstance, I could only cry 'Winnie! my poor Winnie!' while over my head seemed to pass Necessity and her black ages of despair (Watts-Dunton, *Aylwin*, 301).

The next chapter is entitled "The Revolving Cage of Circumstance," and simply pursues the consequences of Henry's grief, his encounter with his remorseful mother, and his reading of his father's mystical writings. Desperate in his longing for some sense of Winifred, he goes to Mount Snowden, a place associated with her in his mind, accompanied by his gypsy friend Sinfi Lovell. In that beautiful natural setting, Henry *sees* Winifred but immediately regards the vision as a hallucination—the consequence of his own prostration and Sinfi's mesmerically powerful will that has enslaved "his will and his senses" (Watts-Dunton, *Aylwin*, 358). But even believing the vision false, identifying Winifred's face with the beauty of nature helps Henry to shed his morose view of the world as a charnel house and to recover instead a sense of the world's beauty.

Henry stays some weeks in the vicinity of Snowdon and then is surprised by Sinfi's return with a live and healthy Winifred, explaining that with the help of the painter D'Arcy (patterned on D. G. Rossetti), Winifred's curse was transferred magnetically to Sinfi, who was able to overcome it. D'Arcy's letter to Henry summarizes this solution to his problem. "As Job's faith was tried by Heaven, so has your love been tried by the power which you call 'circumstance' and which Wilderspin calls 'the spiritual world.' All that death has to teach the mind and the heart of man you have learnt to the very full, and yet she you love is restored to you, and will soon be in your arms" (Watts-Dunton, *Aylwin*, 442). Henry could find no consolation in materialism for the loss of his great love, D'Arcy says. He himself underwent a similar suffering, discovering his consolation in a power that transcends death.

Yes, my dear Aylwin, I knew that when the issues of Life are greatly beyond the common, and when our hearts are torn as yours has been torn, and when our souls are on fire with a flame such as that which I saw was consuming you, the awful possibilities of this universe—of which we, civilized men or savages, know nothing—will come before us, and tease our hearts with strange wild hopes, though all the "proofs" of all the logicians should hold them up to scorn. (Watts-Dunton, *Aylwin*, 444)

Sinfi, in making Winifred's *dukkeripen* (or fate-sign) come true, has also conquered her own. Winifred's fate is to marry Henry; Sinfi's was to love him in vain. The story ends happily with the loving pair viewing the symbol of their happiness—a cross-shaped, rose-colored cloud and light over Snowdon.

Watts-Dunton's novel must be read with considerable suspension of disbelief. The philosophy it expresses appears to be direct, but in fact is clouded by unresolved issues on the questionable margin of "philosophical" thought. Henry Aylwin's greatest torment is that he finds no satisfaction in materialism, yet can only fear the teaching of traditional faith. He cannot decide for certain if man's destiny is shaped by heredity, malign fate, supernatural powers recognized by the gypsies, or only by random circumstance. Like Henry, the reader too must juggle a complex of competing beliefs, because he knows no more than the first-person narrator, except for a few forecasts of events to come and backward reflections. Unlike Henry, the reader does not have a recovered sweetheart to help him affirm his trust in the prevailing power of love in the universe. We must trust not Henry himself but D'Arcy, who interprets Henry's story for him. D'Arcy sees life the way he sees paintings—as symbolic renderings of the veil of nature. Watts-Dunton's romance aspires to this same condition. There are enough symbolic hints and structural clues for us to interpret *Aylwin* as Watts-Dunton intended, but that interpretation can never be reduced to a summary or epitome. William Sharp wrote to Watts-Dunton that he might have called his novel *Destiny* if the title had not already been used by a famous author (probably Susan Ferrier). "The irresistibility of Fate, the overwhelming power of Circumstance, find genuine expression in your pages. As through Aeschylus, as through Omar Khayyam, there is beyond the general light an ominous shadow—of inevitable descent."[62] There is no ignoring that shadow in the novel, but ultimately it is the light that triumphs. The novel is called *Aylwin*, not *Destiny*; it names its central character and transfers emphasis from destiny to individual will. There are fates, but they maybe altered and even overcome. Man lives in the face of mystery and must exert his will as though he is free because to yield to materialist determinism is to abandon that freedom. Just as the reader follows a bizarre tale with many strange turnings, discontinuities, and coincidences, trusting that a narrative design will finally emerge, so man must assume a design arising out of his experiences in a manner he will never be able to define but in which he can place his trust. Watts-Dunton's narrative leaps to its conclusion by inexplicable events that override the relentless approach of destiny. The inexplicable cancels fate because it suspends causation. It is miracle brought within reach of those eager to believe. Whereas Hardy declared all interpretations of cosmic designs temporary fictions that men individually and as communities create for themselves and recommended none of them, urging only a faith in the admitted fiction of creative art, Watts-Dunton suggested that, although the story of existence could not be fully known as a work of art may be, it is there to be viewed with all its symbols awaiting our hopeful interpretation.

NOTES

1. George Meredith, *The Letters of George Meredith*, ed. C. L. Cline, 3 vols. (Oxford: Clarendon Press, 1970), 2:866 [22 July 1887].

2. Meredith, *The Egoist*, ed. Robert M. Adams (New York: W. W. Norton and Company, 1979), 4ff. Subsequent references appear in the text.

3. Adams, "A Counter Kind of Book," in *The Egoist*, 557, 553, 552.

4. Walter F. Wright, *Art and Substance in George Meredith: A Study in Narrative* (Lincoln: University of Nebraska Press, 1953), 10.

5. Meredith shared this fascination for illumination by way of metaphor with Carlyle, Eliot, and Henry James.

6. Gillian Beer, *Meredith: A Change of Masks: A Study of the Novels* (London: Athlone Press, 1970), 94. Subsequent references appear in the text. J. Hillis Miller's excellent essay, "'Herself Against Herself' The Clarification of Clara Middleton," in *The Representation of Women in Fiction*, ed. Carolyn G. Heilbrun and Margaret R. Higonnet, Selected Papers from the English Institute, 1981, n.s., no. 7 (Baltimore: Johns Hopkins University Press, 1983), describes how self is not fixed but dissolves into fleeting wishes, etc., all rendered by Meredith through rhetorical figures. Miller indicates that characters in *The Egoist* must learn to read other characters but also suggests that there is no proper language for the self, only figures. "The implicit discovery of *The Egoist* is therefore of the inherence of language in character" (p. 115).

7. See Judith Wilt's *The Readable People of George Meredith* (Princeton: Princeton University Press, 1975), 74ff.

8. Meredith, *Beauchamp's Career* (New York: Charles Scribner's Sons, 1909), 5. Subsequent references appear in the text.

9. Meredith's allusion is to the colossal statue at Thebes in Egypt thought to represent Memnon, in Greek mythology the son of Tithonus and Eos and king of the Ethiopians. When the morning sunlight struck this statue it produced musical sounds, supposed to be the voice of Memnon. These sounds ceased after the Romans restored it. The sounds were supposed to have been made by air passing through crevices in the stone.

10. I have discussed Meredith's humorous use of the systemic metaphor in "Systemic Irregularity: Meredith's *Ordeal*," *Papers on Language and Literature* 7, no. 1 (Winter 1971): 61–71.

11. Meredith, *The Ordeal of Richard Feverel* (New York: Random House, 1950), 590, 588. Subsequent references appear in the text.

12. Joan Williams, ed., *Meredith: The Critical Heritage* (New York: Barnes & Noble, 1971), 41.

13. Lionel Stevenson, *The Ordeal of George Meredith: A Biography* (New York: Charles Scribner's Sons, 1953), 48.

14. Meredith, *The Adventures of Harry Richmond* (New York: Charles Scribner's Sons, 1911), 565.

15. Meredith, "Modern Love," in *Selected Poems*, ed. Graham Hough (London: Oxford University Press, 1962), 31.

16. Judith Wilt observes that here, as in so many of Meredith's characterizations, the key word is "read" (p. 71).

17. Meredith, *The Tragic Comedians: A Study in a Well-Known Story* (New York: Charles Scribner's Sons, 1914), 107.

18. Meredith, *Diana of the Crossways* (New York: Charles Scribner's Sons, 1910), 95. Subsequent references appear in the text.

19. Gillian Beer discusses the Diana myth in the novel and says "Mythology becomes a means of endorsing the *stature* of his heroine while questioning her aspirations" (p. 156).

20. Meredith, *The Amazing Marriage* (New York: Charles Scribner's Sons, 1913), 50. Subsequent references appear in the text.

21. Meredith's picture of man's relationship to nature is most clearly presented in his poem "The Woods of Westermain," and amounts to a progressively inclusive transformation of human nature from Blood (instincts, passions, basic consciousness), to Brain (mind, intellect, ego), to Spirit (energy, vital force). Meredith believed in the mind's ability to encompass nature but also saw the overdevelopment of brain as a danger.

22. Samuel Butler, *Erewhon* (New York: Random House, 1955). Subsequent references appear in the text.

23. See the discussion of Butler's thought in chapter 7 of this study.

24. Peter Morton, *The Vital Science: Biology and the Literary Imagination,*, 1860–1900 (London: George Allen & Unwin, 1984), 183. Subsequent references appear in the text.

25. Thomas L. Jeffers, *Samuel Butler Revalued* (University Park: Pennsylvania State University Press, 1981), 40ff.

26. Butler, *The Way of All Flesh* (New York: Grosset & Dunlap, n.d.), 22. Subsequent references appear in the text.

27. Quoted by J. Hillis Miller in *Thomas Hardy: Distance and Desire* (Cambridge: Harvard University Press, 1970) from a letter to Edward Clodd (p. 15). See Robert Gittings, *Thomas Hardy's Later Years* (Boston: Little, Brown and Co., 1978), 114, and Michael Millgate, *Thomas Hardy: A Biography* (Oxford: Oxford University Press, 1985), 450, concerning Hardy's reading of Schopenhauer, Von Hartmann, and Haekel in the 1890s.

28. Miller, 22.

29. Bert G. Hornback, *The Metaphor of Chance: Vision and Technique in the Works of Thomas Hardy* (Athens: Ohio University Press, 1971), 5–6.

30. Hardy wrote to Florence Henniker about *Jude*, mentioning the theme of heredity:

> It is curious that some papers consider the story a sort of manifesto on the marriage question, though it is really one about two persons who, by a hereditary curse of temperament, peculiar to their family, are rendered unfit for marriage, or think they are. The tragedy is really addressed to those into whose souls the iron of adversity has deeply entered at some time of their lives, and can hardly be congenial to self-indulgent persons of ease and affluence. (*One Rare Fair Woman: Thomas Hardy's Letters to Florence Henniker*, 1893–1922, ed. Evelyn Hardy and F. B. Pinion [Coral Gables, Fla.: University of Miami Press], 47)

31. Hardy denied advocating free love in *Jude* and disclaimed any theory about free love (Hardy, *One Rare Fair Woman*, 52). In his autobiography, he denied having a coherent philosophy at all (Florence Emily Hardy, *The Later Years of Thomas Hardy*, 1892–1928 (London: Macmillan and Co., 1930], 217ff). Subsequent references appear in the text.

32. Florence Emily Hardy, *The Early Life of Thomas Hardy*, 1840–1891 (London: Macmillan and Co., 1928), 232, 146. Dennis Taylor discusses Hardy's web imagery in *Hardy's Poetry*, 1860–1928 (New York: Columbia University Press, 1981), 62ff, 86.

33. Thomas Hardy, *The Complete Poetical Works*, ed. Samuel Hynes, 3 vols. (Oxford: Clarendon Press, 1984), 2:319.

34. Hardy questions the coherence of Nietzsche's philosophy and considers Bergson's philosophy just "our old friend Dualism in a new suit of clothes" (Florence Hardy, *Later Years*, 160, 168).

35. Michael Millgate writes that "Hardy seems to have been constantly drawn towards a 'Laodiceanism' of his own—a reluctance to adopt absolute or even firm positions, a willingness to see virtue in all sides of a question, an insistence upon the provisionality of his opinions and the need to register them rather as a series of tentative impressions than as the systematic formulations of a philosopher" (*Biography*, 220). Hardy said as much himself several times, for example, in the "Apology" that opens *Late Lyrics and Earlier* (1922) where he warns that his poems

present no philosophy but are "a series of fugitive impressions which I have never tried to co-ordinate" or a "juxtaposition of unrelated, even discordant, effusions" (*Poetical Works* 2:319, 321).

36. See Lawrence O. Jones's "Imitation and Expression in Thomas Hardy's Theory of Fiction," for an examination of Hardy's view of his art (*Studies in the Novel* 7, no. 4 [Winter 1975]: 507–25).

37. Charlotte Thompson, "Language and the Shape of Reality in *Tess of the d'Urbervilles*," *ELH* 50, no. 4 (Winter 1983): 732.

38. See chapter 3 of the present study.

39. Thomas Hardy, *Tess of the d'Urbervilles*, ed. Scott Elledge (New York: W. W. Norton & Co., 1979), 43.

40. Edmund Blunden, *Thomas Hardy* (London: Macmillan and Co., 1954), 79.

41. Joseph Warren Beach, *The Technique of Thomas Hardy* (Chicago: University of Chicago Press, 1922), 229.

42. Commenting on Arthur Symons's fiction and the "slice of life" school of writing, Hardy likened Symons to a god in relation to his characters and wondered if he had the right to pretend to less than total knowledge of his own imaginative creations (Millgate, *Biography*, 439).

43. Thomas Hardy, *Far from the Madding Crowd* (New York: New American Library, 1960), 100. Subsequent references appear in the text.

44. Dale Kramer, *Thomas Hardy: The Forms of Tragedy* (Detroit: Wayne State University Press, 1975), 43.

45. Thomas Hardy, *Two on a Tower* (New York and London: Harper & Brothers, n.d.), vii.

46. Thomas Hardy, *The Return of the Native* (New York: W. W. Norton & Co., 1969), 131–32. Subsequent references appear in the text.

47. See Michael Millgate for a discussion of the high/low symbolism in *Two on a Tower* (*Thomas Hardy: His Career as a Novelist* [New York: Random House, 1971], 185ff).

48. Thomas Hardy, *The Mayor of Casterbridge* (W. W. Norton & Co., 1977), 78, 83. Subsequent references appear in the text.

49. Albert J. Guerard, "Henchard, Hardy's Lord Jim," in *Casterbridge*, 319ff.

50. Millgate, *Biography*, 410.

51. Thomas Hardy, *Jude the Obscure* (New York: W. W. Norton & Co., 1978), 267.

52. Thomas Hardy, "The Profitable Reading of Fiction," in *Life and Art: Essays, Notes, and Letters Collected for the First Time*, ed. Ernest Brennecke, Jr. (New York: Haskell House, 1966), 66.

53. Roy Morrell, *Thomas Hardy: The Will and the Way* (Kuala Lumpur: University of Malaya Press, 1965), 142.

54. J. T. Laird, *The Shaping of Tess of the d'Urbervilles* (Oxford: Clarendon Press, 1975), 45.

55. Morrell, 153.

56. Laird, 46–48.

57. Hardy worked out a comic version of this pursuit of the ideal in *The Well-Beloved*.

58. Millgate, *Biography*, 279.

59. Millgate, *Career*, 230.

60. Marlene Springer, *Hardy's Use of Allusion* (Lawrence: University Press of Kansas, 1983), 174.

61. Theodore Watts-Dunton, *Aylwin: The Renascence of Wonder* (London: Oxford University Press, 1934), 41. Subsequent references appear in the text.

62. Thomas Hake and Arthur Compton-Rickett *The Life and Letters of Theodore Watts-Dunton*, 2 vols. (New York: G. P. Putnam's Sons, 1916) 2:309.

T.S. ELIOT

Wilkie Collins and Dickens

It is to be hoped that some scholarly and philosophic critic of the present generation may be inspired to write a book on the history and aesthetic of melodrama. The golden age of melodrama passed, it is true, before any person living was aware of its existence: in the very middle of the last century. But there are many living who are not too young to remember the melodramatic stage before the cinema replaced it; who have sat entranced, in the front stalls of local or provincial theatres, before some representation of *East Lynne*, or *The White Slave*, or *No Mother to Guide Her*; and who are not too old to have observed with curious interest the replacement of dramatic melodrama by cinematographic melodrama, and the dissociation of the elements of the old three-volume melodramatic novel into the various types of the modern 300-page novel. Those who have lived before such terms as "highbrow fiction," "thrillers" and "detective fiction" were invented realize that melodrama is perennial and that the craving for it is perennial and must be satisfied. If we cannot get this satisfaction out of what the publishers present as "literature," then we will read—with less and less pretence of concealment—what we call "thrillers." But in the golden age of melodramatic fiction there was no such distinction. The best novels *were* thrilling; the distinction of *genre* between such-and-such a profound "psychological" novel of today and such-and-such a masterly "detective" novel of today is greater than the distinction of *genre* between *Wuthering*

From *T.S. Eliot: Selected Essays*. © 1950 by Harcourt, Inc., and renamed 1978 by Esme Valorie Eliot.

Heights, or even *The Mill on the Floss*, and *East Lynne*, the last of which "achieved an enormous and instantaneous success, and was translated into every known language, including Parsee and Hindustani." We believe that several contemporary novels have been "translated into every known language"; but we are sure that they have less in common with *The Golden Bowl*, or *Ulysses*, or even *Beauchamp's Career*, than *East Lynne* has in common with *Bleak House*.

In order to enjoy and to appreciate the work of Wilkie Collins, we ought to be able to reassemble the elements which have been dissociated in the modern novel. Collins is the contemporary of Dickens, Thackeray, George Eliot; of Charles Reade and almost of Captain Marryat. He has something in common with all of these novelists; but particularly and significantly with Dickens. Collins was the friend and sometimes the collaborator of Dickens; and the work of the two men ought to be studied side by side. There is, unhappily for the literary critic, no full biography of Wilkie Collins; and Forster's *Life of Dickens* is, from this point of view, most unsatisfactory. Forster was a notable biographer; but as a critic of the work of Dickens his view was a very narrow view. To any one who knows the bare facts of Dickens's acquaintance with Collins, and who has studied the work of the two men, their relationship and their influence upon one another is an important subject of study. And a comparative study of their novels can do much to illuminate the question of the difference between the dramatic and the melodramatic in fiction.

Dickens's "best novel" is probably *Bleak House;* that is Mr. Chesterton's opinion, and there is no better critic of Dickens living than Mr. Chesterton. Collins's best novel—or, at any rate, the only one of Collins's novels which every one knows—is *The Woman in White*. Now *Bleak House* is the novel in which Dickens most closely approaches Collins (and after *Bleak House*, *Little Dorrit* and parts of *Martin Chuzzlewit*); and *The Woman in White* is the novel in which Collins most closely approaches Dickens. Dickens excelled in character; in the creation of characters of greater intensity than human beings. Collins was not usually strong in the creation of character; but he was a master of plot and situation, of those elements of drama which are most essential to melodrama. *Bleak House* is Dickens's finest piece of construction; and *The Woman in White* contains Collins's most real characterization. Every one knows Count Fosco and Marion Halcombe intimately; only the most perfect Collins reader can remember even half a dozen of his other characters by name.

Count Fosco and Marion are indeed real personages to us; as "real" as much greater characters are, as real as Becky Sharp or Emma Bovary. In comparison with the characters of Dickens they lack only that kind of reality which is almost supernatural, which hardly seems to belong to the character by natural right, but seems rather to descend upon him by a kind of inspiration or grace. Collins's best characters are fabricated, with consumate skill, before our eyes; in Dickens's greatest figures we see no process or calculation. Dickens's figures belong to poetry, like figures of Dante or Shakespeare, in that a single phrase, either by them or about them, may be enough to set them wholly before us. Collins has no phrases. Dickens can with a phrase make a character as real as flesh and blood—*"What a Life Young Bailey's Was!"*—like Farinata

Chi fur gli maggior tui?

or like Cleopatra,

*I saw her once
Hop forty paces through the public street.*

Dickens's characters are real because there is no one like them; Collins's because they are so painstakingly coherent and lifelike. Whereas Dickens often introduces a great character carelessly, so that we do not realize, until the story is far advanced, with what a powerful personage we have to do, Collins, at least in these two figures in *The Woman in White*, employs every advantage of dramatic effect. Much of our impression of Marion is due to the words in which she is first presented:

> "The instant my eyes rested on her I was struck by the rare beauty of her form, and by the unaffected grace of her attitude. Her figure was tall, yet not too tall; comely and well developed, yet not fat; her head set on her shoulders with an easy, pliant firmness; her waist, perfection in the eyes of a man, for it occupied its natural place, it filled out its natural circle, it was visibly and delightfully undeformed by stays. She had not heard my entrance into the room, and I allowed myself the luxury of admiring her for a few moments before I moved one of the chairs near me as the least embarrassing means of attracting her attention. She turned towards me immediately. The easy elegance of every movement of her limbs and body, as soon as she began to advance from the far end of the room, set me in a flutter

> of expectation to see her face clearly. She left the window—and I
> said to myself, 'The lady is dark.' She moved forward a few
> steps—and I said to myself, 'The lady is young.' She approached
> nearer, and I said to myself (with a sense of surprise which words
> fail me to express), 'The lady is ugly!'"

The introduction of Count Fosco—too long to quote in full—requires many
more small strokes; but we should observe, Marion Halcombe being already
given, that our impression of the Count is made very much stronger by being
given to us as Marion's impression of him:

> "There are peculiarities in his personal appearance, his habits,
> and his amusements, which I should blame in the boldest terms,
> or ridicule in the most merciless manner, if I had seen them in
> another man. What is it that makes me unable to blame them, or
> to ridicule them in *him?*"

After this who can forget the white mice or the canaries, or the way in which
Count Fosco treated Sir Percival's sulky bloodhound? If *The Woman in White*
is the greatest of Collins's novels, it is so because of these two characters. If
we examine the book apart from Marion and Fosco, we must admit that it is
not Collins's finest work of construction, and that certain of his peculiar
melodramatic gifts are better displayed in other books. The book is dramatic
because of two characters; it is dramatic in the way in which the dramatic
differs from the melodramatic. Sir Percival Glyde is a figure of pasteboard,
and the mystery and the plot of which he is the centre are almost grotesque.
The one of Collins's books which is the most perfect piece of construction,
and the best balanced between plot and character, is *The Moonstone;* the one
which reaches the greatest melodramatic intensity is *Armadale.*
     The Moonstone is the first and greatest of English detective novels. We
say *English* detective novels, because there is also the work of Poe, which has
a *pure* detective interest. The detective story, as created by Poe, is something
as specialized and as intellectual as a chess problem; whereas the best English
detective fiction has relied less on the beauty of the mathematical problem
and much more on the intangible human element. In detective fiction
England probably excels other countries; but in a *genre* invented by Collins
and not by Poe. In *The Moonstone* the mystery is finally solved, not altogether
by human ingenuity, but largely by accident. Since Collins, the best heroes
of English detective fiction have been, like Sergeant Cuff, fallible; they play
their part, but never the sole part, in the unravelling. Sherlock Holmes, not

altogether a typical English sleuth, is a partial exception; but even Holmes exists, not solely because of his prowess, but largely because he is, in the Jonsonian sense, a humorous character, with his needle, his boxing, and his violin. But Sergeant Cuff, far more than Holmes, is the ancestor of the healthy generation of amiable, efficient, professional but fallible inspectors of fiction among whom we live today. And *The Moonstone*, a book twice the length of the "thrillers" that our contemporary masters write, maintains its interest and suspense at every moment. It does this by devices of a Dickensian type; for Collins, in addition to his particular merits, was a Dickens without genius. The book is a comedy of humours. The eccentricities of Mr. Franklin Blake, the satire on false philanthropy in the character of Mr. Godfrey Ablewhite (to say nothing of the Life, Letters and Labours of Miss Jane Ann Stamper), Betteridge with his "Robinson Crusoe," and his daughter Penelope, support the narrative. In other of Collins's novels, the trick of passing the narration from one hand to another, and employing every device of letters and diaries, becomes tedious and even unplausible (for instance, in *Armadale*, the terrific villain, Miss Gwilt, commits herself to paper far too often and far too frankly); but in *The Moonstone* these devices succeed, every time, in stimulating our interest afresh just at the moment when it was about to flag.

And in *The Moonstone* Collins succeeds in bringing into play those aids of "atmosphere" in which Dickens (and the Brontës) exhibited such genius, and in which Collins has everything except their genius. For his purpose, he does not come off badly. Compare the description of the discovery of Rosanna's death in the Shivering Sands—and notice how carefully, beforehand, the *mise-en-scène* of the Shivering Sands is prepared for us—with the shipwreck of Steerforth in *David Copperfield*. We may say, "There is no comparison!" but there *is* a comparison; and however unfavourable to Collins, it must increase our estimation of his skill.

There is another characteristic of Wilkie Collins which also brings him closer to Dickens, and it is a characteristic which has very great melodramatic value: compare the work of Collins with the work of Mrs. Henry Wood, already mentioned, and one sees how important for melodrama is the presence or absence of this. Forster, in his *Life of Dickens*, observes:

> "On the coincidences, resemblances and surprises of life Dickens liked especially to dwell, and few things moved his fancy so pleasantly. The world, he would say, was so much smaller than we thought it; we were all so connected by fate without knowing it; people supposed to be far apart were so constantly elbowing

each other; and tomorrow bore so close a resemblance to nothing
half so much as to yesterday."

Forster mentions this peculiarity early in the life of Dickens, long before
Dickens became acquainted with Collins. We may take it that this feeling was
common to Dickens and Collins, and that it may have been one of the causes
of their being drawn so sympathetically together, once they had become
acquainted. The two men had obviously in common a passionate feeling for
the drama. Each had qualities which the other lacked, and they had certain
qualities in common. It is perfectly reasonable to believe that the relations of
the two men—of which Forster gives us only the barest and most
unsatisfactory hints—affected profoundly the later work of each. We seem to
find traces of it in *Little Dorrit* and *The Tale of Two Cities*. Collins could never
have invented Durdles and Deputy; but Durdles and Deputy were obviously
to play their part in a whole, *bien charpentè* as Collins's work is, and as the
work of Dickens prior to *Bleak House* is not.

    One of the minor works of Collins which illustrates especially this
insistence upon the "coincidences, resemblances and surprises of life" is *The
Frozen Deep*. The story, as we read it, was patched up from the melodrama
which Collins wrote first; which was privately performed with great success
on several occasions, and in which Dickens took the leading part. Collins was
the cleverer at writing stage pieces; but we may imagine that Dickens was the
cleverer at acting them; and Dickens may have given to the *rôle* of Richard
Wardour, in acting it, an individuality which it certainly lacks in the story.
This story, we may add for the benefit of those who have not read it, depends
upon coincidence with a remarkably long arm; for the two men who ought
not to meet—the accepted and the rejected lover—do meet, and under the
most unlikely conditions they join, without knowing each other's identity,
the same Polar Expedition.

    In *The Frozen Deep* Collins wrote a piece of pure melodrama. That is to
say, it is nothing but melodrama. We are asked to accept an improbability,
simply for the sake of seeing the thrilling situation which arises in
consequence. But the frontier of drama and melodrama is vague; the
difference is largely a matter of emphasis; perhaps no drama has ever been
greatly and permanently successful without a large melodramatic element.
What is the difference between *The Frozen Deep* and *Oedipus the King?* It is
the difference between coincidence, set without shame or pretence, and
fate—which merges into character. It is not necessary, for high drama, that
accident should be eliminated; you cannot formulate the proportion of
accident that is permissible. But in great drama character is always felt to

be—not more important than plot—but somehow integral with plot. At least, one is left with the conviction that if circumstances had not arranged the events to fall out in such and such a way, the personages were, after all, such that they would have ended just as badly, or just as well, and more or less similarly. And sometimes the melodramatic—the accidental—becomes for Collins the dramatic—the fatal. There is one short tale, not one of his best known, and far from being his best—a tale with an extremely improbable ghost—which nevertheless is almost dramatic. It is called *The Haunted Hotel*; what makes it better than a mere readable second-rate ghost story is the fact that fatality in this story is no longer merely a wire jerking the figures. The principal character, the fatal woman, is herself obsessed by the idea of fatality; her motives are melodramatic; she therefore compels the coincidences to occur, feeling that she is compelled to compel them. In this story, as the chief character is internally melodramatic, the story itself ceases to be merely melodramatic, and partakes of true drama.

There is another characteristic of certain tales of Collins's, which may be said to belong to melodrama, or to the melodramatic part of drama. It consists in delaying, longer than one would conceive it possible to delay, a conclusion which is inevitable and wholly foreseen. A story like *The New Magdalen* is from a certain moment merely a study in stage suspense; the *dénouement* is postponed, again and again, by every possible ingenuity; the situations are in the most effective sense theatrical, without being in the profounder sense dramatic. They are seldom, as in *The Woman in White*, situations of conflict between significant personalities; they are more often conflicts between chessmen which merely occupy hostile positions on the board. Such, for instance, is the prolonged battle between Captain Wragge and Mrs. Lecomte at Aldburgh, in *No Name*.

The one of Collins's novels which we should choose as the most typical, or as the best of the more typical, and which we should recommend as a specimen of the melodramatic fiction of the epoch, is *Armadale*. It has no merit beyond melodrama, and it has every merit that melodrama can have. If Miss Gwilt did not have to bear such a large part of the burden of revealing her own villainy, the construction would be almost perfect. Like most of Collins's novels, it has the immense—and nowadays more and more rare— merit of being never dull. It has, to a very high degree, the peculiar Collins merit above mentioned, which we might call the air of spurious fatality. The machinery of the book is operated by the Dream. The mind of the reader is very carefully prepared for acceptance of the Dream; first by the elaborately staged coincidence of the two cousins getting marooned on the wreck of the ship on which the father of the one had long before entrapped the father of the other; secondly by the way in which the Dream is explained away by the doctor. The doctor's explanation is so reasonable that the reader immediately reacts in favour of the Dream. Then, the character of the dreamer himself is made plausibly intuitive; and the stages by which the various parts of the Dream are realized are perfectly managed. Particularly is this true of the scene in which, after some excellent comedy of humours on the boating party, Miss Gwilt arrives at sunset on the desolate shore of the Norfolk Broads. By means of the Dream, we are kept in a state of tension which makes it possible to believe in characters which otherwise we should find preposterous.

The greatest novels have something in them which will ensure their being read, at least by a small number of people, even if the novel, as a literary form, ceases to be written. It is not pretended that the novels of Wilkie Collins have this permanence. They are interesting only if we enjoy "reading novels." But novels are still being written; and there is no contemporary novelist who could not learn something from Collins in the art of interesting and exciting the reader. So long as novels are written, the possibilities of melodrama must from time to time be re-explored. The contemporary "thriller" is in danger of becoming stereotyped; the conventional murder is discovered in the first chapter by the conventional butler, and the murderer is discovered in the last chapter by the conventional inspector—after having been already discovered by the reader. The resources of Wilkie Collins are, in comparison, inexhaustible.

And even if we refused to take Collins very seriously by himself, we can hardly fail to treat him with seriousness if we recognize that the art of which he was a master was an art which neither Charles Reade nor Dickens despised. You cannot define Drama and Melodrama so that they shall be reciprocally exclusive; great drama has something melodramatic in it, and the best melodrama partakes of the greatness of drama. *The Moonstone* is very near to *Bleak House*. The theft of a diamond has some of the same blighting effect on the lives about it as the suit in Chancery; Rosanna Spearman is destroyed by the diamond as Miss Flite is destroyed by Chancery. Collins's novels suggest questions which no student of "the art of fiction" can afford to neglect. It is possible that the artist can be too conscious of his "art." Perhaps Henry James—who in his own practice could be not only "interesting," but had a very cunning mastery of the finer melodrama—may have had as a critic a bad influence. We cannot afford to forget that the first—and not one of the least difficult—requirements of either prose or verse is that it should be interesting.

SANDRA M. GILBERT AND SUSAN GUBAR

A Dialogue of Self and Soul:
Plain Jane's Progress

I dreamt that I was looking in a glass when a horrible face—the face of
an animal—suddenly showed over my shoulder. I cannot be sure if this
was a dream, or if it happened.

—Virginia Woolf

Never mind.... One day, quite suddenly, when you're not expecting it, I'll
take a hammer from the folds of my dark cloak and crack your little skull
like an egg-shell. Crack it will go, the egg-shell; out they will stream, the
blood, the brains. One day, one day.... One day the fierce wolf that walks
by my side will spring on you and rip your abominable guts out. One day,
one day.... Now, now, gently, quietly, quietly....

—Jean Rhys

I told my Soul to sing—
She said her Strings were snapt—
Her bow—to Atoms blown—
And so to mend her—gave me work
Until another Morn—
—Emily Dickinson

If *The Professor* is a somewhat blurred trance-statement of themes and
conflicts that dominated Charlotte Brontë's thought far more than she
herself may have realized, *Jane Eyre* is a work permeated by angry, *Angrian*

From *The Madwoman in the Attic: The Woman Writer and the Nineteeth-Century Literary
Imagination.* © 1979 by Yale University.

fantasies of escape-into-wholeness. Borrowing the mythic quest-plot—but not the devout substance—of Bunyan's male *Pilgrim's Progress*, the young novelist seems here definitively to have opened her eyes to female realities within her and around her: confinement, orphanhood, starvation, rage even to madness. Where the fiery image of Lucia, that energetic woman who probably "once wore chains and broke them," is miniaturized in *The Professor*, in *Jane Eyre* (1847) this figure becomes almost larger than life, the emblem of a passionate, barely disguised rebelliousness.

Victorian critics, no doubt instinctively perceiving the subliminal intensity of Brontë's passion, seem to have understood this point very well. Her "mind contains nothing but hunger, rebellion, and rage," Matthew Arnold wrote of Charlotte Brontë in 1853[1]. He was referring to *Villette*, which he elsewhere described as a "hideous, undelightful, convulsed, constricted novel,"[2] but he might as well have been speaking of *Jane Eyre*, for his response to Brontë was typical of the outrage generated in some quarters by her first published novel.[3] "Jane Eyre is throughout the personification of an unregenerate and undisciplined spirit," wrote Elizabeth Rigby in *The Quarterly Review* in 1848, and her "autobiography ... is preeminently an anti-Christian composition.... The tone of mind and thought which has fostered Chartism and rebellion is the same which has also written *Jane Eyre*."[4] Anne Mozley, in 1853, recalled for *The Christian Remembrancer* that "Currer Bell" had seemed on her first appearance as an author "soured, coarse, and grumbling; an alien ... from society and amenable to none of its laws."[5] And Mrs. Oliphant related in 1855 that "Ten years ago we professed an orthodox system of novel-making. Our lovers were humble and devoted ... and the only true love worth having was that ... chivalrous true love which consecrated all womankind ... when suddenly, without warning, *Jane Eyre* stole upon the scene, and the most alarming revolution of modern times has followed the invasion of *Jane Eyre*."[6]

We tend today to think of *Jane Eyre* as moral gothic, "myth domesticated," *Pamela's* daughter and *Rebecca's* aunt, the archetypal scenario for all those mildly thrilling romantic encounters between a scowling Byronic hero (who owns a gloomy mansion) and a trembling heroine (who can't quite figure out the mansion's floor plan). Or, if we're more sophisticated, we give Charlotte Brontë her due, concede her strategic as well as her mythic abilities, study the patterns of her imagery, and count the number of times she addresses the reader. But still we overlook the "alarming revolution"—even Mrs. Oliphant's terminology is suggestive—which "followed the invasion of *Jane Eyre*." "Well, obviously *Jane Eyre* is a feminist tract, an argument for the social betterment of governesses and equal rights for women," Richard Chase somewhat grudgingly admitted in 1948. But like most other modern critics, he believed that the novel's power arose from its mythologizing of Jane's confrontation with masculine sexuality.[7]

Yet, curiously enough, it seems not to have been primarily the coarseness and sexuality of *Jane Eyre*, which shocked Victorian reviewers (though they disliked those elements in the book), but, as we have seen, its "anti-Christian" refusal to accept the forms, customs, and standards of society—in short, its rebellious feminism. They were disturbed not so much by the proud Byronic sexual energy of Rochester as by the Byronic pride and passion of Jane herself, not so much by the asocial sexual vibrations between hero and heroine as by the heroine's refusal to submit to her social destiny: "She has inherited in fullest measure the worst sin of our fallen nature—the sin of pride," declared Miss Rigby.

> Jane Eyre is proud, and therefore she is ungrateful, too. It pleased God to make her an orphan, friendless, and penniless—yet she thanks nobody, and least of all Him, for the food and raiment, the friends, companions, and instructors of her helpless youth.... On the contrary, she looks upon all that has been done for her not only as her undoubted right, but as falling far short of it.[8]

In other words, what horrified the Victorians was Jane's anger. And perhaps they, rather than more recent critics, were correct in their response to the book. For while the mythologizing of repressed rage may parallel the mythologizing of repressed sexuality, it is far more dangerous to the order of society. The occasional woman who has a weakness for black-browed Byronic heroes can be accommodated in novels and even in some drawing rooms; the woman who yearns to escape entirely from drawing rooms and patriarchal mansions obviously cannot. And Jane Eyre, as Matthew Arnold, Miss Rigby, Mrs. Mozley, and Mrs. Oliphant suspected, was such a woman.

Her story, providing a pattern for countless others, is—far more obviously and dramatically than *The Professor*—a story of enclosure and escape, a distinctively female *Bildungsroman* in which the problems encountered by the protagonist as she struggles from the imprisonment of her childhood toward an almost unthinkable goal of mature freedom are symptomatic of difficulties Everywoman in a patriarchal society must meet and overcome: oppression (at Gateshead), starvation (at Lowood), madness (at Thornfield), and coldness (at Marsh End). Most important, her confrontation, not with Rochester but with Rochester's mad wife Bertha, is the book's central confrontation, an encounter—like Frances Crimsworth's fantasy about Lucia—not with her own sexuality but with her own imprisoned "hunger, rebellion, and rage," a secret dialogue of self and soul on whose outcome, as we shall see, the novel's plot, Rochester's fate, and Jane's coming-of-age all depend.

Unlike many Victorian novels, which begin with elaborate expository paragraphs, *Jane Eyre* begins with a casual, curiously enigmatic remark: "There was no possibility of taking a walk that day." Both the occasion ("that day") and the excursion (or the impossibility of one) are significant: the first is the real beginning of Jane's pilgrim's progress toward maturity; the second is a metaphor for the problems she must solve in order to attain maturity. "I was glad" not to be able to leave the house, the narrator continues: "dreadful to me was the coming home in the raw twilight ... humbled by the consciousness of my physical inferiority" (chap. 1).[9] As many critics have commented, Charlotte Brontë consistently uses the opposed properties of fire and ice to characterize Jane's experiences, and her technique is immediately evident in these opening passages.[10] For while the world outside Gateshead is almost unbearably wintry, the world within is claustrophobic, fiery, like ten-year-old Jane's own mind. Excluded from the Reed family group in the drawing room because *she* is not a "contented, happy, little child"—excluded, that is, from "normal" society—Jane takes refuge in a scarlet-draped window seat where she alternately stares out at the "drear November day" and reads of polar regions in Bewick's *History of British Birds*. The "death-white realms" of the Arctic fascinate her; she broods upon "the multiplied rigors of extreme cold" as if brooding upon her own dilemma: whether to stay in, behind the oppressively scarlet curtain, or to go out into the cold of a loveless world.

Her decision is made for her. She is found by John Reed, the tyrannical son of the family, who reminds her of her anomalous position in the household, hurls the heavy volume of Bewick at her, and arouses her passionate rage. Like a "rat," a "bad animal," a "mad cat," she compares him to "Nero, Caligula, etc." and is borne away to the red-room, to be imprisoned literally as well as figuratively. For "the fact is," confesses the grownup narrator ironically, "I was [at that moment] a trifle beside myself; or rather *out* of myself, as the French would say.... like any other rebel slave, I felt resolved ... to go all lengths" (chap. 1).

But if Jane was "out of" herself in her struggle against John Reed, her experience in the red-room, probably the most metaphorically vibrant of all her early experiences, forces her deeply into herself. For the red-room, stately, chilly, swathed in rich crimson, with a great white bed and an easy chair "like a pale throne" looming out of the scarlet darkness, perfectly represents her vision of the society in which she is trapped, an uneasy and elfin dependent. "No jail was ever more secure," she tells us. And no jail, we soon learn, was ever more terrifying either, because this is the room where Mr. Reed, the only "father" Jane has ever had, "breathed his last." It is, in other words, a kind of patriarchal death chamber, and here Mrs. Reed still keeps "divers parchments, her jewel-casket, and a miniature of her dead husband." in a secret drawer in the wardrobe (chap. 2). Is the room haunted, the child wonders. At least, the narrator implies, it is realistically if not gothically haunting, more so than any chamber in, say, *The Mysteries of Udolpho*, which established a standard for such apartments. For the spirit of a society in which Jane has no clear place sharpens, the angles of the furniture, enlarges the shadows, strengthens the locks on the door. And the deathbed of a father who was not really her father emphasizes her isolation and vulnerability.

Panicky, she stares into a "great looking glass," where her own image floats toward her, alien and disturbing. "All looked colder and darker in that visionary hollow than in reality," the adult Jane explains. But a mirror, after all, is also a sort of chamber, a mysterious enclosure in which images of the self are trapped like "divers parchments." So the child Jane, though her older self accuses her of mere superstition, correctly recognizes that she is doubly imprisoned. Frustrated and angry, she meditates on the injustices of her life, and fantasizes "some strange expedient to achieve escape from insupportable oppression—as running away, or, if that could not be effected, never eating or drinking more, and letting myself die" (chap. 2). Escape through flight, or escape through starvation: the alternatives will recur throughout *Jane Eyre* and, indeed, as we have already noted, throughout much other nineteenth- and twentieth- century literature by women. In the red-room, however, little Jane chooses (or is chosen by) a third, even more terrifying, alternative: escape through madness. Seeing a ghostly, wandering light, as of the moon on the ceiling, she notices that "my heart beat thick, my head grew hot; a sound filled my ears, which I deemed the rushing of wings; something seemed near me; I was oppressed, suffocated: endurance broke down." The child screams and sobs in anguish, and then, adds the narrator coolly, "I suppose I had a species of fit," for her next memory is of waking in the nursery "and seeing before me a terrible red glare crossed with thick black bars" (chap. 3), merely the nursery fire of course, but to Jane Eyre the child a terrible reminder of the experience she has just had, and to Jane Eyre the adult narrator an even more dreadful omen of experiences to come.

For the little drama enacted on "that day" which opens *Jane Eyre* is in itself a paradigm of the larger drama that occupies the entire book: Jane's anomalous, orphaned position in society, her enclosure in stultifying roles and houses, and her attempts to escape through flight, starvation, and—in a sense which will be explained—madness. And that Charlotte Brontë quite consciously intended the incident of the red-room to serve as a paradigm for the larger plot of her novel is clear not only from its position in the narrative but also from Jane's own recollection of the experience at crucial moments throughout the book: when she is humiliated by Mr. Brocklehurst at Lowood, for instance, and on the night when she decides to leave Thornfield. In between these moments, moreover, Jane's pilgrimage consists of a series of experiences which are, in one way or another, variations on the central, red-room motif of enclosure and escape.

As we noted earlier, the allusion to pilgriming is deliberate, for like the protagonist of Bunyan's book, Jane Eyre makes a life-journey which is a kind of mythical progress from one significantly named place to another. Her story begins, quite naturally, at *Gates-head*, a starting point where she encounters the uncomfortable givens of her career: a family which is not her real family, a selfish older "brother" who tyrannizes over the household like a substitute patriarch, a foolish and wicked "stepmother," and two unpleasant, selfish "stepsisters." The smallest, weakest, and plainest child in the house, she embarks on her pilgrim's progress as a sullen Cinderella, an angry Ugly Duckling, immorally rebellious against the hierarchy that oppresses her: "I know that had I been a sanguine, brilliant, careless, exacting, handsome, romping child—though equally dependent and friendless—Mrs. Reed would have endured my presence more complacently," she reflects as an adult (chap. 2).

But the child Jane cannot, as she well knows, be "sanguine and brilliant." Cinderella never is; nor is the Ugly Duckling, who, for all her swansdown potential, has no great expectations. "Poor, plain, and little," Jane Eyre—her name is of course suggestive—is invisible as air, the heir to nothing, secretly choking with ire. And Bessie, the kind nursemaid who befriends her, sings her a song that no fairy godmother would ever dream of singing, a song that summarizes the plight of all real Victorian Cinderellas:

> My feet they are sore, and my limbs they are weary,
> Long is the way, and the mountains are wild;
> Soon will the twilight close moonless and dreary
> Over the path of the poor orphan child.

A hopeless pilgrimage, Jane's seems, like the sad journey of Wordsworth's Lucy Gray, seen this time from the inside, by the child herself rather than by the sagacious poet to whom years have given a philosophic mind. Though she will later watch the maternal moon rise to guide her, now she imagines herself wandering in a moonless twilight that foreshadows her desperate flight across the moors after leaving Thornfield. And the only hope her friend Bessie can offer is, ironically, an image that recalls the patriarchal terrors of the red-room and hints at patriarchal terrors to come—Lowood, Brocklehurst, St. John Rivers:

> Ev'n should I fall o'er the broken bridge passing,
> Or stray in the marshes, by false lights beguiled,
> Still will my Father, with promise and blessing
> Take to His bosom the poor orphan child.

It is no wonder that, confronting such prospects, young Jane finds herself "whispering to myself, over and over again" the words of Bunyan's Christian: "What shall I do?—What shall I do?" (chep. 4).[11]

What she does do, in desperation, is burst her bonds again and again to tell Mrs. Reed what she thinks of her, an extraordinarily self-assertive act of which neither a Victorian child nor a Cinderella was ever supposed to be capable. Interestingly, her first such explosion is intended to remind Mrs. Reed that she, too, is surrounded by patriarchal limits: "What would Uncle Reed say to you if he were alive?" Jane demands, commenting, "It seemed as if my tongue pronounced words without my will consenting to their utterance: something spoke out of me over which I had no control" (chap. 4). And indeed, even imperious Mrs. Reed appears astonished by these words. The explanation, "something spoke out of me," is as frightening as the arrogance, suggesting the dangerous double consciousness—"the rushing of wings, something ... near me"—that brought on the fit in the red-room. And when, with a real sense that "an invisible bond had burst, and that I had struggled out into unhoped-for liberty," Jane tells Mrs. Reed that "I am glad you are no relation of mine" (chap. 4), the adult narrator remarks that "a ridge of lighted heath, alive, glancing, devouring, would have been a meet emblem of my mind"—as the nursery fire was, flaring behind its black grates, and as the flames consuming Thornfield also will be.

Singnificantly, the event that inspires little Jane's final fiery words to Mrs. Reed is her first encounter with that merciless and hypocritical patriarch Mr.

Brocklehurst, who appears now to conduct her on the next stage of her pilgrimage. As many readers have noticed, this personification of the Victorian superego is—like St. John Rivers, his counterpart in the last third of the book—consistently described in phallic terms: he is "a black pillar" with a "grim face at the top ... like a carved mask," almost as if he were a funereal and oddly Freudian piece of furniture (chap. 4). But he is also rather like the wolf in "Little Red Riding Hood." "What a face he had.... What a great nose! And what a mouth! And what large prominent teeth!" Jane Eyre exclaims, recollecting that terror of the adult male animal which must have wrung the heart of every female child in a period when all men were defined as "beasts."

Simultaneously, then, a pillar of society and a large bad wolf, Mr. Brocklehurst has come with news of hell to remove Jane to *Lowood*, the aptly named school of life where orphan girls are starved and frozen into proper Christian submission. Where else would a beast take a child but into a wood? Where else would a column of frozen spirituality take a homeless orphan but to a sanctuary where there is neither food nor warmth? Yet "with all its privations" Lowood offers Jane a valley of refuge from "the ridge of lighted heath," a chance to learn to govern her anger while learning to become a governess in the company of a few women she admires.

Foremost among those Jane admires are the noble Miss Temple and the pathetic Helen Burns. And again, their names are significant. Angelic Miss Temple, for instance, with her marble pallor, is a shrine of ladylike virtues: magnanimity, cultivation, courtesy—and repression. As if invented by Coventry Patmore or by Mrs. Sarah Ellis, that indefatigable writer of conduct books for Victorian girls, she dispenses food to the hungry, visits the sick, encourages the worthy, and averts her glance from the unworthy. "'What shall I do to gratify myself—to be admired—or to vary the tenor of my existence' are not the questions which a woman of right feelings asks on first awaking to the avocations of the day," wrote Mrs. Ellis in 1844.

> Much more congenial to the highest attributes of woman's character are inquiries such as these: "How shall I endeavor through this day to turn the time, the health, and the means permitted me to enjoy, to the best account? Is any one sick? I must visit their chamber without delay.... Is any one about to set off on a journey? I must see that the early meal is spread.... Did I fail in what was kind or considerate to any of the family yesterday? I will meet her this morning with a cordial welcome."[12]

And these questions are obviously the ones Miss Temple asks herself, and answers by her actions.

Yet it is clear enough that she has repressed her own share of madness and rage, that there is a potential monster beneath her angelic exterior, a "sewer" of fury beneath this temple.[13] Though she is, for instance, plainly angered by Mr. Brocklehurst's sanctimonious stinginess, she listens to his sermonizing in ladylike silence. Her face, Jane remembers, "appeared to be assuming ... the coldness and fixity of [marble]; especially her mouth, closed as if it would have required a sculptor's chisel to open it" (chap. 7). Certainly Miss Temple will never allow "something" to speak through her, no wings will rush in her head, no fantasies of fiery heath disturb her equanimity, but she will feel sympathetic anger.

Perhaps for this reason, repressed as she is, she is closer to a fairy godmother than anyone else Jane has met, closer even to a true mother. By the fire in her pretty room, she feeds her starving pupils tea and emblematic seedcake, nourishing body and soul together despite Mr. Brocklehurst's puritanical dicta. "We feasted," says Jane, "as on nectar and ambrosia." But still, Jane adds, "Miss Temple had always something ... of state in her mien, of refined propriety in her language, which precluded deviation into the ardent, the excited, the eager: something which chastened the pleasure of those who looked on her and listened to her, by a controlling sense of awe" (chap. 8). Rather awful as well as very awesome, Miss Temple is not just an angel-in-the-house; to the extent that her name defines her, she is even more house than angel, a beautiful set of marble columns designed to balance that bad pillar Mr. Brocklehurst. And dispossessed Jane, who is not only poor, plain, and little, but also fiery and ferocious, correctly guesses that she can no more become such a woman than Cinderella can become her own fairy godmother.

Helen Burns, Miss Temple's other disciple, presents a different but equally impossible ideal to Jane: the ideal—defined by Goethe's Makarie—of self-renunciation, of all-consuming (and consumptive) spirituality. Like Jane "a poor orphan child" ("I have only a father; and he ... will not miss me" [chap. 9]), Helen longs alternately for her old home in Northumberland, with its "visionary brook," and for the true home which she believes awaits her in heaven. As if echoing the last stanzas of Bessie's song, "God is my father, God is my friend," she tells Jane, whose skepticism disallows such comforts, and "Eternity [is] a mighty home, not a terror and an abyss" (chap. 7). One's duty, Helen declares, is to submit to the injustices of this life, in expectation of the ultimate justice of the next: "it is weak and silly to say you *cannot bear* what it is your fate to be required to bear" (chap. 7).

Helen herself, however, does no more than *bear* her fate. "I make no effort [to be good, in Lowood's terms]," she confesses. "I follow as inclination guides me" (chap. 7). Labeled a "slattern" for failing to keep her drawers in ladylike order, she meditates on Charles I, as if commenting on all inadequate fathers ("what a pity ... he could see no father than the prerogatives of the crown") and studies *Rasselas*, perhaps comparing Dr. Johnson's Happy Valley to the unhappy one in which she herself is immured. "One strong proof of my wretchedly defective nature," she explains to the admiring Jane, "is that even [Miss Temple's] expostulations ... have no influence to cure me of my faults." Despite her contemplative purity, there is evidently a "sewer" of concealed resentment in Helen Burns, just as there is in Miss Temple. And, like Miss Temple's, her name is significant. Burning with spiritual passion, she also burns with anger, leaves her things "in shameful disorder," and dreams of freedom in eternity: "By dying young, I shall escape great sufferings," she explains (chap. 9). Finally, when the "fog-bred pestilence" of typhus decimates Lowood, Helen is carried off by her own fever for liberty, as if her body, like Jane's mind, were "a ridge of lighted heath ... devouring" the dank valley in which she has been caged.

    This is not to say that Miss Temple and Helen Burns do nothing to help Jane come to terms with her fate. Both are in some sense mothers for Jane, as Adrienne Rich has pointed out,[14] comforting her, counseling her, feeding her, embracing her. And from Miss Temple, in particular, the girl learns to achieve "more harmonious thoughts: what seemed better regulated feelings had become the inmates of my mind. I had given in allegiance to duty and order. I appeared a disciplined and subdued character" (chap. 10). Yet because Jane is an Angrian Cinderella, a Byronic heroine, the "inmates" of her mind can no more be regulated by conventional Christian wisdom than Manfred's or Childe Harold's thoughts. Thus, when Miss Temple leaves Lowood, Jane tells us, "I was left in my natural element." Gazing out a window as she had on "that day" which opened her story, she yearns for true liberty: "for liberty I uttered a prayer." Her way of confronting the world is still the Promethean way of fiery rebellion, not Miss Temple's way of ladylike repression, not Helen Burns's way of saintly renunciation. What she has learned from her two mother is, at least superficially, to compromise. If pure liberty is impossible, she exclaims, "then ... grant me at least a new servitude" (chap. 10).

It is, of course, her eagerness for a new servitude that brings Jane to the painful experience that is at the center of her pilgrimage, the experience of *Thornfield*, where, biblically, she is to be crowned with thorns, she is to be cast out into a desolate field, and most important, she is to confront the demon of rage who has haunted her since her afternoon in the red-room.

Before the appearance of Rochester, however, and the intrusion of Bertha, Jane—and her readers—must explore Thornfield itself. This gloomy mansion is often seen as just another gothic trapping introduced by Charlotte Brontë to make her novel saleable. Yet not only is Thornfield more realistically drawn than, say, Otranto or Udolpho, it is more metaphorically radiant than most gothic mansions: it is the house of Jane's life, its floors and walls the architecture of her experience.

Beyond the "long cold gallery" where the portraits of alien unknown ancestors hang the way the specter of Mr. Reed hovered in the red-room, Jane sleeps in a small pretty chamber, harmoniously furnished as Miss Temple's training has supposedly furnished her own mind. Youthfully optimistic, she notices that her "couch had no thorns in it" and trusts that with the help of welcoming Mrs. Fairfax "a fairer era of life was beginning for me, one that was to have its flowers and pleasures, as well as its thorns and toils" (chap. 11). Christian, entering the Palace Beautiful, might have hoped as much.

The equivocal pleasantness of Mrs. Fairfax, however, like the ambiguous architecture of Thornfield itself, suggests at once a way in which the situation at Thornfield reiterates all the other settings of Jane's life. For though Jane assumes at first that Mrs. Fairfax is her employer, she soon learns that the woman is merely a house*keeper*, the surrogate of an absent master, just as Mrs. Reed was a surrogate for dead Mr. Reed or immature John Reed, and Miss Temple for absent Mr. Brocklehurst. Moreover, in her role as an extension of the mysterious Rochester, sweet-faced Mrs. Fairfax herself becomes mysteriously chilling. "Too much noise, Grace," she says peremptorily, when she and Jane overhear "Grace Poole's" laugh as they tour the third story. "Remember directions!" (chap. 11).

The third story is the most obviously emblematic quarter of Thornfield. Here, amid the furniture of the past, down a narrow passage with "two rows of small black doors, all shut, like a corridor in some Bluebeard's castle" (chap. 11), Jane first hears the "distinct formal mirthless laugh" of mad Bertha, Rochester's secret wife and in a sense her own secret self. And just above this sinister corridor, leaning against the picturesque battlements and looking out over the world like Bluebeard's bride's sister Anne, Jane is to long again for freedom, for "all of incident, life, fire, feeling that I ... had not in my actual existence" (chap. 12). These upper regions, in other words, symbolically miniaturize one crucial aspect of the world in which she finds herself. Heavily enigmatic, ancestral relics wall her in; inexplicable locked rooms guard a secret which may have something to do with *her*; distant vistas promise an inaccessible but enviable life.

Even more importantly, Thornfield's attic soon becomes a complex focal point where Jane's own rationality (what she has learned from Miss Temple) and her irrationality (her "hunger, rebellion and rage") intersect.[15] She never, for instance, articulates her rational desire for liberty so well as when she stands on the battlements of Thornfield, looking out over the world. However offensive these thoughts may have been to Miss Rigby—and both Jane and her creator obviously suspected they would be—the sequence of ideas expressed in the famous passage beginning "Anybody may blame me who likes" is as logical as anything in an essay by Wollstonecraft or Mill. What is somewhat irrational, though, is the restlessness and passion which, as it were, italicize her little meditation on freedom. "I could not help it," she explains,

> the restlessness was in my nature, it agitated me to pain sometimes. Then my sole relief was to walk along the corridor of the third story, backwards and forwards, safe in the silence and solitude of the spot, and allow my mind's eye to dwell on whatever bright visions rose before it.

And even more irrational is the experience which accompanies Jane's pacing:

> When thus alone, I not unfrequently heard Grace Poole's laugh: the same peal, the same low, slow ha! ha! which, when first heard, had thrilled me: I heard, too, her eccentric murmurs; stranger than her laugh. [chap. 12]

Eccentric murmurs that uncannily echo the murmurs of *Jane's* imagination, and a low, slow ha! ha! which forms a bitter refrain to the tale *Jane's* imagination creates. Despite Miss Temple's training, the "bad animal" who was first locked up in the red-room is, we sense, still lurking somewhere, behind a dark door; waiting for a chance to get free. That early consciousness of "something near me" has not yet been exorcised. Rather, it has intensified.

Many of Jane's problems, particularly those which find symbolic expression in her experiences in the third story, can be traced to her ambiguous status as a governess at Thornfield. As M. Jeanne Peterson points out, every Victorian governess received strikingly conflicting messages (she was and was not a member of the family, was and was not a servant).[16] Such messages all too often caused her features to wear what one contemporary observer called "a fixed sad look of despair."[17] But Jane's difficulties arise also, as we have seen, from her constitutional *ire*; interestingly, none of the women she meets at Thornfield has anything like that last problem, though all suffer from equivalent ambiguities of status. Aside from Mrs. Fairfax, the three most important of these women are little Adèle Varens, Blanche Ingram, and Grace Poole. All are important negative "role-models" for Jane, and all suggest problems she must overcome before she can reach the independent maturity which is the goal of her pilgrimage.

The first, Adèle, though hardly a woman, is already a "little woman," cunning and doll-like, a sort of sketch for Amy March in Louisa May Alcott's novel. Ostensibly a poor orphan child, like Jane herself, Adèle is evidently the natural daughter of Edward Rochester's dissipated youth. Accordingly, she longs for fashionable gowns rather than for love or freedom, and, the way her mother Céline did, sings and dances for her supper as if she were a clockwork temptress invented by E. T. A. Hoffman. Where Miss Temple's was the way of the lady and Helen's that of the saint, hers and her mother's are the ways of Vanity Fair, ways which have troubled Jane since her days at Gateshead. For how is a poor, plain governess to contend with a society that rewards beauty and style? May not Adèle, the daughter of a "fallen woman," be a model female in a world of prostitutes?

Blanche Ingram, also a denizen of Vanity Fair, presents Jane with a slightly different female image. Tall, handsome, and wellborn, she is worldly but, unlike Adèle and Céline, has a respectable place in the world: she is the daughter of "Baroness Ingram of Ingram Park," and—along with Georgiana and Eliza Reed—Jane's classically wicked stepsister. But while Georgiana and Eliza are dismissed to stereotypical fates, Blanche's history teaches Jane ominous lessons. First, the charade of "Bridewell" in which she and Rochester participate relays a secret message: conventional marriage is not only, as the attic implies, a "well" of mystery, it is a Bridewell, a prison, like the Bluebeard's corridor of the third story. Second, the charade of courtship in which Rochester engages her suggests a grim question: is not the game of the marriage "market" a game even scheming women are doomed to lose?

Finally, Grace Poole, the most enigmatic of the women Jane meets at Thornfield—"that mystery of mysteries, as I considered her"—is obviously associated with Bertha, almost as if, with her pint of porter, her "staid and taciturn" demeanor, she were the madwoman's public representative. "Only one hour in the twenty four did she pass with her fellow servants below," Jane notes, attempting to fathom the dark "pool" of the woman's behavior; "all the rest of her time was spent in some low-ceiled, oaken chamber of the third story; there she sat and sewed ... as companionless as a prisoner in her dungeon" (chap. 17). And that Grace is as companionless as Bertha or Jane herself is undeniably true. Women in Jane's world, acting as agents for men, may be the keepers of other women. But both keepers and prisoners are bound by the same chains. In a sense, then, the mystery of mysteries which Grace Poole suggests to Jane is the mystery of her own life, so that to question Grace's position at Thornfield is to question her own.

Interestingly, in trying to puzzle out the secret of Grace Poole, Jane at one point speculates that Mr. Rochester may once have entertained "tender feelings" for the woman, and when thoughts of Grace's "uncomeliness" seem to refute this possibility, she cements her bond with Bertha's keeper by reminding herself that, after all, "*You* are not beautiful either, and perhaps Mr. Rochester approves you" (chap. 16). Can appearances be trusted? Who is the slave, the master or the servant, the prince or Cinderella? What, in other words, are the real relationships between the master of Thornfield and all these women whose lives revolve around his? None of these questions can, of course, be answered without reference to the central character of the Thornfield episode, Edward Fairfax Rochester.

Jane's first meeting with Rochester is a fairytale meeting. Charlotte Brontë deliberately stresses mythic elements: an icy twilight setting out of Coleridge or Fuseli, a rising moon, a great "lion-like" dog gliding through the shadows like "a North-of-England spirit, called a 'Gytrash' which ... haunted solitary ways, and sometimes came upon belated travellers," followed by "a tall steed, and on its back a rider." Certainly the Romanticized images seem to suggest that universe of male sexuality with which Richard Chase thought the Brontës were obsessed.[18] And Rochester, in a "riding-cloak, fur-collared, and steel-clasped," with "a dark face ... stern features and a heavy brow" himself appears the very essence of patriarchal energy, Cinderella's prince as a middle-aged warrior (chap. 12). Yet, what are we to think of the fact that the prince's first action is to fall on the ice, together with his horse, and exclaim prosaically "what the deuce is to do now?" Clearly the master's mastery is not universal. Jane offers help, and Rochester, leaning, on her shoulder, admits that "necessity compels me to make you useful." Later, remembering the scene, he confesses that he too had seen the meeting as a mythic one, though from a perspective entirely other than Jane's. "When you came on me in Hay Lane last night, I ... had half a mind to demand whether you had bewitched my horse" (chap. 13). Significantly, his playful remark acknowledges *her* powers just as much as (if not more than) her vision of the Gytrash acknowledged *his*. Thus, though in one sense Jane and Rochester begin their relationship as master and servant, prince and Cinderella, Mr. B. and Pamela, in another they begin as spiritual equals.

As the episode unfolds, their equality is emphasized in other scenes as well. For instance, though Rochester imperiously orders Jane to "resume your seat, and answer my questions" while he looks at her drawings, his response to the pictures reveals not only his own Byronic broodings, but his consciousness of hers. "Those eyes in the Evening Star you must have seen in a dream.... And who taught you to paint wind? ... Where did you see Latmos?" (chap. 13). Though such talk would bewilder most of Rochester's other dependents, it is a breath of life to Jane, who begins to fall in love with him not because he is her master but in spite of the fact that he is, not because he is princely in manner, but because, being in some sense her equal, he is the only qualified critic of her art and soul.

Their subsequent encounters develop their equality in even more complex ways. Rudely urged to entertain Rochester, Jane smiles "not a very complacent or submissive smile," obliging her employer to explain that "the fact is, once for all, I don't wish to treat you like an inferior ... I claim only such superiority as must result from twenty years difference in age and a century's advance in experience" (chap. 14). Moreover, his long account of his adventure with Céline—an account which, incidentally, struck many Victorian readers as totally improper, coming from a dissipated older man to a virginal young governess[19]—emphasizes, at least superficially, not his superiority to Jane but his sense of equality with her. Both Jane and Charlotte Brontë correctly recognize this point, which subverts those Victorian charges: "The ease of his manner," Jane comments, "freed me from painful restraint; the friendly frankness ... with which he treated me, drew me to him. *I felt at [these] times as if he were my relation rather than my master*" (chap. 15 [ital. ours]). For of course, despite critical suspicions that Rochester is seducing Jane in these scenes, he is, on the contrary, solacing himself with her unseduceable independence in a world of self-marketing Cèlines and Blanches.

His need for her strength and parity is made clearer soon enough—on, for instance, the occasion when she rescues him from his burning bed (an almost fatally symbolic plight), and later on the occasion when she helps him rescue Richard Mason from the wounds inflicted by "Grace Poole." And that these rescues are facilitated by Jane's and Rochester's mutual sense of equality is made clearest of all in the scene in which only Jane of all the "young ladies" at Thornfield fails to be deceived by Rochester in his gypsy costume: "With the ladies you must have managed well," she comments, but "You did not act the character of a gypsy with me" (chap. 19). The implication is that he did not—or could not—because he respects "the resolute, wild, free thing looking out of" Jane's eyes as much as she herself does, and understands that just as he can see beyond her everyday disguise as plain Jane the governess, she can see beyond his temporary disguise as a gypsy fortune-teller—or his daily disguise as Rochester the master of Thornfield.

This last point is made again, most explicitly, by the passionate avowals of their first betrothal scene. Beginning with similar attempts at disguise and deception on Rochester's part ("One can't have too much of such a very excellent thing as my beautiful Blanche") that encounter causes Jane in a moment of despair and ire to strip away her own disguises in her most famous assertion of her own integrity:

> "Do you think, because I am poor, obscure, plain, and little, I am soulless and heartless? You think wrong!—I have as much soul as you,—and full as much heart! And if God had gifted me with some beauty, and much wealth, I should have made it as hard for you to leave me, as it is now for me to leave you. I am not talking to you now through the medium of custom, conventionalities, or even of mortal flesh:—it is my spirit that addresses your spirit; just as if both had passed through the grave, and we stood at God's feet equal,—as we are!" [chap. 23]

Rochester's response is another casting away of disguises, a confession that he has deceived her about Blanche, and an acknowledgment of their parity and similarity: "My bride is here," he admits, "because my *equal* is here, and my *likeness*." The energy informing both speeches is, significantly, not so much sexual as spiritual; the impropriety of its formulation is, as Mrs. Rigby saw, not moral but political, for Charlotte Brontë appears here to have imagined a world in which the prince and Cinderella are democratically equal, Pamela is just as good as Mr. B., master and servant are profoundly alike. And to the marriage of such true minds, it seems, no man or woman can admit impediment.

But of course, as we know, there is an impediment, and that impediment, paradoxically, pre-exists in both Rochester and Jane, despite their avowals of equality. Though Rochester, for instance, appears in both the gypsy sequence and the betrothal scene to have cast away the disguises that gave him his mastery, it is obviously of some importance that those disguises were necessary in the first place. Why, Jane herself wonders, does Rochester have to trick people, especially women? What secrets are concealed behind the charades he enacts? One answer is surely that he himself senses his trickery is a source of power, and therefore, in Jane's case at least, an evasion of that equality in which he claims to believe. Beyond this, however, it is clear that the secrets Rochester is concealing or disguising throughout much of the book are themselves in Jane's—and Charlotte Brontë's—view secrets of inequality.

The first of these is suggested both by his name, apparently an allusion to the dissolute Earl of Rochester, and by Jane's own reference to the Bluebeard's corridor of the third story: it is the secret of masculine potency, the secret of male sexual guilt. For, like those pre-Byron Byronic heroes the real Restoration Rochester and the mythic Bluebeard (indeed, in relation to Jane, like any experienced adult male), Rochester has specific and "guilty" sexual knowledge which makes him in some sense her "superior." Though this point may seem to contradict the point made earlier about his frankness to Jane, it really should not. Rochester's apparently improper recounting of his sexual adventures *is* a kind of acknowledgment of Jane's equality with him. His possession of the hidden details of sexuality, however—his knowledge, that is, of the *secret* of sex, symbolized both by his doll-like daughter Adèle and by the locked doors of the third story behind which mad Bertha crouches like an animal—qualifies and undermines that equality. And though his puzzling transvestism, his attempt to impersonate a *female* gypsy, may be seen as a semi-conscious effort to reduce this sexual advantage his masculinity gives him (by putting on a woman's clothes he puts on a woman's weakness), both he and Jane obviously recognize the hollowness of such a ruse. The prince is inevitably Cinderella's superior, Charlotte Brontë saw, not because his rank is higher than hers, but because it is *he* who will initiate *her* into the mysteries of the flesh.

That both Jane and Rochester are in some part of themselves conscious of the barrier which Rochester's sexual knowledge poses to their equality is further indicated by the tensions that develop in their relationship after their betrothal. Rochester, having secured Jane's love, almost reflexively begins to treat her as an inferior, a plaything, a virginal possession—for she has now become his initiate, his "mustard-seed," his "little sunny-faced ... girl-bride." "It is your time now, little tyrant," he declares, "but it will be mine presently: and when once I have fairly seized you, to have and to hold, I'll just— figuratively speaking—attach you to a chain like this" (chap. 24). She, sensing his new sense of power, resolves to keep him "in reasonable check": "I never can bear being dressed like a doll by Mr. Rochester," she remarks, and, more significantly, "I'll not stand you an inch in the stead of a seraglio.... I'll [prepare myself] to go out as a missionary to preach liberty to them that are enslaved" (chap. 24). While such assertions have seemed to some critics merely the consequences of Jane's (and Charlotte Brontë's) sexual panic, it should be clear from their context that, as is usual with Jane, they are political rather than sexual statements, attempts at finding emotional strength rather than expressions of weakness.

Finally, Rochester's ultimate secret, the secret that is revealed together with the existence of Bertha, the literal impediment to his marriage with Jane, is another and perhaps most surprising secret of inequality: but this time the hidden facts suggest the master's inferiority rather than his superiority. Rochester, Jane learns, after the aborted wedding ceremony, had married Bertha Mason for status, for sex, for money, for everything but love and equality. "Oh, I have no respect for myself when I think of that act!" he confesses. "An agony of inward contempt masters me. I never loved, I never esteemed, I did not even know her" (chap. 27). And his statement reminds us of Jane's earlier assertion of her own superiority: "I would scorn such a union [as the loveless one he hints he will enter into with Blanche]: therefore I am better than you" (chap. 23). In a sense, then, the most serious crime Rochester has to expiate is not even the crime of exploiting others but the sin of self-exploitation, the sin of Céline and Blanche, to which he, at least, had seemed completely immune.[20]

That Rochester's character and life pose in themselves such substantial impediments to his marriage with Jane does not mean, however, that Jane herself generates none. For one thing, "akin" as she is to Rochester, she suspects him of harboring all the secrets we know he does harbor, and raises defenses against them, manipulating her "master" so as to keep him "in reasonable check." In a larger way, moreover, all the charades and masquerades—the secret messages—of patriarchy have had their effect upon her. Though she loves Rochester the man, Jane has doubts about Rochester the husband even before she learns about Bertha. In her world, she senses, even the equality of love between true minds leads to the inequalities and minor despotisms of marriage. "For a little while," she says cynically to Rochester, "you will perhaps be as you are now, [but] ... I suppose your love will effervesce in six months, or less. I have observed in books written by men, that period assigned as the farthest to which a husband's ardor extends" (chap. 24). He, of course, vigorously repudiates this prediction, but his argument—"Jane: you please me, and you master me, [because] you seem to submit"—implies a kind of Lawrentian sexual tension and only makes things worse. For when he asks "Why do you smile [at this], Jane? What does that inexplicable ... turn of countenance mean?" her peculiar, ironic smile, reminiscent of Bertha's mirthless laugh, signals an "involuntary" and subtly hostile thought "of Hercules and Samson with their charmers." And that hostility becomes overt at the silk warehouse, where Jane notes that "the more he bought me, the more my cheek burned with a sense of annoyance and degradation.... I thought his smile was such as a sultan might; in a blissful and fond moment, bestow on a slave his gold and gems had enriched" (chap. 24).

Jane's whole life-pilgrimage has, of course, prepared her to be angry in this way at Rochester's, and society's, concept of marriage. Rochester's loving tyranny recalls John Reed's unloving despotism, and the erratic nature of Rochester's favors ("in my secret soul I knew that his great kindness to me was balanced by unjust severity to many others" [chap. 15]) recalls Brocklehurst's hypocrisy. But even the dreamlike paintings that Jane produced early in her stay at Thornfield—art works which brought her as close to her "master" as Helen Graham (in *The Tenant of Wildfell Hall*) was to hers—functioned ambiguously, like Helen's, to predict strains in this relationship even while they seemed to be conventional Romantic fantasies. The first represented a drowned female corpse; the second a sort of avenging mother goddess rising (like Bertha Mason Rochester or *Frankenstein's* monster) in "electric travail" (chap. 13); and the third a terrible paternal specter carefully designed to recall Milton's sinister image of Death. Indeed, this last, says Jane, quoting *Paradise Lost*, delineates "the shape which shape had none," the patriarchal shadow implicit even in the Father-hating gloom of hell.

Given such shadowings and foreshadowings, then, it is no wonder that as Jane's anger and fear about her marriage intensify, she begins to be symbolically drawn back into her own past, and specifically to reexperience the dangerous sense of doubleness that had begun in the red-room. The first sign that this is happening is the powerfully depicted, recurrent dream of a child she begins to have as she drifts into a romance with her master. She tells us that she was awakened "from companionship with this baby-phantom" on the night Bertha attacked Richard Mason, and the next day she is literally called back into the past, back to Gateshead to see the dying Mrs. Reed, who reminds her again of what she once was and potentially still is: "Are you Jane Eyre? ... I declare she talked to me once like something mad, or like a fiend" (chap. 21). Even more significantly, the phantom-child reappears in two dramatic dreams Jane has on the night before her wedding eve, during which she experiences "a strange regretful consciousness of some barrier dividing" her from Rochester. In the first, "burdened" with the small wailing creature, she is "following the windings of an unknown road" in cold rainy weather, straining to catch up with her future husband but unable to reach him. In the second, she is walking among the ruins of Thornfield, still carrying "the unknown little child" and still following Rochester; as he disappears around "an angle in the road," she tells him, "I bent forward to take a last look; the wall crumbled; I was shaken; the child rolled from my knee, I lost my balance, fell, and woke" (chap. 25).

What are we to make of these strange dreams, or—as Jane would call them—these "presentiments"? To begin with, it seems clear that the wailing child who appears in all of them corresponds to "the poor orphan child" of Bessie's song at Gateshead, and therefore to the child Jane herself, the wailing Cinderella whose pilgrimage began in anger and despair. That child's complaint—"My feet they are sore, and my limbs they are weary;/ Long is the way, and the mountains are wild"—is still Jane's, or at least the complaint of that part of her which resists a marriage of inequality. And though consciously Jane wishes to be rid of the heavy problem her orphan self presents, "I might not lay it down anywhere, however tired were my arms, however much its weight impeded my progress." In other words, until she reaches the goal of her pilgrimage—maturity, independence, true equality with Rochester (and therefore in a sense with the rest of the world)—she is doomed to carry her orphaned alter ego everywhere. The burden of the past cannot be sloughed off so easily—not, for instance, by glamorous lovemaking, silk dresses, jewelry, a new name. Jane's "strange regretful consciousness of a barrier" dividing her from Rochester is, thus, a keen though disguised intuition of a problem she herself will pose.

Almost more interesting than the nature of the child image, however, is the *predictive* aspect of the last of the child dreams, the one about the ruin of Thornfield. As Jane correctly foresees, Thornfield *will* within a year become "a dreary ruin, the retreat of bats and owls." Have her own subtle and not-so-subtle hostilities to its master any connection with the catastrophe that is to befall the house? Is her clairvoyant dream in some sense a vision of wishfulfilment? And why, specifically, is she freed from the burden of the wailing child at the moment *she* falls from Thornfield's ruined wall?

The answer to all these questions is closely related to events which follow upon the child dream. For the apparition of a child in these crucial weeks preceding her marriage is only one symptom of a dissolution of personality Jane seems to be experiencing at this time, a fragmentation of the self comparable to her "syncope" in the red-room. Another symptom appears early in the chapter that begins, anxiously, "there was no putting off the day that advanced—the bridal day" (chap. 25). It is her witty but nervous speculation about the nature of "one Jane Rochester, a person whom as yet I knew not," though "in yonder closet ... garments *said* to be hers had already displaced [mine]: *for not to me appertained that ... strange wraith-like apparel*" (chap. 25 [ital. ours]). Again, a third symptom appears on the morning of her wedding: she turns toward the mirror and sees "a robed and veiled figure, so unlike my usual self that it seemed almost the image of a stranger" (chap. 26), reminding us of the moment in the red-room when all had "seemed colder and darker in that visionary hollow" of the looking glass "than in reality." In view of this frightening series of separations within the self—Jane Eyre splitting off from Jane Rochester, the child Jane splitting off from the adult Jane, and the image of Jane weirdly separating from the body of Jane—it is not surprising that another and most mysterious specter, a sort of "vampyre," should appear in the middle of the night to rend and trample the wedding veil of that unknown person, Jane Rochester.

Literally, of course, the nighttime specter is none other than Bertha Mason Rochester. But on a figurative and psychological level it seems suspiciously clear that the specter of Bertha is still another—indeed the most threatening—avatar of Jane. What Bertha now *does*, for instance, is what Jane wants to do. Disliking the "vapoury veil" of Jane Rochester, Jane Eyre secretly wants to tear the garments up. Bertha does it for her. Fearing the inexorable "bridal day," Jane would like to put it off. Bertha does that for her too. Resenting the new mastery of Rochester, whom she sees as "*dread* but adored," (ital. ours), she wishes to be his equal in size and strength, so that she can battle him in the contest of their marriage. Bertha, "a big woman, in stature almost equalling her husband," has the necessary "virile force" (chap. 26). Bertha, in other words, is Jane's truest and darkest double: she is the angry aspect of the orphan child, the ferocious secret self Jane has been trying to repress ever since her days at Gateshead. For, as Claire Rosenfeld points out, "the novelist who consciously or unconsciously exploits psychological Doubles" frequently juxtaposes "two characters, the one representing the socially acceptable or conventional personality, the other externalizing the free, uninhibited, often criminal self."[21]

It is only fitting, then, that the existence of this criminal self imprisoned in Thornfield's attic is the ultimate legal impediment to Jane's and Rochester's marriage, and that its existence is, paradoxically, an impediment raised by Jane as well as by Rochester. For it now begins to appear, if it did not earlier, that Bertha has functioned as Jane's dark double *throughout* the governess's stay at Thornfield. Specifically, every one of Bertha's appearances—or, more accurately, her manifestations—has been associated with an experience (or repression) of anger on Jane's part. Jane's feelings of "hunger, rebellion, and rage" on the battlements, for instance, were accompanied by Bertha's "low, slow ha! ha!" and "eccentric murmurs." Jane's apparently secure response to Rochester's apparently egalitarian sexual confidences was followed by Bertha's attempt to incinerate the master in his bed. Jane's unexpressed resentment at Rochester's manipulative gypsy-masquerade found expression in Bertha's terrible shriek and her even more terrible attack on Richard Mason. Jane's anxieties about her marriage, and in particular her fears of her own alien "robed and veiled" bridal image, were objectified by the image of Bertha in a "white and straight" dress, "whether gown, sheet, or shroud I cannot tell." Jane's profound desire to destroy Thornfield, the symbol of Rochester's mastery and of her own servitude, will be acted out by Bertha, who burns down the house and destroys *herself* in the process as if she were an agent of Jane's desire as well as her own. And finally, Jane's disguised hostility to Rochester, summarized in her terrifying prediction to herself that "you shall, yourself, pluck out your right eye; yourself cut off your right hand" (chap. 27) comes strangely true through the intervention of Bertha, whose melodramatic death causes Rochester to lose both eye and hand.

These parallels between Jane and Bertha may at first seem somewhat strained. Jane, after all, is poor, plain, little, pale, neat, and quiet, while Bertha is rich, large, florid, sensual, and extravagant; indeed, she was once even beautiful, somewhat, Rochester notes, "in the style of Blanche Ingram." Is she not, then, as many critics have suggested, a monitory image rather than a double for Jane? As Richard Chase puts it, "May not Bertha, Jane seems to ask herself, be a living example of what happens to the woman who [tries] to be the fleshly vessel of the [masculine] *élan*?"[22] "Just as [Jane's] instinct for self-preservation saves her from earlier temptations," Adrienne Rich remarks, "so it must save her from becoming this woman by curbing her imagination at the limits of what is bearable for a powerless woman in the England of the 1840s."[23] Even Rochester himself provides a similar critical appraisal of the relationship between the two. "That is *my wife*," he says, pointing to mad Bertha,

> "And *this* is what I wished to have ... this young girl who stands so grave and quiet at the mouth of hell, looking collectedly at the gambols of a demon. I wanted her just as a change after that fierce ragout.... Compare these clear eyes with the red balls yonder—this face with that mask—this form with that bulk...." [chap. 26]

And of course, in one sense, the relationship between Jane and Bertha is a monitory one: while acting out Jane's secret fantasies, Bertha does (to say the least) provide the governess with an example of how not to act, teaching her a lesson more salutary than any Miss Temple ever taught.

Nevertheless, it is disturbingly clear from recurrent images in the novel that Bertha not only acts *for* Jane, she also acts *like* Jane. The imprisoned Bertha, running "backwards and forwards" on all fours in the attic, for instance, recalls not only Jane the governess, whose only relief from mental pain was to pace "backwards and forwards" in the third story, but also that "bad animal" who was ten-year-old Jane, imprisoned in the red-room, howling and mad. Bertha's "goblin appearance"—"half dream, half reality," says Rochester—recalls the lover's epithets for Jane: "malicious elf," "sprite," "changeling," as well as his playful accusation that she had magically downed his horse at their first meeting. Rochester's description of Bertha as a "monster" ("a fearful voyage I had with such a monster in the vessel" [chap. 27]) ironically echoes Jane's own fear of being a monster ("Am I a monster? ... is it impossible that Mr. Rochester should have a sincere affection for me?" [chap. 24]). Bertha's fiendish madness recalls Mrs. Reed's remark about Jane ("she talked to me once like something mad or like a fiend") as well as Jane's own estimate of her mental state ("I will hold to the principles received by me when I was sane, and not mad—as I am now [chap. 27]"). And most dramatic of all, Bertha's incendiary tendencies recall Jane's early flaming rages, at Lowood and at Gateshead, as well as that "ridge of lighted heath" which she herself saw as emblematic of her mind in its rebellion against society. It is only fitting, therefore, that, as if to balance the child Jane's terrifying vision of herself as an alien figure in the "visionary hollow" of the red-room looking glass, the adult Jane first clearly perceives her terrible double when Bertha puts on the wedding veil intended for the second Mrs. Rochester, and turns to the mirror. At that moment, Jane sees "the reflection of the visage and features quite distinctly in the dark oblong glass," sees them as if they were her own (chap. 25).

For despite all the habits of harmony she gained in her years at Lowood, we must finally recognize, with Jane herself, that on her arrival at Thornfield she only "*appeared* a disciplined and subdued character" [ital. ours]. Crowned with thorns, finding that she is, in Emily Dickinson's words, "The Wife—without the Sign,"[24] she represses her rage behind a subdued facade, but her soul's impulse to dance "like a Bomb, abroad," to quote Dickinson again,[25] has not been exorcised and will not be exorcised until the literal and symbolic death of Bertha frees her from the furies that torment her and makes possible a marriage of equality—makes possible, that is, wholeness within herself. At that point, significantly, when the Bertha in Jane falls from the ruined wall of Thornfield and is destroyed, the orphan child too, as her dream predicts, will roll from her knee—the burden of her past will be lifted—and she will wake. In the meantime, as Rochester says, "never was anything at once so frail and so indomitable ... consider the resolute wild free thing looking out of [Jane's] eye.... Whatever I do with its cage, I cannot get at it—the savage, beautiful creature" (chap. 27).

That the pilgrimage of this "savage, beautiful creature" must now necessarily lead her away from Thornfield is signalled, like many other events in the novel, by the rising of the moon, which accompanies a reminiscent dream of the red-room. Unjustly imprisoned now, as she was then, in one of the traps a patriarchal society provides for outcast Cinderellas, Jane realizes that this time she must escape through deliberation rather than through madness. The maternal moon, admonishing her ("My daughter, flee temptation!") appears to be "a white human form ... inclining a glorious brow," a strengthening image, as Adrienne Rich suggests, of the Great Mother.[26] Yet—"profoundly, imperiously, archetypal"[27]—this figure has its ambiguities, just as Jane's own personality does, for the last night on which Jane watched such a moon rise was the night Bertha attacked Richard Mason, and the juxtaposition of the two events on that occasion was almost shockingly suggestive:

> [The moon's] glorious gaze roused me. Awaking in the dead of night, I opened my eyes on her disk.... It was beautiful, but too solemn: I half rose, and stretched my arm to draw the curtain.
>   Good God! What a cry! [chap. 20]

Now, as Jane herself recognizes, the moon has elicited from her an act as violent and self-assertive as Bertha's on that night. "What was I?" she thinks, as she steals away from Thornfield. "I had injured—wounded—left my master. I was hateful in my own eyes" (chap. 28). Yet, though her escape may seem as morally ambiguous as the moon's message, it is necessary for her own self-preservation. And soon, like Bertha, she is "crawling forwards on my hands and knees, and then again raised to my feet—as eager and determined as ever to reach the road."

Her wanderings on that road are a symbolic summary of those wanderings of the poor orphan child which constitute her entire life's pilgrimage. For, like Jane's dreams, Bessie's song was an uncannily accurate prediction of things to come. "Why did they send me so far and so lonely,/Up where the moors spread and grey rocks are piled?" Far and lonely indeed Jane wanders, starving, freezing, stumbling, abandoning her few possessions, her name, and even her self-respect in her search for a new home. For "men are hard-hearted, and kind angels only / Watch'd o'er the steps of a poor orphan child." And like the starved wanderings of Hetty Sorel in *Adam Bede*, her terrible journey across the moors suggests the essential homelessness—the nameless, placeless, and contingent status—of women in a patriarchal society. Yet because Jane, unlike Hetty, has an inner strength which her pilgrimage seeks to develop, "kind angels" finally do bring her to what is in a sense her true home, the house significantly called *Marsh End* (or Moor House) which is to represent the end of her march toward selfhood. Here she encounters Diana, Mary, and St. John Rivers, the "good" relatives who will help free her from her angry memories of that wicked stepfamily the Reeds. And that the Rivers prove to be literally her relatives is not, in psychological terms, the strained coincidence some readers have suggested. For having left Rochester, having torn off the crown of thorns he offered and repudiated the unequal charade of marriage he proposed, Jane has now gained the strength to begin to discover her real place in the world. St. John helps her find a job in a school, and once again she reviews the choices she has had: "Is it better, I ask, to be a slave in a fool's paradise at Marseilles ... or to be a village schoolmistress, free and honest, in a breezy mountain nook in the healthy heart of England?" (chap. 31). Her unequivocal conclusion that "I was right when I adhered to principle and law" is one toward which the whole novel seems to have tended.

The qualifying word *seems* is, however, a necessary one. For though in one sense Jane's discovery of her family at Marsh End does represent the end of her pilgrimage, her progress toward selfhood will not be complete until she learns that "principle and law" in the abstract do not always coincide with the deepest principles and laws of her own being. Her early sense that Miss Temple's teachings had merely been superimposed on her native vitality had already begun to suggest this to her. But it is through her encounter with St. John Rivers that she assimilates this lesson most thoroughly. As a number of critics have noticed, all three members of the Rivers family have resonant, almost allegorical names. The names of Jane's true "sisters," Diana and Mary, notes Adrienne Rich, recall the Great Mother in her dual aspects of Diana the huntress and Mary the virgin mother;[28] in this way, as well as through their independent, learned, benevolent personalities, they suggest the ideal of female strength for which Jane has been searching. St. John, on the other hand, has an almost blatantly patriarchal name, one which recalls both the masculine abstraction of the gospel according to St. John ("in the beginning was the *Word*") and the disguised misogyny of St. John the Baptist, whose patristic and evangelical contempt for the flesh manifested itself most powerfully in a profound contempt for the *female*. Like Salome, whose rebellion against such misogyny Oscar Wilde was later also to associate with the rising moon of female power, Jane must symbolically, if not literally, behead the abstract principles of this man before she can finally achieve her true independence.

At first, however, it seems that St. John is offering Jane a viable alternative to the way of life proposed by Rochester. For where Rochester, like his dissolute namesake, ended up appearing to offer a life of pleasure, a path of roses (albeit with concealed thorns), and a marriage of passion, St. John seems to propose a life of principle, a path of thorns (with no concealed roses), and a marriage of spirituality. His self-abnegating rejection of the worldly beauty Rosamund Oliver—another character with a strikingly resonant name—is disconcerting to the passionate and Byronic part of Jane, but at least it shows that, unlike hypocritical Brocklehurst, he practices what he preaches. And what he preaches is the Carlylean sermon of self-actualization through work: "Work while it is called today, for the night cometh wherein no man can work."[29] If she follows him, Jane realizes, she will substitute a divine Master for the master she served at Thornfield, and replace love with labor—for "you are formed for labour, not for love," St. John tells her. Yet when, long ago at Lowood, she asked for "a new servitude" was not some such solution half in her mind? When, pacing the battlements at Thornfield she insisted that "women [need] a field for their efforts as much as their brothers do" (chap. 12), did she not long for some such practical "exercise"? "Still will my Father with promise and blessing, /Take to his bosom the poor orphaned child," Bessie's song had predicted. Is not Marsh End, then, the promised end, and St. John's way the way to His bosom?

Jane's early repudiation of the spiritual harmonies offered by Helen Burns and Miss Temple is the first hint that, while St. John's way will tempt her, she must resist it. That, like Rochester, he is "akin" to her is clear. But where Rochester represents the fire of her nature, her cousin represents the ice. And while for some women ice may "suffice," for Jane, who has struggled all her life, like a sane version of Bertha, against the polar cold of a loveless world, it clearly will not. As she falls more deeply under St. John's "freezing spell," she realizes increasingly that to please him "I must disown half my nature." And "as his wife," she reflects, she would be "always restrained ... forced to keep the fire of my nature continually low, ... though the imprisoned flame consumed vital after vital" (chap. 34). In fact, as St. John's wife and "the sole helpmate [he] can influence efficiently in life, and retain absolutely till death" (chap. 34), she will be entering into a union even more unequal than that proposed by Rochester, a marriage reflecting, once again, her absolute exclusion from the life of wholeness toward which her pilgrimage has been directed. For despite the integrity of principle that distinguishes him from Brocklehurst, despite his likeness to "the warrior Greatheart, who guards his pilgrim convoy from the onslaught of Apollyon" (chap. 38), St. John is finally, as Brocklehurst was, a pillar of patriarchy, "a cold cumbrous column" (chap. 34). But where Brocklehurst had removed Jane from the imprisonment of Gateshead only to immure her in a dank valley of starvation, and even Rochester had tried to make her the "slave of passion," St. John wants to imprison the "resolute wild free thing" that is her soul in the ultimate cell, the "iron shroud" of principle (chap. 34).

Though in many ways St. John's attempt to "imprison" Jane may seem the most irresistible of all, coming as it does at a time when she is congratulating herself on just that adherence to "principle and law" which he recommends, she escapes from his fetters more easily than she had escaped from either Brocklehurst or Rochester. Figuratively speaking, this is a measure of how far she has traveled in her pilgrimage toward maturity. Literally, however, her escape is facilitated by two events. First, having found what is, despite all its ambiguities, her true family, Jane has at last come into her inheritance. Jane Eyre is now the heir of that uncle in Madeira whose first intervention in her life had been, appropriately, to define the legal impediment to her marriage with Rochester, now literally as well as figuratively an independent woman, free to go her own way and follow her own will. But her freedom is also signaled by a second event: the death of Bertha.

Her first "presentiment" of that event comes, dramatically, as an answer to a prayer for guidance. St. John is pressing her to reach a decision about his proposal of marriage. Believing that "I had now put love out of the question, and thought only of duty," she "entreats Heaven" to "Show me, show me the path." As always at major moments in Jane's life, the room is filled with moonlight, as if to remind her that powerful forces are still at work both without and within her. And now, because such forces are operating, she at last hears—she is receptive to—the bodiless cry of Rochester: "Jane! Jane! Jane!" Her response is an immediate act of self-assertion. "I broke from St. John.... It was *my* time to assume ascendancy. *My* powers were in play and in force" (chap. 35). But her sudden forcefulness, like her "presentiment" itself, is the climax of all that has gone before. Her new and apparently telepathic communion with Rochester, which many critics have seen as needlessly melodramatic, has been made possible by her new independence and Rochester's new humility. The plot device of the cry is merely a sign that the relationship for which both lovers had always longed is now possible, a sign that Jane's metaphoric speech of the first betrothal scene has been translated into reality: "my spirit ... addresses your spirit, just as if both had passed through the grave, and we stood at God's feet, equal—as we are!" (chap. 23). For to the marriage of Jane's and Rochester's true minds there is now, as Jane unconsciously guesses, no impediment.

Jane's return to Thornfield, her discovery of Bertha's death and of the ruin her dream had predicted, her reunion at Ferndean with the maimed and blinded Rochester, and their subsequent marriage form an essential epilogue to that pilgrimage toward selfhood which had in other ways concluded at Marsh End, with Jane's realization that she could not marry St. John. At that moment, "the wondrous shock of feeling had come like the earthquake which shook the foundations of Paul and Silas' prison; it had opened the doors of the soul's cell, and loosed its bands—it had wakened it out of its sleep" (chap. 36). For at that moment she had been irrevocably freed from the burden of her past, freed both from the raging specter of Bertha (which had already fallen in fact from the ruined wall of Thornfield) and from the self-pitying specter of the orphan child (which had symbolically, as in her dream, rolled from her knee). And at that moment, again as in her dream, she had *wakened* to her own self, her own needs. Similarly, Rochester, "caged eagle" that he seems (chap. 37), has been freed from what was for him the burden of Thornfield, though at the same time he appears to have been fettered by the injuries he received in attempting to rescue Jane's mad double from the flames devouring his house. That his "fetters" pose no impediment to a new marriage, that he and Jane are now, in reality, equals, is the thesis of the Ferndean section.

Many critics, starting with Richard Chase, have seen Rochester's injuries as "a symbolic castration," a punishment for his early profligacy and a sign that Charlotte Brontë (as well as Jane herself), fearing male sexual power, can only imagine marriage as a union with a diminished Samson. "The tempo and energy of the universe can be quelled, we see, by a patient, practical woman," notes Chase ironically.[30] And there is an element of truth in this idea. The angry Bertha in Jane *had* wanted to punish Rochester, to burn him in his bed, destroy his house, cut off his hand and pluck out his overmastering "full falcon eye." Smiling enigmatically, she had thought of "Hercules and Samson, with their charmers."

It had not been her goal, however, to quell "the tempo and energy of the universe," but simply to strengthen herself, to make herself an equal of the world Rochester represents. And surely another important symbolic point is implied by the lovers' reunion at Ferndean: when both were physically whole they could not, in a sense, *see* each other because of the social disguises—master/servant, prince/Cinderella—blinding them, but now that those disguises have been shed, now that they are equals, they can (though one is blind) see and speak even beyond the medium of the flesh. Apparently sightless, Rochester—in the tradition of blinded Gloucester—now sees more clearly than he did when as a "mole-eyed blockhead" he married Bertha Mason (chap. 27). Apparently mutilated, he is paradoxically stronger than he was when he ruled Thornfield, for now, like Jane, he draws his powers from within himself, rather than from inequity, disguise, deception. Then, at Thornfield, he was "no better than the old lightning-struck chestnut tree in the orchard," whose ruin foreshadowed the catastrophe of his relationship with Jane. Now, as Jane tells him, he is "green and vigorous Plants will grow about your roots whether you ask them or not" (chap. 37). And now, being equals, he and Jane can afford to depend upon each other with no fear of one exploiting the other.

Nevertheless, despite the optimistic portrait of an egalitarian relationship that Brontë seems to be drawing here, there is "a quiet autumnal quality" about the scenes at Ferndean, as Robert Bernard Martin points out.[31] The house itself, set deep in a dark forest, is old and decaying: Rochester had not even thought it suitable for the loathsome Bertha, and its valley-of-the-shadow quality makes it seem rather like a Lowood, a school of life where Rochester must learn those lessons Jane herself absorbed so early. As a dramatic setting, moreover, Ferndean is notably stripped and asocial, so that the physical isolation of the lovers suggests their spiritual isolation in a world where such egalitarian marriages as theirs are rare, if not impossible. True minds, Charlotte Brontë seems to be saying, must withdraw into a remote forest, a wilderness even, in order to circumvent the strictures of a hierarchal society.

Does Brontë's rebellious feminism—that "irreligious" dissatisfaction with the social order noted by Miss Rigby and *Jane Eyre's* other Victorian critics—compromise itself in this withdrawal? Has Jane exorcised the rage of orphanhood only to retreat from the responsibilities her own principles implied? Tentative answers to these questions can be derived more easily from *The Professor, Shirley*, and *Villette* than from *Jane Eyre*, for the qualified and even (as in Villette) indecisive endings of Brontë's other novels suggest that she herself was unable clearly to envision viable solutions to the problem of patriarchal oppression. In all her books, writing (as we have seen) in a sort of trance, she was able to act out that passionate drive toward freedom which offended agents of the status quo, but in none was she able consciously to define the full meaning of achieved freedom—perhaps because no one of her contemporaries, not even a Wollstonecraft or a Mill, could adequately describe a society so drastically altered that the matured Jane and Rochester could really live in it.

What Brontë could not logically define, however, she could embody in tenuous but suggestive imagery and in her last, perhaps most significant redefinitions of Bunyan. Nature in the largest sense seems now to be on the side of Jane and Rochester. *Ferndean*, as its name implies, is without artifice— "no flowers, no garden-beds"—but it is green as Jane tells Rochester he will be, green and ferny and fertilized by soft rains. Here, isolated from society but flourishing in a natural order of their own making, Jane and Rochester will become physically "bone of [each other's] bone, flesh of [each other's] flesh" (chap. 38), and here the healing powers of nature will eventually restore the sight of one of Rochester's eyes. Here, in other words, nature, unleashed from social restrictions, will do "no miracle—but her best" (chap. 35). For not the Celestial City but a natural paradise, the country of Beculah "upon the borders of heaven," where "the contract between bride and bridegroom [is] renewed," has all along been, we now realize, the goal of Jane's pilgrimage.[32]

As for the Celestial City itself, Charlotte Brontë implies here (though she will later have second thoughts) that such a goal is the dream of those who accept inequities on earth, one of the many tools used by patriarchal society to keep, say, governesses in their "place." Because she believes this so deeply, she quite consciously concludes *Jane Eyre* with an allusion to *Pilgrim's Progress* and with a half-ironic apostrophe to that apostle of celestial transcendence, that shadow of "the warrior Greatheart," St. John Rivers. "His," she tells us, "is the exaction of the apostle, who speaks but for Christ when he says—'Whosoever will come after me, let him deny himself and take up his cross and follow me'" (chap. 38). For it was, finally, to repudiate such a crucifying denial of the self that Brontë's "hunger, rebellion, and rage" led her to write *Jane Eyre* in the first place and to make it an "irreligious" redefinition, almost a parody, of John Bunyan's vision.[33] And the astounding progress toward equality of plain Jane Eyre, whom Miss Rigby correctly saw as "the personification of an unregenerate and undisciplined spirit," answers by its outcome the bitter question Emily Dickinson was to ask fifteen years later: "'My husband—women say—/Stroking the Melody—/Is *this*—the way?'"[34] No, Jane declares in her flight from Thornfield, *that* is not the way. *This*, she says—this marriage of true minds at Ferndean—this is the way. Qualified and isolated as her way may be, it is at least an emblem of hope. Certainly Charlotte Brontë was never again to indulge in quite such an optimistic imagining.

NOTES

Epigraphs: Moments of Being (New York: Harcourt Brace Jovanovich, 1977), p. 69; *Good Morning, Midnight* (New York: Vintage, 1974), p. 52; *Poems*, J. 410.

1. Matthew Arnold, *Letters of Matthew Arnold*, ed. George W. E. Russell (New York and London: Macmillan, 1896), 1:34.

2. Matthew Arnold, *The Letters of Matthew Arnold to Arthur Hugh Cloguh*, ed. Howard Foster Lowry (London and New York: Oxford University Press, 1932), p. 132.

3. Significantly, in view of comments by other contemporary critics, Arnold added in the same letter that "Religion or devotion or whatever it is to be called may be impossible for such people now: but they have at any rate not found a substitute for it, and it was better for the world when they comforted themselves with it." It should of course be noted, however, that *Jane Eyre* (like *Villette*) was warmly praised by many reviewers, usually for what George Henry Lewes, writing in *Fraser's Magazine* 36 (December 1847), called its "deep, significant reality."

4. *Quarterly Review* 84 (December 1848): 173–74.

5. *The Christian Remembrancer* 25 (June 1853): 423–43.

6. *Blackwood's Magazine* 77 (May 1855): 554–68.

7. Richard Chase, "The Brontës, or Myth Domesticated," in *Jane Eyre*, ed. Richard J. Dunn (New York: Norton, 1971), pp. 468 and 464.

8. *Quarterly Review* 84 (December 1848): 173–74. That Charlotte Brontë was herself quite conscious of the "revolutionary" nature of many of her ideas is clearly indicated by the fact that, as we shall see, she puts some of Miss Rigby's words into the mouth unpleasant and supercilious Miss Hardman in *Shirley*.

9. All references to *Jane Eyre* are to the Norton Critical Edition, ed. Richard J. Dunn (New York: Norton, 1971).

10. See, for instance, David Lodge, "Fire and Eyre: Charlotte Brontë's War of Earthly Elements," in *The Brontës*, ed. Ian Gregor, pp. 110–36.

11. (If *The Pilgrim's Progress*: "behold I saw a man clothed with rags ... he brake out with a lamentable cry, saying, 'What shall I do?'" Charlotte Brontë made even more extensive references to *Pilgrim's Progress* in *Villette*, and in her use of Bunyan she was typical of many nineteenth-century novelists, who—from Thackeray to Louisa May Alcott—relied on his allegory to structure their own fiction. For comments on Charlotte Brontë's allusions to *Pilgrim's Progress in Villette* see Q. D. Leavis, "Introduction" to *Villette* (New York: Harper & Row, 1972), pp. vii–xli.

12. Mrs. Sarah Ellis, *The Family Monitor*, pp. 9–10.

13. See de Beauvoir (on Tertullian), *The Second Sex*, p. 156.

14. Adrienne Rich, "Jane Eyre: The Temptations of a Motherless Woman," *Ms.* 2, no. 4 (October 1973):69–70.

15. In *The Poetics of Space* Gaston Bachelard speaks of "the rationality of the roof" as opposed to "the irrationality of the cellar." In the attic, he notes, "the day's experiences can always efface the fears of the night," while the cellar "becomes buried

madness, walled-in tragedy" (pp. 18–20). Thornfield's attic is, however, in his sense both cellar and attic, the imprisoning lumber-room of the past and the watch-tower from which new prospects are sighted, just as in Jane's mind mad "restlessness" coexists with "harmonious" reason.

16. See M. Jeanne Peterson, "The Victorian Governess: Status Incongruence in Family and Society," in *Suffer and Be Still: Women in the Victorian Age*, ed. Martha Vicinus (Bloomington, Ind.: Indiana University Press, 1972), pp. 3–19.

17. See C. Willet Cunnington, *Feminine Attitudes in the Nineteenth Century*, p. 119.

18. Chase, "The Brontës, or Myth Domesticated," p. 464.

19. See, for instance, Mrs. Oliphant, *Women Novelists of Queen Victoria's Reign* (London: Hurst & Blackett, 1897), p. 19: "The chief thing ... that distressed the candid and as yet unaccustomed reader in "Jane Eyre" ... was the character of Rochester's confidences to the girl whom he loved ... that he should have talked to a girl so evidently innocent of his amours and his mistresses."

20. In a sense, Rochester's "contemptible" prearranged marriage to Bertha Mason is also a consequence of patriarchy, or at least of the patriachal custom of primogeniture. A younger son, he was encouraged by his father to marry for money and status because sure provisions for his future could be made in no other way.

21. Claire Rosenfeld, "The Shadow Within: The Conscious and Unconscious Use of the Double," in *Stories of the Double*, ed. Albert J. Guerard (Philadelphia: J. B. Lippincott, 1967), p. 314. Rosenfeld also notes that "When the passionate uninhibited self is a woman, she more often than not is dark." Bertha, of course, is a Creole—swarthy, "livid," etc.

22. Chase, "The Brontës, or Myth Domesticated," p. 467.

23. Rich, "Jane Eyre: The Temptations of a Motherless Woman," p. 72. The question of what was "bearable for a powerless woman in the England of the 1840s" inevitably brings to mind the real story of Isabella Thackeray, who went mad in 1840 and was often (though quite mistakenly) thought to be the original of Rochester's mad wife. Parallels are coincidental, but it is interesting that Isabella was reared by a Bertha Mason-like mother of whom it was said that "wherever she went, 'storms, whirlwinds, cataracts, tornadoes' accompanied her," and equally interesting that Isabella's illness was signalled by mad inappropriate laughter and marked by violent suicide attempts, alternating with Jane Eyre-like docility. That at one point Thackeray tried to guard her by literally *tying* himself to her ("a riband round her waist, & to my waist, and this always woke me if she moved") seems also to recall Rochester's terrible bondage. For more about Isabella Thackeray, see Gordon N. Ray, *Thackeray: The Uses of Adversity, 1811–1846* (New York: McGraw-Hill, 1955), esp. pp. 182–85 (on Isabella's mother) and chap. 10. "A Year of Pain and Hope," pp. 250–77.

24. See Emily Dickinson, *Poems*, J. 1072, "Title divine—is mine!/The Wife—without the sign!"

25. See Emily Dickinson, *Poems*, J. 512, "The Soul has Bandaged Moments."

26. Rich, "Jane Eyre; The Temptations of a Motherless Woman," p. 106.

27. Ibid.

28. Ibid.

29. *Sartor Resarlus*, chap. 9, "The Everlasting Yea."

30. Chase, "The Brontës, or Myth Domesticated," p. 467.

31. Robert Bernard Martin, *The Accents of Persuasion: Charlotte Brontës Novels* (New York: Norton, 1966), p. 90.

32. *The Pilgrim's Progress* (New York: Airmont Library, 1969), pp. 140–41.

33. It should be noted here that Charlotte Brontës use of *The Pilgrim's Progress* in *Villette* is much more conventional. Lucy Snowe seems to feel that she will only find true bliss after death, when she hopes to enter the Celestial City.

34. See Emily Dickinson, *Poems*, J. 1072, "Title divine—is mine!"

GEORGE LEVINE

Dickens and Darwin

Dickens is the great novelist of entanglement, finding in the mysteries of the urban landscape those very connections of interdependence and genealogy that characterize Darwin's tangled bank. Certainly, Dickens is not self-evidently a Darwinian novelist—much of his catastrophist and apocalyptic imagination is incompatible with Darwin's gradualist world. Yet in many respects, particularly in his energetic tendencies to multitudinousness and the mysteries of imperceptible connection, he is close indeed to Darwin's "nature," far from the ordered world of natural theology. Even his "catastrophism," with its implicit recognition of progressive change rather than Lyellian stasis, belongs to Darwin's world, for, as I have suggested, Darwin's achievement was in part the absorption into uniformitarianism of catastrophist progression.

From the start Dickens's preoccupation with irrepressible multiplicity contends against an aspiration to order and meaning. When Mr. Pickwick slams the door on the suffering outside his prison room, Dickens dramatizes the loss of an unambiguous sense that the world makes sense and is ultimately ordered and just. He yearns for a "nature" that is indeed God's second book, as in the tradition of natural theology. But, like Darwin, he describes a world that resists such ordering. Unlike Darwin, he is often driven to arbitrary manipulation of plot to reinstate what his imagination has expelled.

From *Darwin and the Novelists: Patterns of Science in Victorian Fiction.* © 1988 by the Presidents and Fellows of Harvard College.

The refrain "What connexion can there be?"[1] which echoes implicitly through all of *Bleak House* is answered by genealogy, just as Darwin's question about the meaning of the "natural system" is answered: "All true classification is genealogical; ... community of descent is the hidden bond which naturalists have been unconsciously seeking, and not some unknown plan of creation" (*Origin*, p. 404). The juxtaposition of the separate worlds of Chesney Wold and Tom-All-Alone's in sequential chapters implies just such a "hidden bond," which is laden with moral implications.

Esther is the natural daughter who links the apparently unrelated city and rural life, poverty and wealth, lower class and aristocracy, and she is a figure for the moral bond that society ignores. Many in Dickens's society thought that Darwin's establishment of such natural connections of descent implied the destruction of the very moral bonds Dickens used genealogy to affirm. Both *Bleak House* and the *Origin* bespeak, in their different ways, the culture's preoccupations with "connexion" where physical juxtaposition, as in the cities, seemed to reveal startling spiritual, even biological discontinuity. What has Jo the crossing sweep got to do with Tulkinghorn the rich and powerful lawyer? Much of the battle about evolutionary theory implied the culture's deep discomfort with its new social juxtapositions, its attempt to deny the implicit religious context of the "hidden bond" as it appears in Dickens, its unwillingness to know that we are all literally one family.[2] Dickens's preoccupation with discovering connections links him in one way with a tradition of narrative that goes back to Oedipus, in another, with the Judaco-Christian insistence that we are our brothers' keepers, and in yet another, to Darwinian styles of investigation and explanation.

Dickens certainly admired Darwin's theory, as Darwin took pleasure in Dickens's novels. There is no evidence that Dickens, like the more austere and dogmatic Carlyle, found Darwinism anathema. And it has been suggested that "the organisation of *The Origin of Species* seems to owe a good deal to the example of one of Darwin's most frequently read authors, Charles Dickens."[3] No literate person living between 1836 and 1870 could have escaped knowing about Dickens. After 1859, the same would have been true about Darwin. While Darwin rewrote for nineteenth-century culture the myth of human origins, secularizing it yet giving it a comic grandeur and a tragic potential, Dickens was the great mythmaker of the new urban middle class, finding in the minutiae of the lives of the shabby genteel, the civil servants, the "ignobly decent," as Gissing's novelist Biffin called them, great comic patterns of love and community, and great tragic possibilities of dehumanization and impersonal loss.

Given the pervasiveness of their fame, Dickens and Darwin had to have known each other's myths. In the crucial period of the late 1830s, in the notebooks that show him developing his theory, Darwin recorded that reading a review of Comte "made me endeavour to remember and think deeply," an activity that gave him an "intense headache." In contrast, he noted "the immediate manner in which my head got well when reading article by Boz."[4] The pleasures of Dickens remained with Darwin permanently. Although Darwin claimed that later in life he lost the power to enjoy poetry, he was a constant reader of literature from his youth,[5] and to the end, as he indicates in his *Autobiography*, he read novels steadily—or had them read to him.[6] In a well-known passage in his letters, he returns casually to *Pickwick Papers*—one of his favorite books—for a little philosophy: "As a turnkey remarked in one of Dickens's novels, 'Life is a rum thing'" (*Life and Letters*, II, 446). He even uses a Dickens description of a snarling mob in *Oliver Twist* to support his argument that human expressions are ultimately derived from rudimentary animal behavior.

What matters far more is that Dickens's development implies a confrontation with the very kinds of problems that Darwin, in his much different way, was also addressing. Dickens would turn the preoccupation with connections into moral parables, but his major narrative and moral difficulty had to do with the problem of change, about which he was much more ambivalent than Darwin. Although he supported the developments of the new science, that greatest instrument of change, and he despised the ignorance and prejudices of the past, there remains a strain of essentialism in his writing that led to trouble when he tried to imagine change of character; and though he brilliantly satirizes those who deny change, his style itself often denies it.

Dickens greeted with eagerness the radical developments in knowledge and communications that marked the nineteenth century. It would have been impossible for anyone, no less someone as imaginatively alive as Dickens, to have written without absorbing into his language something of the way science had been changing it. But he always regarded science as means to a human end, and he characteristically used scientific fact and method for moral purposes. According to Jonathan Arac, Dickens absorbs and transmutes the development in late eighteenth-century discourse by which scientific language was transferred to social theory. Arac points out, for example, how in the description of Tom-All-Alone's, Dickens "conveys less a specific physical description of the slum ... than an attitude of scientific precision about it ... Dickens's insistence on 'truth' in his preface to *Bleak House* ... leads him to draw wherever possible on scientific authorities, for he was convinced that there was no conflict between science, rightly understood, and the imagination."[7] The megalosaurus waddling up Holborn Hill, to take an obvious but minor example, was a discovery of nineteenth-century geology and paleontology, and was named by William Buckland, apparently no earlier than 1824. Dickens's friend, the famous anatomist Richard Owen, made megalosaurs an important element in his own theorizing and regarded them as the highest forms of reptile, with real affinities to mammals. Moreover, there are signs on the very first page of *Bleak House* that Dickens was aware of and could use for his own purposes the early-century debate among geologists over the question of whether the mineral world and the fossil record are to be accounted for by flood or fire. At first Dickens seems a Neptunist, as Ann Wilkinson points out,[8] but his Neptunism is opposed by Vulcanism, as, for example, in the fires of Rouncewell's mill, Mr. Krook's spontaneous combustion, and the "transferred" spontaneous combustion of the whole Jarndyee and Jarndyee case. These more or less plausible and respectable geological positions were scientifically argued and subserved traditional religious ends. Part of Dickens's materials for imagining the world, they are evidence that he used science as much for metaphor as for the latest news about the cosmos. But he did turn to it, he would not be reckless about what science had already revealed. His Neptunism and Vulcanism are a literary convenience that required no belief, but "spontaneous combustion" did. On that, too, Dickens thought he had science on his side.[9]

He was in fact extremely alert to modern scientific and technological developments. As Alexander Welsh has noted, it would be unwise "to underestimate the degree to which Dickens was aware of the intellectual ferment of his time."[10] Harvey Sucksmith points out that Dickens was "receptive to biological ideas throughout his life."[11] Unlike Carlyle and Ruskin, with whom he is often associated, Dickens does not look back nostalgically to a golden past. There is a strain in him that does praise "merrie olde England" and revere the old-fashioned. But the old, old fashion, Paul Dombey discovers, is death. Dickens was very much a man of his time, "a pure modernist," Ruskin notoriously complained,—"a leader of the steam-whistle party *par excellence*—and he had no understanding of any power of antiquity except a sort of jackdaw sentiment for cathedral towers."[12] Despite the wonderful extravagance, Ruskin was right. The savage satire at the start of book II of *The Tale of Two Cities* is only one example of Dickens's attitude toward the past; the more complex celebration of the railroad in *Dombey and Son* is another.

The bias of Dickens's world is toward the new. His attack on modern bureaucracy is more often than not an attack on a system that madly repeats the worst of ancient practices and traditions: the circumlocution office, chancery, charity schools, and new poor law, almost invariably reenforce the values and methods of the old. Even Dickens's vendetta against utilitarianism and laissez-faire economics is directed not at the new and industrious middle class, but, rather, at the heartlessness of bureaucratic and institutional England. And these Dickens shows to be reflected and abetted by obstinate support of obsolete procedures and structures that confirm old class divisions and generate new ones. Society sets up against competent and innovative minds like Daniel Doyce and Mr. Rouncewell obstructive relies like Tite Barnacle or (with some vestiges of dignity) Sir Leicester Dedlock. Worse, it produces a new breed of villain, ostensibly "modern" but by gestures at respectability merely exploiting ancient injustices in pursuit of success for Number One: Fagin, Mr. Carker, Uriah Heep, Mr. Vholes, Mr. Bounderby, Bradley Headstone.

Science, for Dickens, was a means to help dispel superstition and ancient prejudice and habit. Ignorance is the enemy of morality. In a speech as late as 1869, at a point in his career when, if he had been as disillusioned with contemporary materialism as he is sometimes purported to have been, that disillusion would have emerged, he objects strenuously to the characterization of the age as "materialistic." Instead, he celebrates the scientific and technological discoveries that had improved the quality of life. The speech was an implicit attack on a recent speech by Francis Close, Dean of Carlisle, who had complained about the secularization of knowledge. "There were those," the dean had complained, "who would prefer any dream, however foolish or vain, to the testimony of God respecting the origin of our species."[13] Dickens argues energetically for the continuing expansion of scientific knowledge, always seeing it as a means to important human ends. "I confess," he says,

> that I do not understand this much used phrase, a "material age,"
> I cannot comprehend—if anybody can: which I very much
> doubt—its logical signification. For instance: has electricity
> become more material in the mind of any sane, or moderately
> insane man, woman, or child, because of the discovery that in the
> good providence of God it was made available for the service and
> use of man to an immeasurably greater extent than for his
> destruction? Do I make a more material journey to the bedside of
> my dying parents or my dying child, when I travel at the rate of
> sixty miles an hour, than when I travel thither at the rate of six?[14]

Here, if anywhere, is the credo of the "steam-whistle party." But Dickens was not unambivalent, and the treatment of Dombey's ride in the train that seems hurtling toward death, if not its personification, can give some sense of why the problem of change was never a simple one for him. Nevertheless, the speech is unequivocal in embracing the new. And it is not merely an endorsement of technological application of scientific ideas. Practical as Dickens's orientation was, the speech shows that he believed that the practical grew from a willingness to entertain and seek new ideas, whatever their apparent application. Darwinism and the secular interpretation of nature are not the problem; the problem is dogmatic traditionalism. "Do not let us be discouraged or deceived by vapid empty words," he urges. "The true material age is the stupid Chinese age, in which no new grand revelation of nature is granted, because such revelations are ignorantly and insolently repelled, instead of being humbly and diligently sought."[15] Dickens, too, believed that science is compatible with religion: the true irreligion is conventional dogmatic religiosity.

That he was not an intellectual, in our usual sense of the word, is obvious enough. Although some of his more mature comments on science (particularly on "spontaneous combustion") may seem both ignorant and prejudiced, Dickens maintained a warm relation with science and scientists. He enlisted important scientists for help with his weekly journals—not only Owen, who wrote several pieces for *Household Words*, but also, for example, Michael Faraday, who sent him the notes for his famous lectures on the candle, which eventually became *The Chemical History of a Candle*. Dickens published a kind of summary of it in *Household Words*, a summary that Wilkinson has found useful in understanding the structure and significance of *Bleak House*.

The details of Dickens's novels often reveal that he had absorbed, like an intelligent layman, some of the key ideas issuing from contemporary developments in geology, astronomy, and physics. The evidence is most obvious in *Household Words* and *All the Year Round*, where scientific matters are taken as significant despite the homely and domestic emphases. Often surprisingly sophisticated despite their popularizing strategies, the scientific essays stressed the relation of science to ordinary life and made his journals important popularizers of scientific ideas.

This is not to deny the complicating antiscientific strain in his writing. Mr. Pickwick begins as a butt of satire, and one of his persistently satirized characteristics is scientific ambition. He is introduced, in a gently Swiftian way, as the author of "Speculations on the Source of the Hampstead Ponds, with some Observations on the Theory of Tittlebats." On his first adventure, a cab ride, he solemnly accepts and notes the cabman's sardonic exaggeration that his horse is forty-two years old, or that the horse stays out two or three weeks at a time and only can keep standing because the cab supports it. A bit later, he becomes deeply excited about an "archaeological" discovery, which turns out to read BILL STUMPS HIS MARK. Some of the animosity to trivial science is diverted later in the book to "the scientific gentleman" who manages to mistake Mr. Pickwick's lantern in the garden for "some extraordinary and wonderful phenomenon of nature."[16]

In 1846, Dickens published his last Christmas book, *The Haunted Man*. It gave him the opportunity to carry out further that attack on the scientific character comically announced in *Pickwick Papers*, for the central character is the chemist, Redlaw, who has bargained away his power of memory. The connection between the scientific pursuit and dehumanization that follows is implicit, but Dickens makes very little of it. Here was a subject designed to explore the anaesthetizing consequences of exclusively analytic mental activity such as we find in the actual autobiographies of Darwin and Mill. But Dickens does not seem very interested in pursuing it. The hard look at life is painful, so the moral goes; implicitly, the scientist sees the pain and, sensitive enough, feels it. For the most part in this very thin tale Redlaw is a sympathetic figure, whose decision to give up memory is treated with understanding, although, of course, implicitly criticized. A willingness to take a good look at the worst is as essential as a celebration of the virtuous. Thus, in appealing for a restoration of his memory, Redlaw cries: "In the material world, as I have long taught, nothing can be spared; no step or atom in the wondrous structure could be lost, without a blank being made in the great universe. I know, now, that it is the same with good and evil, happiness and sorrow, in the memories of men."[17] With the conventional moral application of excessive reliance on science, the speech is nevertheless couched in the terms of science itself; and it reveals Dickens's awareness of one of the fundamental principles of contemporary science, the conservation of matter, demonstrated by Lavoisier late in the eighteenth century. Lavoisier had shown that the actual amount of material in a chemical transformation remains the same before and after: "We must always suppose an exact equality between the elements of the body examined and those of the product of its analysis," Lavoisier said.[18] In Dickens, the indestructibility of the physical universe, like all other scientifically affirmed ideas, becomes moral metaphor. For Redlaw and Dickens the physical world signifies, as it did for the natural theologians. Here, at least, Dickens's ambivalence about "God" does not inhibit him from using the physical as a sanction and even a model for the moral; rather, as for the natural theologians, faith that what turned up would be meaningful encourages further scientific pursuit of knowledge.

Similarly, in the very year of the *Origin*, Dickens published in *All the Year Round* an essay called "Gamekeeper's Natural History," which mocks in a traditional way the abstractness of most scientific thought. "No one can paint a thing which is not before him as he paints," says the author, and "natural history is not to be written by professors in spectacles—timid, twittering, unsophisticated men—from stuffed animals and bleached skeletons."[19] But it *is* to be written from life, by naturalists, so the author says, like "Audubon, White of Selbourne, Gould." Sharing his culture's Baconian commitment to "experience" as the source of knowledge, Dickens implicitly sees the writer's and the scientist's task of representing the real as deriving from the same powers, leading to the same places.

The coverage of science in the journals does not suggest that scientific thought and experiment were dehumanizing. Taken together the essays show that Dickens was familiar with and sympathetic to the large ideas which, though not strictly anticipations of Darwin's theory, were conditions for it. For example, Darwin needed, above all, the large infusion of time that Lyell's *Principles of Geology* gave him; and Dickens was not retrograde in accepting it, as is manifest in the comfortable allusions in *Bleak House* to geological time. The essay "The World of Water" talks about the "thousand, thousand years ago" in which fossil creatures lived. It casually refers to man as a latecomer into the world (although this is true even in Genesis), and it accepts the position of Cuvier and Lyell that there has been large-scale extinction of species, even forecasting the ultimate extinction of man himself.[20]

In the essays Dickens seems particularly fascinated by the minutiae revealed under the microscope—the dramatic disparity between what is visible to the naked eye and what is really there. In essay drawing on Philip Gosse's *Evening with the Microscope* Dickens describes the similarity in all vertebrate blood. And he gives a series of dramatic and pleasantly horrific pictures of the natural world, as, for example: "We venture to say that the poet who spoke of butterflies kissing the sweet lips of the flower &c. never looked through a microscope at that flat coiled tongue bristling with hairs and armed with hooks, rifling and spoiling like a thing of worse fame, but of no worse life."[21] Dickensian gothic is merely an entertaining way to emphasize that the natural wonders revealed by science were evidence of its value, and, indeed, of its value as entertainment; it further expresses Dickens's instinctive view that matter of fact is really mysterious and wonderful and not fully visible to any but an intense and imaginative moral vision.

Thus, while Dickens was willing to consider the pursuit of knowledge for its own sake, there was a touch of the Gradgrind in him; he always wanted to know to what use the knowledge would be put. His dislike of Gradgrindian "science" is dislike for the privileging of the intellect, which turns human complexity into abstraction and allows brutality under the sanction of "Truth." Dickens wants science in his fictions as metaphor, and this is true even for such burning theological questions as whether man is a child, cousin, or sibling of the apes. The opening chapter of *Martin Chuzzlewit*, as Sucksmith reminds us, alludes comically to the theory that man is descended from the apes (probably drawing on Dr. Johnson's description of Lord Monboddo).[22] Concluding his genealogical chapter about the Chuzzlewits, Dickens writes: "It may be safely asserted, and yet without implying any direct participation in the Mondboddo doctrine touching the probability of the human race having once been monkeys, that men do play very strange and extraordinary tricks."[23]

A much later essay in *All the Year Round* called "Our Nearest Relation" comfortably accepts the biological closeness of gorilla to man. Even the essayist's misapprehension that the gorilla is a ferocious and aggressive animal is what most naturalists' accounts at the time would have asserted. Dickens and his journal take the facts where they find them, but convert them quickly into moral metaphor. The gorilla essay concludes with this passage:

> Again and again it strikes the fancy—strikes deeper than the fancy—that the honey-making architectural bee, low down in the scale of life with its insignificant head, its little boneless body, and gauzy wing, is our type of industry and skill: while this apex in the pyramid of the brute creation, this near approach to the human form, what can it do? The great hands have no skill but to clutch and strangle; the complex brain is kindled by no divine spark; there, amid the unwholesome luxuriance of a tropical forest, the creature can do nothing but pass its life in fierce sullen isolation—eat, drink, and die?[24]

The essay takes up the idealist anatomy or transcendental biology of Richard Owen, the view, as Peter Bowler describes it, that similarity in structure among living creatures expresses an "'archetype' or ground plan on which all forms of life ... are modeled."[25] Several essays in *Household Words* expound and argue for transcendental biology. One such concludes exuberantly in this way: "Thus, beyond and above the law of design in creation, stands the law of unity of type, and unity of structure. No function so various, no labours so rude, so elaborate, so dissimilar, but this cell can build up the instrument, and this model prescribes the limits of its shape. Through all creation the microscope detects the handwriting of power and of ordnance. It has become the instrument of a new revelation in science, and speaks clearly to the soul as to the mind of man."[26] The similarity among organisms, like the similarity between gorilla and human, does not imply consanguinity, and certainly not descent, for the essential pre-Darwinian tenet of almost all thinkers aware of the similarities was that there is, nevertheless, an absolute gap between humanity and anthropoid, a gap to be filled only by the "divine spark" so manifestly missing in the gorilla's brain (a position which, remarkably, A. R. Wallace also took up later in his career, to Darwin's deep disappointment).[27] Even the most partisan Darwinians would concede what Huxley, for example, called "the vast intellectual chasm" between Man and the ape; but Huxley was to argue that the similarity in physical structure of the brains was evidence of consanguinity. There was no need to assume that an intellectual difference would entail "an equally immense difference between their brains."[28]

Nevertheless, Dickens's enthusiasm for new "grand revelations" of nature seems to have led him to publish in *All the Year Round* a remarkably fair-minded review of the *The Origin of Species* only a few months after the book first appeared. The review congratulates Darwin for living not "in the sixteenth century" and not in "Austria, Naples, or Rome," but in "more tolerant times." It proceeds to a reasonably skeptical but very careful presentation of the theory (using, without quotation marks, much of Darwin's own language), and concludes in a splendidly Victorian way, with sentiments worthy of Dickens:

> Timid persons, who purposely cultivate a certain inertia of mind, and who love to cling to their preconceived ideas fearing to look at such a mighty subject from an unauthorized and unwonted point of view, may be reassured by the reflection that, for theories, as for organised beings, there is also a Natural Selection and a Struggle for Life. The world has seen all sorts of theories rise, have their day, and fall into neglect. Those theories only survive which are based on truth, as far as our intellectual faculties can at present ascertain; such as the Newtonian theory of universal gravitation. If Mr. Darwin's theory be true, nothing can prevent its ultimate and general reception, however much it may pain and shock those to whom it is propounded for the first time.[29]

Although Dickens tried to avoid controversy in any of the essays he published in the journals, one can only infer that he was willing to risk controversy on this issue. A month earlier he had published another essay, called "Species," which, without reference to Darwin, quotes him at length as though in the essay writer's voice. The prose is judiciously impartial, but it employs Darwin's own words as its own: "It may be just as noble a conception of the Deity to believe that he created a few original forms capable of self-development into other and needful forms, as to believe that He required a fresh act of creation to supply the voids caused by the action of His laws."[30] Two essays so generously indulgent of the development theory in a journal as tightly controlled as *All the Year Round* seem very unlikely unless Dickens were ready to endorse the idea himself. The strategy of the review, carefully considering objections, but proceeding with a long and unquestioned set of quotations from Darwin in the voice of the reviewer, and concluding with an open evocation of a Darwinian metaphor, suggests a far greater commitment to the idea of evolution by natural selection than is explicitly affirmed. Even as it questions Darwin's theory, it uses his dominant metaphor to predict its future.

The attitudes implicit in the language and structure of Dickens's books are, like the attitudes essayed in his journals and afloat in scientific thought in the 1830s and 1840s, premonitory of the argument Darwin was constructing; they are also often in tension with it.

Dickens's openness to science is reflected in the qualities that characterize his fiction. His novels, in their way, work with the materials that Darwin transformed in another. What Dickens could not have accepted—and *Hard Times*, for example, is in part a tract against it—is the "scientific" treatment of the human subject, although in Bucket, an ultimately sympathetic character, Dickens prepares the way even for this; and the satirical strain of the third person narrator in *Bleak House*, like the sardonic voice at the opening of *Oliver Twist*, provides rhetorical form for such detached treatment. The human in Dickens largely escapes the reduction Darwin's theory implies, but the bleaker his vision the more ready Dickens is to regard the human as scientific (that is, merely material) subject. To avoid such a fate, he leaves open rationally inexplicable avenues of plotting and characterization. Nevertheless, many of the major characteristics of Dickens's way of seeing and writing about the world are reflected in major elements of Darwin's theory. The cultural theme of connection, with its implication in genealogy, is a major concern of both writers, for example, and suggests again that the possibilities of imagination in science and literature are mutually bounded, mutually derived. Science and literature help create the conditions necessary for each other's development.

The differences between Dickens and Austen are not merely the differences of individual genius. Both may have used contrivances necessary to resolve narrative problems; but Austen's self-consciousness allows her to affirm the intelligible design of the world. Parody is possible for her because she is easy with what is parodied. Dickens, by contrast, thinks less about the contrivance of the coincidences that drive so much of his plotting because they are essential to him if he is to find any shape for a world of profusion, multiplicity, and apparent disorder, a world in which, despite his celebrations of order, he is at home. The landscapes and the architecture of these worlds are far from those ordered eighteenth-century houses and gardens that define and place the characters in *Mansfield Park*. They are the view from Todgers, the chaos of Barnaby's London, Tom-All-Alone's, the dust heaps of *Our Mutual Friend*. Dickens is closer to Darwin than Austen, and not merely chronologically.

Some of the elements of Darwin's vision that I isolated in the first chapter have their counterparts in Dickensian narrative, and for the rest of this chapter I want to consider the parallels and the points of divergence. What is true for Dickens, a writer brilliantly outside the main stream of Victorian realism, is true more emphatically for the realists. Discussion of the Darwinian elements in Dickens, even of the ways he averts Darwinian treatment, should throw light on the other novelists, as well.

First, Dickens the "catastrophist" has much of the Darwinian uniformitarian in his vision. Like the great domestic novelists of the century, Dickens is fascinated by the most trivial domestic and social details—food, furnishings, manners, and all the particularities of ordinary life. The whole movement of narrative toward these details is very much part of the movement that led to evolutionary theory, and it is evident in the rhetoric of Darwin's own argument. Second, the emphasis on the ordinary is often accompanied by a preoccupation with mystery. Somehow, the familiar resonates through all of Dickens with tones of the unfamiliar; things are and are not what they seem. As Dickens himself says (in the Preface of *Bleak House*), he is concerned with "the romantic side of familiar things." To this I juxtapose Darwin's program of defamiliarization, discussed in detail in the preceding chapter, the attempt to discover new principles of order in the midst of what we have long taken for granted. Third, the mystery of the familiar seems to generate complicated plots, full of coincidence, as amidst the multitudinous populations of each novel jostling against each other, new relationships are perceived. The whole seems to move toward catastrophe and a reversal when everything is explained; yet, on the whole, everything *is* explained and what has seemed like chance at the level of story acquires a meaning in an overall plot or design. Dickens does not quite accept the Darwinian rejection of teleology and the need for chance as explanation; chance is there, to be sure, but Dickens makes it work for teleology, even if under strain. Fourth, Dickens struggles with the cultural and Darwinian tendency to blur boundaries. The familiar Dickensian "character" has a sharply defined nature, a singular essence normally conveyed in a few tricks of manner: Pecksniff is invariably a hypocrite, although his hypocritical invention is wonderfully various; Mr. Dombey is invariably proud, Amy Dorrit invariably angelic. The reading of the essential nature of characters seems related by contrast to Darwin's nominalism, and here the question of "change," raised at the start of this chapter becomes prominent. Fifth, the question of connection is critical in both writers: things hang together in Dickens's world, stories converge, unlikely connections are made, entanglements and dependencies are inevitable. In modern jargon, Dickens has an ecological vision; and so, of course, has Darwin. Finally, sixth, all of the elements I have been noting become part of a world overwhelmingly vital because abundant, multitudinous, diverse, full of aberration, distortions, irrationality, which may or may not be ultimately reducible to the large patterns.

The importance of uniformitarianism to the Darwinian argument should by now be clear; it is worth emphasizing, however, that preoccupation with the ordinary is the very heart of romanticism, Wordsworth's responsibility in the division of labor in the *Lyrical Ballads*. Wordsworth's songs and ballads began to emerge only a few years after James Hutton's paper, in 1785, giving the gist of his position in *The Theory of the Earth* (1795). Dickens begins his career as a reporter whose skills are based on his powers of observation, with an uncanny eye for the ordinary. In his eyes the ordinary is transformed, not by miraculous or catastrophic intrusions, but by intense and minute perception. So in his sketches he examines door knobs and reports on the behavior of cabbies, shopkeepers, marginal gentlemen. Wherever he looks, even in the Vauxhall Gardens by daylight, when the ordinariness leads to pervasive disenchantment, the ordinary carries its own enchantment. Describing "early coaches," for example, he notes that "the passengers change as often in the course of one journey as the figures in a kaleidoscope, and though not so glittering, are far more amusing."[31]

The extraordinary popularity of such trivia presupposes a shift to an audience concerned with middle-class domesticity and to the recognition from that perspective of how completely the largest events of our lives evolve from the accumulation of precisely such minutiae. The essay from *Household Words* already alluded to, "Nature's Greatness in Small Things," explores the similarity between the minutest microscopic organism and the largest. "Not unfrequently," says the author, "it is seen that forms the most minute are most essential," capable of working "immeasurable changes."[32] The popular fascination with books about what the microscope revealed is also related to the preoccupation with the domestic and the ordinary. All of these phenomena are part of the same movement that made concern for the domestic the dominant motif of the self-consciously "realist" fiction of the high Victorian period.

Aesthetically, the fulfillment of the uniformitarian vision was articulated in the Victorian novel's constant reversion to the ordinary, and to its treatment of it as normative. We find it most completely formulated in George Eliot's celebration of the art of the Dutch realist school of painting as a kind of model for her fiction. The antirevolutionary implications of this aesthetic are worked out in Eliot (see her handling of politics in *Felix Holt* as the most obvious example). Later, when Razumov of Conrad's *Under Western Eyes* scrawls "Evolution not Revolution," Conrad is affirming both a political and an aesthetic tradition that, by late in the century, was breaking down. I will be taking Razumov's attempt to affirm evolution against the revolutionary substance and style of the novel he occupies as a convenient marking point for a shift from Darwinian thinking in fiction. Evolutionary theory, Victorian realism, and antirevolutionary ideology go together very tightly through the century. Ironically, the materialist and secularizing implications of the revolutionary views that Jane Austen was resisting, when embodied in evolutionary theory, become conservative.

While it is common to see realist and Dickensian art in opposition, Dickens, with what Arac describes as a "scientific" attitude, seems even more concerned to insist on the literal truth of his writings than the more conventionally realistic writers.[33] For however much Dickens is to be regarded as a great entertainer or as metaphysical novelist, he *claimed* that he was a realist. Perhaps the earliest claim is in the preface to *Oliver Twist*, in which he attacks those who cannot stand the unhappy truths he has revealed. "There are people of so refined and delicate a nature, that they cannot bear the contemplations of such horrors," he says contemptuously. But he would not for those readers "abate one hole in the Dodger's coat, or one scrap of curl-paper in the girl's dishevelled hair." And as for the character of Nancy, "it is useless to discuss whether the conduct and character of the girl seems natural or unnatural, probable or improbable, right or wrong. IT IS TRUE."

He bases this claim on his own experience of watching "these melancholy shades of life." Notice that here, in the defense of the reality of his fiction, Dickens rejects romance literature, which ignores surface details, and that this rejection entails mimetic particularity, attention to the minutiae of ordinary life. Have these sordid facts he has revealed "no lesson," Dickens asks, "do they not whisper something beyond the little-regarded warning of an abstract moral precept?"[34] The ordinary—the hole in the Dodger's coat, Nancy's disheveled hair—is given in Dickens some of the quality of allegory.

In the preface to *Martin Chuzzlewit* Dickens makes a similar point, emphaizing how perspective determines what is to be considered "realistic." "What is exaggeration to one class of minds and perceptions, is plain truth to another ... I sometimes ask myself whether it is *always* the writer who colours highly, or whether it is now and then the reader whose eye for colour is a little dull." This eagerness to assert the literal truth of his fictions continued to the end of Dickens's career. In the postscript to *Our Mutual Friend* he talks of the "odd disposition in this country to dispute as improbable in fiction, what are the commonest experiences in fact," and he proceeds to defend as realistic old Harmon's will and his treatment of the Poor Law with evidence from *The Lancet.*[35]

Perhaps the most famous and egregious instance of Dickens's defense of the literal reality of his stories comes in the preface to *Bleak House*, where he defends the scientific validity of spontaneous combustion. "Before I wrote that description," he says, "I took pains to investigate the subject" (p. 4). It is particularly strange that an episode that has such coherent symbolic significances should seem to require from Dickens a defense of its literal truth. The spontaneous combustion of Krook is formally like the shooting of the albatross, and in the novel it is self-evidently the physical equivalent of the consumption in "costs" of the case of Jarndyce and Jarndyce, and the externalization of the moral nature of "justice" in Chancery. But again it suggests that while a "Coleridgean" novelist, showing himself most advantageously in extreme and quasi-supernatural situations, Dickens always saw himself as a realist, committed to the truthful representation of commonly experienced particulars. Thematically, his enterprise *was* very similar to that of the realists.

But Dickens had the confidence of natural theology, in which material reality corresponds meaningfully to a moral reality. The great analogy of natural theology, between physical and spiritual nature, is embedded in his imagination; the Darwinian disanalogy is the threat. If it is not quite the designed world of the natural theologians, it is nevertheless a world in which the fall into secularity is not inevitably a fall from grace. Allegory is not so much an invention as a representation, a mirror as much as a lamp.

In realist fiction of the kind Eliot wrote, "Nature has her language, and she is not unveracious; but we don't know all the intricacies of her syntax just yet."[36] In Darwin's writing nature is not illegible, but its syntax is difficult, and its meaning does not imply a moral reality inherent in the material, only its own nature. Eliot, through her conception of nemesis, often tries to infuse nature with moral meaning. But equally often she can sound like Darwin reminding us of the difference between "the face of nature bright with gladness"—the face that the natural theologian tends to see—and the destruction and devouring that accompany that "gladness." So she tells also of "what a glad world this looks like," but how "hidden behind the apple blossoms, or among the golden corn, or under the shrouding boughs of the wood, there might be a human heart beating with anguish."[37] In the wooden roadside cross Eliot finds a fit "image of agony" for the representation of what lies beneath the visible loveliness. It is a human symbol for a nonhuman nature. That is, the realist can find symbolic representations of the moral implication, but the symbol and the moral reality are human inventions. Nature is Darwinian. For Eliot, as for Dickens, the novelist was to make the ordinary resonant with myth, to show that the dream of romance is an absurd distortion and inferior to the romance of the ordinary, which contains within it forms of myth. But the romance of the ordinary is never inherent in nature. Nature's language is neutral.

The romantic-uniformitarian leaning of Dickens is partly undercut in the longer novels in which the traditions of stage melodrama are used to allow for quite literal catastrophe. Yet the distance between the uniformitarian and catastrophist position is much less absolute than it may at first seem. Both are romantic positions—the Wordsworth and Coleridge of science, as it were. In Dickens, the "catastrophe" of the murder of Tulkinghorn, for example, or the literal collapse of the Clennam house, can be seen as a metaphor for the consequences of the tedious daily accumulation of depressing facts—the slow grinding of Chancery, the moral bankruptcy of the deadening, static, circumlocutory world of bureaucracy and business. Dickens saw that the ordinary world was full of the extraordinary; he saw, too, that the extraordinary was the inevitable consequence of what seemed merely trivial, as an earthquake is caused by minute, almost undetectable movements over long periods of time. The argument between uniformitarians and catastrophists was, thus, double-edged, and we can feel analogous ambivalence in Dickens. If all extremes are merely accumulations of the ordinary, all the ordinary is potentially extreme.

The ordinary, then, is latent with possibilities of the extraordinary. It is a trick of contemporary horror movies, whose fundamental strategy is to focus on recognizable people in recognizable situations and then intrude something monstrous upon them. In Dickens, it is not only such gothic strategies (the talking chair in the *Pickwick Papers*, for example). But it is also Mrs. Copperfield bringing home a second husband who becomes, in his Puritanical austerity, a monster to the child. It is Boffin's dust heap, the dreary refuse of a recognizably ugly city, which becomes a mysterious treasure to Wegg; it is the clock greeting young Paul Dombey with "How-is-my-little-friend?"; it is Boz's superb account of the clothing in the window of the "emporium for second hand wearing apparel," which suddenly enact their melodramatic and yet commonplace histories. Like Darwin, who said, we must "no longer look at an organic being as a savage looks at a ship, as at something wholly beyond his comprehension," and must learn "to regard every production of nature as one which has had a history" (*Origin*, p. 456), Dickens makes us see the history—and the melodrama—in the commonplace object. He often affirms a world beyond the secular, but his works for the most part lose their touch with that world beyond, and with any authority except time, chance, and personal avarice. The world he creates—even Amy Dorrit's—is, like Darwin's, time-bound. Truth is not on the surface, after all, except as the surface offers to the keen observer clues to its history. All things imply histories but hide their pasts. By the time of *Bleak House*, only the professionally trained—police inspectors, like Bucket—can pierce through appearances with any confidence.

As he puts it at the start of his sketch "A Visit to Newgate," "force of habit" exercises great power "over the minds of men" and prohibits them from "reflection" on "subjects with which every day's experience has rendered them familiar." The essay "Character" is almost archaeological in that it infers whole lives from mere surfaces: "There was something in the man's manner and appearance which told us, we fancied, his whole life, or rather his whole day."[38] These attitudes and strategies are characteristic of Dickens's method throughout his career.

Such strategies parallel the views of the most advanced thinkers about science at the time. Herschel does sound occasionally like a romantic poet, or, perhaps more precisely, he formulates in the language of science ideas that were powerful in both poetry and fiction. If undisciplined experience leaves us open to our prejudices of opinion and of sense, a close look at nature—the glitter of a soap bubble, the fall of an apple—under the restraint of rational discipline, transforms it into a wonderland. "To the natural philosopher there is no natural object unimportant or trifling. From the least of nature's work he may learn the greatest lessons."[39] But the mysteries of the ordinary are only there for those who, like the readers of Dickens's novels, have been taught to look for clues.

As I pointed out in the last chapter, Darwin learned from Herschel and tried to emulate him. And although Herschel was not entirely pleased with Darwin's theory, he would have found in Darwin's work the same fascination with details, the same recognition of the miraculous nature of the ordinary, that he had tried to imbue in his readers. Darwin not only investigated the most ordinary phenomena—seeds in his garden, worm castings, bird excrement, bees' nests, pigeon breeding—but as a consequence discovered and persistently revealed that the details are not what they seem: plants travel; and organisms are frequently maladapted to their environment, or have organs irrelevant to adaptation. The strategy of defamiliarization so central to the *Origin* in its reeducating of natural philosophers and weaning them from creationism and natural theology, is akin to the strategies of domestic novels—as in Eliot's reminder in "Amos Barton" to learn to see some of "the poetry and the pathos ... lying in the experience of a human soul that looks out through dull grey eyes."[40] The poetry and the pathos of natural history are evident in this piece of domesticated science, in which Darwin builds his argument about the way seeds can be transported: "I took in February three tablespoonfuls of mud from three different points, beneath water, on the edge of a little pond; this mud when dry weighed 6 3/4 ounces; I kept it covered up in my study for six months, pulling up and counting each plant as it grew; the plants were of many kinds, and were altogether 537 in number; and yet the viscid mud was all contained in a breakfast cup!" (*Origin*, p. 377). Such defamiliarization, characteristic of Darwin as well as of Dickens, makes it impossible to tuck nature into the neat formulas of natural theology. It is not only that the distribution of vegetation all over the world can be accounted for by natural means, but that nature is extravagant, wasteful, busy in activities not perceptible to the casual observer. Domestic detail changes under rigorous scrutiny. And such a passage is part of an overall strategy that suggests once more that there is nothing stable in the world around us. Species are not fixed but endlessly varying. All the stable elements of our gardens, our domestic animals, our own bodies are mysteriously active, aberrant, plastic.

On the issue of teleology Dickens tried not to be Darwinian. In novels so chance-ridden as his, one would expect to find real compatibility with Darwin, whose theory posited a world without design, generated out of chance variations. But since Darwinian variation occurs without reference to need, environment, or end, Darwin's chance is antiteleological. Contrarily, in traditional narrative of the sort Dickens wrote, chance serves the purpose not of disorder, but of meaning—from Oedipus slaying his father to the catastrophic flood at the end of *The Mill on the Floss*. The order "inside" the fiction might be disrupted—Oedipus's reign, or the life of Maggie—but the larger order of the narrative depends on such disruptions.

The difference might best be indicated by the fact that while both Dickens and Darwin describe worlds in which chance encounters among the myriad beings who populate them are characteristic, for Dickens chance is a dramatic expression of the value and ultimate order in nature, and it belongs recognizably to a tradition that goes back to Oedipus. Each coincidence leads characters appropriately to catastrophe or triumph and suggests a designing hand that sets things right in the course of nature. The "contrivances" in Darwin, however, though they tend to move the species toward its current state of adaptation or extinction, appear to be undesigned. Chance in nature drains it of meaning and value. The variations even in domestic animals, carefully bred, are inexplicable. Only close attention of a breeder, who discards variations he doesn't want, leads to the appearance of design. But the breeder is entirely dependent on the accidents of variation. Darwin and Dickens in a way tell the same story, yet the implications are reversed.

Working in a theatrical and literary tradition, Dickens must use apparent chance to create a story with a beginning, a middle, and an end. And it is a story much like that told by natural theologians, which makes "chance" part of a larger moral design, thus effectively denying its chanciness by making it rationally explicable in terms of a larger structure. The feeling of coincidence is merely local. Such manipulation is a condition of storytelling, where "chance" must always contradict the implications of the medium itself. Even in narratives that seem to emphasize the power of chance over human design, narrative makes chance impossible. Design is intrinsic to the language of storytelling, with its use of a narrative past tense. "Once upon a time" already implies design. Moreover, the focus of narrative attention on particular characters makes everything that happens in the narrative relate to them. It may be that the relation is a negative one: the character, like Micawber, waits for something to turn up, and it never does; but in the end, of course, Micawber has been in the right place at the right time, and while the narrator might applaud Micawber's sudden energy, what happened is not because he chose it. At the same time, the narrative certainly did choose it, both because it in fact helps Micawber achieve the condition to which he has always aspired, and because it allows the exposure of Uriah

Heep and the righting of all the wrongs with which that part of the story has been concerned. Ultimately, it is all for the sake of David Copperfield as the happy resolutions of *Mansfield Park* are for Fanny.

Chance in narrative has at least two contradictory aspects. When Eliot's narrator condemns "Favourable Chance" in *Silas Marner*, she is among other things suggesting (what Darwin would have agreed to) that the world is not designed for any individual's interest. What Godfrey or Dunstan wants has no more to do with the way the world operates than what the giraffe wants. The giraffe's long neck does not develop because he wants it, but because longer-necked giraffes had on the whole survived better than shorter-necked ones. Nothing is going to shorten the trees for any given giraffe; nothing, presumably, will put gold in Dunstan's hands or rid Godfrey of his wife. Dickens, I believe, would subscribe to this way of seeing, although his attacks on chance are less obvious and direct. Yet in *Silas Marner* all the major events are the result of "chance."[41] The narrative does not make credible a necessary connection between the events and the behavior of the characters, nor does it try. The fabular structure of the story is outside the realistic mode that the expressed sentiments of the narrator affirm. In being much more self-consciously a "tale," and less a "realistic" representation of the world in all its complexity, *Silas Marner* exposes boldly what is usually more disguised in realistic fiction, where the necessary "coincidences" are normally made to appear natural and causally related.

The "chance" events in *Silas Marner* self-consciously work out a parable (complex as it becomes), in which they all reflect moral conditions and shadow forth a world in which the principle of nemesis, works, in which we bear moral responsibility for what we do; and that moral responsibility is worked out in nature and society. The effect of the narrative is to convey the sense that the "chance" events were determined by a designing power, intrinsic to nature itself, that used to be called God.

Narrative, it is assumed, is different from life, however, and presumably "real" coincidences would not imply the design of some "author." But any language used to describe events will turn into narrative and import design once more. Sudden catastrophes invariably evoke the question, "Why?" "Why did he have to die?" The question implies that there are "reasons" beyond the physiological and that the explanation, he was hit by a car, or his heart stopped, is not satisfactory or complete. What moral end was served? Where is the justice in the death? Or, if catastrophe is avoided, the language is full of "luck," the remarkable luck that we canceled off the plane that crashed, and the accompanying sense that we weren't "meant" to die yet. Often, others' catastrophes inspire guilt, as though the survivors are responsible, or could have managed to swap positions had they the courage. Even in trivial affairs, this tendency of ordinary language is powerful. We talk about bad weather as though it were designed to ruin our one day off, or we carry umbrellas and half believe that this will trick the rain away.

Such anthropocentric language is characteristic of natural theology, and Dickens does not resist it. But Dickens still uses chance to project a world governed by a great designer, even if he often has difficulty doing so. Putting aside the random abundance of the earlier works, we find that the self-consciously less episodic and more thematically coherent later novels use mysterious and apparently inexplicable details for the sake of human significance. Inevitably, Dickens does produce a Darwinian excess, which he needs to ignore or compress into order to achieve the comfort of significance; but his plotting is determined by the illumination and intelligible explanation of *apparently* random detail. The collapse of Mrs. Clennam's house is both literal and figurative, of course. Oliver's innocence is preserved and triumphant. Carker is crushed by the new railway, which we earlier learned opens for all to see the ugliness and misery of London. Dickensian narrative derives much of its energy from the gradual revelation of the design that incorporates all accidents, just as Herschelian science derives its energy from the attempt to explain all of the minutest natural phenomena in terms of general law. Characters struggle to discover its existence, and to work out its particular meaning, while the reader is always several steps ahead of the characters and several behind the author. We know that there is meant to be nothing chancy about Dickensian chance.[42]

Whereas Dickens, then, could exploit the metaphorical implications of language with confidence in its power to reveal design, Darwin had to resist language's intentionality and implications of design in order to describe a world merely there—without design or meaning. We have seen how in the very act of developing his theory and rejecting arguments from design he fell into the metaphorical and storytelling structures of the language to talk about "Natural Selection" as a "being." But the development of genetic variations, as Waddington points out, is not causally connected with the selective process that will determine whether the variations survive. In narrative terms this suggests that there can be no moral explanation, no superphysical "justification" of the development. The gene and its phenotype develop regardless of their narrative context. Such a separation drains nature of its moral significance and links Darwinism with the realist project that Dickens resisted even as he more than half participated in it. The matter of chance and teleology constituted the core of Dickens's defense, his attempt to keep nature from being merely neutral.

But Dickens did not reject science in order to resist that cold neutrality. It was Darwin, most effectively, who split scientific from theological discourse on this issue: science would not allow any "explanation" that depended on unknown principles that might be invoked, erratically, whenever empirical investigation failed. Scientific faith in law need not extend to scientific belief in the good intentions of the natural world. Dickens, like Darwin, would exclude mere caprice from the universe, but Darwinian "law" might well be regarded as capricious from the human point of view.

Yet another essay in *All the Year Round* provides a typical Victorian affirmation of the value of science, which grows from "Patience," while "Magic," its ancient forebear in the quest for meaning and control, is based on "Credulity." For science to emerge, the essay argues, "the phenomena of Nature, at least all the most ordinary phenomena, must have been disengaged from this conception of an arbitrary and *capricious* power, similar to human will, and must have been recognized as *constant*, always succeeding each other with fatal regularity."[43] These are certainly principles to which Darwin, like Lyell and Herschel before him, would have subscribed. The writer here, in eagerness to dispel "caprice," is not considering the full human implications of this apparently unimpeachable, modern, scientific position. In narrative, ironically, the ultimate effect of the "scientific" view of order and regularity is that the world begins to feel humanly erratic. That is, it becomes a fatalistic or deterministic world, like Hardy's, in which events do indeed develop inexorably from the slow accumulation of causes; yet they are, from the human perspective, entirely a matter of chance, because they are not subject to the control either of will or consciousness. Such a world is not, strictly, disordered, but it is, as Mayr has argued, probabilistic: "No one will ever understand natural selection until he realizes that it is a statistical phenomenon."[44] Not only does it work regardless of the interests of individual members of the population, but its working can only be described statistically, without explanation of why in any case or in the majority of cases, things develop as they do. Natural selection is humanly meaningless. Narrative forces what abstract discourse can avoid, a recognition of the difficulty and potential self-contradictoriness of the very ideas of chance and order.

The radical difference between Darwin and Dickens, despite Dickens's predisposition both to science and to the overall Darwinian vision, is simply in that Darwin's "laws" have no moral significance. Although they can be adapted for moral purposes (and were, immediately and continuingly), they do not answer questions like "Why?" except in physical or probabilistic terms. Birds can carry seeds in their talons, or deposit them thousands of miles away in their excrement. But what design is there in these particular seeds, these particular species making the trip? Why did the bird eat this plant rather than that, travel to this island rather than that? Survival in Darwin's nature is not *morally* significant. Adaptiveness is not designed, being the mere adjustment of the organism to its particular environment, and it has no direction. There is no perfection in Darwin's world, no intelligent design, no purpose. Fact may not be converted to meaning.[45]

This is a very tough sort of "chance," and its toughness evoked resistance from scientists as well as writers and theologians. In Dickens, while Darwinian chance threatens almost instinctively to overwhelm order, chance largely derives from another tradition, the one, in fact, that Darwin was self-consciously combatting. His novels tend to act out the arbitrariness of the connections they want to suggest are natural (and in that unintended sense, even here they are Darwinian). Dickens tries to tie event to meaning in a way that removes from chance its edge of inhumanity. This is the very tradition that Darwin identifies when, in *The Descent of Man*, he explains why he had perhaps overestimated the power of natural selection in the early editions of the *Origin*: "I was not able to annul the influence of my former belief, then widely prevalent, that each species had been purposely created; and this led to my tacitly assuming that every detail of structure, excepting rudiments, was of some special, though unrecognised, service" (I, 15). Every detail, on that earlier model, means something. Insofar as Dickens's later novels begin to suggest a chasm between event and meaning (delicately intimated in the "usual uproar" that concludes *Little Dorrit*), Dickens moves, like the later Darwin, away from the natural-theological tradition that had dominated his imaginative vision.

It is perhaps a measure of how far Dickens has traveled from Austen's way of seeing, however, that even where he persists in the contrivances of coincidence, their discontinuity with the worlds he is creating is disturbing. Such discontinuity is particularly striking in *Little Dorrit* and *Our Mutual Friend*. In most cases, while there are no naturalistic laws by which to account for the "chances" in Dickens's novels, coincidence feels too often like a matter of the conventions of narrative. Of course, Lady Dedlock *must* die at the gate of the wretched source of all plagues, where Jo had given off one ray of light in his gratitude to the now dead Nemo. The characters cannot perceive the design, but it is really there. Still, though there are scientific laws that make the development of organisms intelligible, the comfort of intelligibility does not lead to the comfort of meaning and purpose: in Darwin's world, it is random.

Darwin could get nowhere with his theory as long as language was taken to imply an essential reality it merely named. As Gillian Beer points out, in this respect, as with the question of chance, Darwin was forced to use a language that resisted the implications of his argument. Language, she says, "always includes agency, and agency and intention are frequently impossible to distinguish in language."[46] Yet more generally, to borrow a page from Derrida, language implies "presence." It assumes an originary reality ultimately accessible. Here as elsewhere, Darwin avoided epistemology to stick to his biological business, and here again he was forced to resist the implications of the language with which he made his arguments.

I have shown how at the center of his theory is a redefinition of the word "species," by which he almost undefined it. Species can have no Platonic essence, and Darwin was content to use the word as others used it, while demonstrating that species could be nothing but time-bound and perpetually transforming aggregations of organisms, all of which are individually different. For the most part, Darwin tried to do without a definition of species at all, for a definition would have got him into the kinds of serious difficulties already discussed, leading to the view that his book, as Louis Agassiz claimed, was about nothing: if "species" is merely an arbitrary term not corresponding to anything in nature, then *The Origin of Species* is about nothing.

Definition would have implied an essentialist view of the world, one entirely compatible with natural theology, and incompatible with evolution by natural selection. Essentialism, as Mayr has noted, implies a "belief in discontinuous, immutable essences,"[47] and this belief is reenforced by the reifying nouns characteristic of our language. John Beatty, in a revision of his argument that Darwin in fact was denying the existence of species, points out that Darwin could "use the term 'species' in a way that agreed with the use of the term by his contemporaries, but not in a way that agreed with his contemporaries' *definitions* of the term."[48] Darwin was not a poststructuralist and would not have argued that there is nothing out there to correspond to his language. But he knew he would have been paralyzed by accepting the definitions of "species" current among fellow naturalists. Recall that when Darwin talks of the "something more" naturalists think is implied by the natural system, he is working with their general nonevolutionary understanding of "natural system" and classifications within it; what he does, to follow Beatty's point, is accept their usage but not their definition so that he can replace the essentialist "something more" with the "hidden bond" of "propinquity of descent."

Essentialism was the enemy of evolutionary thinking, creating the greatest obstacle to conceptions of change. Mayr singles out Platonic essentialism, "the belief in constant *eide*, fixed ideas, separate from and independent of the phenomena of appearance," as having had "a particularly deleterious impact on biology through the ensuing two thousand years." Essentialism made it almost impossible to name a *kind* of animal—say, horse—without implying both its permanence and the "real" nature of its identity in all important qualities with all other horses, regardless of its merely accidental, that is, its particular physical and living characteristics. "Genuine change, according to essentialism" notes Mayr, "is possible only through the saltational origin of new essences,"[49] and clearly Darwin, for whom nature made no leaps, found essentialism a large obstruction.[50]

In plotting and characterization, change (as I have earlier said) was Dickens's greatest difficulty. His narratives and his characters seem to belong to a saltational world. For the narratives do make leaps, and when characters change they often do so (particularly in the earlier work) through abrupt conversion, as, for example, Scrooge. As opposed to a realist like Eliot, who writes from within a tradition much more clearly related to Darwinian thought and to the advanced science and psychology of the time, and whose narrator claims that "character is not cut in marble," Dickens writes out of an essentialist tradition. Barbara Hardy has pointed out that his novels rarely escape some tinge of the tradition of the *Bildungsroman*, but Dickens's use of that tradition of character development and change rarely explores the slow processes by which characters in that tradition learn and grow.[51]

Typically, Dickensian characters behave as though they had single, discoverable selves that constitute their essence. Mr. Jarndyce is a good and generous man, all of whose strategies in the world are designed to reaffirm that goodness. To be sure, this also entails a certain deviousness, for if he is to accept congratulations on his goodness, he can no longer regard himself as disinterested. But this ambivalence is built into his essence, and one of his most characteristic self-expressions is his complaint about the wind being in the East, which signals either bad news or the self-division that comes when he is about to receive praise or gratitude. So it is, in other ways, with most of Dickens's characters, who have been criticized through the years by critics seeking more fluid, complex, unstable, and I would say Darwinian, "selves."

The essentialist nature of Dickens's imagination is perhaps most evident in the clarity with which he usually distinguishes goodness and badness. Dickens's tendency is to read character into these categories, even when by virtue of his extraordinary sympathetic imagination he creates sequences like that of Sikes on the run or Fagin in prison, which shift our perspective on the melodramatic narrative. But the moral borders are firmly drawn. As Leo Bersani has observed, "In Dickens, the mental faculties dramatized in allegory are concealed behind behavior which *represents* those faculties. And the critical method appropriate to this literary strategy is one which treats the words and acts of literary characters as signs of the allegorical entities which make up these characters."[52] In this respect Dickens is most distant from Darwin and realism. Eliot's emphasis on mixed conditions, mixed natures, and her virtual incapacity (until Grandcourt in *Daniel Deronda*) to create a figure of unequivocal evil, fairly represents the difference. Dickens, writing within the "metaphysical mode" as Edward Eigner defines it, is heavily dependent on plot and emphasizes the external rather than the internal, but only because he counts on the adequacy of the natural to express meaning. In keeping with the natural-theological tradition, the emphasis on the external itself depends on strong confidence in the legibility of the material world, its expression of spiritual and moral realities comprehensible to those who choose to see. Ironically, when the world is secularized, as in the Darwinian scheme, narrative must turn inward because the material world becomes increasingly unintelligible. In Dickens, whom I have been characterizing as essentialist, there is visible a growing inability to be satisfied with the essentialist imagination.

The process of making narrative more literal by turning from allegorical representation to psychological mimesis under the pressures of secularization parallels the strategies Darwin uses in breaking with essentialism. One of the great Christian metaphors, and one of the central concerns of Victorian writers, becomes in Darwin a literal fact: we are all one family. Not the idea, but physical inheritance connects all living organisms. The move severed event from meaning (in a way contrary to Dickens's largely allegorical use of event) and destabilized all apparently permanent values by thrusting them into nature and time. Essentialism and nominalism were, therefore, no merely abstract metaphysical problems. On the whole, common sense and tradition required a world in which the ultimate realities remained outside time, and in which an ideal essence (as opposed to biological inheritance) defined the self. The concept of "character" itself implies such an essence.

The implications of this distinction extend into every aspect of narrative art. The essentialist mode is, for the most part, metaphorical. On the one hand, it depends on the likeness between physical and moral states, and the Dickensian emphasis on the physical peculiarities belongs to such a metaphorical tradition. On the other hand, the nominalist position, like Darwin's, severs the physical from the moral, and Darwin begins to make the connection metonymically. That is, in *The Expression of the Emotions in Man and Animals*, Darwin tries to read feeling from expression. But his reading is predominantly physiological. For example:

> Although ... we must look at weeping as an incidental result, as purposely as the secretion of tears from a blow outside the eye, or as a sneeze from the retina being affected by a bright light, yet this does not present any difficulty in our understanding how the secretion of tears serves as a relief of suffering. And by as much as the weeping is more violent or hysterical, by so much will the relief be greater—on the same principle that the writhing of the whole body, the grinding of the teeth, and the uttering of piercing shrieks, all give relief under an agony of pain.[53]

Just as, for Darwin, organisms are connected by physical inheritance, so moral and emotional states are expressed by physiological activity directed at physical defense and relief. All those aspects of human identity and experience that are traditionally regarded as uniquely human, connected with spiritual states unavailable to lower organisms, are in fact physical conditions shared by other organisms. Darwin had observed monkeys in zoos, for example, to discover whether "the contraction of the orbicular muscles" was similarly connected with "violent expiration and the secretion of tears." He notes that elephants sometimes weep and contract their orbicular muscles! Of course, novelists in the realist tradition did not need to accept Darwin's extension of the "uniquely" human to the rest of the natural world, but their emphasis on close analysis of character, increasingly from the inside, corresponded to a decreasing (but never extinguished) reliance on the conformity of physical and moral states, of the sort so characteristic of Dickens.

Nevertheless, Dickens's fiction does participate in the move toward a Darwinian imagination of the world, a growing uncertainty about the notion of an "essential" self or about the possibility of detecting the moral through the physical (a quest that is increasingly professionalized, requiring a Bucket to do the work); and he is thematically urgent about the need for change. Abruptness remains characteristic, yet his preoccupation with the slow but inevitable movements in nature toward change, and with the consequences of refusing it is something more than a throwback to old comic literary traditions. It is as though he accepts uniformitarianism but rejects the gradualism that Lyell imposed upon it; like Darwin he seems to be reconciling the progressivism of catastrophism with the naturalism of uniformitarianism. Several of his most wonderful narratives focus on this problem: Mrs. Skewton in *Dombey and Son*, Miss Havisham in *Great Expectations*, and Mrs. Clennam all succumb to the forces of change their whole lives would have denied. And yet the very figures Dickens uses to

thematize change are static (essentialist in conception) and require
extravagances of plot to force them into time. They dwell in worlds not
where change evolves slowly through time, but where it comes
catastrophically, through melodrama, revelation, conversion. In a world of
Bagstock and Barnacle, Captain Cuttle and Flora Finching, Mr. Toots and
Mr. Merdle, it is hard to imagine that each of us does not have some
essential, inescapable selfhood. But Clennam, Sidney Carton, and John
Harmon, not to speak of Pip and Eugene Wrayburn, all flirt with doubts
about the self so profound that they verge on self-annihilation. Each of them
either literally or metaphorically dies, almost as though it were suicide. The
question of change, even of the reality of the self, moves from the periphery
to the center of Dickens's art and brings him to the edge of the Darwinian
world, which feels like a threat, but can also, as for Clennam, be a liberation.

In other respects Dickens's worlds often seem to be narrative enactments of
Darwin's theory. Beer makes the connection by pointing to the "apparently
unruly superfluity of material" in Dickens's novels, "gradually and
retrospectively revealing itself as order, its superfecundity of instances
serving an argument which can reveal itself only through instance and
relations."[54] *Bleak House* is only Dickens's most elaborate working out of the
way all things are connected, and connected by virtue of mutual dependence
and relationship. The answer to the question, "What connexion can there
be?" we have noted, is a genealogical one, that Esther is Lady Dedlock's
daughter. Mr. Guppy and Mr. Tulkinghorn detect it immediately. But all
characters eventually connect, in other literal ways, from the brickmakers,
who deceive Bucket in his pursuit, to Jo, the literal bearer of the plague, to
the lawyers who drain the life from Richard, to Mr. Jarndyce, Skimpole,
Boythorn, and Sir Leicester himself.

 Bleak House embodies in every aspect of its plots and themes the
preoccupation with connections, across place, class, and institutions. But
almost all of Dickens's novels from *Dombey and Son* to *Our Mutual Friend* are
novels of crossing and interconnection and responsibility. And throughout
these works Dickens employs devices beyond the plot to enforce an
overwhelming sense of hidden bonds, dependencies that have about them
the quality of mystery appropriate to both religious intensity and gothic
narratives.

 The great dramatic moments in Dickens are often framed by
apparently irrelevant natural scenes. Among the most vivid is the passage in
Bleak House that precedes the ominous image of Allegory pointing above Mr.
Tulkinghorn's heads on the evening of the murder. It wanders, by way of the

moon, far from Mr. Tulkinghorn: He looks up casually, thinking "what a fine night, what a bright large moon, what multitudes of stars! A quiet night, too." And the passage moves across the whole of the English landscape, hill summits, water meadows, gardens, woods, island, weirs, shore, the steeples of London. The universal silence is violated by the shot, and when the dogs stop barking, "the fine night, the bright large moon, and multitudes of stars, are left at peace again" (pp. 584–585).

The passage effectively intensifies the event, implying merely by description some larger significance, but it does not express in its physical nature the moral condition at the center of the narrative. The vast silent panorama, disrupted only by the barking of the dogs, is antithetical to the murder going on. And surely it is not mere ornamentation. Passages such as this (there are equivalent ones in *Little Dorrit*) are the scenic counterpart of Dickens's commitment to multiple plots. The natural world, for Dickens, contains and limits human action. Often, as in the passage just quoted, it comments ironically on the action. But the effect is always larger than irony. The world is larger than anyone's imagination of it; connections extend out endlessly. In its vast and serene movement, it seems indifferent to human ambition. Regardless of the arbitrariness and violence of human action, nature continues its regular movement, has its own plot, as it were, which inevitably crosses with and absorbs the human plot.

The novels from Dickens's great middle period forward, with one or two possible exceptions, build thematically on the conception of society as integrally unified, with the revelation of that unification a central element of plot as well as theme. It is clear in the relation between the Toodles and the Dombeys, as in that between Esther and the Dedlocks. Even in *Hard Times* the circus and Mr. Bounderby's past confirm connections among classes and types denied by social convention. *Little Dorrit* explores in William Dorrit's genteel ambitions and in the fate of the Marshalsea and Bleeding Heart Yard the inevitability of connections. *The Tale of Two Cities* acts out melodramatically and in the context of revolutionary action the undeniable mutual dependence of class on class. And *Our Mutual Friend*, in its river and dust heaps, in its tale of the crossing of classes, makes the theme of "connections" both symbolic and literal. The mutual dependencies on which organic life depends in Darwin are dramatized socially in Dickens through his elaborate and multiple plotting and through his gradual revelations, often through the structure of a mystery plot, of the intricacy of relations disguised by sharp demarcations and definitions of classes.

Dickens's world, then, is as much a tangled bank as that evoked by Darwin at the end of the *Origin*. Of course, Dickens takes the metaphorical,

Christian view, that Darwin was to make literal, that we are all one and deny our brotherhood at our peril. And he strains his plotlines to do it. Darwin tells us that seeing all organisms as "lineal descendants of some few beings which lived long before the first bed of Cambrian system was deposited," makes them seem to him "ennobled" (*Origin*, p. 458). The world is a tangled bank on which "elaborately constructed forms, so different from each other, and dependent upon each other in so complex a manner," struggle and evolve yet further into the "most beautiful and wonderful of forms" (p. 460). Had Darwin not written this passage in almost the same form ten years before *Bleak House*, one might have thought he was trying to sum up that great novel.

It is not, however, simply in the fact of complex interrelationship and interdependence that Dickens's and Darwin's worlds seem akin. In both there is an almost uncontrollable energy for life. Dickens's novels are densely populated, full of eccentrics, variations from the norm, and, as in the case of Jo or the retarded Maggie of *Little Dorrit*, or Barnaby Rudge, or Smike of *Nicholas Nickleby*, marginal figures who test the validity of the whole society. Darwin, for his part, needs to locate the unaccountable variation, the deviant figure or organ that will not be accommodated in an ideal and essentialist taxonomy, like woodpeckers who do not peck wood, vestigial organs that serve no adaptive function. Relentless in the pursuit of detail, he qualifies almost all generalization, even his own charting of the descent of species, with the muted and powerful "nature is never that simple."

Victorian clutter and Dickensian grotesque are akin to Darwin's encyclopedic urge to move beyond the typical. In this quality Darwin transcends again the kind of rationalist law-bound science that he inherited from Herschel. Darwin is not very interested in types. I would argue that although Dickens's characters seem to be "types," they are atypical in their excesses. Old Jocy B, Josh Bagstock, is not so much a type as a grotesque— an aberration from the norm whose fictional strength lies in the way the excesses echo recognizable and more apparently normal human behavior. That sort of grotesque, in its multiple manifestations, is very much in the Darwinian mode. As Michael Ghiselin has suggested, the Darwinian revolution, in its overthrow of essentialism, lays "great emphasis on the 'atypical' variants which the older taxonomy ignored."[55] Distortion, excess, and clutter are the marks of Victorian design, of Dickens's novels, and of Darwin's world.

For both Dickens and Darwin, knowledge (and humanity) are not attainable unless one learns to see the multiplicity of variants that lie beyond the merely typical. Biology revolutionized nineteenth-century science because it displaced mathematical models (however briefly) as an ultimate resting place for belief. Darwin's book insisted that one could not understand the development of species unless one recognized that individual variations were always occurring, and that the world is filled with developments from variations which might once have been considered aberrant.

Thus, for Darwin—and the pressure for this is evident in the sheer abundance of Dickens's novels as well—variety is not aberration but the condition for life. Dombey attempts to limit the Dombey blood, and in rejecting the fresh blood and milk of Mrs. Toodles causes his son's death. *Our Mutual Friend* concludes with one of the most remarkable moments in Dickens: Wrayburn is redeemed and brought back to life by crossing the class boundary to marry Lizzie Hexam. In the final scene Twemlow is forced to redefine language in a Darwinian way, moving the idea of "gentleman" from a fixed and permanent class definition to a vital (and indeed sexual) one that becomes so wide-ranging as to lose its exclusivity. "Sir," returns Twemlow to the permanently Podsnapian Podsnap, "if this gentleman's feelings of gratitude, of respect, of admiration, and affection, induced him (as I presume they did) to marry this lady ... I think he is the greater gentleman for the action, and makes the greater lady. I beg to say, that when I use the word, gentleman, I use it in the sense in which the degree may be attained by any man" (p. 891).

Mixing and denial of absolute boundaries become the conditions of life in Dickens's novels as they will be in Darwin's biology. In Darwin, the unaccountable variation, the crossing—of sexes and varieties, if not of species—increases vitality. On the old model life was determined by separate creation and eternal separation into ideal and timeless orders. On the Darwinian model life is enhanced by slight disturbances of equilibrium, by change.

Learning to confront change and to make it a principle of life was Dickens's great trial as a novelist. It is a long way from Pickwick to the timid Twemlow, who affirms the value of mixing in a society constructed to deny it. Twemlow is, moreover, one of the very few minor characters in Dickens who actually change, and whose change is not abrupt reversal, but the quiet consequence of a long accumulation of frustrations. While Pickwick's novel happens episodically and manages to return to the moral condition of innocence by slamming the door, the later Dickens moves increasingly to the structure of Paradise Lost—you can't go home again; change is irrevocable. The Darwinian revolution entailed the rejection of cyclical history, or ideal history: time moved in one direction only (and in this respect, it made a powerful companion to the otherwise initially hostile science of thermodynamics, which introduced the irreversible "arrow of time" into physics—a development I will discuss in the next chapter, on *Little Dorrit*). And yet Dickens goes on, as in the Christian dispensation, to make the change he can no longer avoid facing, the loss of stasis and ideal innocence, into the condition of a greater redemption.

The resistance of Victorian intellectuals to Dickens as a truly serious novelist might be attributed, partially, to two different emphases that can be traced conveniently in the reading of Darwin. The one, the more strictly intellectual, exemplified by G. H. Lewes and George Eliot, absorbed Darwin into the uniformitarian-scientific mode and, as it were, domesticated him and the chancy dysteleological world he offered. The other reads Darwin within a fully comic vision, lights instinctively on the aberrant and extreme cases of the sort that Darwin had to emphasize to disrupt contemporary religious and scientific thought and to reveal a world prolific and dynamic in the production of endless and sometimes grotesque varieties of life. Yet Dickens always struggled back toward the possibilities of essentialist thought and morality. The aberrant comes round to the ideal, at last.

While Dickens often strains toward the comfort of design, he has an astonishing eye for the aberrant and energy for abundance and for life. Perhaps equally remarkable, like Darwin, he managed to use inherited idealist and design-permeated conventions to build almost mythic structures of crossing and recrossing appropriate to the sense of modern urban life (Ruskin deplores this in his "Fiction, Fair and Foul," where he totes up the number of deaths and diseases in *Bleak House*) Dickens's capacity to imagine himself beyond the conventions of order that dominated Victorian social and political life allowed him to write in a way that helped open the culture for the Darwinian vision toward which, in his increasingly courageous confrontation with change, he himself was moving. Podsnap's relation to Twemlow parallels society's first response to Darwin. We should not be surprised that Dickens did not play Podsnap himself.

Notes

1. Charles Dickens, *Bleak House*, ed. George Ford and Sylvere Monod (New York: W. W. Norton, 1977), p. 197. Page numbers in text refer to this edition.

2. Stephen Jay Gould, in "Flaws in a Victorian Veil" (in *The Panda's Thumb*), discusses Louis Agassiz's resistance to Darwin's theory in this context. Agassiz was appalled that blacks might be related to whites and as a consequence he turned unscientifically to the idea of polygeny (we cannot *all* be descended from the same original sources). Gould quotes Agassiz:

I shudder from the consequences. We have already to struggle, in our progress, against the influence of universal equality, in consequence of the difficulty of preserving the acquisitions of individual eminence, the wealth of refinement and culture growing out of select association. What would be our condition if to these difficulties were added the far more tenacious influences of physical disability. Improvements in our system of education ... may sooner or later counterbalance the effects of the apathy of the uncultivated and of the rudeness of the lower classes and raise them to a higher standard. But how shall we eradicate the stigma of a lower race when its blood has once been allowed to flow freely into that of our children. (pp. 174–175)

3. Beer, *Darwin's Plots*, p. 8.

4. Charles Darwin, *Metaphysics, Materialism, and the Evolution of Mind: Early Writings of Charles Darwin*, ed. Paul H. Barrett (Chicago: University of Chicago Press, 1974), p. 20.

5. See Gillian Beer, "Darwin's Reading and the Fictions of Development," in *The Darwinian Heritage*, pp. 543–588.

6. Nora Barlow, ed., *The Autobiography of Charles Darwin* (New York: W. W. Norton, 1958), pp. 138–139.

7. See Jonathan Arac, *Commissioned Spirits: The Shaping of Social Motion in Dickens, Carlyle, Melville, and Hawthorne* (New Brunswick, N.J.: Rutgers University Press, 1979), pp. 126, 131. Arac offers an interesting discussion of how scientific language pervades the novel.

8. Ann Wilkinson, "*Bleak House*: From Faraday to Judgment Day," *ELH*, 34 (1967): 225–247. I draw on this excellent essay frequently in my discussion of *Bleak House*.

9. See E. Gaskell, "More about Spontaneous Combustion," *Dickensian*, 69 (1973): 23–35.

10. Alexander Welsh, *The City of Dickens* (Oxford: Oxford University Press, 1971), p. 117.

11. Harvey Sucksmith, *The Narrative Art of Charles Dickens* (Oxford: Oxford University Press, 1970), p. 171.

12. E.T. Cook and Alexander Wedderburn, eds., *The Library Edition of the Works of John Ruskin*, 39 vols. (London: George Allen, 1905), VII, 7.

13. K.J. Fielding, ed., *The Speeches of Charles Dickens* (Oxford: Oxford University Press, 1960), p. 403.

14. Ibid., p. 404.

15. Ibid.

16. Charles Dickens, *The Posthumous Papers of the Pickwick Club*, ed. Robert L. Patten (Harmondsworth: Penguin Books, 1972), pp. 73–74, 647.

17. Charles Dickens, *The Haunted Man*, in *The Christmas Books*, 2 vols. (Harmondsworth: Penguin Books, 1971) II, 322.

18. Lavoisier quoted in Gerald Holton, *Introduction to Concepts and Theories in Physical Science* (Princeton: Princeton University Press, 1985), p. 231.

19. Charles Dickens, "Gamekeeper's Natural History," *All the Year Round* (September 10, 1859): 474.

20. Charles Dickens, "The World of Water," reprinted from *Household Words*, in *Home and Social Philosophy; or, Chapters on Everyday Topics* (New York: G. P. Putnam, 1852), p. 245.

21. See *All the Year Round* (September 17, 1859): 490.

22. Stephen Toulmin and June Goodfield (in *The Discovery of Time*) cite Boswell quoting Johnson: "But, sir, it is as possible that the Ourang-Outang does not speak, as that he speaks. However, I shall not dispute the point. I should have thought it not possible to find a Monboddo; yet he exists" (p. 98).

23. Charles Dickens, *The Life and Adventures of Martin Chuzzlewit* (London: Thomas Nelson, n.d.), p. 7.

24. Charles Dickens, "Our Nearest Relation," *All the year Round* (May 28, 1859): 114–115.

25. Bowler, *Evolution*, pp. 123–124.

26. Charles Dickens, "Nature's Greatness in Small Things," *Household Words* (November 28, 1857): 513.

27. Cf. Bowler, *Evolution*, p. 222.

28. T.H. Huxley, *Man's Place in Nature* (1863; repr., Ann Arbor: University of Michigan Press, 1959), p. 122.

29. Review of *The Origin of Species*, *All the Year Round* (July 7, 1860): 293, 299.

30. "Species," *All the Year Round* (June 2, 1860): 176.

31. Charles Dickens, *Sketches by "Boz"* (London: Macmillan and Co., 1958), p. 128.

32. Dickens, "Nature's Greatness," p. 511.

33. Cf. John Romano, *Dickens and Reality* (New York: Columbia University Press, 1978): "A single-minded stress on the separation of Dickens' fictive world from our own slights the realistic or representational elements in the novels and their persistent claim, like the claim in Tolstoy, that they are set in the real world" (p. 3). Romano's important claims for Dickens as realist locate a crucial distinction of the realist's enterprise: "The realist puts in doubt the very enterprise of art. As a corollary of the affirmation of the real, realism discredits the precondition of its own existence, that form which confines, distorts, de-actualizes reality in the process of assimilating it" (p. 84). But it is precisely here where the claims for Dickens as a realist might be most usefully assimilated to my argument about natural theology and uniformitarianism. Dickens's commitment to realism is combined with something like a natural-theological faith in the order of experience itself; hence, there is no real sign in Dickens of that characteristic Thackerayan irony at the expense of art itself.

34. Charles Dickens, *Oliver Twist* (Harmondsworth: Penguin Books, 1966), pp. 36, 35.

35. Charles Dickens, *Our Mutual Friend* (Harmondsworth: Penguin Books, 1971), p. 893. Page numbers in the text refer to this edition.

36. George Eliot, *Adam Bede* (Harmondsworth: Penguin Books, 1980), p. 198.

37. Ibid., p. 410.

38. Dickens, *Sketches*, pp. 185, 199.

39. Herschel, *Preliminary Discourse*, p. 14.

40. George Eliot, "The Sad Fortunes of the Reverend Amos Barton," in *Scenes of Clerical Life* (Harmondsworth: Penguin Books, 1973), p. 81.

41. Two recent essays discuss this contradiction in the novel. The form of the novel itself seems to run counter to expressed narrative intent. This problem deserves yet fuller treatment. See Susan R. Cohen, "A History and a Metamorphosis: Continuity and Discontinuity in *Silas Marner,*" *Texas Studies in Literature and Language*, 25 (Fall 1983): 410–446; Donald Hawes, "Chance in *Silas Marner,*" *English*, 31 (1982): 213–218.

42. "The effect of Dickens's characteristic method," says Harland Nelson, "is an impression of an all-pervading design in human affairs, unexpectedly encompassing and harmonizing the profusely various elements of the story; not (as in a novel by Collins) an impression of an unbroken chain of events, unobtrusively laid down and given a final shake to bring the whole linked series at once into view" ("Dickens's Plots: 'The Ways of Providence' or the Influence of Collins?" *Victorian Newsletter*, 19, 1961: 11). But the strain to make the harmony is evident in the great novels, and the ways of providence or of natural theology are often challenged by the methods designed to affirm them.

43. Charles Dickens, "Magic and Science," *All the Year Round* (March 23, 1861): 562.

44. Mayr, *The Diversity of Life*, p. 37.

45. Manier's summary of Darwin's views on the wars of nature that help further natural selection demonstrates how inappropriate moral and generalizing application of Darwinian theory was:

Success in these wars of organic being could *not* be traced to variations which were *favorable* in some *absolute* sense; on the contrary, a variation must be understood to be *successful in relation* to some particular segment of the range of alternative variations, and in the context of the chances of life which happened to be available in the given physical circumstances or conditions. Such expression as "chance offspring" or "round of chances" alluded to the complexity of the predictions used in Darwin's hypothesis, and implied that this complexity could not be reduced in the way that Newton had reduced the complexity of planetary motion by formulating a few generally applicable laws. (*The Young Darwin*, pp. 121–122)

46. Beer, *Darwin's Plots*, p. 53.

47. Mayr, *The Diversity of Life*, p. 283.

48. Beatty, "Speaking of Species," p. 265.

49. Mayr, *The Growth of Biological Thought*, pp. 304–305, 38.

50. Darwin was not totally consistent in his rejection of essentialism. Not only is such consistency impossible given the nature of our language, but Darwin could himself employ arguments that imply an essentialist reality. This is particularly so when, under the pressure of antievolutionary arguments, he revises the *Origin* in later editions and makes many more concessions on the inheritance of acquired characteristics. Daniel Simberloff emphasizes the importance of the rejection of essentialist typology in the Darwinian revolution and points to various Darwinian ideas that nevertheless revert to essentialism. See "A Succession of Paradigms in Ecology: Essentialism to Materialism and Probabilism," *Synthese*, 43 (1980): 3–29, where he cites Richard Lewontin in arguing that Darwin's belief in the blending (not particularistic) theory of inheritance is "readily traced to [his] attachment to essentialist, typological thought." Darwin was hampered by his lack of knowledge of genetics and of Mendelian theory, which made evident that inheritance was not a blending but a 1:2:1 distribution of genetic materials, some of which would not be visible in the parent. Simberloff also notes Lewontin's description of Darwin's "retreat to idealism or essentialism" in his theory of "pangenesis," for the hypothetical "gemmules" are "egregiously ideal essence-conferring entities" (pp. 6–7). See also R. D. Lewontin, "Darwin and Mendel—the Materialist Revolution," in *The Heritage of Copernicus: Theories "More Pleasing to the Mind,"* ed. J. Neyman (Cambridge, Mass.: MIT Press, 1974), pp. 166–183.

51. Barbara Hardy, "*Martin Chuzzlewit*," in *Dickens and the Twentieth Century*, ed. John Gross and Gabriel Pearson (Toronto: University of Toronto Press, 1962), pp. 107–120. Hardy points out that the abruptness of Martin's conversion is typical of Dickens: "There is no point in comparing Dickens's conversions here with the slow and often eddying movement traced in George Eliot or Henry James. But I think this change is even more abrupt in exposition, relying heavily on compressed rhetoric, than the fairly abrupt conversions of David Copperfield or Bella Wilfer, though the important difference lies in the context of dramatized moral action. Dombey, Steerforth, Gradgrind, Pip, and other major and minor examples of flawed character—not necessarily changing—are demonstrated in appropriate action, large and small" (p. 114). Hardy is criticizing not the abruptness but the way the abrupt change is dramatized and contextualized. The Dickensian mode of change, belonging to a very different tradition, has its own constraints.

52. Bersani, *A Future for Astyanax*, p. 18.

53. Charles Darwin, *The Expression of the Emotions in Man and Animals* (1872; repr., Chicago: University of Chicago Press, 1965), p. 175.

54. Beer, *Darwin's Plots*, p. 8.

55. Ghiselin, *The Triumph of the Darwinian Method*, p. 61.

Chronology

1832	Passage of the First Reform Bill in Parliament, doubling the electorate; Lord Tennyson, *Poems*; Thomas Carlyle, *Biography*.
1833	Abolition of slavery; Thomas Carlyle, *Sartor Resartus*; Robert Browning, *Pauline*.
1835	Browning, *Paracelsus*.
1836	Factory Act limits children under 13 to no more than 48 hours per week in textile mills; first train in London; Charles Dickens, *Sketches by Boz*, *Pickwick Papers*.
1837	Death of William IV; Accession of Queen Victoria; Carlyle, *French Revolution*; Dickens, *Oliver Twist*; William Makepeace Thackeray, *Yellowplush Correspondence*; Browning, *Strafford*.
1838	Great Western Railway opens; Anti-Corn Law League founded; Dickens, *Nicholas Nickleby*.
1839	First Chartist petition presented to Parliament; Fox Talbot and Daguerre announce rival photographic processes; Opium War; Carlyle, *Chartism*; Thackeray, *Catherine*.
1840	Marriage of Victoria and Prince Albert; annexation of New Zealand; Penny Post established; Thomas Hardy born; Dickens, *The Old Curiosity Shop*, *Master Humphrey's Clock*; Browning, *Sordello*; Thackeray, *Paris Sketch Book*.
1841	London Library established; *Punch* begins publication;

Carlyle, *On Heroes and Hero Worship*; Dickens, *Barnaby Rudge*; Thackeray, *Samuel Titmarsh and the Great Hoggarty Diamond*; Browning, *Pippa Passes*.

1842   Chartist Riots; second presentation of Charter to Parliament; Copyright Act; Tennyson, *Poems*; Browning, *Dramatic Lyrics*.

1843   Wordsworth named Poet Laureate; Carlyle, *Past and Present*; John Ruskin, *Modern Painters* (vol .1); Dickens, *A Christmas Carol*; Thomas Babington Macaulay, *Critical and Historical Essays*.

1844   Thackeray, *Barry Lyndon*; Benjamin Disraeli, *Coningsby*; Elizabeth Barrett Browning, *Poems*.

1845   Irish potato famine; Carlyle, *Oliver Cromwell*; Disraeli, *Sybil*; Dickens, *Cricket on the Hearth*; Friedrich Engels, *The Condition of the Working Class in England*.

1846   Corn Laws repealed; beginning of railway boom; Dickens, *Dombey and Son*; Edward Bulwer, *Lucretia*; the Brontë sisters, *Poems*; Edward Lear, *Book of Nonsense*; Thackeray, *Snobs of England*.

1847   Ten Hours Act limits women and children under 18 to ten hour work days in textile mills; Tennyson, *The Princess*; Charlotte Brontë, *Jane Eyre*; Emily Brontë, *Wuthering Heights*; Anne Brontë, *Agnes Grey*; Thackeray, *Vanity Fair*.

1848   Chartist demonstration in London (third presentation of Charter); Public Health Act; revolutions in France, Germany, Poland, Hungary, and Italy; Pre-Raphaelite Brotherhood founded; Mrs. Elizabeth Gaskell, *Mary Barton: A Tale of Manchester Life*; A. Brontë, *The Tenant of Wildfell Hall*; Thackeray, *Pendennis*; Karl Marx and Engels, *Communist Manifesto*.

1849   Corn Laws abolished; C. Brontë, *Shirley*; Ruskin, *Seven Lamps of Architecture*; Dickens, *David Copperfield*; Macaulay, *History of England*, volumes 1 and 2.

1850   Tennyson succeeds Wordsworth as Poet Laureate, Carlyle, *Latter-Day Pamphlets*; Elizabeth Barrett Browning, *Sonnets from the Portuguese*; Charles Kingsley, *Alton Locke*.

1851   Great Exhibition in London; Louis Napoleon, *coup d'état*; Gaskell, *Cranford*; Ruskin, *The Stones of Venice*; George Meredith, *Poems*.

1852	New Houses of Parliament open; Thackeray, *Henry Esmond*; Matthew Arnold, *Empedocles on Etna*; Dickens, *Bleak House*.
1853	Charlotte Brontë, *Villette*; Gaskell, *Ruth*; Arnold, *Poems*; Thackeray, *English Humorists of the 18th Century*.
1854	Crimean War breaks out; construction of the London Underground (the first subway) begins; Dickens, *Hard Times*.
1855	Stamp Tax abolished; Tennyson, *Maud*; Kingsley, *Westward Ho!*; Robert Browning, *Men and Women*; Anthony Trollope, *The Warden*; Dickens, *Little Dorrit*; Gaskell, *North and South*; Thackeray, *The Newcomes*.
1856	Treaty of Paris (ending Crimean War).
1857	Indian Mutiny; Matrimonial Causes Act makes divorce available without a special act of Parliament; E.B. Browning, *Aurora Leigh*; Trollope, *Barchester Towers*; Gaskell, *The Life of Charlotte Brontë*; Eliot, *Scenes from Clerical Life*; Thackeray, *The Virginians*; C. Brontë, *The Professor*; Ruskin, *Political Economy of Art*.
1858	India transferred to British Crown; Carlyle, *Frederick the Great* (vols I–II); Trollope, *Three Clerks, Dr. Thorne*.
1859	Charles Darwin, *Origin of Species*; Dickens, *A Tale of Two Cities*; Eliot, *Adam Bede*; Meredith, *The Ordeal of Richard Feverel*; John Stuart Mill, *On Liberty*, Tennyson, *Idylls of the King*.
1860	Eliot, *The Mill on the Floss*; Wilkie Collins, *The Woman in White*; Ruskin, *Unto This Last*; Dickens, *Great Expectations*; Thackeray, *Lovel the Widower*; Meredith, *Evan Harrington*.
1861	American Civil War (–1865); Prince Albert dies; Elizabeth Barrett Browning dies; Eliot, *Silas Marner*; Trollope, *Framley Parsonage*.
1862	Death of William Makepeace Thackeray; Christina Rossetti, *Goblin Market*; Meredith, *Modern Love*; Eliot, *Romola*.
1863	Gaskell, *Sylvia's Lovers*; Kingsley, *The Water-Babies*.
1864	Gaskell, *Wives and Daughters*; Dickens, *Our Mutual Friend*; Thackeray, *Denis Duval*; Trollope, *Can You Forgive Her?*

1865	Assassination of President Lincoln; Reform League founded to promote extension of the vote for working class men; Arnold, *Essays in Criticism, I*; Algernon Charles Swinburne, *Atalanta in Calydon*; Lewis Carroll, *Alice in Wonderland*.
1866	Women's suffrage petition presented to Parliament by John Stuart Mill; Eliot, *Felix Holt*; Swinburne, *Poems and Ballads*; Ruskin, *Crown of Wild Olive*; Trollope, *The Claverings*.
1867	Passage of the Second Reform Bill, furthering reducing property qualification for the vote; typewriter invented; Arnold, *New Poems*; Trollope, *The Last Chronicle of Barset*.
1868	Collins, *The Moonstone*; Browning, *The Ring and The Book*; Morris, *Earthly Paradise*.
1869	Suez Canal opens; Trollope, *Phineas Finn*; Mill, *On the Subjection of Women*; Tennyson, *Holy Grail*; Arnold, *Culture and Anarchy*.
1870	Franco-Prussian War; First Married Woman's Property Act, women gain rights to their own wages earned after marriage; death of Dickens; Dickens, *Edwin Drood*; Dante Gabriel Rosetti, *Poems*.
1871	Trade unions legalized; abolition of religious test at universities; Lear, *The Owl and The Pussy Cat*; Eliot, *Middlemarch*; Carroll, *Through the Looking Glass*; Darwin, *Descent of Man*, Swineburne, *Songs Before Sunrise*.
1873	Arnold, *Literature and Dogma*; Mill, *Autobiography*.
1874	Thomas Hardy, *Far From the Madding Crowd*; Trollope, *The Way We Live Now*.
1875	Public Health Act; agricultural depression; Arnold, *God and The Bible*.
1876	Telephone invented; Victoria declared Empress of India; Eliot, *Daniel Deronda*.
1877	Russo-Turkish war; Meredith, *Idea of Comedy*.
1878	Electric lights installed on some London streets; Matrimonial Causes Act allows judicial separation for cruelty and assault; University of London opens all degrees and prizes to women; Hardy, *The Return of the Native*; Henry James, *The Europeans*; Swinburne, *Poems and Ballads*.
1879	First telephone exchange opens in London; Meredith, *The Egoist*.

1880	First Boer War; Tennyson, *Ballads*; James, *The Portrait of a Lady*; Robert Browning, *Dramatic Idyls, II.*
1881	Browning Society founded; death of Benjamin Disraeli; Robert Louis Stevenson, *Treasure Island*; Carlyle, *Reminiscences.*
1882	Married Women's Property Act, women have right to all their property earned before or after marriage; Hardy, *Two on a Tower*; Swinburne, *Tristram of Lyonesse.*
1884	James, *The Art of Fiction*; J.A. Froude, *Carlyle: Life in London.*
1885	Criminal Law Amendment Act raises the age of consent for girls to 16 and makes sexual acts between men illegal; radio waves discovered; internal combustion engine invented; Tennyson, *Tiresias.*
1886	Stevenson, *Kidnapped, Dr. Jekyll and Mr. Hyde*; Hardy, *The Mayor of Casterbridge, The Woodlanders.*
1887	Victoria's Golden Jubilee; Meredith, *Ballads and Poems of Tragic Life.*
1888	"Jack the Ripper" murders five women in London; death of Matthew Arnold; Arnold, *Essays in Criticism, II.*
1889	Prevention of Cruelty to Children prohibits employment of the children under 10; George Bernard Shaw, *Fabian Essays*, Swinburne, *Poems and Ballads.*
1890	Rudyard Kipling, *Soldiers Three.*
1891	Oscar Wilde, *The Picture of Dorian Gray*; Hardy, *Tess of the D'Urbervilles*; Kipling, *The Light that Failed.*
1892	Tennyson dies; Shaw, *Widowers' Houses.*
1893	Shaw, *Mrs Warren's Profession.*
1894	Stevenson dies.
1895	Oscar Wilde's trial results in his conviction and imprisonment; X-rays discovered; Wilde, *The Importance of Being Earnest, An Ideal Husband*; H.G. Wells, *The Time Machine*; Hardy, *Jude the Obscure.*
1896	Wireless telegraphy invented; both Oxford and Cambridge reject proposals to grant degrees to women; Shaw, *You Never Can Tell.*
1897	Victoria's Diamond Jubilee; Bram Stoker, *Dracula*; Wells, *Invisible Man.*

1898	Hardy, *Wessex Poems;* death of William Gladstone.
1899	Second Boer War; school attendance mandatory to age 12; Joseph Conrad, *Heart of Darkness*.
1900	British Labor Party founded; Sigmund Freud, *The Interpretation of Dreams*; Conrad, *Lord Jim*.
1901	Death of Victoria; accession of Edward VII; Kipling, *Kim*.

Contributors

HAROLD BLOOM is Sterling Professor of the Humanities at Yale University and Henry W. and Albert A. Berg Professor of English at the New York University Graduate School. He is the author of over 20 books, including *Shelley's Mythmaking* (1959), *The Visionary Company* (1961), *Blake's Apocalypse* (1963), *Yeats* (1970), *A Map of Misreading* (1975), *Kabbalah and Criticism* (1975), *Agon: Toward a Theory of Revisionism* (1982), *The American Religion* (1992), *The Western Canon* (1994), and *Omens of Millennium: The Gnosis of Angels, Dreams, and Resurrection* (1996). *The Anxiety of Influence* (1973) sets forth Professor Bloom's provocative theory of the literary relationships between the great writers and their predecessors. His most recent books include *Shakespeare: The Invention of the Human* (1998), a 1998 National Book Award finalist, *How to Read and Why* (2000), *Genius: A Mosaic of One Hundred Exemplary Creative Minds* (2002), and *Hamlet: Poem Unlimited* (2003). In 1999, Professor Bloom received the prestigious American Academy of Arts and Letters Gold Medal for Criticism, and in 2002 he received the Catalonia International Prize.

LIONEL STEVENSON has published many articles and books on British literature, including *The Pre-Raphaelite Poets* (1974), *The English Novel: A Panorama* (1960), and *The Ordeal of George Meredith: A Biography* (1967).

MICHAEL WHEELER is a visiting Professor of English Literature at the University of Southampton. His publications include *The Art of Allusion in*

Victorian Fiction (1979), *Death and the Future Life in Victorian Literature and Theology* (1990), *A Digital Edition of Ruskin's Modern Painters*, volume I (2000). He is also editor of *Ruskin and Environment: The Storm Cloud of the Nineteenth Century* (1995) and *Time and Tide: Ruskin Studies* (1996).

JULIA PREWITT BROWN is Associate Professor of English at Boston University. She is the author of *Jane Austen's Novels: Social Change and Literary Form* (1979). Her book on Oscar Wilde's philosophy of art is forthcoming from the University Press of Virginia.

CHRISTOPHER S. NASSAAR, Associate Professor of English at the American University of Beirut, is the author of *Into the Demon Universe: A Literary Exploration of Oscar Wilde* (1974), and *Oscar Wilde: The Importance of Being Earnest*, a study guide reprinted annually. He is also the editor of *The English Literacy Decadence: An Anthology*.

ROBIN GILMOUR is author of *The Victorian Period: The Intellectual and Cultural Context, 1830–1890* (1994) and *The Idea of the Gentleman in the Victorian Novel* (1981).

FREDERICK R. KARL, a renown literary biographer and critic, is Professor of English at New York University. His biographies include *Joseph Conrad* (1979), *William Faulkner* (1989), *Franz Kafka* (1991), and *George Eliot* (1995).

S. DIANA NEILL taught at the University of London. She is the author of *A Short History of the English Novel* (1951).

J. HILLIS MILLER is Distinguished Professor of English and Comparative Literature at the University of California, Irvine. He is also Honorary Professor of Peking University and past president of the Modern Language Association. A Fellow of the American Academy of Arts and Sciences, he has published many essays and reviews and is an editor of various literary journals. Among J. Hillis Miller's books are *Charles Dickens: The World of His Novels* (1958), *The Disappearance of God*; *Poets of Reality* (1965), *Fiction and Repetition* (1982), *The Linguistic Moment* (1985), *The Ethics of Reading* (1986), *Hawthorne and History* (1991), *Ariadne's Thread* (1992), *Illustration* (1992), *Victorian Subjects* (1990), *Tropes, Parables, Performatives* (1990), *Theory Now and Then* (1990), *New Starts* (1993), *Topographies* (1994) and *Black Holes* (1999).

ELAINE SHOWALTER is Professor of English at Princeton University. She is the author of *Speaking of Gender* (1989), *Sister's Choice: Tradition and Change in American Women's Writing* (1991), *Daughters of Decadence* (1993), *Sexual Anarchy: Gender and Culture at the "Fin De Siecle"* (1995), *Hystories: Hysterical Epidemics and Modern Culture* (1997), and editor of *The New Feminist Criticism: Essays on Women, Literature, and Theory* (1985).

JEFF NUNOKAWA teaches English literature at Princeton University. *He is author of The Afterlife of Property: Domestic Securities and Victorian Fiction* (1994).

JOHN R. REED is Distinguished Professor of English at Wayne State University. His publications include *Victorian Conventions* (1975), *The Natural History of H.G. Wells* (1982), and *Decadent Style* (1985).

The American-British poet and critic T.S. ELIOT (Thomas Stearns Eliot) was one of the most distinguished literary figures of the 20th century. His first book of poems, *Prufrock and Other Observations*, was published in 1917, and *The Waste Land*, considered by many to be the single most influential poetic work of the twentieth century, was published in 1922. T. S. Eliot received the Nobel Prize for Literature in 1948, and died in London in 1965.

Poet and critic SANDRA M. GILBERT teaches English at the University of California, Davis. Along with Susan Gubar, she published *The Madwoman in the Attic: The Woman Writer and the 19th-Century Literary Imagination* in 1979, a runner-up for both The Pulitzer Prize and the National Book Critics Circle Award. Gilbert is the author of a prose memoir, *Wrongful Death: A Medical Tragedy* (1995), and many books of poetry including *Ghost Volcano* (1995), *Inventions of Farewell: A Book of Elegies* (2001), *Kissing the Bread: New and Selected Poems* (2000), *Blood Pressure* (1988), *The Summer Kitchen* (1983), and *In the Fourth World* (1978).

SUSAN GUBAR, Distinguished Professor of English and Women's Studies, has taught at Indiana University for more than twenty years. Along with Sandra M. Gilbert, she published *The Madwoman in the Attic: The Woman Writer and the 19th-Century Literary Imagination* in 1979, a runner-up for both The Pulitzer Prize and the National Book Critics Circle Award. Gilbert and Gubar also co-authored *No Man's Land: The Place of the Woman Writer in the Twentieth Century: The War of the Words* (1988), *Sexchanges* (1989), and *Letters from the Front* (1994). The recipient of awards from the National

Endowment for the Humanities and the Guggenheim Foundation, Gubar is also the author of *Racechanges: White Skin, Black Face in American Culture* (1997), and the editor of *Critical Condition: Feminism at the Turn of the Century* (2000).

GEORGE LEVINE is Kenneth Burke Professor of Literature and Director of the Center for the Critical Analysis of Contemporary Culture, Rutgers University. He has written on science, the history of science, and on literature.

Bibliography

Altick, Richard D. *The English Common Reader: A Social History of the Mass Reading Public, 1800–1900.* Columbus: Ohio State University Press, 1998.

Allott, Miriam Farris, ed. *The Brontës: The Critical Heritage.* London: Routledge & Kegan Paul, 1974.

Armstrong, Nancy. *Desire and Domestic Fiction: A Political History of the Novel.* New York: Oxford University Press, 1987.

Bailin, Miriam. *The Sickroom in Victorian Fiction.* New York: Cambridge University Press, 1994.

Barickman, Richard, Susan MacDonald, and Myra Stark. *Corrupt Relations: Dickens, Thackeray, Trollope, Collins and the Victorian Sexual System.* New York: Columbia University Press, 1982.

Beckson, Karl. *London in the 1890s: A Cultural History.* New York: W.W. Norton, 1992.

Beer, Gillian. *Darwin's Plots: Evolutionary Narrative in Darwin, George Eliot, and Nineteenth-Century Fiction.* London: Routledge & Kegan Paul, 1983.

Beer, Patricia. *Reader, I Married Him: A Study of the Women Characters of Jane Austen, Charlotte Brontë, Elizabeth Gaskell and George Eliot.* London: Macmillan, 1974.

Bloom, Harold, ed. *British Women Fiction Writers of the 19th Century.* Philadephia, PA: Chelsea House Publishers, 1998.

Bodenheimer, Rosemarie. *The Politics of Story in Victorian Social Fiction.* Ithaca: Cornell University Press, 1988.

Brantlinger, Patrick. *The Spirit of Reform: British Literature and Politics, 1832–1867.* Cambridge: Harvard University Press, 1977

———. *Rule of Darkness: British Literature and Imperialism, 1830–1914.* Ithaca, N.Y.: Cornell University Press, 1988.

——— and William B. Thesing. *A Companion to The Victorian Novel.* Oxford: Blackwell Publishers Ltd., 2002.

Brinton, Crane. *English Political Thought in the Nineteenth Century*. London: E. Benn, 1933.

Brown, Julia Prewitt. *A Reader's Guide to the Nineteenth-Century English Novel*. New York: Macmillan Publishing Company, 1985.

Chapple, J.A.V. *Science and Literature in the Nineteenth Century*. Hampshire, UK: Macmillan, 1986.

Church, Richard. *The Growth of the English Novel*. London: Methuen, 1951.

Christ, Carol T and John O. Jordan, eds. *Victorian Literature and the Victorian Visual Imagination*. Berkeley: University of California Press, 1995.

Cosslett, Tess. *Woman To Woman: Female Friendship in Victorian Fiction*. Brighton, Sussex: Harvester, 1988.

Craft, Christopher. *Another Kind Of Love: Male Homosexual Desire In English Discourse, 1850–1920*. Berkeley: University of California Press, 1994.

David, Deirdre, ed. *The Cambridge Companion to the Victorian Novel*. Cambridge: Cambridge University Press, 2001.

Duncan, Ian. *Modern Romance and Transformations of the Novel: The Gothic, Scott, Dickens*. Cambridge, UK: Cambridge University Press, 1992.

Eagleton, Terry. *Myths of Power: A Marxist Study of the Brontës*. Macmillan: London, 1975.

Eliot, T.S. *Selected Essays*. New York: Harcourt, Brace and Company, 1932.

Ford, George H. and Lauriat Lane Jr, eds. *The Dickens Critics*. Ithaca, NY: Cornell University Press, 1961.

Gallager Catharine, *The Industrial Reformation of English Fiction: Social Discourse and Narrative Form, 1832–1867*. Chicago: University of Chicago Press, 1985.

Gilmour, Robin. *The Novel in the Victorian Age: A Modern Introduction*. London: Edward Arnold, 1986.

———. *The Victorian Period: The Intellectual and Cultural Context of English Literature 1830–1890*. London: Longman, 1993.

Gilbert, Sandra M. and Susan Gubar. *The Madwoman in the Attic: The Woman Writer and the Nineteenth-Century Literary Imagination*. New Haven: Yale University Press, 1979.

Haight, Gordon, ed. *A Century of George Eliot Criticism*. Boston: Houghton Mifflin, 1965.

Helsinger, Elizabeth, Robin Lauterbach Sheets, and William Veeder. *The Woman Question: Society and Literature in England and America, 1837–1883*, 3 vols. New York: Garland, 1983.

Himmelfarb, Gertrude. *Marriage and Morals Among the Victorians: Essays*. New York: Knopf, 1986.

Houghton, Walter. *The Victorian Frame of Mind, 1830–1870*. New Haven: Yale University Press, 1957.

Hughes, Winifred. *The Maniac in the Cellar: Sensation Novels of the 1860s*. Princeton, N.J.: Princeton University Press, 1980.

Hurley, Kelly. *The Gothic Body: Sexuality, Materialism, and Degeneration at the Fin De Siècle*. Cambridge: Cambridge University Press, 1996.

Jay, Elisabeth. *Faith and Doubt in Victorian Britain*. Hampshire: Macmillan, 1986.

Jenkins, Alice and Juliet John, eds. *Rereading Victorian Fiction*. New York: St. Martins Press, 2000.

Karl, Frederick R. *An Age of Fiction: The Nineteenth Century British Novel*. New York: Farrar, Strous and Giroux, 1964.

Levine, George. *Darwin and the Novelists: Patterns of Science in Victorian Fiction*. Cambridge: Harvard University Press, 1988.

————, ed. *Realism and Representation: Essays on the Problem of Realism in Relation to Science, Literature, and Culture*. Madison: University of Wisconsin Press, 1993.

———— and William Madden, eds. *The Art of Victorian Prose*. New York: Oxford University Press, 1968.

Levine, Philippa. *Victorian Feminism 1850–1900*. London: Hutchinson Education, 1987.

Marcus, Steven. *The Other Victorians: A Study of Sexuality and Pornography in Mid-nineteenth-Century England*. New York: Basic Books, 1966.

Miller, J. Hallis. *Charles Dickens: The World of His Novels*. Cambridge, MA: Harvard University Press, 1958.

————. *The Form of Victorian Fiction*. Notre Dame: University of Notre Dame Press, 1968.

Nassaar, Christopher S. *The Victorians: A Major Authors Anthology*. Lanham: University Press of America, 2000.

Neff, Emery. *Carlyle and Mill: An Introduction to Victorian Thought*. New York, Columbia University Press, 1926.

Neill, S. Diana. *A Short History of the English Novel*. New York: The Macmillan Company, 1952.

Newsome, David. *The Victorian World Picture: Perceptions and Introspections in an Age of Change*. London: J. Murray, 1997.

Poovey, Mary. *Uneven Developments: The Ideological Work of Gender in Mid-Victorian England*. Chicago: University of Chicago Press, 1988.

Reed, John R. *Victorian Will*. Athens: Ohio University Press, 1989.

Robbins, Ruth and Julian Wolfreys, eds. *Victorian Gothic: Literary and Cultural Manifestations in the Nineteenth Century*. New York: Palgrave, 2000.

Sedgwick Eve Kosofsky. *Between Men: English Literature and Male Homosocial Desire*. New York: Columbia University Press, 1985.

Showalter, Elaine. *A Literature of Their Own: British Women Novelists From Brontë to Lessing*. Princeton: Princeton University Press, 1977.

————. *The Female Malady: Women, Madness, and English Culture, 1830–1980*. New York: Pantheon Books, 1985.

————. *Sexual Anarchy: Gender and Culture at the Fin de Siècle*. London: Viking, 1990.

Small, Helen. *Love's Madness: Medicine, the Novel, and Female Insanity, 1800–1865*. New York: Oxford University Press, 1996.

Stang, Richard. *The Theory of the Novel in England 1850–1870*. New York, Columbia University Press, 1959.

Stevenson, Lionel. *The English Novel, A Panorama*. Boston: Houghton Mifflin, 1960.

——. "The Modern Values of Victorian Fiction." *CLA Journal* IV, no. 1, 1960.

Tillotson, Kathleen. *Novels of the Eighteen-Forties*. Oxford: Clarendon Press, 1956.

Tucker, Herbert F. *A Companion to Victorian Literature and Culture*. Malden, MA: Blackwell Publishers, 1999.

Vargish, Thomas. *The Providential Aesthetic in Victorian Fiction*. Charlottesville: University of Virginia, 1985.

Warhol, Robyn R. *Gendered Interventions: Narrative Discourse in the Victorian Novel*. New Brunswick: Rutgers University Press, 1989.

Watt Ian, ed. *The Victorian Novel: Modern Essays in Criticism*. London: Oxford University Press, 1971.

Wheeler, Michael. *The Art of Allusion in Victorian Fiction*. London: Macmillian, 1979.

——. *Death and the Future Life in Victorian Literature and Theology*. Cambridge: Cambridge University Press, 1994.

——. *English Fiction of the Victorian Period*. UK: Longman Group Limited, 1985.

Williams, Raymond. *Culture and Society: 1780–1950*. New York: Columbia University Press, 1983.

Yeazell, Ruth B. *Fictions of Modesty: Women and Courtship in the English Novel*. Chicago: University of Chicago Press, 1991.

——, ed. *Sex, Politics, and Science in the Nineteenth-Century Novel, Selected Papers from the English Institute, 1983–4*. Baltimore: Johns Hopkins University Press, 1986.

Acknowledgments

"The Modern Values of Victorian Fiction" by Lionel Stevenson. From *CLA Journal* 4:1 (September 1960): 1–7. © 1960 by the College Language Association. Reprinted by permission.

"Mid-Century Fiction: A Victorian identity: social-problem, religious and historical novels" by Michael Wheeler. From *English Fiction of Victorian Period 1830–1890*: 35–46. © 1994 by Longman Group UK Limited. Reprinted by permission.

"Class and Money" by Julia Prewitt Brown. From *A Reader's Guide to the Nineteenth Century English Novel*: 1–26. © 1985 by Julia Prewitt Brown. Reprinted by permission.

"Introduction to *The Victorians: A Major Authors Anthology*" by Christopher S. Nassaar, ed. From *The Victorians: A Major Authors Anthology*: xiii–xxiii. © 2000 by University Press of America, Inc. Reprinted by permission.

"The Novel in the Age of Equipoise: Wilkie Collins, Trollope, George Eliot" by Robin Gilmour. From *The Novel in the Victorian Age: A Modern Introduction*: 107–145. © 1986 by Robin Gilmour. Reprinted by permission.

"The Brontës: The Outsider as Protagonist" from *An Age of Fiction: The Nineteenth Century British Novel* by Frederick R. Karl: 77–103. © 1964, renewed 1992 by Frederick R. Karl. Reprinted by permission of Farrar, Straus and Giroux, LLC.

"London by Gaslight" by S. Diana Neill. From *A Short History of the English Novel*: 137–163. © 1952 by The Macmillan Company. Reprinted by permission.

"Time and Intersubjectivity" by J. Hillis Miller. From *The Form of Victorian Fiction*: 1–27. © 1968 by the University of Notre Dame Press, Notre Dame, Indiana. Used by permission.

"Feminine Heroines: Charlotte Brontë and George Eliot" by Elaine Showalter. From *A Literature of Their Own: British Women Novelists from Brontë to Lessing*: 100–132. © 1977 by Princeton University Press. Reprinted by permission of Princeton University Press.

"Sexuality in the Victorian Novel" by Jeff Nunokawa. From *The Cambridge Companion to The Victorian Novel*, ed. Deirdre David: 125–148. © 2001 by Cambridge University Press. Reprinted with the permission of Cambridge University Press.

"George Meredith, Samuel Butler, Thomas Hardy, and Theodore Watts-Dunton" by John R. Reed. From *Victorian Will*: 328–358. © 1989 by John R. Reed. Reprinted with the permission of Ohio University Press, Athens, Ohio.

"Wilkie Collins and Dickens (1927)" from *Selected Essays*, by T.S. Eliot: 409–418. © 1950 by Harcourt, Inc., and renewed 1978 by Esme Valorie Eliot, reprinted by permission of the publisher.

"A Dialogue of Self and Soul: Plain Jane's Progress" by Sandra M. Gilbert and Susan Gubar. From *The Madwoman in the Attic: The Woman Writer and the Nineteenth-Century Literary Imagination*: 336–371. © 1979 by Yale University. Reprinted by permission.

"Dickens and Darwin" by George Levine. From *Darwin and the Novelists: Patterns of Science in Victorian Fiction*: 119–152. © 1988 by the President and Fellows of Harvard College. Reprinted by permission.

Index